Thinking about Deterrence

Enduring Questions in a Time of Rising Powers, Rogue Regimes, and Terrorism

EDITED BY
ADAM LOWTHER

Air University Press
Air Force Research Institute
Maxwell Air Force Base, Alabama

Project Editor
James S. Howard

Cover Art, Book Design, and Illustrations
Daniel Armstrong

Composition and Prepress Production
Nedra Looney

Print Preparation and Distribution
Diane Clark

AIR FORCE RESEARCH INSTITUTE

AIR UNIVERSITY PRESS

Director and Publisher
Allen G. Peck

Editor in Chief
Oreste M. Johnson

Managing Editor
Demorah Hayes

Design and Production Manager
Cheryl King

AFRI /AU PRESS
AIR FORCE RESEARCH INSTITUTE

Disclaimer

Contents

Illustrations

Figure

Table

CONTENTS

About the Authors

Kevin R. Beeker is a US Air Force senior combat pilot in the A/OA-10 and has also completed a joint tour flying F/A-18s with the US Navy. He currently works in the Combat Targeting Division at US Cyber Command, Fort Meade, Maryland. He received his MS degree in cyber warfare from the Air Force Institute of Technology, Wright-Patterson AFB, Ohio.

James A. Blackwell is special advisor to the assistant chief of staff, strategic deterrence and nuclear integration, at Headquarters US Air Force. He received his PhD and MALD from the Fletcher School of International Law and Diplomacy and BS from the US Military Academy. He previously served as executive director of the Secretary of Defense Task Force on DOD Nuclear Weapons Management. He co-edited *Making Defense Reform Work* with Barry Blechman (Brassey's, 1990) and has authored numerous books and articles.

Elbridge A. Colby is a principal analyst at the Center for Naval Analysis, where he advises a number of US government entities on deterrence and nuclear weapons issues. He previously served in a number of government positions, including the New START negotiations and ratification team for the Department of Defense and as an advisor to the Congressional Strategic Posture Commission. He is a graduate of Harvard College and Yale Law School.

Anne Fitzpatrick earned her PhD in science and technology studies from Virginia Tech in 1998. Her research includes high-performance computing and strategic science and technology analyses. She has lived and worked in the former Soviet Union and is fluent in Russian.

Michael R. Grimaila is an associate professor of systems engineering at the Air Force Institute of Technology, Wright-Patterson AFB, Ohio. He received his PhD in electrical engineering from Texas A&M University. His research interests include mission assurance, network management and security, quantum cryptography, and systems engineering.

Michael W. Haas is a principal electronics engineer at the 711th Human Performance Wing, Air Force Research Laboratory, Wright-Patterson AFB, Ohio. He received his PhD in engineering and applied science from the University of Southampton, United Kingdom. His research interests include cyberspace operations, information operations, and human interface technology.

Dale Hayden is the deputy director of the Air Force Research Institute (AFRI). He has authored a number of articles on Air Force topics, with a focus on space issues. Colonel Hayden completed a distinguished Air Force career in 2008 after more than 25 years of service as a space and missile officer. He holds a PhD in administration of higher education from the University of Alabama.

Hunter Hustus is technical advisor to the assistant chief of staff, strategic deterrence and nuclear integration at Headquarters US Air Force. He received his MA in political science from the University of South Dakota. He previously served as foreign policy and congressional affairs advisor to US Air Forces in Europe and served as a B-52 electronic warfare officer and NATO staff officer before retiring from active duty.

Kamal T. Jabbour is senior scientist for information assurance in the Information Directorate, Air Force Research Laboratory, Rome, New York. He taught and conducted research for two decades on the computer engineering faculty at Syracuse University, including a three-year term as department chair. Dr. Jabbour has received one US patent, published more than 60 papers in refereed journals and conference proceedings, and penned 317 articles on running.

Adam B. Lowther is a research professor at the AFRI. He is the author of numerous books, chapters, journal articles, and editorials on contemporary defense issues. Before joining AFRI, Dr. Lowther taught international relations and security studies at two universities. He also served in the US Navy at several shipboard and shore commands. He holds a PhD in international relations from the University of Alabama.

Robert F. Mills is an associate professor of electrical engineering at the Air Force Institute of Technology, Wright-Patterson AFB, Ohio. He received his PhD in electrical engineering from the University of Kansas. His research interests include network management and security, electronic warfare, and systems engineering.

James D. Perry holds an MA degree in security policy studies and a PhD in history from George Washington University and was a visiting fellow at the Hoover Institution, Stanford University, 1996–97. He is currently a senior analyst for Northrop Grumman Corporation, where he conducts defense policy, operational, and budgetary analyses to support company programs. His particular areas of expertise include long-range strike, unmanned systems, and emerging antiaccess threats to power projection.

E. Paul Ratazzi is a principal engineer in the Cyber Assurance Branch of the Air Force Research Laboratory in Rome, New York. His research interests include access control and security for mobile devices and assured cloud computing. He holds BSEE and MS degrees in management from Rensselaer Polytechnic Institute and an MSEE from Syracuse University and is currently a PhD candidate (ABD) in electrical and computer engineering at Syracuse University.

Keith B. Payne is the president of the National Institute for Public Policy, a professor and the head of the Graduate Department of Defense and Strategic Studies, Missouri State University (Washington Campus), the chairman of the US Strategic Command's Strategy and Policy Panel, the editor-in-chief of *Comparative Strategy: An International Journal*, and a co-chair of the US Nuclear Strategy Forum. He has served as the Deputy Assistant Secretary of Defense for Forces Policy. He served on the bipartisan Congressional Commission on the Strategic Posture of the United States and on the Secretary of State's International Security Advisory Board. He is the author, co-author, or editor of over one hundred and fifty published articles and seventeen books and monographs. Payne received a PhD in international relations from the University of Southern California.

Edward H. Robbins is a supervisory management analyst for the assistant chief of staff, strategic deterrence and nuclear integration, at Headquarters US Air Force. He holds a PhD in business (decision sciences/financial economics) from Stanford University and several degrees in differing areas of applied mathematics. He has worked more than a decade for the US military—conducting logistical systems analyses, evaluating the functionality of aircraft weapons systems, forecasting Air Force capabilities under future constrained budgets, and carrying out/supervising research on strategic deterrence.

Gary Schaub Jr. is a senior researcher at the Centre for Military Studies of the University of Copenhagen, Denmark. He is a former faculty member of the Air War College and the School of Advanced and Space Studies, as well as performing a research sabbatical at the Air Force Research Institute, Maxwell AFB, Alabama. He holds a PhD from the University of Pittsburgh.

Jonathan Trexel is program manager of the Strategic Deterrence Assessment Lab of Science Applications International Corporation. He has over 25 years' experience in intelligence analysis and in deterrence and other national security policy. He holds a bachelor's degree in political science, a master's in strategic intelligence, and is a PhD candidate at the University of Nebraska, specializing in US national security and foreign policy.

Foreword

We are in the post–post–Cold War era, and the strategic environment continues to shift before our very eyes. The US *National Military Strategy* notes that "ongoing shifts in relative power and increasing interconnectedness in the international order indicate a strategic inflection point." The landscape at this inflection point is a mix of the familiar and the foreign.

The United States remains the world's preeminent power, as nation-states play the primary role in the globalized world they created. However, there are nation-states of increasing influence that were not co-authors of the existing rule sets and international norms. Many have a regional, not a global perspective, but their regional interests cannot be pursued without global effect. We do not yet know for certain how they will adapt and where they will challenge current structures.

Instant global reach is a defining characteristic of the twenty-first century. It reinforces our interconnectedness and, at the same time, provides asymmetric opportunity to nonstate actors. Even now, there remain non-status-quo states that keep their populaces in the dark or subject them to information manipulation.

Nuclear weapons and deterrence remain characteristics of the post–post-Cold War era. On 5 April 2009 in Prague, President Obama stated, "the United States will take concrete steps towards a world without nuclear weapons. To put an end to Cold War thinking, we will reduce the role of nuclear weapons in our national security strategy, and urge others to do the same. Make no mistake: As long as these weapons exist, the United States will maintain a safe, secure and effective arsenal to deter any adversary, and guarantee that defense to our allies."

Those few words capture many of the challenges facing those who study and conduct deterrence in a global environment comprised of multiple nuclear-armed states, rising regional non-status-quo powers, nonstate actors, and an intertwined network of allies and partners. There are regions where multiple states possess nuclear weapons for divergent reasons, with conflicting doctrines and beliefs regarding their efficacy, and where geography and operational reach shape—or shake—stability.

The United States remains the sole power able to reach and influence every one of these regions, but our own historical and cultural values are manifest in offshore hesitancy which sometimes produces a distinct lag in the development of both grand strategy and operational concepts. We will find ourselves in situations simultaneously conducting deterrence (to prevent a power from considering harm against us), extending deterrence (to protect allies and partners), and underwriting assurance (to maintain security relationships and support nonproliferation). Tailoring twentieth-century platforms and weapon systems to such a problem set requires fresh thinking.

To transcend Cold War thinking, we need to move beyond reliance solely on deterrence through imposition of costs to integrate denial of benefits and other methods for encouraging restraint. This sort of thinking requires diversity in our analytical tool kits. We should retain effective classic methodologies (e.g., game theory) and at the same time integrate newer behavioral approaches outside a *rational* state-based actor construct.

This transformation in thinking also requires an understanding that reductions in arsenal sizes change the problem itself and in a nonlinear manner. The combination of smaller arsenals and multiple nuclear-armed states is not a matter of arithmetic.

We will see continued efforts to decrease our and our allies' military expenditures. This demands we increase the rigor behind our analysis of the capabilities needed to deter and the platforms, personnel, and concepts sufficient to generate those capabilities. While we require sufficiency, we have little room for overcapacity.

A major challenge of deterrence in the twenty-first century lies in understanding the contributions of nonnuclear capabilities and proper integration of defensive systems. Success will also require the right mix of specific capabilities across air, cyber, and space domains that influence adversary decision calculus. Employing conventional and nuclear force structures, postures, and doctrines to create synergistic effect across these domains will require innovation. Not only will freedom to maneuver in these domains provide the president valuable options for influencing an adversary's decision-making process, but it is prerequisite to successfully reducing our reliance on nuclear weapons.

Perhaps it is counterintuitive, but as we "reduce the role of nuclear weapons in our national security strategy, and urge others to do the same," we must increase our commitment to improving expertise and modernizing our forces. With smaller arsenals, we can afford less risk in either systems or personnel. The illusionary, but logical, tension between decreasing the role of nuclear weapons, while at the same time strengthening deterrence, means it will remain challenging to recruit and retain the best. An encouraging sign is the number of young academics conducting new analysis, openly debating, and publishing on nuclear issues and twenty-first-century deterrence.

As we continue the work of reducing the size of the world's nuclear arsenals and analyze the rich complexity of our current strategic setting, efforts such as this volume are welcome additions to the much needed discussion and debate of deterrence concepts. This work provides much for the serious student of deterrence to contemplate, imposing several ideas and methods to meet the challenges of deterrence in the twenty-first century.

WILLIAM A. CHAMBERS
Major General, USAF
Assistant Chief of Staff for
Strategic Deterrence and Nuclear Integration

SECTION 1

The Prospects for Deterrence

in Cyberspace

Chapter 1

Introduction

The Evolution of Deterrence

Adam Lowther

Rapidly evolving strategic challenges, difficult fiscal conditions, and a desire to refashion national security policy are giving new life to an old concept—deterrence. While two decades of constant military operations in Iraq, Afghanistan, and elsewhere are largely responsible for American decision makers' focusing on present conflicts, scholars and strategists are beginning to undertake a long-overdue reexamination of Washington's approach to national security. This renaissance in strategic thinking is leading many to reconsider deterrence theory and practice.

Joint Publication 1-02, *Department of Defense Dictionary of Military and Associated Terms*, defines *deterrence* as "the prevention from action by fear of the consequences. . . . a state of mind brought about by the existence of a credible threat of unacceptable counteraction." From this definition it is easy to see that deterrence can incorporate a wide range of means focused on an equally wide array of actors. Unfortunately for deterrence theory, the concept has often been seen as synonymous with Cold War nuclear strategy, which played a major role in post–Cold War stagnation. Efforts are now under way to expand the context in which deterrence may prove useful in defending national interests against a host of new and developing threats.

During the half-century-long Cold War, the United States and the Soviet Union maintained an uneasy peace, largely because each country relied on a deterrence theory and policies that focused on preventing nuclear war. Theorists such as Bernard Brodie, Herman Kahn, and Thomas Schelling clearly emphasized that conventional conflict could escalate into nuclear war, thus requiring careful attention on the part of statesmen.[1] The special circumstances of the Cold War kept attention focused on *preventing* nuclear war rather than analyzing the continuities between nuclear and "lesser included" conflicts.

The watershed events represented by the end of the Cold War and the terrorist attacks of 11 September 2001 called into question the relevance of deterrence as a strategic approach. It began falling out of favor soon after the collapse of the Soviet Union, as democratization, globalization, and a focus on second- and third-world economic development displaced the decades-long emphasis on hard power.[2] Nuclear operations seemed less relevant in a world characterized by such diverse challenges as failed states, humanitarian disaster, genocidal conflict, counter/nonproliferation, terrorism, and asymmetric conflict. Amidst this changing strategic milieu, few sought to adapt deterrence's central premise—altering an ally's or adversary's behavior—to remain a relevant strategic approach. Instead, a new paradigm was needed for a "new world order."[3]

A generation later, optimism has faded as conflict and strife have proven as persistent as ever. Thus, a new opportunity for deterrence is presenting itself. However, if deterrence theory is to be relevant, it must move well beyond the vestiges of its Cold War past and focus on linking deterrence to desired effects—regardless of the actor being deterred. In other words, states that adopt deterrence as part of a comprehensive strategy should be able to determine, with a fair degree of certainty, that the policies and initiatives intended to deter certain behavior actually achieve their objective. Accomplishing this task is a difficult one and makes the success of deterrence difficult to determine.

While theorists and practitioners agree that, at its core, deterrence is about convincing adversaries and allies that the cost of an undesirable action is greater than the rewards, demonstrating success remains so elusive that a number of policy makers are reluctant to invest in new deterrence concepts and strategies. As in the past, moving deterrence forward will require an understanding of an adversary's motives, decision-making processes, and objectives.[4] While the Cold War structure may have evolved to give strategists some degree of confidence that the principal adversary was deterred by American capability, force structure, and alliances, today's diversity of challenges increases the complexity of formulating successful deterrence strategies.[5] In fact, not all adversaries may be deterrable. This may be particularly true of some nonstate actors.

Several analysts postulate that globalization has fundamentally transformed the security environment, making unilateral state action impractical and ineffective.[6] Those who adopt this perspective often argue that the threat-based nature of deterrence creates a diplomatic and military environment that precludes constructive conflict resolution.[7] Others claim that the fiscal costs of developing and maintaining the military platforms necessary to sustain a credible deterrent are prohibitively expensive and ineffectively consume limited resources that could be more efficiently used to better humanity.[8] Others see the primary utility of deterrence as remaining focused on nuclear weapons and their potential to prevent or cause major conflicts.

The lack of a post–Cold War "school of thought" has produced a situation in which the understanding of deterrence has stagnated. Thus, deterrence is receiving woefully inadequate consideration as a potential approach to the defense of the nation's vital, major, and peripheral interests. Ultimately, this could lead to policies that do not consider the full range of available options. Preventing such an outcome by encouraging deterrence thinking is the objective of this volume. Before turning to the specific chapters, which take a more granular look at specific aspects of deterrence, addressing four broad questions may serve to set the baseline for understanding.

What Is Twenty-First-Century Deterrence?

When it comes to deterrence, there are more questions than answers. Those who expect concise and immediate answers are destined to be frustrated by the highly theoretical nature of deterrence thinking. Those who would like to move deterrence into new areas may experience similar frustration as the conversation quickly becomes constrained to notions of nuclear deterrence, arms control, and counter/nonproliferation. There are, however, several insights that can inform policy discussions.

First, deterrence may not work in all situations. Some adversaries are simply unlikely to be deterred by the means available to the state. When such an adversary arises, containment or eradication may be the only viable options. However, understanding the culture, interests, and objectives of adversaries has the potential to decrease the number that cannot be deterred.[9] Possession of a value system that differs from Western norms does not make an adversary irrational. It simply requires greater knowledge and understanding on the part of the United States and its allies if deterrence is to be successful.

For those instances in which statecraft does apply, situations can and should be shaped without resorting to the threats inherent in deterrence interactions. This suggests that states should develop coherent and comprehensive approaches that are applicable to the global security environment and that they should deliberately employ all instruments of power to achieve preferred objectives. In such a context, states would focus and tailor their strategies according to the demands of the threat.[10]

In those situations where deterrence may apply, policy makers must determine the appropriate instruments, ensuring that the desired state of affairs (status quo) is effectively communicated and accepted by the target audience. Additionally, the success of deterrence depends on the ability to understand an adversary's behavior and possible counter moves. Absent such assessment, deterrence will remain a theoretical construct with little relation to conditions as they actually exist.

Second, although it may not be possible to deter all nonstate actors, it may be possible to deter many.[11] This is an area requiring further research aimed at developing an understanding of objectives and values. Only by understanding a nonstate actor can the United States and its allies target what it values most. While it is often said that Islamic fundamentalists are undeterrable, they do seek to achieve tangible worldly objectives.[12] This presents an opportunity to develop an effective set of deterrence policies that may include all aspects of diplomacy, information, military action, and economics. To the extent that criminals, insurgents, terrorists, and other groups represent challenges to state and international security, they operate outside the accepted laws of conflict due to weakness, not an inherent preference for the "tactics of the weak." To suggest that nonstate actors are—by nature— irrational would be a grave mistake.[13]

Finally, as long as states possess nuclear weapons and as long as there are those willing to share information and technology about weapons of mass destruction (WMD), deterrence remains a valid strategic approach. Where states have acquired such capabilities, deterrence is the primary approach that provides a foundation for governing interaction with adversaries. For those states that seek to acquire WMD, deterrence provides an approach that can be used to counter the proliferation threat.

What Means Are Available for Deterrence?

During the Cold War, the means of deterrence would not have generated significant interest. They were simple, straightforward, and well understood. However, the collapse of the Soviet Union on Christmas Day 1991, followed a decade later by the 9/11 terrorist attacks on the United States, left many within the academic and policy communities searching for new solutions to current problems. Most importantly, these events undermined the foundation upon which Cold War deterrence was built. Before 25 December 1991, it was widely understood that deterrence and nuclear weapons went hand in hand and were reliable partners. The end of the Cold War decoupled the two.

During the 1990s, globalization and democratization filled the void left by the Cold War's end. Although the United States experienced terrorist attacks on more than a few occasions before 9/11, it was not until the attacks on New York City and Washington, DC, that national security policy focused on the defeat of Islamic fundamentalist violence. Nonstate actors became the primary threat to American security. The elimination of al-Qaeda and other terrorist networks rose to preeminence among foreign policy and military objectives. Kinetic force became the primary instrument of power.

The mood in Washington changed, however, when a new administration took office in January 2009. This presented an opportunity to examine the usefulness of deterrence in an international system where the primary threats to security and stability are, and will remain, rogue regimes and nonstate actors—with the potential for a peer competitor down the line.[14] For deterrence to once again play a prominent role in defense policy, the instruments of deterrence must be applicable to current threats.

Unlike the Cold War, violent Islamic fundamentalism does not pose an existential threat to the United States. However, this does not mean that the United States should not maintain its capabilities (means) at all levels of conflict (fig. 1.1).

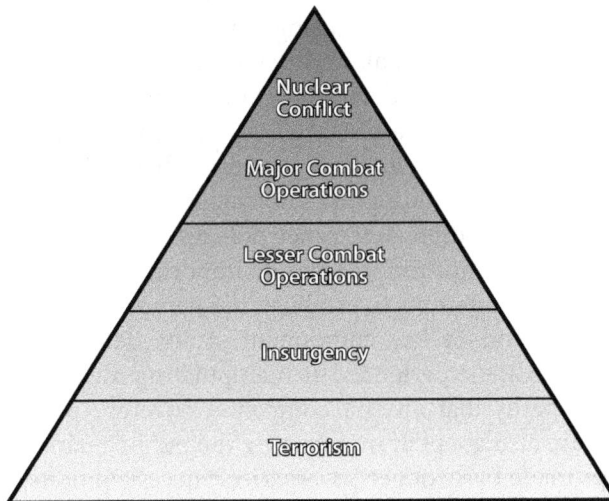

Figure 1.1. Conflict pyramid

Nuclear deterrence will remain the capstone of defense policy for many years to come. Determining the correct number of weapons and the proper mix of delivery platforms is a critical challenge for maintaining credible nuclear deterrence. While the threat of nuclear conflict is greatly diminished from its Cold War height, nuclear disarmament would allow and encourage adversaries operating at the lower end of the conflict spectrum to seek equality with the United States. Thus, it may be possible to deter nuclear proliferation by maintaining a credible nuclear deterrent.

With a wide variety of threats to security and stability in the international system, a new set of "redlines" that effectively communicate boundaries to potential adversaries is required. Not only do rogue regimes and nonstate actors pose significant threats to American interests, but their tactics (e.g., terrorism and cyber attack) are among the more difficult to deter. These adversaries operate from a rationale that is difficult for Americans to understand and develop effective deterrence policies to counter.[15]

Thinking in terms of weapons of *mass effect* rather than weapons of mass destruction may be a better approach. In an era where cyber warfare is becoming an increasingly important capability of state and nonstate actors—even as terrorism remains a key threat—the role of kinetic force is diminishing. Deterring current and future adversaries will require an expanded set of tools that rely more on the diplomatic, informational, and economic elements of national power.[16]

Intelligence will play an increasingly important role in supporting policies of dissuasion, denial, and deterrence. American Cold War strategists believed they understood rational Soviet leaders. The same cannot be said of modern adversaries who do not operate within the same rational framework as their Western adversaries. Intelligence plays a vital role in providing the knowledge and understanding required to develop credible deterrence policies.

Strategic communication will play an important role in undermining an adversary's attempts to establish the narrative and capture the moral high ground—a key component of any deterrence strategy. Nonstate actors are experienced at manipulating media coverage to gain the sympathy that often accompanies coverage of the "underdog." They are also adept at maximizing the public relations benefits of mistakes made by stronger adversaries. Successful nonstate actors are masterful in articulating a set of grievances that draw support from target audiences. Effectively countering the communications and public relations efforts of nonstate actors has the potential to undermine their cause and deter their efforts.

Rather than allowing nonstate actors to deter states through superiority in information/communication operations, states must develop the capability to deter nonstate actors through similar advantages. This may prove particularly difficult for democracies that are often unwilling to develop effective propaganda capabilities.[17]

Modernizing the instruments of deterrence for an international security environment different from its Cold War predecessor is long overdue and may yield unanticipated benefits. Doing so does not, however, guarantee the success of deterrence. Like all strategies, deterrence is prone to shortcomings that require alternative courses of action. As the next section illustrates, deterrence is not a magic bullet.

Why Does Deterrence Fail?

Actors operate within a strategic environment where incomplete information and suboptimal choices are characteristic of decision making. Some scholars suggest that decision makers operate within a framework of bounded rationality where variables such as stress, fear, exhaustion, and imperfect information abound.[18] Decision makers may see their adversaries very differently from what they actually are due to the importance of cultural, historical, linguistic, political, or religious differences. These limits in rationality and understanding can lead to a lack of situational awareness, poor signaling, misinformation, confusion, and the misreading of signals.[19]

Deterrence may fail because the United States, or any actor, does not understand its adversary. As mentioned earlier, American decision makers often operate without understanding the culture, history, language, politics, and religion of an adversary. Mirror imaging frequently occurs, leading decision makers to develop deterrence policies that are less effective than they could be.[20] The war in Iraq is one example of where a more complete understanding of these variables may have led to the development of policies that could have deterred a domestic-led and/or foreign-led insurgency.

There may also be a "credibility gap" between capability and will. Although the United States possesses unrivaled economic and military might, American decision makers, for many reasons, often respond to deterrence failures with insufficient punitive action to restore the status quo and credibility. This creates a gap between capability and will. Thus, future adversaries may not be deterred because of a history of unconvincing American action. For example, Osama bin Laden stated in a post–9/11 interview that weak American responses to previous al-Qaeda attacks created an expectation that President Bush would respond in a limited fashion to the 9/11 attacks, as had previous administrations.[21]

While ambiguity is a necessary element of a deterrence strategy, communicating a message that is too ambiguous can mislead an adversary and suggest that the United States, for example, will accept a change in the status quo when it will not. Ambiguity has worked best when uncertainty surrounds the severity of a response, not the possibility of a response. One of the most widely cited examples of too great a degree of ambiguity is the 25 July 1990 comments of the US ambassador to Iraq, April Glaspie, to Saddam Hussein that the United States had "no opinion" on the conflict between Iraq and Kuwait, thus opening the door for the Iraqi dictator's invasion of his neighbor.

One scholarly study suggests that approximately 30 percent of conflicts are initiated by a weaker power attacking a stronger.[22] Despite the probability of defeat or annihilation, weaker states frequently fail to be deterred by stronger adversaries because they are highly motivated (asymmetry of interests), they misperceive the probable response, and/or they seek to take advantage of an acute military vulnerability. Although risks often outweigh rewards, weaker states frequently feel risks more acutely.[23] The Japanese attack on Pearl Harbor is the most familiar example of a weaker state attacking a much stronger adversary despite an admittedly low probability of winning a prolonged conflict. For the Japanese, the risks of not attacking far outweighed the risks of an American response.[24] This was clearly the result of misperception of American will by the Japanese High Command.

Often deterrence fails because of a combination of the above points. Rarely does a single variable cause an adversary to seek a change in the status quo despite an articulated deterrence policy. It is clear, however, that the United States and others can reduce deterrence failures by more effectively communicating with an adversary. Successfully deterring current and future adversaries will depend on these variables.

What Impacts a Deterrence Strategy?

Undoubtedly, this final question is the most difficult of the four. The breadth of the question allows for varying interpretations of its meaning, which is useful in making three final points.

First, decision makers (political and military) in democracies are particularly guilty of focusing almost solely on current threats rather than long-term strategic interests. Deterrence, on the other hand, is dependent on developing effective policies well in advance of an adversary's attempt to alter the status quo. This requires decision makers to devise a tailored strategy and policy, effectively communicate objectives, and respond to potential threats well in advance of any adversary taking action.[25]

Second, the nuclear umbrella and extended deterrence remain a critical component of American foreign policy. As Japan remains committed to a nonnuclear defense posture—despite growing threats—the credibility of US extended deterrence weighs heavily in the strategic calculations of all nuclear umbrella beneficiaries. Further reduction in the operationally deployed strategic nuclear force is of great concern to the Japanese, for example, and poses a risk of encouraging proliferation if extended deterrence loses credibility. Japan and other allies have the potential to rapidly join the nuclear club should perceived threats and a lack of US commitment warrant such a response.

Third, public debate of deterrence concepts, policy, and strategy is a difficult task that often devolves into emotion-laden arguments. During the Cold War, Herman Kahn, the respected nuclear strategist, advocated a policy that would have enabled the United States to survive and win a nuclear conflict with the Soviet Union. His frank and calculating approach led policy makers, journalists, and scholars to dismiss his ideas. Today, it is equally difficult to discuss deterrence in public venues. The often unpleasant policy choices that are required lead policy makers, journalists, academics, and the American public to reject the entire discussion.

Although Herman Kahn found fostering a public debate on nuclear strategy difficult, there was at least some interest in the topic by the public at- large. Today, nuclear issues are passé and often seen as a relic of the Cold War. As in the past, today's threats require that decision makers contemplate unseemly options that the public finds at odds with our values. In part, this volume seeks to further an often stagnant debate.

Deterrence in the Twenty-First Century

To shed new light on deterrence—moving beyond the Cold War—the contributors to this work were asked to address specific questions relating to one or more of the many applications or characteristics of deterrence. While a broad consensus exists among the contributors that deterrence will remain relevant throughout the twenty-first century, there are differences in perspective when it comes to the prospects of successfully deterring peer competitors, rogue regimes, and nonstate actors across all domains with conventional and nuclear forces. Each chapter focuses on a contemporary question that is relevant to the current debate and assumes at least some knowledge of deterrence. The work is divided into three sections:

1. The Prospects for Deterrence in Cyberspace

2. The Relevance of Nuclear Deterrence in the Twenty-First Century, and

3. New Approaches To Conventional Deterrence

Section 1 begins by asking, "Can an operationally responsive cyberspace deter adversaries?" Kevin R. Beeker, Robert F. Mills, Michael R. Grimaila, and Michael W. Haas suggest that deterrence in cyberspace should look much like the current approach to deterrence in space. They argue for the creation of an operationally responsive cyberspace capability that brings government and private-sector cyber assets together to focus on a three-tiered approach. Tier 1 centers on the employment of capabilities, Tier 2 focuses on reconstitution efforts, and Tier 3 incorporates efforts to develop new capabilities. In all, the authors suggest that cyber deterrence is possible, if the right actions are taken.

The next chapter, "Does the United States Need a New Model for Cyber Deterrence?," begins by examining the distinct differences between the cyber domain and those of air, land, sea, and space. Kamaal T. Jabbour and E. Paul Ratazzi point out how some of the differences in fundamental characteristics make traditional approaches to deterrence unlikely to succeed. They offer alternatives that are more likely to succeed, given the current state of technology and understanding.

Section 2 begins with "Is Nuclear Deterrence Still Relevant?" Elbridge Colby argues that those who posit a fundamentally different strategic environment in which major war is no longer possible are mistaken; liberal values, economic globalization, and the international community have not changed the nature of conflict. Colby argues that human nature has not changed, making fear, honor, and interest no less drivers of human action today than they were in the time of Thucydides. Thus, nuclear deterrence and the nuclear arsenal remain as relevant today as they were during the Cold War.

In "How Much Is Enough?" Keith Payne challenges the current approach to sizing the nuclear arsenal, arguing that today's challenges make it difficult to determine the "right" size for the US stockpile. He argues that a more flexible approach is needed. Taking into account deterrence, assurance, damage limitation, and dissuasion will prove critical in determining the optimum size for the arsenal in an ever-changing strategic environment.

Jonathan Trexel moves beyond the strict limitations of nuclear deterrence to suggest that a new approach to long-term deterrence is necessary in "Can Tailored Deterrence and Smart Power Succeed against the Long-Term Nuclear Proliferation Challenge?" In keeping with the approach laid out in the 2006 *Deterrence Operations Joint Operating Concept*, Trexel seeks to move deterrence beyond its Cold War roots, making it a concept that can be employed against a wide array of actors that challenge US interests. One particular challenge he discusses is the proliferation of nuclear weapons in the years and decades ahead.

The next chapter in this section asks, "Is a new focus on nuclear weapons research and development necessary?" In addressing this question, Anne Fitzpatrick examines the changing nature of knowledge in nuclear weapons science and research, development, test, and evaluation (RDT&E) since the end of underground testing. She focuses on the nuclear weapons enterprise and stockpile stewardship programs, exploring recent developments in knowledge generation.

In what ways does Cold War logic inform the US military about strategic deterrence challenges of the twenty-first century? Edward Robbins, Hunter Hustus, and James Blackwell advance the mathematical foundations of strategic deterrence theory by revising and extending a crisis stability model that originated in the 1960s. Their game-theoretic analysis discovers a set of mathematical conditions through which strategic deterrence will be achieved, and they apply those rules to varying issues of force structure, nuclear warfare operations, and executive-level nuclear warfare decision making.

Section 3 examines deterrence in relation to nontraditional actors and tools, beginning with Gary Shaub's "Are Rogue Regimes Deterrable?" Shaub examines the deterrence literature, highlighting the fact that it often explains adversary intent from the perspective of one of two frameworks: strategic intent or internal logic. Actors were either motivated by a desire to change the status quo to mitigate external threats or because they sought to influence an internal audience. He suggests that both have explanatory power and are incorporated into the US Strategic Command's *Deterrence Operations Joint Operating Concept*. This, he argues, is the right approach.

This editor suggests that a layered approach to deterrence is required in "How Can the United States Deter Nonstate Actors?" We must address the threat posed by nonstate actors at the international, domestic, and individual levels. And at each level, policies that employ dissuasion, denial, and threat are critical to ensuring that deterrence does not fail if one particular effort is unsuccessful. In creating a layered approach that employs multiple methods, deterrence has a greater chance to succeed.

In "Is Space Deterrence Science Fiction?" Dale Hayden argues that the Cold War approach to deterrence is insufficient for the challenges posed by space. With the United States committed to keeping space weapon-free, Hayden suggests that a new approach to deterring adversaries from attacking US space assets is required. He proposes creating a space force that is resilient, responsive, and cost-effective. If successful, the United States will deter adversaries by demonstrating that it can rapidly reconstitute any loss of space-based capabilities.

"Can Unmanned Aerial Systems Contribute to Deterrence?" takes an innovative look at the role of remotely piloted aircraft (RPA) in a conventional deterrence strategy. James Perry suggests that they can serve either as strike or as intelligence, surveillance, and reconnaissance (ISR) platforms that can be employed against peer competitors, rogue regimes, and nonstate actors. RPA can play an important role in holding at risk that which an adversary values. Because these systems are unmanned, the United States can take much greater risks with these assets, a fact that may improve the effectiveness of a conventional deterrence strategy.

In summary, the central theme of this work is simple. Deterrence remains relevant. Those who advocate deterrence are not stuck in the

Cold War. In fact, in difficult fiscal times, deterrence may be more relevant than ever. The liberal dream held by neoconservatives and internationalists alike is an expensive one that the United States may no longer have the resources to fulfill. If this is true, expending greater energy on deterrence strategies that are often cost-effective strategies may be the best approach for the United States.

SECTION 1

The Prospects for Deterrence

in Cyberspace

Chapter 2

Operationally Responsive Cyberspace

A Critical Piece in the Strategic Deterrence Equation

Kevin R. Beeker, Robert F. Mills, Michael R. Grimaila, and Michael W. Haas

> *Cyber superiority ensures freedom of action in all domains (and denies freedom of action to adversaries) . . . predicate to all military and national security ops.*
>
> —Lt Gen Robert L. Elder

Introduction

Strategic deterrence is a well-established concept in military doctrine and an essential element of national power. However, deterrence in cyberspace is proving challenging due to several factors: the asymmetric nature of the domain, difficulties in the accurate and timely attribution of hostile activities, lack of established thresholds on what constitutes an act of war in cyberspace, an overemphasis on technology, and the growing number of adversaries that have access to cyberspace. In this chapter, we draw parallels between the domains of space and cyberspace for the purpose of identifying deterrence strategies that can impose costs, deny benefits, and encourage adversary restraint. We propose the establishment of an operationally responsive cyberspace (ORC) capability, similar in nature to operationally responsive space (ORS), which would significantly contribute to cyber deterrence by promoting cyber mission assurance activities that reduce or deny an adversary the benefits of cyber attacks. An ORC office would be responsible for coordinating and directing the research, development, testing, operational deployment, and coordination of cyber mission assurance efforts within the United States and ensure that holistic solutions are developed that account for the organizational systems composed of people, processes, and technology. A focused effort to develop a resilient cyberspace infrastructure prepares us to fight through cyber attacks and sends a strong deterrence message to potential adversaries that seek to gain benefits through asymmetric cyber attacks.

Superiority does not imply complete dominance in a war-fighting domain; if superiority in any domain were easily gained, there would be little need for our military to deter an adversary from conducting attacks against the United States and its interests, both at home and abroad. In Operation Desert Storm, the Iraqis flew 122 aircraft to Iran to avoid destruction by coalition air forces.[1] This demonstrates a successful deterrence strategy on our part because the Iraqis knew full well that the cost of attacking the coalition's air forces would be far higher than any benefit to be gained by having them fight directly. Granted, those 122 aircraft did not comprise the entire Iraqi air defense capability; Iraq retained and employed other air defense capabilities, resulting in the loss of 37 fixed-wing aircraft and five helicopters by the United States and its allies.[2]

At a micro level, the coalition's loss of these aircraft might represent a "prohibitive interference" for accomplishment of tactical missions, but at a macro level, most would accept that the coalition had achieved air superiority and was not prohibitively restricted from accomplishing its goals. Going into the conflict, we knew there would be opposition, and we were prepared to operate in a contested environment. Air superiority had to be established in varying degrees in different geographical areas to ensure overall mission accomplishment.

As we mature our understanding of military operations in cyberspace, a number of questions arise. For example, what does cyberspace superiority really mean, and how is it achieved? How can and should we deter attacks in and through cyberspace against our national interests? Assuming that deterrence fails, how do we conduct operations (fight through) in a contested cyberspace environment? What lessons can we learn from deterrence concepts in other domains that might shed some light on cyberspace "fight through"? The purpose of this chapter is to examine some of these concepts as they relate to cyberspace. First, we discuss a deterrence strategy based on denying the benefits of an adversary's actions. This strategy is highly applicable to the cyberspace environment because it avoids some of the problems associated with attribution and instead focuses on mission assurance. Next, we discuss what the space community has done in terms of developing a mission assurance strategy, the cornerstone of which is called operationally responsive space, or ORS. We then show the ways in which many of the problems and challenges of cyberspace deterrence and security are actually quite similar to space and describe how an operationally responsive cyberspace capability will go far in addressing many of our deterrence needs.

Deterrence Strategy: Denial of Benefits

Deterrence is all about convincing an adversary to not do something undesirable. A useful framework for developing a deterrence strategy is the Department of Defense (DOD) *Deterrence Operations Joint Operating Concept (DOJOC)*, which provides the military's doctrinal foundation for deterrence operations. The central idea of the *DOJOC* is "to decisively influence the adversary's decision-making calculus in order to prevent hostile actions against US vital interests."[3] The *DOJOC* seeks to accomplish this deterrence through a combination of denying benefits, imposing costs, and encouraging restraint.[4] Each of these is viewed from the adversary's point of view, because it is in the adversary's mind that the decision to commit the act is made. The concept is illustrated in figure 2.1. Deterrence is successful when the perceived costs incurred by an adversary outweigh the perceived benefits in regard to the consequences of restraint (fulcrum). Deterrence fails if an adversary perceives that a benefit of taking an action outweighs any associated costs and then commits those actions.

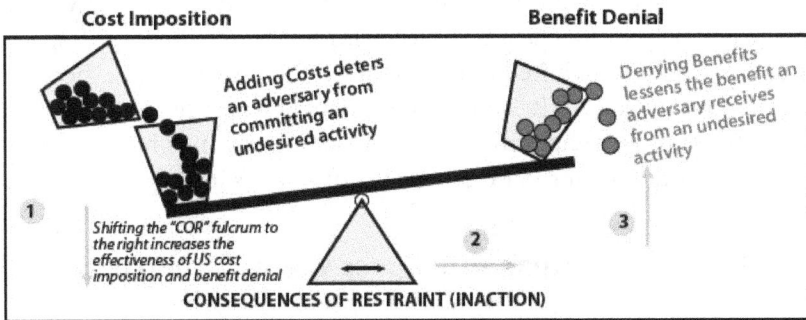

Cost Imposition   **Benefit Denial**

Adding Costs deters an adversary from committing an undesired activity

Denying Benefits lessens the benefit an adversary receives from an undesired activity

1

Shifting the "COR" fulcrum to the right increases the effectiveness of US cost imposition and benefit denial

2

3

CONSEQUENCES OF RESTRAINT (INACTION)

Deterrence Strategy
Successful deterrence is maintained by countering an adversary's perceived benefits with credible costs (1) or by denying the adversary benefits that may have been gained (2). The US can also induce adversary restraint by taking actions to 'shift the fulcrum' (3)

Figure 2.1. *DOJOC* **model of deterrence** (Adapted from LCDR Hal Okey, "Strategic Deterrence [SD] Joint Operating Concept [JOC] Version 2.0," Power-Point presentation, http://www.dtic.mil/futurejointwarfare/strategic/sd_joc.ppt.)

Beeker et al., in "Applying Deterrence in Cyberspace," provide a more detailed discussion of how the *DOJOC* model can apply in cyberspace.[5] In this chapter, we focus primarily on the denial of benefits. A prime example of how denying benefits can support deterrence and mission assurance is our approach to chemical or biological weapons. The US military equips its forces with mission-oriented protective posture (MOPP) gear and trains its members to carry out their missions despite the potential use of these weapons on the battlefield. These actions demonstrate to an enemy that their use of such weapons may make it more inconvenient for us to conduct our mission, but we *will get it done* nonetheless. In other words, the adversary will be denied whatever reward it seeks by employing such weapons and, we would hope, decide not to use them in the first place. If the adversary is not deterred from using those weapons, then our training and exercising will ensure that our forces can operate safely and continue the mission with minimal casualties.

Similarly, our cyberspace deterrence strategies should seek to deny the adversary benefits from its actions against us in and through cyberspace. Exercising and proving capabilities to operate while under duress or fight through cyberspace attacks will contribute to cyberspace deterrence. We must be able to fight through attacks in cyberspace, to include being able to carry the fight to the adversary when required. This in turn will deny the adversary benefits should it desire to attack. Demonstrating an ability to operate in a contested network environment will help influence any adversaries not to conduct cyberspace attacks against the United States, because there will be little permanent or lasting effect. The ability to recover from and generate a quick, effective, and overwhelming response to an attack in cyberspace will be an important factor in deterring an adversary's initiation of attack.

Domain Comparison: Space versus Cyberspace

As we examine deterrence within cyberspace, it is useful to examine the common ground between space and cyberspace strategies. Space and cyberspace are "utility domains" in that they enable operations in other domains. It is difficult to imagine trying to conduct operations in the air, land, or sea domains without our space and cyberspace capabilities. A Government Accountability Office (GAO) report on military space operations recognized that space systems play an "increasingly important role in DOD's overall war-fighting capability as well as the economy and the nation's critical infrastructure" and that "this growing dependence, however, is also making commercial and military space systems attractive targets for adversarial attacks."[6] Similarly, President Obama, in his remarks on securing the nation's information technology (IT) infrastructure, said,

> From now on, our digital infrastructure—the networks and computers we depend on every day—will be treated as they should be: as a strategic national asset. Protecting this infrastructure will be a national security priority. We will ensure that these networks are secure, trustworthy and resilient. We will deter, prevent, detect, and defend against attacks and recover quickly from any disruptions or damage.[7]

But space and cyberspace are also war-fighting domains in their own right—contested domains at that. Military commanders realize that space dominance can no longer be assumed. Consequently, ADM Michael Mullen, chairman of the Joint Chiefs of Staff, introduced a new special area of emphasis, titled "Space as a Contested Environment," on 30 March 2009. Space systems are vulnerable to a variety of attack vectors, including electronic jamming, dazzling, and debris fields causing kinetic destruction. Cyberspace is similar, and perhaps even more complicated, because the cost of entry for a cyberspace actor is much lower than for space. Costs include gaining the required technical expertise, the ability to command and control attacks, and the time to develop attack capabilities as well as the monetary costs to participate in the given domain. The interdependency between space and cyberspace is significant. Barriers to entry in the form of costs are traditionally higher in space, and it becomes much easier for someone to attack our space capabilities through the cyberspace domain, which fundamentally changes the deterrence equation. Deterrence strategies must recognize and address these cross-domain attacks; further, space and cyberspace planners must work together to explore and understand these issues.

To help ensure we have unfettered access to space, US Strategic Command (USSTRATCOM) created an operationally responsive space capability, shown in figure 2.2 and 2.3. ORS uses activities in three tiers to improve robustness and enhance our deterrence posture. Conceptually, Tier 1 involves leveraging existing capabilities (employment) to meet the needs of a joint force commander (JFC); an example might be adjusting a satellite orbit to provide better coverage in a war-fighting region. Tier 2 involves replacing a damaged satellite or providing capability via small launchers within weeks (launch/ deploy). Finally, Tier 3 addresses rapid development and deployment, such as deploying a new satellite to fill a capability gap within months. USSTRATCOM works closely with all of the combatant commands and JFCs to identify requirement gaps in the space infrastructure and prioritize requests for space capabilities.

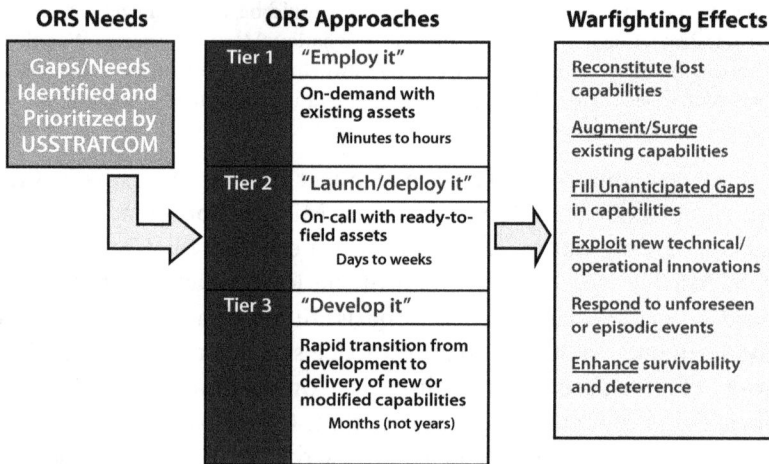

ORS Needs	ORS Approaches		Warfighting Effects
Gaps/Needs Identified and Prioritized by USSTRATCOM	**Tier 1** "Employ it" On-demand with existing assets Minutes to hours		Reconstitute lost capabilities Augment/Surge existing capabilities
	Tier 2 "Launch/deploy it" On-call with ready-to-field assets Days to weeks		Fill Unanticipated Gaps in capabilities Exploit new technical/ operational innovations
	Tier 3 "Develop it" Rapid transition from development to delivery of new or modified capabilities Months (not years)		Respond to unforeseen or episodic events Enhance survivability and deterrence

Figure 2.2. ORS concept (Adapted from Peter Wegner, "Operationally Responsive Space: Meeting the Joint Force Commanders' Needs," US Department of Defense, October 2008, http://www.responsivespace.com/ors/reference /ORS%20Office%20Overview_PA_Cleared%20notes.pdf.)

A key element of the Tier 2 ORS strategy is the Rapid Response Space Center (RRSC), or the Chile Works.[8] The RRSC should be fully operational in 2015, and its purpose is to use prebuilt components, solar arrays, power sources, and control mechanisms to attach to payloads (such as imagery and communications) to rapidly field a satellite in a matter of days. While establishing an ORS office to develop contingency plans may better position the United States in the space domain—and to some extent affect adversary decision making— building and funding a project like the Chile Works sends a much stronger message by demonstrating our resolve and ability to sustain capabilities in a contested environment.

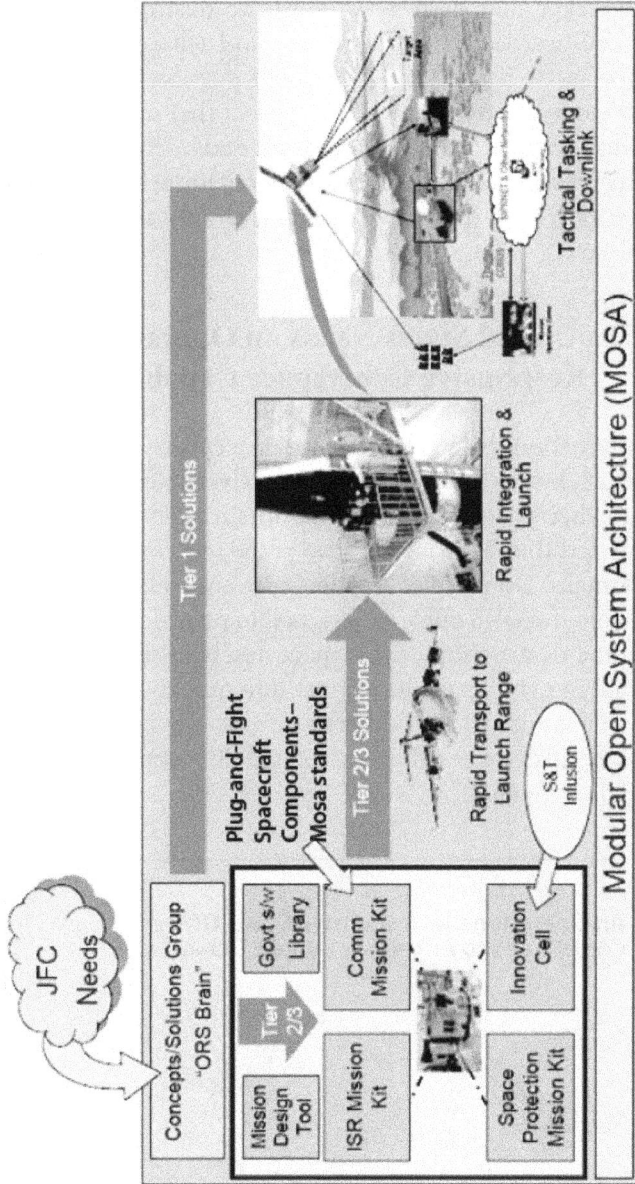

Figure 2.3. Implementation of the ORS concept (Adapted from Wegner, "Operationally Responsive Space.")

A rapid satellite development and launch capability communicates to our adversary that despite its efforts to destroy or degrade our space capabilities, we have the resolve and wherewithal to replace those space assets if needed. The benefit portion of the adversary's deterrence calculation is reduced by the fact that satellite destruction or disruption will not achieve its desired ends. This affects the decision to attempt satellite destruction or degradation; it might even deter the adversary from pursuing a destructive antisatellite program in the first place.

The United States Needs an Operationally Responsive Cyberspace Capability

Given our nation's heavy dependence on a cyberspace infrastructure, one might ask how we are posturing ourselves to continue operating given that cyberspace is a contested domain. Cyberspace is perhaps more contested than is space because of the much lower cost of entry into the domain. Do we have a cyberspace equivalent of ORS? In the same way that the ORS office is designed to provide quick reconstitution upon the destruction of our space assets, is there anything that can be done in cyberspace to reconstitute quickly after the destruction or compromise of key cyberspace infrastructure? Creating an operationally responsive cyberspace capability would be a step in the right direction (fig. 2.4).

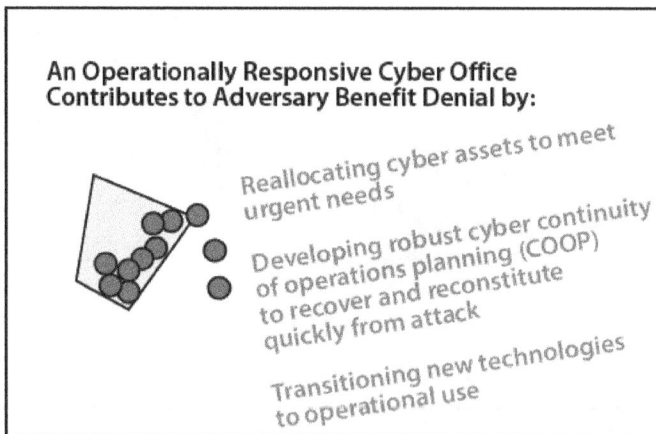

An Operationally Responsive Cyber Office Contributes to Adversary Benefit Denial by:

Reallocating cyber assets to meet urgent needs

Developing robust cyber continuity of operations planning (COOP) to recover and reconstitute quickly from attack

Transitioning new technologies to operational use

Figure 2.4. ORC contributes to benefit denial

ORC would be based upon similar principles to those of the ORS (table 2.1), but it would likely not operate in the exact same capacity. For example, ORS includes the ability to build and deploy satellites within weeks to replace damaged assets or provide new capabilities. It is unlikely that an ORC office would "build" equipment or software that is commonly associated with cyberspace infrastructure (e.g., routers and computer operating systems). This is primarily due to the much more widely pervasive and varying nature of cyberspace, to include large diversity in applications, information databases, network layouts, and actual hardware.

Table 2.1. Comparison of ORS to ORC

Tier	Operationally Responsive Space	Operationally Responsive Cyberspace
1	Retasking of a remote sensing satellite to provide reconnaissance photos	Reallocating satellite or "backbone" network bandwidth toward urgent communication need
	Requesting additional bandwidth from civilian communications satellites	Assigning extra computing processors across organizational boundaries
2	Building a new satellite with off-the-shelf components in weeks or days	Developing of robust cyber infrastructure continuity of operations plans to recover and reconstitute quickly
		Using virtual servers and desktop thin clients
		Storing data storage in backup sites
		Creating and applying Net Force maneuver concepts
3	Transition of new intelligence, surveillance, reconnaissance / communications capability to operational use in less than one year	Continual transition of new cyber reconstitution/recovery technologies to operational use

Adapted from Beeker et al., "Applying Deterrence in Cyberspace."

Instead, ORC would contribute more in the areas of providing leadership and focus for cyberspace operations and capability development. Cyberspace is a created domain—created by governments, businesses, organizations, and individuals—which represents another significant difference between the domains of space and cyberspace. Within the DOD alone, there are many entities responsible for creating, sustaining, and defending the cyberspace domain, including the services, combatant commands, and combat support agencies. Defending and sustaining the domain is a shared responsibility, and focusing the capability to reconstitute our cyber infrastructure in a single ORC office, even in a limited sense, would be problematic. With that said, we need to think about how ORC principles could be achieved. If the network or key services are not available, whether due to an attack, accident, or self-induced maintenance action, the response to such events should not be to send people home until the "IT guys" could figure out workarounds at the local level. The ability to fight through such events is critical.

While there may not be a direct one-to-one comparison between ORC and ORS functionality, an ORC office can still be modeled on similar principles. ORC could still have the same three-tier focus, but instead of being directly involved in recovery and reconstitution efforts, the ORC office would be a focal point for coordinating and encouraging activities and providing guidance throughout government and our national critical infrastructure sectors. The ORC office would also advocate policy and priorities to ensure that activities in each of the tiers requiring national-level attention and investment are pursued. This would include developing principles, lessons learned, and best practices (e.g., doctrine) to better help the nation prepare and respond to attacks in and through cyberspace. As these principles are implemented, exercised, and promoted, they will have an increasing deterrent effect upon an adversary's desire to attack the nation's cyberspace infrastructure. The objective is to convince our adversaries that any attempt to attack our systems would be a wasted effort because of a demonstrated ability to reconstitute affected cyber resources quickly.

Although ORC in this context is centralized at the national level, the concept can—and probably should—be decentralized in its application. USSTRATCOM oversees space reconstitution and recovery efforts for the DOD; the US Cyber Command (USCYBERCOM) could fulfill a similar role in reconstituting DOD cyber capabilities to a certain extent without intruding upon the services' organize, train, and equip responsibilities. In this instance, ORC looks very similar to ORS. Reconstitution and recovery capabilities must be pushed beyond and below the USCYBERCOM commander and should conceptually be constituted at the lowest possible levels. Examples abound and include backup servers for information and cyber-specific continuity of operations planning (COOP). Some thoughts and ideas related to activities that could be pursued in each of the tiers are discussed below.

Tier 1

As with ORS, ORC Tier 1 focuses on how to employ existing capabilities to achieve a desired effect. For example, a particular organization may need additional bandwidth across satellite communication networks for a period of time to support a task requiring increased data rates. Or an organization may need additional computer processors beyond its current capability to complete a modeling and simulation run and may require processors from other organizations to accomplish the task.

Both of these examples would contribute to our deterrence posture. Cyberspace is a malleable, constructed domain, and the ability to change the domain quickly—whether in response to an attack or to meet near-term mission requirements—demonstrates a high degree of agility and adaptability. Retasking cyber infrastructure assets can be extremely complicated due to highly shared resources and the intertwined nature of cyberspace. Cyberspace assets, such as satellite communications and Internet "backbone" pipes, are used by a variety of customers that cross organizational boundaries. In these instances, there is rarely a single authority or process that can reallocate resources quickly to support emergency requests. An ORC-type office could have the responsibility to establish procedures and define authorities for making decisions to reallocate/retask cyber infrastructure assets across organizational boundaries at the national level (e.g., government versus private sector or DOD versus Department of Homeland Security). At lower levels, single authorities may be easier to identify, such as in the DOD, where USCYBERCOM has been given the responsibility for securing and defending the Global Information Grid (GIG). Even then, however, the authority to secure and defend the GIG may not provide the authority to reallocate assets within the GIG. As a result, a similar ORC reallocation function may be required at lower organizational levels as well.

Tier 2

With ORS, Tier 2 focuses on deployment, to include the ability to launch new satellite capabilities rapidly. In a similar way, we must be prepared to reconstitute our cyberspace capabilities to prove and demonstrate to an adversary our ability to fight through an attack with little or no degradation in capability. To do this, ORC must focus on all elements of the cyberspace infrastructure. This includes not only the network links over which information flows and the hardware/ computers which process the information, but also the information itself stored in various databases and computer systems.

Significant strides have already been made in handling reconstitution of equipment, software, and data. Best practices for network operations include automatic failover, hot swappable storage devices, mirroring of databases and websites, and offsite storage of critical data, just to name a few. For example, if information at a primary operations center is destroyed or compromised, a backup copy of the information can be retrieved from an off-site location. In a worst-case scenario where the primary operations center is physically destroyed or needs to be moved due to a high threat environment, backup sites can even function as alternate operations centers. Private companies such as Carbonite, DriveHeadquarters, and others are providing similar data storage backup capabilities to both individuals and organizations.

A vast majority of the IT professionals at all levels (unit, major command, service, USCYBERCOM, etc.) are primarily concerned with keeping the network operational—keeping the bits and packets flowing. This activity is necessary but not sufficient for cyberspace fight through. There is a dichotomy in the perception between network defenders and operations personnel in military operations.[9] Network defenders are typically focused on assuring the health of the networked information infrastructure with a limited view of the operational importance of the missions supported. In contrast, operations personnel tend to be focused upon their own missions with limited understanding of how the missions depend upon the cyberspace infrastructure. These communities are inherently linked because, while network operations personnel focus upon maintaining the health and safety of the network and information systems, the mission operations personnel, who inherently rely upon the network and information systems, focus on assuring their mission operations through command decision making. Since the network exists to support organizational missions, there needs to be a stronger focus upon mission assurance and mission situational awareness.[10]

The DOD defined *mission assurance* for the first time in DOD Directive 3020.40, *DoD Policy and Responsibility for Critical Infrastructure*, as

a process to ensure that assigned tasks or duties can be performed in accordance with the intended purpose or plan. It is a summation of the activities and measures taken to ensure that required capabilities and all supporting infrastructures are available to the Department of Defense to carry out the National Military Strategy. It links numerous risk management program activities and security-related functions, such as force protection; antiterrorism; critical infrastructure protection; IA continuity of operations; chemical, biological, radiological, nuclear, and high explosive defense; readiness; and installation preparedness to create the synergy required for the Department of Defense to mobilize, deploy, support, and sustain military operations throughout the continuum of operations.[11]

While this definition is broad and focused on all critical infrastructure, it clearly identifies that the ability to perform operations is what is being protected, not just the information and communications infrastructure. While this sounds like a trivial difference, it is not, because its understanding requires a much stronger link between the operations and communications communities. This is one of many reasons behind the creation of the cyber operations career field within the US Air Force.[12] This increased mission focus represents a significant culture change from traditional communications and IT support.

An often-overlooked part of the mission assurance puzzle is business continuity planning (BCP) or continuity of operations planning. The purpose of BCP is to mitigate operational risks and help organizations stay in business when confronted with natural disasters, fire, data loss, cyber attacks, or other serious events. Effective mission assurance planning requires significant introspection by the end users. We must not forget that the whole point of building cyberspace is to enable information sharing among diverse and distributed users, and only they understand the context of the information being transmitted through the network.

BCP should be nothing new for most organizations in the DOD and should be included in any organization's continuity plans, especially those dealing with critical infrastructure. The Center for Strategic and International Studies (CSIS) Commission on Cybersecurity for the 44th Presidency summarizes the philosophy of COOP: "We will never be fully secure in cyberspace, but much can be done to reduce risk, increase resiliency, and gain new strengths."[13] The 2009 *National Infrastructure Protection Plan*, along with the underlying plans that focus on the nation's critical infrastructure sectors, also state the need for COOP and resiliency plans. However, the primary emphasis in these documents continues to be on *protection* of cyber assets, not *recovery*.[14] As a result, these documents contain little detail or guidance for generating robust COOPs which adequately meet cyber infrastructure requirements.

A strategic-focused ORC office would be an ideal location to develop appropriate COOP guidance for the DOD and national critical infrastructure and provide experts to assist governmental and private organizations in developing such plans. The need for an ORC office to provide this functionality is highlighted by the fact that COOP robustness regarding cyber infrastructure is often lacking.[15] A classic example of inadequate business continuity planning for cyberspace infrastructure came to light in the aftermath of Hurricane Katrina when emergency response efforts were crippled by a lack of communications: companies were unable to contact their employees to coordinate a response, and municipal websites normally used to disseminate disaster recovery and other information were unavailable for weeks.[16] In these areas, an ORC office could provide needed expertise and assistance to organizations and governmental entities to ensure their COOP plans sufficiently provide for reconstituting cyber infrastructure following attacks or other events. Further, the ORC could take on the role of developing curriculum and training for cyber infrastructure disaster recovery. This would help solve the lack of cyber infrastructure disaster recovery material within most IT curricula and help ensure that personnel entering the IT career fields are able to assist their employers with robust cyber COOP plans.[17] As robust cyber infrastructure COOPs are implemented, exercised, and updated, they will assist in creating a deterrent effect by demonstrating our will, resolve, and ability to continue operations in the face of determined opposition. These efforts will frustrate an adversary's attack and call into question its judgment for initiating such attacks.

In addition to continuity planning, the ORC could also take a lead role in leveraging new technologies that enable rapid reconstitution and service restoration. One example would be encouraging the use of virtual servers. Virtual servers can help provide quick recovery because a server with a hardware failure can be replaced with a spare and reimaged in a matter of minutes. Thin clients can provide the same type of recovery capability to desktops. Within the USAF, the Combat Information Transport System (CITS) is designed to provide these technologies and capabilities throughout much of the USAF's cyberspace infrastructure.[18] An ORC office could take lessons learned and successes from efforts such as CITS and provide insights and advice to other governmental and private organizations on how to implement similar systems. As implementation of these technologies becomes more ingrained within the United States, our ability to respond and reconstitute quickly from cyber attacks will improve.

The previous discussion refers to reconstitution of cyberspace infrastructure and data, that is, protection of the data at rest. Another significant issue is the ability to fight through attacks that degrade or deny our communication links. Since more and more of our communication capabilities are becoming IP-based (i.e., the Internet), our critical infrastructure has become less redundant and has fewer alternatives for passing information in the event that IP-based networks fail. Also, unlike data backups and computer hardware, it is difficult (and expensive) for organizations to quickly deploy new physical network infrastructure. Further, creating redundant network links, especially at the backbone level, is unlikely since the companies that run and maintain the current links operate on thin margins that do not justify significant investment to build redundant links. This is where an ORC office could advocate for funding and developing policy to assist in establishing redundant links and improved capability. Without government investment, it is unlikely that redundant links at the backbone level will ever be built. Private companies are unlikely to provide significant investment in redundant links based only upon "proposed" scenarios that have yet to occur. The ORC's role would be to identify the most critical points where redundant links are needed and ensure they are appropriately resourced.

Finally, the ORC could assist in identifying and implementing strategies for building resiliency in organizational networks. An interesting concept is Net Force Maneuver,[19] which is based on the idea of polymorphic networks. The objective is to provide the adversary a confusing picture of our cyberspace infrastructure, thereby causing it to have an incorrect picture of how portions of our cyberspace infrastructure tie to certain missions and operational tasks. An adversary's network reconnaissance and attacks will then be directed at the wrong points due to misperception of our network operations, resulting in a diminishing return for its efforts. Hence, the adversary sees its cost portion of the deterrence calculation increase, creating a situation where it is less likely to attack our critical cyber infrastructure.

Typically, maneuver warfare is seen as "a warfighting philosophy that seeks to shatter the enemy's cohesion through a variety of rapid, focused, and unexpected actions which create a turbulent and rapidly deteriorating situation with which the enemy cannot cope."[20] In the traditional war-fighting perspective, offensive maneuver is used to arrange conflict at the most advantageous time and location. However, from a cyberspace perspective, maneuver can be used in a defensive manner to frustrate the abilities of the attacker to identify and successfully attack the right resources. Different strategies for conducting this deception could be pursued. For example, fake (but realistic) operating environments could be created to alter the adversary's perception of key network operations and the location or existence of important data. These fake environments, also known as honeypots or honeynets, could be placed on alternate links upon which the main operations do not rely. In this case, the adversary could be led to attack the wrong targets with little or no effect on main operations. Another potential strategy could be virtually maneuvering among different links, networks, and databases, and so forth to provide the enemy with uncertainty as to where the real cyber operations are occurring at any given time. The ORC office could be responsible for maturing these types of strategies and developing new techniques for Net Force Maneuver, to include developing doctrine for employment.

Tier 3

The focus of Tier 3 ORS capabilities is the rapid transition of new space capabilities from development to delivery in a time frame of months versus years. A Tier 3 capability in cyberspace is even more critical due to the quick-changing technology throughout the cyberspace domain. Governmental reviews continue to highlight the need for research and innovation, including President Obama's recent 60-day cyberspace policy review, which has, as part of its near-term action plan, the following:

> Develop a framework for research and development strategies that focus on game-changing technologies that have the potential to enhance the security, reliability, resilience, and trustworthiness of digital infrastructure; provide the research community access to event data to facilitate developing tools, testing theories, and identifying workable solutions.[21]

It is important to note that "resiliency" is included in the research efforts, to include "developing options for additional services the Federal government could acquire or direct investments the government could make to enhance the survivability of communications during a time of natural disaster, crisis or conflict."[22] Also, an action to "coordinate with international partners and standards bodies to support next-generation national security/emergency preparedness communications capabilities in a globally distributed next-generation environment" is included.[23]

It is encouraging to see an increased focus being devoted to cyber infrastructure resiliency and recovery efforts, in addition to the usual heavy emphasis on network protection. However, there are several foundational research themes that must be addressed in depth to support the implementation of ORC. A significant challenge is to understand fully the cause-and-effect relationship between a given action to be undertaken and the subsequent "decision-making calculus" of the adversary. The cyberspace domain has many more nation-states, nongovernmental organizations (NGO), and ad hoc groups interconnected than does the space domain; there are exponentially more interrelated responses that could be triggered by any single action or set of actions. In addition, it is not beyond the realm of possibility that a set of actions could induce one or more of these interrelated nation-states, NGOs, or ad hoc groups to move from a neutral mindset to an adversarial mind-set, adding complexity and potentially deepening a conflict. This is true of either defensive or offensive actions if made public.

Effects caused by offensive cyber actions can be classified as affecting the physical domain and the cognitive domain. Physical domain effects of a cyber action can be evaluated on test hardware and software that replicate, as closely as possible, the hardware and software environment being targeted. It is much more difficult to predict how future cyber actions will affect the cognitive domain. In addition, uncertainty exists regarding cascading effects in the cognitive domain—that is, subsequent (higher order) effects caused by cognitive domain effects that are directly attributable to the initial cyber actions. Cognitive domain effects are a function of many variables, such as culture, perceived conditions of one's environment, the perceived target of the attack, level of belief in the knowledge of the attacker's identity, content of any present internal media coverage, and reaction by governmental, secular, or religious leaders.

Accelerated development and then high-level maintenance of a robust understanding of the cause-and-effect link between defensive and offensive cyber actions for deterrence and influence on potential adversaries is required to keep pace with rapid advances in cyberspace technology. This increased understanding of cause-and-effect links within the cognitive domain will reduce the potential of deepening future conflicts by presenting combatant commanders with a more predictable set of cognitive effects achievable through the use of offensive and defensive cyber actions. In essence, the increased understanding of achievable cognitive domain effects associated with a particular set of cyber actions increases the level of security by increasing the assurance that the desired cognitive domain effects will be achieved and by reducing the risk of generating unwanted initial or cascading cognitive domain effects, as discussed earlier. An ORC office would take the lead in increasing the emphasis on research into cyber infrastructure recovery and reconstitution, and transitioning new technologies, capabilities, and processes to both the governmental and private sectors. Through these efforts, the ORC could fulfill Tier 3–type activities and contribute to deterrence by proving to our adversaries our commitment to recovery and reconstitution capabilities and mission accomplishment. A comparison of efforts within each tier across the space and cyberspace domains is presented in table 2.1 as an enabling concept.

Conclusion

The domains of space and cyberspace have such great similarities that when policy makers, leaders, and strategists develop deterrence policies, they should consider how they could complement and support each other. Deterrence efforts impose costs, deny benefits, and encourage adversary restraint. In space, USSTRATCOM's Joint Operationally Responsive Space Office contributes to deterrence by denying the adversary the benefits of a space attack. ORS efforts signal to others that attacks against our satellites and space assets will be less effective, because these attacks can be mitigated using a three-tiered approach to developing, deploying, and employing space capabilities.

An operationally responsive cyberspace construct could afford much the same result for our nation in cyberspace. ORC would contribute to denying benefit to potential adversaries through a combination of robust cyber infrastructure continuity of operation plans, focused research and development of new recovery and reconstitution technologies, exercises that demonstrate and advance Net Force Maneuver and related concepts, and dedicated research efforts focused on cyber infrastructure recovery. The establishment of a national ORC office (within USCYBERCOM perhaps) would be a positive first step that would contribute to a strategic cyberspace deterrence strategy in a very real way. Organizing to fight through cyber attacks not only prepares the United States to operate under duress, but sends a strong deterrence message to potential adversaries that the nation aims to deny the benefit derived from an adversary's cyberspace attacks.

Notes

1. "Airpower in Operation Desert Storm," *Air Force Fact Sheets.*
2. "The Operation Desert Shield/Desert Storm Timeline," American Forces Press Service.
3. Department of Defense (DOD), *Deterrence Operations Joint Operating Concept.*
4. US Strategic Command, Policy, Doctrine and International Affairs Division (USSC PDIAD), "Strategic Deterrence (SD) Joint Operating Concept (JOC) Version 2.0."
5. Beeker, Mills, and Grimaila, "Applying Deterrence in Cyberspace."
6. USSC PDIAD, "SD JOC Version 2.0."
7. "Remarks by the President on Securing our Nation's Cyber Infrastructure."
8. Holmes, "Lab to Build Special Order Satellites in Days."
9. Tinnel, Saydjari, and Haines, "An Integrated Cyber Panel System."
10. Hale, Grimaila, Mills, Haas, and Maynard, "Communicating Potential Mission Impact Using Shared Mission Representations."
11. DOD Directive 3020.40, *DoD Policy and Responsibility for Critical Infrastructure.*
12. US Air Force Public Affairs, "Communications Airmen Meet to Discuss Career Field's Transformation."
13. Center for Strategic and International Studies (CSIS), *Securing Cyberspace for the 44th Presidency.*
14. Department of Homeland Security, *National Infrastructure Protection Plan.*
15. Vijayan, "Data Security Risks Missing from Disaster Recovery Plans"; and Government Accountability Office, *Internet Infrastructure.*
16. Landry and Koger, "Dispelling 10 Common Disaster Recovery Myths."
17. Ibid.
18. Paone, "CITS Key to Air Force Cyber Superiority Goal."
19. Hunt, Bowes, and Gardner, "Net Force Maneuver."
20. Marine Corps Doctrinal Publication 1, *Warfighting.*
21. The White House, *Cyberspace Policy Review: Assuring a Trusted and Resilient Information and Communications Infrastructure.*
22. Ibid., 35.
23. Ibid.

Chapter 3

Deterrence in Cyberspace

Kamal T. Jabbour and E. Paul Ratazzi

History teaches that wars begin when governments believe the price of aggression is cheap.

—Pres. Ronald Reagan, 1984

Cyberspace is a domain where cyber operations are conducted to enable or achieve military effects and objectives. While traditional warfare concepts and doctrine should be expanded to include this domain, they must account for its unique properties. These include both fundamental differences as well as evolving technical characteristics. As the first line of any defensive strategy, deterrence is an important concept that is of particular interest in this regard. Following a review of cyberspace, cyberspace operations, and key differences between this and other domains, this chapter discusses the various types of deterrence that are possible in cyberspace.

Introduction to Cyberspace

Joint Publication (JP) 1-02, *Dictionary of Military and Associated Terms*, defines *cyberspace* as "a global domain within the information environment consisting of the interdependent networks of information technology infrastructures, including the Internet, telecommunications networks, computer systems, and embedded processors and controllers," and *cyberspace operations* as "the employment of cyber capabilities where the primary purpose is to achieve military objectives or effects in or through cyberspace. Such operations include computer network operations and activities to operate and defend the Global Information Grid."[1]

We view cyberspace first and foremost as a foundational domain that enables US military superiority and secondarily as another warfighting domain in its own right, where specific effects can be achieved through cyberspace operations. In the past, cyberspace has been viewed as a largely *uncontested* environment.[2] However, a recent Air Force Scientific Advisory Board (SAB) study concluded that during a conflict the nature and availability of this environment could and would change dramatically.[3] Furthermore, there is mounting evidence that our national approach to security in this domain is not keeping pace with the threat,[4] our military networks have widespread vulnerabilities,[5] and the strategy to protect our national interests in this new environment has been largely unsuccessful.[6]

A new strategy for securing cyberspace must employ new technical solutions that implement many of the war-fighting concepts that have served us well in other domains. Presumably, deterrence, as the first line of defense and a fundamental element of defensive strategy, must be explored as the foundation for this new strategy.[7] Unfortunately, traditional notions of separate offensive and defensive cyber forces serve to limit artificially the full potential of a deterrence strategy in cyberspace. Since various areas of cyberspace can be simultaneously occupied by both red and blue forces, offensive and defensive operations must likewise occur simultaneously and in concert and not be treated as separate endeavors. A framework for integration of offense and defense is thus required to go beyond a Maginot Line model.[8]

Cyber Operations Vision

In 2009, we developed a science and technology–based vision for cyberspace operations.[9] This vision identified nine key technical capabilities that form an enabling framework for the Air Force's strategic imperatives of global vigilance, global power, and global reach, as shown in table 3.1.

Table 3.1. USAF strategic imperatives are enabled by nine primary technical capabilities

Global Vigilance	the ability to keep an unblinking eye on any entity—to provide warning on capabilities and intentions, as well as identify needs and opportunities	Situational Awareness
		Assurance
		Avoidance
Global Power	the ability to move, supply, and position assets—with unrivaled velocity and precision anywhere	Access
		Survival
		Cross-Domain Operations
Global Reach	the ability to hold at risk or strike any target, anywhere, and project swift, frequently decisive, precise effects	Precision Effects
		Effects Assessment
		Response Action

Adapted from Norton A. Schwartz, "Fly, Fight and Win," CSAF's Vector, September 2008, http://www.af.mil /library/viewpoints/csaf.asp?id=405.

One feature of this new framework is that it blends offense and defense within each imperative and thus optimizes the use of both capabilities in support of cyberspace operations. Several of the nine technical capabilities directly support deterrence strategy. Specifically, assurance and avoidance technologies can significantly raise the costs of attacks while simultaneously lowering the probability of success.

Assurance. A credible fighting force does not conduct warfare with unreliable, untrustworthy, and untested weapons that fail under adversary attack. Assurance in cyberspace demands building war-fighting systems that ensure specific missions, even in a contested environment, using formal, requirements-driven systems engineering processes. When performed properly, assurance results in systems that guarantee the ability to execute mission-essential functions (MEF), even where the adversary is attempting to deny our use of cyberspace. War-fighting systems developed with this approach will be inherently more difficult and costly to attack, therefore decreasing the benefits of attempting attacks.

Avoidance. Unlike a traditional cyber defense mind-set that assumes the extent of the attack surface to be fixed and that addresses risks with additional intrusion and attack detection mechanisms, avoidance seeks to create a *strategic* advantage in cyberspace by avoiding threats altogether. Threat avoidance reduces or eliminates the need to fight, increases the difficulty of attacking, and lowers the probability of a successful attack. Threat avoidance may be accomplished by way of three interrelated approaches: reducing the target-system cross section, increasing agility, and implementing deterrence.[10]

In reducing the target-system cross section, we make many threats irrelevant by eliminating vulnerabilities and their exposure beforehand. As with assurance, vulnerabilities can be "designed out" through a systematic, requirements-based process. However, mission dynamics and ever-changing threats dictate that these secure configurations be maintained constantly and automatically to ensure minimum exposure and responsiveness to system-level mission requirements.[11] Furthermore, legacy protocols and architectures can be replaced with those that favor defense and support defensive prerequisites that are standard in other domains. When nonrepudiation is deemed important, protocols that guarantee attribution and facilitate geolocation must be employed. Likewise, if broad classes of threats exploit stored-program computer architectures, then architectures using physically separate memories must be considered. In effect, many "laws" that govern cyberspace operations consist of synthetic protocols, interfaces, devices, and architectures that can be redesigned to avoid attacks by ensuring a defensive advantage through "threat noninteroperability."

Agility in cyberspace implies maneuverability and the capability to evade attacks. Attacks are avoided by denying the adversary the advantage of time and the benefit of previously collected intelligence. A study of activities across the lifecycle of an attack showed that an attacker spends up to 95 percent of that time in *preparation* for the actual attack execution.[12] A conclusion based on this estimate asserts that mechanisms designed to frustrate the intelligence-gathering and preparation phases of an attack are highly effective in increasing the probability that the attack will never occur.[13] Real-time agility is accomplished through the use of polymorphic techniques at multiple points within the system and network architecture to present an agile, evasive "moving target" that forces an attacker to spend 100 percent of the time in the "find" state of the kill chain.* As an example, rapid address and port hopping among peers across untrustworthy internetworks can thwart an attacker's ability to find, fix, track, and target key systems and allow these systems to deploy escape tactics when faced with a viable threat.[14]

The third element of threat avoidance, cyber deterrence, is the subject of this chapter. Although assurance and threat avoidance contribute to deterrence by way of increased cost and decreased benefit, deterrence is arguably more complex and more difficult to implement than these purely technological means. This is because deterrence includes considerations beyond those that are strictly technological, such as expressed intent and political will.[15] Furthermore, fundamental differences between cyberspace and other domains add to this complexity and render many assumptions of traditional deterrence theory invalid. As such, a brief examination of the properties of cyberspace is warranted.

Properties of Cyberspace

As a war-fighting domain, cyberspace is fundamentally different from other domains. An understanding of these differences is an important prerequisite to developing approaches to cyber deterrence. Several of them have a significant impact on the underlying assumptions of traditional deterrence theory.

---

*Based on the Air Force–centric definition of the kill chain: (1) find, (2) fix, (3) track, (4) target, (5) engage, and (6) assess (F2T2EA).

Cyberspace Is Unbounded and Changes Rapidly. Unlike air, space, sea, and land, which are essentially fixed in size, cyberspace is a technological domain that changes and expands every time humans touch it. Although limited by physical laws, cyberspace operations become useful through the protocols, devices, and architectures that harness them. It is through these designs that we connect, communicate, process, store, attack, and defend in cyberspace.

These "laws" of cyberspace operations dictate how we interface systems, how links and nodes behave, and what works and what does not work. This is analogous to how we harness the physical laws of other domains for the conduct of warfare. However, unlike in other domains, the laws of cyberspace operations change as technology changes.

The result of this evolution is that the threat environment and the means for defense are constantly changing. A zero-day attack executed 30 years ago against an IBM System/360 via malicious punch cards would not be effective today for the same reason Windows malware propagated via a USB thumb drive would not have been effective 30 years ago. While the laws of physics have not changed in 30 years, their technical applications have changed. In cyberspace, technological change brings new capabilities and threats at the same time it obsolesces current ones.

Cyberspace Is Nongeographic. Possibly the most challenging aspect of cyberspace for the application of traditional concepts is that it has no geographic dimensions or boundaries. For millennia, almost every aspect of warfare has been intimately tied to geography. Strategic advantage, doctrine, success, failure, the element of surprise, and many other characteristics and results of warfare have depended on geographic features. Like space, cyberspace has no defined range of operations or areas of responsibility.[16] However, unlike even space, cyber has none of the geographic dimensions so familiar in other domains. The frames of reference that do exist in cyberspace (e.g., logical connectivity) are highly dynamic.

Cyberspace Is Jurisdictionally Complex. Determining jurisdictional boundaries in cyberspace is complicated and not yet well defined. On one hand, some argue that cyberspace is international space (i.e., global commons) that lacks territorial jurisdiction and that its jurisdiction should be based on nationality, much like the high seas or outer space.[17] On the other hand, because cyberspace exists only where technology exists, every piece is privately owned and operated and subject to the owners' laws, regulations, and terms of service. On this premise, jurisdiction would be determined based on the owner of a given piece of cyberspace.

Cyberspace Is Nonattributional. Although not an inherent trait of cyberspace, many aspects of current cyberspace operations lack attribution and favor anonymity. Moreover, an overall global move toward technology that would provide a high degree of nonrepudiation in cyberspace is unlikely due to its status as a global commons and increasing trends toward digital anonymity.[18]

The United States Is Asymmetrically Dependent on Cyberspace. Our increasing reliance on cyberspace, usually viewed as an indicator of technological superiority, has become a vulnerability.[19] The United States is target rich in cyberspace, while many of our adversaries are not.

Cyberspace Has a Low Cost of Entry. No vast arsenals, complex delivery systems, or standing armies are required for an entity to threaten or attack others in cyberspace. In addition, anonymity is virtually guaranteed, further lessening the nonmonetary costs of launching attacks.[20] Finally, there is no significant cost for the adversary to maintain a sustained attack or if an attack fails. Table 3.2 contains a summary of this comparison.

Table 3.2. Cyberspace differs fundamentally from other domains

	Cyberspace	Air, Space, Sea, and Ground
Size	Unbounded	Essentially fixed
Rate of change	High	Low
Governed by	Technology	Physical laws
Ownership and jurisdiction	Private	Sovereign and international
Cost of entry	Low	High
Attribution	Difficult or impossible as currently implemented	High due to physical evidence
Dimension	Connectivity	Geographic
Cost of attack	Little or none	Expended munitions

Cyber Deterrence

Traditional approaches to deterrence include threat of retaliation, assured mutual destruction, denial, increased cost to the adversary, and decreased benefits for the adversary. The inherent characteristics of cyberspace, as well as the ways in which it is currently utilized, will have a significant impact on the viability of these strategies if they are simply borrowed from tradition without revisiting the assumptions behind each. Many of these traditional approaches, especially deterrence through threat of retaliation, have serious shortcomings in the cyber domain because of the fundamental differences outlined previously and summarized here.

1. Lack of attribution.

2. Low cost of aggression with high payoff for success.

3. Inconsequential (due to conflicting, impeding, or nonexistent laws).

4. Low probability of detection.

5. Target has more to lose than the attacker.

6. Emerging technology can instantly "change the game" and invalidate basic assumptions.

In addition, many criticisms of deterrence strategy are based on weaknesses that are only amplified in the cyber domain. Assumptions about the identity, intent, nature, or rationality of a typical cyber adversary can be readily called into question when forming the basis for retaliation.

With all these potential pitfalls, is cyber deterrence worth pursuing or even possible? Obviously, if it can be realized at all, the foundation for deterrence in cyberspace will be much different than for other domains. The basic theory must be reestablished from the ground up, and many of the fundamental assumptions that have been the hallmark of deterrence in the nuclear era will have to be reevaluated. Policy and national strategy must be created and clarified so that adversaries have a basis for decision making and consequence evaluation. Finally, specific technologies must be developed and/or implemented in critical portions of cyberspace to enable cyber deterrence. Beginning with an evaluation of the basic theory, we analyze each of these traditional approaches.

Deterrence through Threat of Retaliation

The current joint definition of deterrence is "the prevention from action by fear of the consequences. Deterrence is a state of mind brought about by the existence of a credible threat of unacceptable counteraction."[21]

This somewhat narrow view of deterrence has its roots in the Cold War. It conjures up images of nuclear Armageddon and a doctrine of deterrence through massive retaliation and mutually assured destruction, especially for those with childhood memories of fallout shelters and duck-and-cover drills. From this definition, which focuses only on consequences through counteraction, one might conclude that deterrence can only be achieved through a threatened counteraction. Some have argued that the geographic and attribution ambiguities in cyberspace make this form of deterrence largely unachievable. These domain characteristics lead to several key difficulties including no actionable basis for deterrence, lack of high confidence, rapid attribution, and lack of a credible and demonstrated capability for response.[22]

Although these problems may indeed preclude effective deterrence of an attacking cyber adversary, this form of deterrence is actually employed routinely and effectively in cyberspace. Every day, millions of DOD and corporate computer users are deterred from violating organizational policy concerning their use of cyberspace. Penalties for misuse are understood and displayed at every login, attribution is virtually certain by way of access credentials, and retribution can be swift and severe. Therefore, deterrence by threat of retaliation does exist in cyberspace but only against users who have a tangible risk and fear certain retaliation. These are authorized users, not the adversary.

Before concluding that deterrence of an adversary by these means is not possible due to the difficulties outlined above, recall from the previous section that cyberspace is a technological domain. In this domain, cyberspace operations must obey laws that are derived from the design of the technology. Because of this, it should be possible to design cyber infrastructure that enables this type of deterrence against even the adversary. Just as authorized users are deterred from misusing corporate resources because of technological means that enable retribution, a properly designed cyberspace would allow unauthorized users to be similarly held at risk.

Assured Mutual Self-Destruction

More and more, cyberspace is becoming interconnected, with many of its users dependent on the proper functioning of shared resources. Cloud computing, for example, offers any individual or organization access to vast computing and storage resources without the added baggage of owning and maintaining the resources. Companies and governments are outsourcing their enterprise applications and storage needs to providers such as Google, Amazon, and Microsoft. The "black box" nature of these services makes it difficult, if not impossible, to know where a particular application is executed or a particular file is stored within the cloud. Even precision attacks against these services may likely have widespread unintended effects, possibly against the interests of an attacker. Similar to the way in which we and our adversaries are mutually dependent on the financial stability of world markets, actors in cyberspace are increasingly dependent on the proper functioning and availability of cyber infrastructure. This mutual dependence translates into a deterrent force if mission-essential functions are placed carefully and securely alongside collateral activities that would be disadvantageous for the adversary to disrupt or destroy.

Deterrence by Denial

This deterrence relies on the buildup of defensive technologies to neutralize or mitigate attacks. Deterrence by denial works well in a "defense-dominant" environment such as missile defense, where the denial of attack success costs more than the expected benefits.[23] Unfortunately, in cyberspace an adversary incurs very little cost when an attack fails and is usually free to keep trying without incurring additional costs. Thus, deterrence by denial is not currently feasible in cyberspace. However, the fact that there is no cost for attempting and failing an attack is simply a result of how cyberspace is currently implemented. If it were implemented in such a way that attack detection was certain and attribution rapid and reliable, the cost for failure might begin to outweigh the expected benefit for some attackers. For example, if a critical function were isolated physically or logically from the rest of cyberspace, the added effort required of an attacker might become prohibitive and expose the attack, thereby providing a deterrent. Similarly, selective substitution of hardware for software in critical systems denies an attacker the ease of remote modification of a target.

Deterrence through Increased Cost to the Adversary

Increasing the cost of attack to the point where an adversary decides it is no longer worthwhile requires an understanding of the adversary's cost model and the level of its relative expertise. Agile cyber systems that break attack planning cycles and render an attacker's knowledge base worthless may increase the cost and/or difficulty of an attack enough to deter. Manipulating how our defenses are presented to affect the adversary's perception of costs can also serve to deter. For example, prepositioning an application on thousands of dissimilar systems across the domain increases disproportionately the cost to an adversary.

Deterrence through Decreased Benefits for the Adversary

In an environment where there will always be some level of vulnerability, deterrence through decreased benefits is based on ensuring that successful attacks do not result in significant payoffs for the adversary. Assuming an attack is detected, this approach might involve deceptive techniques to lure attackers into honeypots or into extracting bogus information. An attacker that perceives (whether true or not) that its costly attacks are producing useless results may be deterred from continuing.

This type of deterrence can also be realized by way of highly resilient systems—systems that have an innate ability to adapt to unexpected inputs, such as those likely presented by an attacker, and continue operating in spite of the attack—for example, genetic algorithms that allow a software system to evolve when new negative test cases are discovered during operation.

Summary and Conclusion

As a fundamental element of defense, deterrence has served as the foundation of US military strategy for decades. With cyberspace now recognized as both an enabling domain and a war-fighting domain in its own right, it is understandable that war fighters and policy makers wish to extend deterrence concepts to cyberspace. Going forward, we must recognize that deterrence models will be unique for every domain, especially cyberspace. Much of the current theory and approach has been built within the context of nuclear deterrence. Blind application of this framework will fail, since the context and very properties of the domain are completely different.

Based on an analysis of the properties of cyberspace, we conclude that there are several opportunities for application of new deterrence. The threat of assured mutual self-destruction of cyberspace assets and approaches that manipulate the adversary's cost-benefit equation seem to hold the most promise. Realization of these will require fundamental technological changes to the cyberspace domain as well as a new set of rational policies that are scientifically sound and enforceable by way of the technical characteristics of the domain.

Notes

1. Joint Publication (JP) 1-02, *Dictionary of Military and Associated Terms*, 141.
2. Shaud, "In Service to the Nation," 35.
3. US Air Force Scientific Advisory Board, *Defending and Operating in a Contested Cyber Domain*, 2.
4. The White House, *Cyberspace Policy Review*, v.
5. Defense Science Board, *Challenges to Military Operations in Support of US Interests*, vol. 2, 320.
6. CSIS, *Securing Cyberspace for the 44th Presidency*, 12.
7. Alberts, *Defensive Information Warfare*, 59; and Tirenin and Faatz, "A Concept for Strategic Cyber Defense."
8. US House, statement of William A. Wulf.
9. Jabbour, "The Science and Technology of Cyber Operations."
10. Air Force Research Laboratory, Information Directorate, *Integrated Cyber Defense & Support Technologies*.
11. Narain, Levin, Malik, and Kaul, "Declarative Infrastructure Configuration Synthesis and Debugging."
12. Lowry, "An Initial Foray into Understanding Adversary Planning and Courses of Action."
13. Air Force Research Laboratory, *Proactive and Predictive Cyber Indications and Warnings*, 82–83.
14. Air Force Research Laboratory, Rome Research Site, "Polymorphic Cyber Defense."
15. For a discussion of *expressed intent*, see Kaufmann, *The Evolution of Deterrence*; and for *political will* see Frederick, "Deterrence and Space-Based Missile Defense."
16. Chilton, "Cyberspace Leadership."
17. Menthe, "Jurisdiction in Cyberspace."
18. Libicki, "Deterrence in Cyberspace."
19. Shaud, "In Service to the Nation."
20. Ibid., 36.
21. JP 1-02, 161.
22. Libicki, "Deterrence in Cyberspace"; and Tirenin and Faatz, *A Concept for Strategic Cyber Defense*.
23. Harknett, "To Deter or Not to Deter."

SECTION 2

The Relevance of Nuclear Deterrence in the Twenty-First Century

Chapter 4

Why Nuclear Deterrence Is Still Relevant

Elbridge A. Colby

Is nuclear deterrence still relevant to US policy? From the heights of its prominence in the depths of the Cold War, nuclear deterrence has fallen into relative obscurity. Given the nature of the conflicts in which the United States is engaged today, attention in defense circles focuses on counterinsurgency, counterterrorism, and high-level conventional conflict. So stark has been the shift that a blue-ribbon panel appointed in the wake of embarrassing incidents within the US nuclear bomber force found "a serious erosion of focus, expertise, mission readiness, resources, and discipline in the nuclear weapons enterprise within the Air Force" and a general lack of interest in nuclear matters within the Defense Department as a whole.[1] The broader intellectual climate has been even less favorable than the neglect suffered within the defense community. Indeed, much of the focus received in recent years by issues relating to nuclear deterrence has been generated by the well-publicized effort to eliminate nuclear weapons entirely, an effort that in one way or another has received the endorsement of both President Obama and his 2008 Republican rival, Senator John McCain, legions of former senior officials, and countless cultural, religious, and other influential figures. Someone not steeped in the intricacies of nuclear deterrence might be forgiven for thinking that the broader military's lack of interest and the testimonies against its necessity by its former high priests and practitioners, like Henry Kissinger, must constitute pretty powerful evidence that nuclear deterrence is no longer relevant—or even needed.

There is an element of truth to this view. The obsessive, at times almost maniacal, focus of the Cold War years on nuclear weapons has passed, and has passed on good grounds. For a variety of reasons, the intense competition between the United States and the Soviet Union

The author would like to thank Bruno Tertrais, George Quester, and Robert Jervis for their helpful comments in preparing the manuscript. Professor Jervis was especially, but characteristically, generous in reviewing a chapter that takes aim at one of his own arguments.

in the years between 1945 and the denouement of the USSR in the late 1980s manifested itself above all in a nuclear weapons arms race. Each side sought to develop and deploy nuclear weapons that could provide what it perceived to be an advantage—not only in military terms but also in the geopolitical perceptual test of strength. This dynamic pushed the two superpowers to field forces with unimaginable destructive capabilities that were well beyond the bounds of any rational strategic goal and demanded the creation of the peculiar neologism "overkill." With each side possessing tens of thousands of thermonuclear weapons, both had the power to annihilate not only each other, but perhaps even civilized life on Earth. Accompanying these arsenals were fervent efforts to develop strategies for their use. Some of these efforts were reasonable attempts to grapple with the contorting challenge of seeking to satisfy political objectives with weapons whose destructiveness transcended the boundaries of the politically sensible; others, however, seemed so untethered from a firm grasp of the weapons' catastrophic power that they imbued nuclear deterrence as a whole with an air of unreality, if not morbid insouciance, perhaps best captured by Stanley Kubrick's *Dr. Strangelove*.[2]

The dissolution of the Soviet Empire and consequent relaxation of tensions between West and East, the disappearance of a credible alternative to socially minded liberal-market systems, and the overweening dominance of the United States in the post–Cold War era, however, have ushered in a radically different perspective on the salience of nuclear deterrence. From being a central concern of geopolitics and, indeed, of humanity, nuclear deterrence suddenly has become marginal and, to many, unnecessary. The chief virtue claimed for it during the dark days of the Cold War had been the prevention of major war, but in the wake of the demise of the great challenger to the free market's ascendancy, such war no longer seems, to many, to be a serious possibility. Indeed, some analysts have gone so far as to claim that war is, in fact, obsolete, a residual vestige of more primitive eras.[3] And one cannot but observe that the rate of wars has declined substantially over the past centuries.[4] This development has been seen as stemming from a variety of roots. Some have emphasized the triumph of pacifying liberal democracy and the eclipse of rival ideologies.[5] Others have stressed a softening of once belligerent social mores and intellectual attitudes and the correlative development of strong "norms" against war.[6] Still others have pointed to the declining economic rationality of war, noting that, in an age of relatively open and free trade, the advantages of territorial conquest in a Malthusian world no longer apply.[7] Such arguments for why major war is no longer a serious possibility may be synthesized into two main thrusts: humanity has moved beyond war, and war no longer pays.

If this view is correct, then it surely follows that nuclear deterrence is indeed irrelevant—and, worse than that, dangerous, given the ever-present chances of accident or miscalculation.[8] A world in which great war is impossible or perhaps even just extremely unlikely would also be a world in which nuclear weapons would serve no rational purpose, for the only justification for maintaining and threatening to use arms of such apocalyptic destructiveness is if they are effective at restraining Mars in the first place. But is it true that major war is no longer possible?

Does War No Longer Pay?

Let us first consider the narrower claim for war's obsolescence—that it no longer pays. According to this argument, traceable to the school of Adam Smith, the long-term gains to be had from trade outweigh those held out by aggressive war. Nations, and interest groups within nations, profit more from the liberal path of specialization and free commerce, which propels the broad enrichment of all parties, than from conquest or subordination.[9] Moreover, especially in a world of highly destructive nonnuclear weaponry and in which nations can mass their populations into great armies, the costs of war are also potentially very high, even without nuclear weapons entering into the equation.

There is much truth to this argument. In a post-Malthusian world in which it is primarily productivity rather than the exploitation of the land that equates to prosperity, it does pay to orient society toward the cultivation of productive and efficient labor rather than military might. Beyond the requirements of defense and the stabilization of the overarching order, it often does not make sense to use the military instrument to extract wealth, even for an order's hegemon, because such use is likely to undermine the free market system itself by spurring countervailing responses by the exploited or those fearing exploitation and by undermining confidence in the stability and market rationality of the order. Even within a country, exploitation may lead to ultimately counterproductive distortions in the economy.[10]

Vesting too much confidence in this argument for the passing of major war, however, might be to confuse the telos of a system with the actual dynamics of its workings. Capitalism, taken to its logical conclusion, would presumably involve the abolition of restraints on the free hiring and firing of labor, the dissipation of international constraints on the movement of persons and goods, and, indeed, even the retirement of the concepts of nationhood and citizenship themselves. Yet is there any reason to think such developments likely, let alone desirable? Are human societies straining to approximate the capitalist ideal of a perfectly rational allocation of capital and effort in the pursuit of the best aggregate outcome, even at the expense of the unproductive? The answer must be a clear no. Quite to the contrary, human beings seem keen to maintain themselves in groupings of one kind or another, above all the nation-state, designed to protect individuals and social groups from a too perfect market rationality and to improve their advantages relative to others.[11] The persistence of this behavior indicates that states and other entities still seek economic protection and advantage from noneconomic sources, and thus may still seek to wrest economic wealth or shelter through military force, including through coercion rather than pure brute force—even if such advantages are less impressive than the absolute gains they might garner in a perfect international market system.[12] This suggests that market suboptimal "errors," ranging from Saddam Hussein's brazen attempt to gain Kuwait's oil riches to variants of the more subtle "Finlandization" feared for West Germany during the 1970s, are still possible.

Nor is the danger of war in liberal capitalism confined to suboptimal "errors." For instance, observers of the international political economy have emphasized that the liberal market system is not reliably self-generating but rather is best sustained by a hegemonic power prepared to enforce the rules of the system, both through economic measures and military force.[13] Yet the exertions of such hegemons tend to sow the seeds of their own demise, leading to weakening of the system, perilous instability, and, ultimately, the breakup of the hegemon's power.[14] The absence of an effective hegemon can, in turn, lead to the balkanization of economic relations and thus to inefficiencies and distortions in the economic system that appear invidious to some members. Even if neither the hegemon nor the system's participants saw the advantages of waging war during a hegemon's ascendancy, the same might not hold true for periods of a hegemon's wane, let alone when there is no hegemon at all. In straightforward terms, states may often have to make do in a world that is not optimally organized on liberal trade principles, a world in which the use of military force might not, from a purely economic point of view, be the per se suboptimal option.

But there is a deeper problem with the argument that war no longer pays—for wars have been waged for reasons other than material gain, and indeed in some cases with the assessment that war would likely result in material loss rather than gain, as in the case of Japan in 1941.[15] In many instances this has resulted from the often tragic nature of the structure of international politics in which states may feel most secure in costly domination or the weakness of their rivals and neighbors rather than in a more prosperous but insecure peace.[16] France's policy of seeking to cripple Germany in the interwar years out of fear of its resurgence stands as a classic example. The policy no doubt was economically suboptimal, but Paris saw it as the safer option, the loss of wealth be damned. If nations still feel insecure in a competitive and anarchic international environment, then there is little reason to see why these classical impulsions to war no longer operate.

Nor is the structure of the international environment the only generator of war. Pride, honor, the *libido dominandi*, the thrill of warfare and conquest, and the like are also primal drivers of human interaction and have historically played important, if not at times dominant, roles in fostering war.[17] The ambitions of Hitler, Mussolini, Napoleon, Genghis Khan, Attila the Hun, Julius Caesar, and Alexander the Great—as well as the armies and peoples they led—simply cannot be understood without reference to the salience of pride, honor, the allure of power and domination, and glory. While calculations of advantage clearly have factored into the considerations of leaders and their populaces, demonstrating that exploitative war is not as profitable as a free-market peace only tinkers at the edges of the calculations of those for whom comfortable prosperity is but one good among others at best, let alone a secondary one, or even, as it was for the Communists, Fascists, and steppe barbarians, an object of disdain.

The proposition that war does not pay may, then, be generally true, but, given the incomplete scope of its applicability and the verity that wars do not stem solely from the pursuit of material gain, it is surely far too narrow a base to conclude that war is passé.

Beyond War? The Issue of Security Communities

What, however, if deeper forces are at work in making war no longer possible, even in a nuclear weapons-free world? Indeed, some argue that not only does war no longer pay, but international politics does not need to generate the insecurities that can lead to war, and the nature of society and mores has so fundamentally changed in advanced liberal democratic systems that great war is no longer a serious option (at least within certain circumstances).

Rather than vainly seeking to survey a vast and variegated literature on this question, it may be more appropriate to focus on a synthesis of these arguments offered by Robert Jervis in his book *American Foreign Policy in a New Era*. Jervis is not only one of the foremost international relations scholars of the era, but he is also highly respected for his judiciousness, wisdom, and immunity to faddishness. Moreover, he is generally identified as a "realist" in political science terms, so taking on his argument for the obsolescence of major war is to take on the argument in its most careful, sophisticated, and resilient form. His arguments for the proposition that "war among the leading great powers—the most developed states of the United States, Western Europe, and Japan—will not occur in the future, and indeed is no longer a source of concern for them," can thus reasonably be taken as a champion for the set of arguments as a whole.[18]

Jervis's basic argument is that war can and, within certain conditions, has become a thing of the past. Drawing from the work of constructivist and liberal as well as realist analysts and scholars, he argues that a "security community" in which war is no longer plausible has emerged as a result of "the destructiveness of war, the benefits of peace, and the changes in values" among the participant nations which more or less correlate with the North Atlantic community and Japan.[19] The outcome has been that, within this community, "neither the publics nor the political elites nor even the military establishments expect war with each other."[20] Indeed, these developments have made "war unthinkable" within the precincts of the security community.[21]

Jervis sees this transcendence of the serious possibility of war as stemming from several factors. Culling from the constructivist school, he first argues that the norms, values, ideas, attitudes, and the like that used to impel nations and peoples to war have been replaced within the security community by those that render war against fellow security community members not only anathema, but unthinkable—

simply not a genuine policy option. As he puts it, "Although war is still seen as necessary when imposed on states by extreme circumstances . . . no one talks about the importance of honor, which sparked many wars in the past, or sees wars as a way to satisfy national or individual quests for glory. States with these outlooks will not fight each other."[22] Moreover, these changes in values are "self-reinforcing," constituting "a benign cycle of behavior, beliefs, and expectations" that allows nations under its influence to get out of the cycle of anxiety and distrust that characterizes states in the suspicious anarchy of realist thought.[23]

The second strand of argument that Jervis draws upon is the liberal one, emphasizing the importance of democratization, economic interdependence, and, to a lesser degree, the role of inter- and supra-national organizations. Jervis is more skeptical of the role of these factors, noting that multiple conditions invariably attach to arguments for the salience of democracy and economic interdependence and dismissing the role of international organizations as "slight."[24] Nonetheless, he contends that the gains brought by peaceful coexistence and the habits of democracy, when operating together with other factors such as the softening of mores, have contributed to making war implausible within the community.[25]

Finally, Jervis points to the critical importance of the traditional realist influences of power and fear. Indeed, his argument is not that nuclear weapons have made no difference. Rather, he judges that "a necessary condition" of great-power peace "is the belief that conquest is difficult and war is terribly costly," and that nuclear weapons in particular have made it "hard for anyone to believe that war could make sense."[26] Yet while Jervis holds that the presence of nuclear weapons *was* essential for the creation and consolidation of the security community of pacific nations, he argues that the progress of "the Community is path-dependent . . . [that] forms of cooperation [have] set off positive feedback and are now self-sustaining."[27] Given that he argues that war among participants in the community is "unthinkable"—a word variously defined as deeming something impossible to conceive or imagine or not capable of being grasped by the mind—it stands to reason that nuclear weapons either are or will become irrelevant and presumably unnecessary among them, and so the same would hold true if the security community were to expand.

Jervis is careful to note that this "community" is composed only of those states which have been subject to the relevant influences, but they are also those states that represent the vanguard of history.[28]

Given that Jervis argues that the security community is self-sustaining in part because its system is superior in delivering value to its members, it stands to reason that the model will expand in one way or another as the rest of the world develops.[29] This is especially so because Jervis emphasizes the critical pacifying importance of nuclear deterrence in making war too costly, a realization that changes in values then work upon to cement the obsolescence of war. Jervis also cautions that war is still possible between members of the security community and outsiders such as China and Russia (as well as smaller nations) but argues that, even here, such disputes are "not like those that characterized great-power conflicts over the past three centuries." Rather than contests for supremacy, he sees these tensions as stemming from advocacy for "milieu goals" and so presumably as more amenable to amelioration and eventual transcendence.[30]

The upshot of Jervis's argument, which synthesizes a vast literature and captures the spirit of a prominent contemporary intellectual attitude, is that the maturation of mores and the progress of democracy and free trade, when combined with the lessons learned from the costliness of war and its limited value, have created a self-sustaining and self-propagating community of nations and peoples for which war is simply unthinkable—as foreign to political and social life as dueling is to interpersonal relations.[31] To this view, while war is still with us as a matter of fact, this is a contingent rather than a necessary aspect of human social interaction. Indeed, the direction of history indicates that it is a passing characteristic; its salience is inversely correlated to the increasing development of human society. Needless to say, a world in which war is simply unimaginable, beyond the pale, is also a world in which nuclear weapons would be unnecessary.

Europe as a Model? The Centrality of Power

But this is not in fact the world in which we live, nor the one in which we can expect to live in the future. The root flaw in Jervis's argument, and in the arguments of those who contend that war is passé, is a conception of history and of human political and social development that markedly overestimates the durability of historically contingent value systems while seriously downplaying the enduring centrality of competition, fear, uncertainty, and power. Jervis is right in marveling at the creation of a pacific community of nations and peoples and at the stark changes in mores and attitudes that have helped propel and cement this community.[32] He is even right in emphasizing that such a community has considerable resilience. But is he right that the basic nature of human politico-social interaction—and to some degree human nature itself—has changed, or is capable of changing, so deeply through the alteration of value systems? The answer is that it has not, nor is it capable of such change. Even as conditions and mores have changed, the same basic competitive dynamics that Hobbes boldly outlined three and a half centuries ago (and that Darwin sketched out in the animal kingdom) remain active today and will continue to remain so as long as human beings are constituted as they have been for millennia.[33] Because of this enduring reality, we must always be acutely aware that war is possible and thinkable and that the most reliable method for minimizing its recurrence is through the prudent manipulation of fear and interest.

Let us first examine the particular case of the "security community" of Europe, for it is within this milieu that Jervis makes his claims of war's impossibility. Jervis is right that Europe has become a continent in which war among its major nations is undesired and indeed implausible. But this is not, at its root, due to changes in the values of Europeans but rather to developments in the European power structure—developments that have not removed the possibility of war as such but rather transferred them to a different plane. The most important factors in explaining the current implausibility of war in Europe are the combination of the essential irrelevance of European state power since the end of the Second World War and the presence of American power. These factors have combined to make serious war between European states pointless, exceptionally difficult to mount, and unnecessary, not to mention unattractive—pointless because such wars would not directly affect the primary, relevant power balance; difficult because European states have not had the power to go to war without American assistance and authorization; and unnecessary because European security has been guaranteed by the hegemon, the United States.

What has happened? Wars throughout history, and particularly major wars in modern Europe, have been driven primarily by the desire to dominate a given state system or to stave off such domination by another.[34] The Thirty Years' War was a struggle by the Habsburg Empire to assert its dominance over Europe and by the Protestant powers and France to resist such domination. The wars of Louis XIV represented successive attempts by France to achieve supremacy over Western Europe. The wars of the French Revolution and especially Napoleon were the apotheosis of this attempt. Finally, World Wars I and II represented efforts by Germany to dominate Europe. Each of these conflicts directly affected the European power balance, was necessary in that the independence or autonomy of the states could not, it was believed, be protected without going to war, and could be initiated at will by any of the major parties to the war. Throughout the modern period, and well before it, state policies on war and peace have been driven above all by such considerations. Great Britain's historical policy of intervening on behalf of the weaker coalition to prevent the consolidation of power on the continent stands as a prime example of this, as do France's policies seeking to counterbalance German power in the years leading up to each of the world wars.

With the end of the Second World War, however, Europe had essentially exhausted itself, leaving the field to the true victors, the giants America and Russia, whom Tocqueville had recognized would come to overawe and outclass Europe.[35] But the European powers were not simply conquered or garrisoned as a matter of contingency; rather, they had been "priced out of the market" of the great power contest.[36] For, after 1945, the European states simply could not stand in the same category as the superpowers militarily or economically. No individual European state or plausible combination of states could match either American or, during the Cold War, Soviet power. Unlike the two superpowers, the states of Europe could not develop secure, effective, and discriminate strategic nuclear and adequate conventional forces, and thus faced, at best, the deathly choice of "suicide or surrender" if abandoned by Washington to Soviet aggression or coercion. As with the princely states of the Holy Roman Empire after Napoleon or the American states in the wake of the Civil War, the European states had been transcended as politico-strategic units. Therefore, instead of a power balance among the European states, after 1945 there ensued first a bipolar structure between the United States and the USSR and then a hegemonic unipolar structure under US auspices, with the European states of Jervis's "security community" serving as allies, irritants, or neutrals, but not leading strategic actors of their own.

These developments, strengthened by the central role of the United States and the dollar in international economic stability, have meant that the contest for power and dominance over Europe since 1945 has taken place at a level beyond which individual European states have been able to play leading roles, a point that was driven home rather harshly by the United States and the Soviet Union during the Suez Crisis of 1956. So dependent upon external protection and leadership have the European states been since 1945, and indeed increasingly over the course of the Cold War, that many astute analysts have regarded them as being part of an American "empire," albeit a liberal one.[37]

In any case, war between European states in the post-1945 world would, unlike those before 1945, have been irrelevant to determining the status of the European system, unnecessary for their preservation, and essentially impossible without US authorization. War among these states would have been pointless, in that it would not have created a more stable or more beneficial strategic environment. It would also have been unnecessary, for the safety and security of the states rested on the guarantee of the United States. Nor would it have been permitted. Neither the United States nor the Soviet Union, during the term of its empire, would have allowed its allies or client states to fight one another.[38] Indeed, most NATO nation-states, and especially the most powerful European state, Germany, have been and are simply incapable of operating substantial military forces independent of US assistance, as evidenced in the 2011 Libyan operation.

This is not to deny the role of changes in values, liberal systems of government, and other factors in propelling and cementing the peace within the European community. Europeans have clearly become less martial (just as Americans have become considerably more martial since assuming a global security role), but this in some ways suits their role as security wards of the United States. And European democratic governments have not pushed for intra-European war and have avoided (with the partial exception of France) directly challenging or excessively undermining the American-led security system. And economic growth has enabled Europeans to focus on prosperity and social welfare. While these factors are important, they are ultimately secondary causes, aids to the underlying dynamic of the transcendence of the intra-European state balance.

Jervis is right, then, that war within the European security community is implausible under current circumstances. But *why* that is negates the proposition that such implausibility means that strategic competition and war can be pushed out of international politics. For the basic reason why Europe is a security community is that the relevant echelon for strategic interaction has risen above intra-European state boundaries to a level at which the European states cannot act autonomously without uniting. The once fiercely independent states of Europe thus resemble the once fractious states of the United States, the patchwork of princely fiefdoms and republics of the Holy Roman Empire, the city-states, and principalities of pre-Risorgimento Italy, the warring tribes of Italy before the Social War, and the proud polises of ancient Greece before Philip of Macedon. In each of these cases, political, social, or economic developments made once-intransigent disputes among states irrelevant and ultimately led to their forming, usually through compulsion, into a larger entity which then directed those energies outward against some common opponent.[39] No one can imagine Virginia fighting Massachusetts and New York today, nor Saxony fighting Bavaria, but that is not because the *potential* for war has disappeared from human affairs; it is rather because these political units cannot compete with more-efficiently organized, larger entities.

Indeed, it is instructive in this respect to note the progress toward the unification of Europe. For centuries, from Charlemagne through Charles V and Louis XIV on to Napoleon and Kaiser Wilhelm, Europeans have dreamed of unification of the states of Europe but have consistently failed. Only today has there been significant, stable progress toward such unification. Why? Clearly the increased fellow-feeling in Europe and the decline of militarism have played roles, but more determinative has been the compulsion to scale. Economically, increased unification through the abolition of trade barriers and synchronization of economic policies has allowed Europe to increase efficiency and thereby seek to compete in a globalized economy. Politically, it has allowed Europe to try to exercise some of its lost influence on the world stage. And, perhaps most revealingly, it has served as a way to try to achieve some autonomy from and balance with the superpower, particularly through the greater, if increasingly uncertain, strength afforded by the euro. Though this unification represents a pacification of intra-European relations, it does not mean the end of strategic competition as such—rather it is in part an attempt to engage on that very strategic plane from which Europe has largely been excluded by its inability to achieve scale—to punch, in more colloquial terms, at the heavyweight level.

Europe's progress toward becoming a security community does not represent, then, a transcendence of war, but rather mainly a displacement of war from its traditional arena among the states of Europe to a broader vista. For better or worse, the United States is Europe's security guarantor and, in key respects, its benign imperial overseer, and the United States is engaged in strategic competition—with a rising China, with a recalcitrant Russia, with an ambitious Iran, and so forth. Europe's development cannot be seen, then, as a model for or an augury of world pacification. It is, rather, another chapter in the long history of the interaction of state power, technology, and strategic competition, one for which war continues to be supremely relevant. Strategic competition and the possibility of great war remain.

The Historical Contingency of Peaceful Europe

The pacific stability of postwar Europe stems primarily, then, from the obsolescence of the European state system and from the security patronage of the United States. Shifts in values and systems of government have helped, but they could not uphold such stability without a favorable power structure. But we would be remiss if we reduced this story to power politics and liberalism alone and dismissed more organic factors in explaining what has happened in Europe, for there may be deeper currents at work in reducing the probability of war within Europe.

Foremost is the possibility that Europe is in a civilizational phase of softening mores, introversion, and complacency. Organic conceptions of the rise, flourishing, and decline of nations and civilizations are woefully unfashionable in an empiricist age, but they have been central to explanations of history and international politics from antiquity until the twentieth century.[40] From Plato to Toynbee, thinkers have observed that powerful nations, peoples, cities, and the like appear to go through stages of development involving some variations of a vigorous and energetic rise, a proud flourishing, and a softening or stultifying decline. The Romans, whose martial prowess, stern discipline, and unwavering determination overpowered every rival in the ancient Mediterranean, became known in the late imperial period rather for their opulence and their unwillingness to shoulder the demands of civic virtue.[41] The Byzantines, who under Justinian reconquered most of the Mediterranean and under Heraclius, took on the Persian Empire, retreated before the Arab invasions in large part because of exhaustion and internal discord before ultimately succumbing to the Ottoman Turks. Machiavelli dedicated himself to understanding why the Italians had declined from the mastery of the Romans to the

disunion and weakness of the city-states and principalities of the Renaissance.[42] Perhaps the best example in the early modern period is
Spain, which became the premier power in Europe in the sixteenth
century before exhausting itself in the confessional wars, debasing its
economy, and yielding to a long decline. Beyond Europe, Chinese
imperial dynasties appeared to past observers to follow a pattern of
vigorous conquest, flourishing, luxuriation, and finally overthrow.
The Ming and the Manchu dynasties followed this pattern. In the
Middle East, the stern and lean Arabs who rode out of the desert and
conquered all before them eventually were seen to become lethargic
and fell to the steppe Turkic peoples.[43]

Europe's current, more pacific phase, then, might be seen as a stage
in its civilizational development.[44] Throughout the history of post-
antique Europe, war as a manifestation of vigorous interstate competition has been a constant, indeed perhaps a driving force, in Europe's
success in gaining world supremacy.[45] But the cataclysms of the two
world wars, the declining influence of and confidence in the traditional sources of Western civilization, and the adoption of modernity
by and consequent rise of non-European nations and peoples, among
other factors, have contributed to what has to be seen as a decline in
civilizational vigor, for lack of a better term, by the European peoples.[46]
This might be particularly intensified by the marked aging of the European population. Europeans are not just less bellicose within Europe,
within the "security community"; they are also less bellicose in general.
In earlier eras, such a civilization would likely have fallen prey to
hungrier, more aggressive peoples or nations, as Rome fell to the
Germanic barbarians, China to Mongols and Manchus, and Arabs to
Mongols and Turks. Even during the Cold War, such a Europe left to
its own devices almost certainly would have fallen under Soviet sway
or outright dominion. But as Europe has been and is protected by the
United States and by nuclear weapons, this did not come to pass.

That Europe has entered into such a historical phase does not,
then, mean that war is passé in general—Europe may be at the end of
its run rather than at the end of history. Peoples and nations have
many times before lost the appetite for war, but that has not meant
that war, to paraphrase Trotsky, was not interested in them. Indeed,
we should not take Europe's development as a one-way ratchet, for
history may be sinusoidal rather than a bell curve. The Chinese, who
were bywords for the "sick men" of Asia in the nineteenth century,
have clearly recovered a civilizational vigor they had lost during the

heyday of Western supremacy. China in recent years has exhibited very clearly an appreciation for the military instrument, even as it promises to surpass Europe in economic success.[47] So we should be extremely cautious about assuming that Europe itself has abandoned its warlike ways for good.

Yet our caution about foretelling the demise of war should not be tied only to views of history, for there are wellsprings of human belligerence that go even deeper than the historical contingency of the security community of Europe.[48] Though the "realists" of neorealism are right that war is endemic to an anarchic state system, man is not driven toward war only by the structure of the international system, which is a relatively recent phenomenon in human development, but also by his deepest instincts and sentiments.[49] Pride, honor, biological necessity, the desire to dominate, the desire to feel "the passion of life to its top," ideological or religious obligations, et cetera have combined to drive people, and especially men, to go to war.[50] It would be inane to try to catalog fully the historical examples of those who have gone to war for more than pure reasons of state, but a few might include Alexander the Great, Julius Caesar, and Louis XIV, who pursued conquests for glory; the religious wars of the Arab Conquests, the Crusades, and the confessional wars, which, while they are certainly not reducible to religious motivations, can hardly be understood without them; and Napoleon and Hitler, whose wars sprang from combinations of vainglory, ideological zeal, and mania. Man is not by nature a pacific animal, as attested by the bloody example of early human history, in which a substantial fraction of deaths—perhaps even as high as half—were caused by violence.[51] Nor must one see human beings as highly instinctive or emotional for war to take place. Hobbes envisioned man in his natural state acting purely out of self-interest and saw that a war of all against all would be the result in the absence of the Leviathan.[52] Changes in values and the application of power are epiphenomenal upon this enduring reality of humanity's native capacity for and inclinations toward bellicosity. Unless our nature is decisively changed to a reliable selfless humility, which seems exceptionally unlikely, human beings will continue to have a propensity toward competition and war.

War remains, in brief, eminently possible, ever potential.[53] Deep structural shifts in power and in the nature of European civilization over the past half-century, and particularly in the past 20 years, have obscured this reality, but it remains.

The Pacifying Effect of Nuclear Weapons

Yet, thankfully, as the past 65 years demonstrate, great war is preventable. But its prevention begins precisely with this recognition that war is always possible, that it is always "thinkable." From this beginning, states can take actions to make war unlikely. Even with their bellicose instincts and incentives, men, especially those who rise to positions of authority, are rarely madmen. Above all, they value survival and the preservation of what they have and love. Threatening these things can serve to turn an adversary away from war.[54] So can superior power, albeit less reliably.[55] Moreover, the *libido dominandi* and the other impulses that drive people toward war can, at least to some extent, be channeled into less destructive pursuits, especially when such attractions are coupled with a clear threat of devastation if the aggressive path is taken.[56] Thus a combination of the exploitation of fear and interest on the one hand and the redirection of warlike instincts toward other endeavors can combine to lessen substantially the probability of war. These are the core verities of deterrence and of enlightened statecraft.

In a nonnuclear world, this task was and would be a great and dubious challenge. Since conventional weapons effect damage at a scale readily cognizable by the human mind and generally tolerable to a committed nation (excepting prodigies of effort available largely only to great states fully mobilized), war in a conventional world was and would be a matter of calculations of foreseeable risks and perceptible gains and losses. Deterring great war in such a world was and would be both very demanding and, in the long term, unreliable. This is because there would always be situations in which a state could see the serious possibility of gaining more through war than it would lose, often justifiably. While catastrophic wars, such as the Thirty Years' War, the Napoleonic Wars, and World War I, would always be possible and thus serve as deterrents, situations would continually arise in which decision makers could assess that their expected benefits would outweigh the possibility of such disaster. These assessments would often be reasonable or at least defensible. Throughout history, for every cataclysmic war, there were multiple smaller but still major wars that advanced the interests of a party—and, equally importantly, multiple instances of the explicit or implicit threat to *go to* war that resulted in an advantage for the threatening party and that decisively shaped the international environment. Bismarck unified Germany under Prussian control through a series of highly successful, contained wars against Denmark, Austria, and France. Similarly, Sardinia and then Italy waged a series of advantageous wars to consolidate control over the peninsula against other Italian states, Austria, and France. Nor would all such wars be wars of conquest or aggrandizement. Rather, they could result from attempts to gain influence or dominance. Bismarck advised against Germany taking possession of Alsace and Lorraine, since he viewed the war against France as primarily a means to assert dominance and secure a unified Germany in Central Europe. In a nonnuclear world, such a strategy might similarly be pursued by a rising power such as China in its near abroad. Nor would all leaders be as restrained as Bismarck. Leaders like Napoleon or Hitler who are fully prepared to countenance massive but still limited (compared to nuclear conflicts) wars could always arise.

In a nonnuclear world, then, war was and would be a potentially attractive policy option—indeed, it might often be the optimal choice, assuming that benevolent or humanitarian impulses do not always prevail in strategic decision making. That implies that the only sure way to deter attack or coercion would be to be so strong as to resist and, ideally, overpower one's opponent. This, of course, is one part of the tragic "security dilemma"—that is, becoming strong enough to mount a formidable defense is highly likely to make one strong enough to molest the very powers that posed the threat in the first place, leading them in turn to build up to avert such a possibility, and so on.[57] In such a nonnuclear world, deterrence was and would be *uncertain*, as calculations of advantage for closely matched conventional conflicts would be speculative and "near run things"; *unstable*, as perturbations in the power balance, technological developments, and differential growth could determine the winner in a fight; and ultimately *unreliable*, as war was and would be effectively inevitable.[58]

This is why nuclear weapons remain as relevant today as they have ever been in the past. For nuclear weapons are by far the most effective method of deterring aggression. The prompt, sure devastation that a major nuclear attack can wreak on a targeted country is so catastrophic that the credible threat to initiate one is almost sure to dissuade any country from aggression. Considerations of state power and security, of glory and honor, of conquest and plunder, all pale in contest against the absolute destruction and defeat of all worldly ends that a major nuclear strike represents. Whereas in a nonnuclear world, aggression and war involve calculations of comparative advantage and calculable risks, great war is much less likely in a nuclear world because no worldly objective can justify the destruction that a large-scale nuclear attack would cause—destruction that in its prompt devastation is thousands of times greater than what conventional weapons can cause. Nuclear weapons cut through calculations of advantage to speak directly to man's most basic instincts of survival and preservation. In a sense, as Robert Jervis himself has pointed out, nuclear deterrence represents the negation of strategy, since it sunders military action from any plausibly commensurate political ends.[59] Needless to say, nuclear deterrence does not prevent every conflict or ensure against war, but when it is implicated, its cautionary pall makes war dramatically less likely.

It is this blunt reality that explains the post-1945 peace, not progressive values or liberalism or economic interdependence. Indeed, postwar history offers a more compelling testimony to the effectiveness of nuclear deterrence than any merely abstract argument can offer. Whereas humanity has suffered great wars from time immemorial, the world has passed through a great and fearsome standoff in the Cold War as well as its aftermath without major conflict precisely because all responsible have recognized the consequences of a full-scale war in a nuclear age. Nor was this recognition cheap or easy, as to be effective nuclear deterrence must rely on a real and fearsome capability and the credible threat to use it. Thus the Cold War is a story of continual imagined wars, with both sides again and again comparing how they would fare in a conflict, balancing each other's force developments, and working to strengthen their capabilities and make manifest their resolve.[60]

Yet it is the very success of nuclear weapons in making great war such an extremely perilous and unattractive endeavor that has, paradoxically, made them seem irrelevant. They have, in a sense, been victims of their own success, so pacifying that they have made the peace seem independent of their influence. Countries spend and focus less on armaments and armies because they know how limited the gains are from such investments as long as nuclear weapons overhang. Yet this has the effect of making it seem like war is simply falling away of its own accord. But we should not confuse the effect with the cause. Nuclear weapons are what make great war unlikely—not new values or economic interdependence.

If nuclear weapons continue to play a salient role in world politics, we might expect this restraint to continue. But if they do not, as those who see the development of self-sustaining security communities presumably would argue, then war will tend to become more of a matter of calculable gains and losses and thus is likely to become more salient again in human affairs. Needless to say, this would be a catastrophe.

The Role of Nuclear Strategy

To say that nuclear weapons remain relevant, indeed central, to peace and stability, however, is not quite to say that nuclear *strategy* is so central, or at least as central as it once was. During the Cold War, debates about nuclear strategy occupied center stage in deliberations about defense policy and even about foreign policy more broadly. The deployment by the United States of the Pershing II intermediate-range ballistic missile and BGM-109B ground-launched cruise missiles to Europe, for instance, was one of the highest-profile foreign policy issues of the late 1970s and early 1980s. Contrarily, the debates today surrounding whether NATO retention of its nuclear capabilities within Europe are mostly for those who till the fields of nuclear weapons and NATO for a living. More broadly, debates about the contours of our nuclear strategy, such as the varying pros and cons of counter-force targeting, the survivability of the land-based strategic force, and the role of tactical nuclear weapons, to name a few, have abated markedly.

This development is likely to endure and, on balance, is a good thing. The strategic stability that preserves the peace is almost certainly less sensitive to changes in nuclear targeting doctrine and other finer aspects of nuclear strategy than was sometimes thought, at least in some quarters, during the Cold War.[61] Nuclear weapons deter above all through the promise of inflicting horrendous destruction. So long as the credible resolve to effect such devastation is firmly established, any additional superior military capability that nuclear weapons provide is effectively irrelevant, as meaningful victory in a true large-scale nuclear exchange is impossible. If so much of what one values is lost, it does not really matter if the other side loses more. Even so steely and determined an opponent as the Soviets seem to have understood this, despite what they said to the contrary.[62]

This is not to say that nuclear strategy is not still very important and relevant. Quite to the contrary—above all because for nuclear deterrence to be effective it must rest on the credible threat to employ nuclear weapons. Thus nuclear capabilities and the plans to use them must bear some relation to the potential conflicts that could arise. This means that defense planners and strategists will continue to need to grapple with the irreducibly complex, unpredictable, and changing issues of how to field, and if necessary employ, nuclear weapons in ways that deter major aggression and coercion.

The rise of China in particular will likely make nuclear strategy again more salient than it has been since 1991. Let us presume that China's rise will, at the very least, create great pressure on American hegemony in the Western Pacific and the East Asian littoral. In such a situation, will the United States be able to continue to extend a credible nuclear umbrella over its allies and associates in East and Southeast Asia as China waxes in strength? Will Washington and these allies and associates want the United States to do so? If they do, what kind of military posture and strategy will be most effective and efficient in deterring Chinese aggression, coercion, or aggrandizement against US-protected states? If the Chinese manage to wrest superiority in conventional military terms away from the United States—which, after all, is located across the Pacific Ocean—will the United States find it attractive to place more reliance on nuclear weapons for extended deterrence purposes? What posture would this entail, and with what kinds of weapons and delivery systems? Will US allies and associates be drawn (again) toward nuclear weapons programs of their own?[63] Would such "friendly" proliferation be more stabilizing than the attempt by the United States to maintain its hegemony? Similar, albeit probably less stressing, questions may well arise about Russia and nuclear-armed regional powers such as Iran and North Korea. Thus, even as it is unlikely to dominate public consciousness as it did during the Cold War, nuclear strategy will remain relevant and indeed probably become more important over the coming decades.

Conclusion

It is a remarkable fact that the mighty scourge of war has, to a degree only dreamt of by earlier ages, passed away. Countries and peoples that had waged and endured war from before recorded history have not suffered its direct effects for over half a century. Needless to say, this is a good to be cherished and one whose preservation we are duty-bound to pursue. Thus we must search out why this peace has descended upon the advanced world and seek to extend its operation.

But in so doing we must exercise the utmost caution when we infer from pacific consequences gentle causes. For we have seen that fear and interest provide a firm grounding for peace and that pacific mores and liberal values can build upon that grounding. But we have not seen, nor does history, biology, or philosophy give us a sturdy basis for believing, that we can safely entrust our security and the vitality of civilization solely to a vision of the new man formed by changes in values and attitudes, economic incentives, and democracy. Prevalent as these influences may be, they are not nearly dominating enough to persuade the prudent to abandon the tested method of deterrence. War remains eminently thinkable and possible; thus it is best kept at bay through the threat of punishing force. Nuclear weapons and the deterrence they provide thus remain not only relevant, but essential. For no other weapon is so fearsome in its destructiveness and thus in its effects so manifestly incommensurate with any worldly gain that would trigger its usage at any significant scale. War as the continuation of political advantage, war as an expression of man's animal nature, war as a manifestation of man's prideful and self-aggrandizing nature—all of these must be restrained in the face of the absolute weapon, for their pursuit is not merely illogical or misguided if it results in nuclear devastation, but actually mad, indeed completely incompatible with the most basic rationality. This is as secure a bind as we are likely to find. War, in a sense, is a caged animal. The beast may seem tamed by its years of confinement, but we would be most unwise to trust our lives to its good graces.

Notes

1. *Report of the Secretary of Defense Task Force on DoD* [Department of Defense] *Nuclear Weapons Management*, 1.

2. For a critique of this way of thinking, see Morgenthau, "The Fallacy of Thinking Conventionally about Nuclear Weapons." For a history of some of the more fervid theorizing (as well as the more solidly grounded), see Kaplan, *The Wizards of Armageddon*.

3. Mueller, *Retreat from Doomsday*; and Mueller, *The Remnants of War*.

4. For a persuasive argument that violence as a whole has declined, see Pinker, *The Better Angels of Our Nature*. While Pinker's argument that violence has declined is compelling, his arguments for *why* it has declined, while containing significant elements of truth (including the important role of nuclear weapons), is nonetheless deeply flawed and in certain respects highly tendentious. A full treatment of Pinker's arguments goes beyond the scope of this chapter, however.

5. Fukuyama, *The End of History and the Last Man*.

6. Wendt, *Social Theory of International Politics*; and Sheehan, *Where Have All the Soldiers Gone?*

7. Rosecrance, *The Rise of the Trading State*. For the classic statement of the argument that commerce would make war impossible, see Angell, *The Great Illusion*. See also Schumpeter, *Capitalism, Socialism, and Democracy*; and Schumpeter, "The Sociology of Imperialism," in his *Imperialism and Social Classes*, 55–98.

8. Sagan, *The Limits of Safety: Organizations, Accidents, and Nuclear Weapons*.

9. For the classic argument along these lines, see Smith, *An Inquiry into the Nature and Causes of the Wealth of Nations*. See also, inter alia, Hume, *Essays Moral, Political, and Literary*, especially "Of the Jealousy of Trade," 327–31; and Ricardo, *On the Principles of Political Economy and Taxation*.

10. For an example of the practical influence of this way of thinking, see Lee, *From Third World to First—The Singapore Story*, 481, 612, inter alia. Lee recounts the central importance of free trade in allowing formerly aggrandizing countries such as Germany and Japan to "grow through trade and investments. They cooperated and competed with other nations and were able to prosper and flourish without wars." But Lee emphasized that this beneficial development is contingent on the active maintenance of open markets and free trade. It is not a given.

11. For an analysis of this, see Huntington, "Why International Primacy Matters."

12. Liberman, for instance, argued that "ruthless invaders can, in fact, successfully exploit industrial societies, at least for short periods of time. Control over industrial societies, moreover, can be maintained for longer periods of time at relatively low expense." Liberman, *Does Conquest Pay*, 4.

13. See, e.g., Robert Gilpin, *Global Political Economy*. As Gilpin summarized, "A liberal international order requires strong leadership and cooperation among the major economic powers. . . . American leadership and interstate cooperation constitute the only possible foundation for an open and stable global economy." Ibid., 388.

14. See Gilpin, *War and Change in World Politics*, chap. 4, 156–85.

15. Kershaw, *Fateful Choices*, chap. 10, 431–70.

16. For explications of this view, see Waltz, *Theory of International Politics*; and Mearsheimer, *The Tragedy of Great Power Politics*.

17. See, for instance, Thucydides, *The Peloponnesian War*, esp. 80; and Augustine, *City of God*, esp. 196–201, 212–14.

18. Jervis, *American Foreign Policy in a New Era*, 12. For another, similarly judicious argument akin to Jervis's, see Schroeder, "Does the History of International Politics Go Anywhere?" For the classic anticipation of this argument, see Kant, *Perpetual Peace*. See also, inter alia, Charles-Irénée Castel, abbe de Saint-Pierre, *A Project for Settling an Everlasting Peace in Europe*.

19. Jervis, *American Foreign Policy in a New Era*, 28. For more on the concept of the "security community," see Deutsch et al., *Political Community and the North Atlantic Area*; and Adler and Barnett, eds., *Security Communities*.

20. Jervis, *American Foreign Policy in a New Era*, 12.

21. Ibid., 17.

22. Ibid.

23. Ibid., 16. For the classic description of states in anarchy, see Morgenthau, *Politics among Nations*.

24. Jervis, *American Foreign Policy in a New Era*, 18–24.

25. Ibid., 26–27.

26. Ibid., 26.

27. Ibid., 29.

28. Ibid., 29–32, inter alia. This argument resembles a variant of the Hegelian argument laid out by Fukuyama in *The End of History*. While Jervis does not predict that all other nations will necessarily track the development of what he refers to as the "leading powers," it is clear that he sees the "leading powers" as representing the most advanced form of social organization. Fukuyama similarly argued that, while history would continue in the contests among nations and peoples, no other form of socio-political organization would supersede social liberal democracy and that the world would tend toward that form of organization over time. Fukuyama, *End of History*, 64, 311, inter alia. Hegel's original argument is laid out in his *The Philosophy of History*.

29. Jervis, *American Foreign Policy in a New Era*, 13–14. Jervis does note that backsliding is possible, but these cautionary remarks cannot be understood as essential, since, if so understood, they would entirely undermine his argument that "war is unthinkable." If backsliding to a situation in which war *is* thinkable is possible, then war itself is eminently possible and eminently thinkable. War cannot be both unthinkable and yet also plausible. As Jervis himself argues, "some of these changes may be irreversible." Ibid., 28.

30. Ibid., 14.

31. Ibid., 28.

32. For a peerless description of this development, see Judt, *Postwar*.

33. Hobbes, *Leviathan*; and Darwin, *The Origin of Species*.

34. See, for instance, Thucydides, *Peloponnesian War*, esp. 49; and Polybius, *The Rise of the Roman Empire*, esp. 535.

35. De Tocqueville, *Democracy in America*, 395–96.

36. For an exceptionally insightful analysis on this point, emphasizing the implications of the military revolution brought on by World War II and the nuclear age for European autonomy, see Schlesinger, *European Security and the Nuclear Threat since 1945*. Schlesinger observed that Europe had been "hopelessly priced out of the game" by the need for sophisticated strategic forces and that the result after 1945 had been an increasing dependence on the United States, 10. This, he saw, had led to the "ultimate strategic dominance of the United States and the Soviet Union," 25.

37. William E. Odom and Robert Dujarric, *America's Inadvertent Empire* (New Haven, CT: Yale University Press, 2004).

38. As Tony Judt put it,

> Western Europeans owed their newfound well-being to the uncertainties of the Cold War. The internationalization of political confrontations, and the consequent engagement of the United States, helped draw the sting from domestic political conflicts. Political issues that in an earlier age would almost certainly have led to violence and war—the unresolved problem of Germany, territorial conflicts between Yugoslavia and Italy, the future of occupied Austria—were all contained, and would in due course be addressed, within the context of Great Power confrontations and negotiations over which Europeans had very little say.

Judt, *Postwar*, 242.

39. For a historical analysis of this development, see van Creveld, *The Rise and Decline of the State*; and Gilpin, *War and Change in World Politics*.

40. See, for instance, Plato, *The Republic*, Book VIII 252–84; Gibbon, *The Decline and Fall of the Roman Empire*; Montesquieu, *Considerations on the Causes of the Greatness of the Romans and Their Decline*; and Toynbee, *A Study of History*. For a more recent, influential example, see Kennedy, *The Rise and Fall of the Great Powers*.

41. Gibbon, *Decline and Fall of the Roman Empire*.

42. Machiavelli, *The Discourses*.

43. See, for instance, Ibn Khaldun, *The Muqaddimah: An Introduction to History*. Trans. F. Rosenthal. Princeton: Princeton University Press, 1967.

44. For a more recent example of this perspective, see Huntington, *The Clash of Civilizations and the Remaking of World Order*, 301–3.

45. Parker, *The Cambridge Illustrated History of Warfare*.

46. For a recent assessment of this dynamic, see Caldwell, *Reflections on the Revolution in Europe: Immigration, Islam, and the West*.

47. See, for instance, DOD, *Annual Report to Congress: Military and Security Developments Involving the People's Republic of China*.

48. For an analysis of the multiple causes of war, see Levy and Thompson, *Causes of War*, who conclude in their analytical survey of explanations of the causes of war that "there are multiple causal paths through which war can occur," 213.

49. See, for instance, Morgenthau, *Politics among Nations*. For a classic statement of neorealism, see Waltz, *Theory of International Politics*.

50. See Keegan, *A History of Warfare*, esp. 3–12; and van Creveld, *The Culture of War*. For "the passion of life to its top," see Holmes, "Memorial Day Speech."

51. Keeley, *War before Civilization*, 88–90. See also Wade, *Before the Dawn*, 9.

52. Hobbes, *Leviathan*, Part I, chap. 13, 82–86.

53. For a similar assessment on the end of war, see Huntington, "No Exit." As Huntington pithily but sagely advised, "To hope for the benign end of history is human. To expect it to happen is unrealistic. To plan on it happening is disastrous."

54. Schelling, *Arms and Influence*, inter alia.

55. Snyder, *Deterrence and Defense*, 14–16.

56. Such ideas were central to the whole thrust of Enlightenment thought on the free market, represented above all in Smith's *Wealth of Nations*. See, for instance, Mandeville, "The Fable of the Bees," 19–154. For a modern appraisal, see Hirschman, *The Passions and the Interests*. A very clear example along different lines is the militaristic Society of Jesus, founded by the ex-soldier Ignatius of Loyola on the military model and commanding perfect obedience from its members to its general and its ultimate commander, the Pope.

57. Herz, "Idealist Internationalism and Security Dilemma."

58. For an analysis of the role of differential growth rates in causing great power conflicts, see Copeland, *The Origins of Major War*.

59. Jervis, *The Illogic of American Nuclear Strategy*.

60. See, for instance, Blackwill and Legro, "Constraining Ground Force Exercises of NATO and the Warsaw Pact."

61. For a similar assessment, see Freedman, *The Evolution of Nuclear Strategy*, especially the conclusion.

62. See interviews of former Soviet officials in Hines et al., *Soviet Intentions 1965–1985*.

63. For a history of some earlier moves toward nuclear weapons by US allies, see Campbell et al., eds., *The Nuclear Tipping Point*.

Chapter 5

How Much Is Enough?

A Goal-Driven Approach to Defining Key Principles for Measuring the Adequacy of US Strategic Forces

Keith B. Payne

A particular approach to identifying deterrence requirements inherited from the Cold War has resulted in frequent proposals regarding US strategic force requirements that are based in general on the number of survivable offensive forces deemed adequate to threaten designated enemy targets. This formula focuses on the number of survivable weapons necessary to threaten a select set of enemy targets, whether urban/industrial, military forces, political centers, or other physical assets. A focus on fewer, soft, unprotected targets—such as urban/industrial—can equate to the requirement for relatively fewer nuclear weapons for deterrence than does a focus on more numerous, hardened, and protected targets—such as military targets. In either case, the logic and formula are clear: Possessing the number of forces necessary to threaten the selected targets essentially is equated to having an adequate deterrent.

Calculating "How Much Is Enough" for Deterrence

Secretary of Defense Robert McNamara was explicit in his use of this formula throughout the 1960s to identify US strategic force requirements, but it continued to be reflected in official assessments of strategic requirements well into the 1980s and continues to dominate unofficial commentary to this day.[1] An entire generation of US officials and commentators was schooled in this methodology. Continued

Portions of this chapter are adapted from Keith B. Payne, *The Great American Gamble: Deterrence Theory and Practice from the Cold War to the Twenty-First Century* (Fairfax, VA: National Institute Press, 2008); Keith B. Payne, study director, *Planning the Future U.S. Nuclear Force*, vols. 1 and 2 (Fairfax, VA: National Institute Press, 2009); and his "How Much Is Enough? A Goal-Driven Approach to Defining Key Principles for Measuring the Adequacy of US Strategic Forces," *Comparative Strategy* 31, no.1 (2012): 3–17.

faith in this Cold War force-sizing formula provides the basis for most contemporary public claims that the force requirements needed to provide nuclear deterrence can be identified with relative precision and confidence.

This familiar Cold War methodology is comforting and convenient. It appears to allow the otherwise very challenging question of "How much is enough?" to be answered with apparent mathematical precision. For example:

> No sane adversary would believe that any political or military advantage would be worth a significant risk of the destruction of his own society. As noted earlier, the delivery of one hundred U.S. warheads would be sufficient to destroy the society and economy of Russia or China, and as few as ten detonations could kill more people than have ever been killed in any country in any previous war. *Thus ten to one hundred survivable warheads should be more than enough to deter any rational leader* from ordering an attack on the cities of the United States or its allies.[2] (emphasis added)

Other commentators may suggest larger numbers, but they still link confidence in the functioning of deterrence to the number of weapons.

> The appropriate mission for U.S. nuclear weapons is deterrence. And the U.S. arsenal of more than 5,000 nuclear weapons has the capacity to deter any threat regardless of how many resources Russia, China, and/or any other country devote to modernizing their arsenals.[3]

There is nothing objectionable to the notion that deterrence planning includes identifying US military threats to enemy assets and using the related number of offensive nuclear weapons to help guide the acquisition requirements for strategic forces. The problem with confidence in this simple Cold War formula, however, is that it presumes a known, reliable, and predictable link between a specific number of US nuclear weapons and the desired deterrent effect and, on that basis, leads to confidence that deterrence will work predictably with some designated number of weapons. In truth, the formula provides no basis for such confidence. In addition, the number of nuclear weapons so identified as adequate for deterrence typically is also presented as the standard for the US nuclear arsenal in general—as if deterrence is the only pertinent goal. It is not.

Using this simplistic formula to define deterrence requirements and US strategic force requirements in general is popular sport in the United States. It is, nevertheless, a flawed and even dangerous approach to answering the question, "How much is enough?" There are too many uncertainties in the functioning of deterrence for confidence in claims that any particular number or types of strategic forces will deter predictably. Answering the question, "How much is enough?" even when done with rigor, involves speculation and a myriad of unavoidable uncertainties. There are, for example, uncertainties involved in the technical estimates of weapon effects and target vulnerabilities. More important, however, is that informed estimates about the deterrent effect of US forces must include assessments of opponent decision-making processes, values, intentions, histories, levels of determination, goals, stakes and worldviews, and the possibilities for reliable communication across a broad spectrum of current and future opponents. Are the opponents in question susceptible to US deterrence threats? If so, are punitive threats to urban/industrial or some other types of targets useful for deterrence? To whom must threats be communicated and how? How might the credibility of US threats be established with any confidence? And how might we understand the level of credibility enemies attribute to our threats?

These types of questions are not minor details with regard to predictions about the functioning of deterrence and related assertions about deterrence requirements. A serious effort to identify those requirements must involve a multidisciplinary examination of such questions with full recognition of the great variation in answers possible across opponents, time, and context. It also may require access to special and occasionally highly classified information. Even the most comprehensive analytic efforts cannot avoid speculation on key variables and, as is discussed below, the contemporary threat environment magnifies the uncertainties.

What Is New and Different? and What Difference Does It Make?

Specific expectations about opponent decision making and behavior are embedded in the Cold War's target-based formula for deterrence. Those expectations foster confident predictions about how opponents will think and behave and, thus, how deterrence will function. On this basis, the formula points to the requirements deemed necessary for deterrence. Some of these embedded expectations about the opponent and context may have been reasonable in the unique conditions of the Cold War, but they are questionable or simply erroneous in the current geopolitical context. Some of the pertinent changes from the

Cold War strategic environment to the present that must move our considerations of deterrence requirements in new directions are explored briefly below.

Detection, Attribution, and Accountability

The conditions of the Cold War facilitated the expectation that the United States would recognize if an attack had occurred, by whom, and with what. Armed with such knowledge, the United States could identify the likely opponent in advance and bring to bear its specified retaliatory deterrence threat. However, if an attack cannot be recognized as such—or the attacker remains unidentified—then punitive retaliatory threats can have little specific direction.

In the contemporary environment there may be little basis for confidence in the attribution of attack, particularly with regard to biological weapons (BW) and limited nuclear threats.[4] It may even be difficult in practice to distinguish between an opponent's employment of a biological agent and a naturally occurring health disaster.[5] How and against whom would US leaders communicate threats to deter an attack that might not be recognized as such or might not be traceable to its source? Generic deterrence threats issued to all who will listen, of course, are possible. But, in such cases, confidence in the old target-based formula to identify "How much is enough?" for deterrence will be unwarranted.

New Opponents and Unprecedented Threats to Be Deterred

During the Cold War the United States pursued efforts to define "stable" deterrence requirements and to "lock in," via arms control, a stable balance of terror based on those requirements. Doing so seemed reasonable during the Cold War because enduring features of that threat environment meant that a relatively set formula could consistently define a balance of terror and the related strategic force requirements.

The contemporary threat environment, however, is far more dynamic than that of the Cold War; it may be more analogous to other historical periods in which the parameters of threat changed quickly.[6] The continuity and centrality of the Soviet threat has been replaced by a kaleidoscope of opponents, threats, and potential threats. US deterrence goals and priorities correspondingly have become more varied, both in the numbers of target audiences and the range of actions to be deterred. The increasingly broad spectrum of opponents in the contemporary era offers more openings for misunderstanding, misperception, ignorance, extreme motivations, distorted communications, highly divergent values, and the lack of mutual familiarity to prevent the reliable functioning of deterrence. Another factor contributing to the uncertainty about the functioning of deterrence is the need to know so much about so many diverse and largely unfamiliar opponents, such as their goals, values, and their decision-making processes.

In such a dynamic geopolitical environment, no single formula can define the set of adequate US forces to be "locked in" for deterrence. There is no easily calculable metric to define deterrence requirements because such assessments must now include a wide spectrum of opponents, contingencies, and possible stakes/goals, all of which may shift as new threats emerge and old threats decline or reemerge. Informed strategies for deterrence must vary according to opponents and contexts as must the corresponding types of deterrent threats and necessary supporting forces. The force levels that might constitute an "adequate" basis for meeting US deterrence goals will depend on these details of the engagement, including opponents' values, vulnerabilities, risk tolerances, perceptions, access to information, and attention. What can reasonably now be said with confidence is that US deterrence threats and supporting strategic forces intended to provide the desired deterrent effect will change and vary depending on the particulars of audience and context.

Implications for Measuring the Adequacy of US Strategic Forces for Deterrence

Deterrence strategies and strategic force standards in the contemporary, fluid environment demand humility in prediction, flexibility in application, and preparation for deterrence failure or irrelevance. The diversity of opponents, circumstances, and threats suggests that contemporary deterrence priorities are for a spectrum of US force options and flexibility in planning, along with the traditional requirements for sufficient force quantity, lethality, and survivability. The threats to be deterred will shift as will opponents' susceptibility to deterrence strategies; this dynamic points to the need for differing approaches to deterrence and a broad spectrum of US capabilities that enable us to adapt deterrence strategies to this variability of opponents, threat conditions, and stakes.

"How Much Do You Know?" Must Precede "How Much Is Enough?"

When diverse and unfamiliar opponents present numerous uncertainties, then seeking to understand the hows and whys of their unique decision making should be the first priority of a deterrence strategy. Information important for deterrence purposes includes understanding an opponent's "mind-set and behavioral style," and anticipating how that unique mind-set and behavioral style will affect the opponent's response to US deterrence threats. The absence of an investigation into such matters "can result in the disintegration of even the best deterrence strategy."[7]

The scope for this necessary investigation is wide-ranging—from the opponent's formal authority structure and processes to the cultural norms that affect decision making. For example, some states and terrorist organizations properly categorized as having "high-intensity aggressive ideologies" can have "propensities toward martyrdom and apocalyptic visions . . . with no risk being too high if top decision makers prefer self-destruction to nonrealization of their vision."[8] Now, gaining insight into such possible opponent characteristics must inform any serious attempt to understand how to deter them and the requirements for doing so.

What Is the Role for Nuclear Weapons in Deterrence?

Confident a priori assertions that nuclear threats are sure to make a decisive difference for deterrence on every occasion, or that they provide little or no significant added value, betray unwarranted certainty regarding how opponents will calculate and behave in the future. Even with a careful assessment of the pertinent details of opponent and context, precise prediction about the link of threat to deterrent effect is subject to uncertainties.

Some general inferences may be made in this regard. A quick review of available evidence points toward the possibly unique value of nuclear weapons for deterrence in some cases. For example, during the 1991 Gulf War the Iraqi leadership believed that the United States would respond to Iraqi WMD use with nuclear weapons—and that expectation appears to have deterred them. That case appears to offer empirical evidence that nuclear deterrence, at least on occasion, can be uniquely effective. Additional evidence may be found in the specific acknowledgement by former Indian army chief, Gen Shankar

Roychowdhury: "Do nuclear weapons deter? Of course they do. Pakistan's nuclear weapons deterred India from attacking that country after the Mumbai strikes."[9] As this and other cases suggest, there is little doubt that on some occasions it has been "the reality of nuclear deterrence" that has had the desired "restraining effect."[10] In the future, as in the past, the working of deterrence on such occasions may be extremely important.

Nuclear weapons also may be necessary to threaten those assets opponents have demonstrated to be of highest value and unsurprisingly seek most to protect. As Defense Secretary Harold Brown emphasized, US deterrence threats in general should be capable of holding at risk those assets valued by the opponent.[11] This may be particularly pertinent to contemporary US deterrence goals, because rogues and other potential opponents are expending considerable effort on hard and deeply buried bunkers, some of which reportedly can be held at risk of destruction only by nuclear weapons.[12]

For deterrence to "work" on those occasions when nuclear deterrence is uniquely decisive in the challenger's decision making—whether those occasions are few or many—could be of great importance, given the potential lethality of emerging WMD threats to the United States. To assert otherwise—that US nuclear weapons now provide no unique added value for deterrence—contradicts available evidence and lays claim to foreknowledge about opponent decision making that cannot exist. Given literally decades of experience, the burden of proof lies with those who now contend that nuclear weapons are of little value for deterrence.

The probability of deterrence failure because of the absence of a US nuclear threat cannot be calculated a priori with precision for any particular case. It may be nonexistent or high, depending on the specific circumstances of the contingency. Even if the risk of deterrence failure for this reason is low, the possibility would still deserve serious consideration because the consequences of a single failure to deter a WMD attack could be measured in thousands to millions of US and allied casualties. Of course, the risk of deterrence failure in the absence of credible US nuclear capabilities may not be low in some cases.

In the contemporary environment when the stakes at risk for the United States in a regional crisis do not include national survival and when postconflict reconstruction and minimization of damage to civilians and neighboring states may be priority goals, the credibility of the US deterrent may rest not on how much damage can be threatened à la the Cold War's "assured destruction" standard, but rather on how controlled is that threatened damage. Consequently, low-yield and highly-accurate nuclear weapons may contribute to a US deterrent threat that is more believable than otherwise would be the case. The US "legacy" Cold War nuclear arsenal's generally high yields and limited precision could threaten to inflict so many innocent casualties that some opponents eager to find a justification for military action may seize on the hope that a US president would not execute an expressed nuclear deterrent threat, given the likely level of collateral damage. An opponent's doubts regarding the US threat in such cases would work against the desired deterrent effect. This possibility points toward the potential value of both advanced nonnuclear and highly discriminate nuclear threat options for deterrence credibility. Some studies conducted late in the Cold War and looking 20 years into the future pointed to the same conclusion.[13]

There can be no promises that nuclear weapons, including more "discriminate" nuclear capabilities, will make the difference between deterrence working or failing on any given occasion. An opponent could miss such fine points regarding US nuclear capabilities or could be so motivated that the specific character of the US nuclear threat is irrelevant to its decision making. What can be said, however, is that no existing study or even series of studies can rightly conclude that nuclear weapons can be dismissed as unnecessary for deterrence purposes. Indeed, such a study is well beyond the art of the possible.

Implications for US Nuclear Force Sizing for Deterrence

This discussion suggests that US nuclear capabilities, including those with accuracy and low yields, may contribute uniquely to US deterrence goals. It does not attempt to identify "the number" of nuclear weapons adequate to ensure deterrence around which the United States can plan for the midterm or long term. As noted above, to do so would be to lay a false claim to knowledge of a specific link between the opponent's decision making and some specific number of US nuclear weapons. More useful than such pretense are the conclusions that:

- US force requirements for deterrence cannot be considered fixed—they are as subject to change as is the threat environment itself.

- There is no number of nuclear weapons that can be linked predictably to the reliable functioning of deterrence.

- Priority measures of merit for US strategic forces should now include sufficient force quantity, lethality, survivability, and flexibility to threaten the wide array of targets potentially important for deterrence.

- US deterrence planning and strategies should have the flexibility and adaptability necessary to adjust to a rapidly changing and surprising threat environment, and to the possibility of deterrence failure.

Any honest effort to answer the more specific question "How much is enough?" in an informed fashion must follow a broad, multidisciplinary net assessment across multiple opponents, deterrence goals, and possible contingencies, and recognize the many uncertainties and limitations involved. Even informed analyses can capture only a "snapshot" in time and require constant review and likely revision to remain pertinent.

Finally, whatever level of US strategic capability may be judged useful for deterrence at a given point in time cannot be the standard of adequacy for US strategic forces, in general, because those forces must serve additional goals beyond deterrence. This last point is a particularly significant departure from Cold War practice when deterrence was the priority among priorities and was the declared basis for formulating strategic force requirements. When US strategic forces must serve additional priority goals that may entail different force requirements, conclusions about deterrence requirements can tell us only part of the story about overall US strategic force requirements.

The Adequacy of US Strategic Forces to Meet Multiple National Goals

In the twenty-first century, deterrence remains an important national goal, but on occasion additional national goals may be equally or even more important and US strategic forces will support these additional goals. Consequently, the sizing and measures of merit for US strategic forces must be informed by the requirements that follow from multiple national goals. The three goals beyond deterrence discussed below are not new; the prioritization of these goals in relation to deterrence and each other has shifted over time and place, but they have been included as US national security goals by Democratic and Republican administrations for decades.[14]

Damage Limitation

In the contemporary environment of multiple potential sources of WMD threat, including limited WMD threats from rogue states and terrorist organizations, the functioning of deterrence is important but uncertain. If and when it fails, the immediate US priority will be the limitation of casualties and damage to the extent possible. The value of strategic forces to support damage limitation directly should now be included in the definition of adequacy and measures of merit for US strategic capabilities. This value was anticipated by the Johnson administration as early as 1964.[15]

The findings from recent studies of limited nuclear attacks against US cities are not surprising—the United States presently is ill-prepared for even a "small" nuclear attack.[16] However, there are numerous practical steps that can be taken to reduce the level of societal vulnerability to limited nuclear attacks.[17] As the author of one recent study concludes, "There actually is quite a bit that we can do [to save lives]. In certain areas, it may be possible to turn the death rate from 90 percent in some burn populations to probably 20 or 30 percent—and those are very big differences—simply by being prepared well in advance."[18]

In this contemporary context, imperfect damage-limitation measures may be the only means of societal protection in the event deterrence fails. In such an instance, they will likely be judged worth the effort whatever the ratio of their cost to the cost of the opponent's offensive capabilities. When the prospective lethality of threat is high, the reliable functioning of deterrence is questionable, and damage-limitation measures can provide appreciable protection, including the goal of damage limitation as a determinant of US strategic force adequacy is the only prudent approach. The Johnson administration identified precisely the same logic and defensive objective in the 1960s. A number of plausible biological and nuclear contingencies now fit this genre of threat, which is why various forms of damage limitation against mass destruction attacks now are potentially so important.

Civil defense measures may now be essential to contemporary US damage-limitation goals. There is no recent precedent of serious US support for civil defense programs but, during the Cold War, Secretary McNamara identified civil defense as the single-most cost-effective approach to societal damage limitation.[19] In the contemporary environment, civil defense preparations against limited nuclear and biological attacks—including nuclear terrorism or bioterrorism—could make a valuable difference in the level of societal destruction and casualties.[20]

In the context of contemporary limited WMD threats, when the alternative of deterrence functioning predictably to prevent war may not exist, the opportunity cost of not pursuing damage-limiting capabilities could be exceedingly high. The possible reduction in societal destruction from damage-limitation capabilities may be a matter of good government and—for the United States—a fundamental responsibility of the federal government as mandated by the Constitution. Of course, the actual value of defenses for any given contingency will be shaped by the nature of the threat, the cost of defenses, their expected effectiveness in reducing casualties and destruction, and the expectation that deterrence will work, fail, or be irrelevant in crisis.

During the Cold War a common notion was that the deployment of strategic defenses for cities would be "destabilizing."[21] If the United States, for example, deployed strategic defenses for its cities, the concern was that the Soviet Union could be motivated to gain a strategic advantage by striking first for fear that the United States—emboldened by its defenses—might itself strike first. Strategic defenses were judged to be one of the few factors that would destabilize an otherwise stable balance of terror.

Despite the widespread acceptance of this notion that US societal defenses are destabilizing, it was at least questionable during the Cold War and makes little sense in the contemporary environment. One way this author illustrates this point for students is to ask them to imagine that the United States and China are in a stable balance of terror relationship; neither country has an incentive to strike first for fear of the other's unacceptable nuclear retaliation. Then the students are asked to imagine that the United States begins to build and deploy strategic defenses. Over the course of months or years, the United States builds defenses that protect from nuclear attack the first 10 percent of the US population, then 20 percent, then 30 percent, and so on to 90 percent of the population. One group of students is selected to represent the Chinese leadership. These students are then asked at what point in this process and along this time line are they motivated to initiate a strategic thermonuclear war with the United States—a war that will result in their own "assured destruction." That point never occurs because the students are quick to realize that despite US defenses, if their priority goal is national and/or personal survival, initiating a strategic nuclear war with the United States that will virtually ensure their own destruction is never in their interest. Even if the United States deploys thick defenses, they recognize that by striking first, Chinese leaders would simply ensure a strategic nuclear war in which they would lose their highest priority value. For these students, unencumbered by Cold War stability dogma, the continuing survivability and effectiveness of US offensive retaliatory forces eliminates any motivation they might otherwise have to strike first; there is no such instability even in the context of robust US defenses.

The point of this exercise is to illustrate why US strategic defenses need not be thought of as destabilizing in this sense, if the United States simultaneously attends to the continuing deterrence effectiveness of its own offensive nuclear forces. The students representing China in this experiment often suggest a wide variety of Chinese reactions to the US deployment of defenses, but their reactions never include initiation of a strategic nuclear war. Indeed, to the extent that the students believe that the United States is emboldened by its strategic defenses, they are quick to reassure the United States by word and deed that China will not engage in any such action lest the United States be provoked. In contrast, in these experiments all bets are off regarding benign Chinese behavior if China can regard US offensive retaliatory nuclear forces as highly vulnerable to attack or ineffective. That, however, is the case with or without the added imagined presence of US strategic defenses. When US offensive forces provide deterrence stability against a first strike, US defenses do not upset that stability.

Assurance

Another national goal that should contribute to the measure of US strategic force adequacy is the assurance of allies, particularly including the contribution of US strategic forces to extended deterrence. This goal is far from new and has great continuity over decades. The 1974 "Schlesinger Doctrine," for example, included the standard of "essential equivalence" for US strategic forces with the Soviet Union, in part to assure allies with regard to US strategic guarantees. The notion was that allied perceptions of US credibility would be strengthened if they viewed US forces as being at least comparable to those of the Soviet Union.[22]

Assurance involves allied perceptions of US power and commitment and the related questions of what and how US strategic capabilities can address the allies' unique fears and circumstances.[23] Useful insight regarding the requirements for assurance may be gained through an effort to understand allied fears and perceptions. The step of asking our allies how the United States might best provide the assurance necessary to help them remain secure and confident in their nonnuclear status is an obvious first step.

Some allies recently have been explicit that the US extended nuclear deterrent is a key to their assurance, and they link their own willingness to remain nonnuclear to the continuation of a credible US extended nuclear deterrent. For example, some senior Japanese officials have become seriously concerned about the continuing credibility of the US extended nuclear deterrent; they have indicated that if the US extended nuclear deterrent loses credibility, other security options will have to be examined. Some in Japan see specific characteristics of US nuclear forces as particularly beneficial for extended deterrence. These force characteristics include a range of nuclear capabilities: flexibility, promptness, low-yield, and precision to allow US deterrence threats that are not made incredible by the prospect of excessive collateral damage. Japanese officials have indicated support for the ultimate elimination of nuclear weapons, but they also believe that this process must be pursued in a careful, step-by-step manner that ensures Japanese security. This mandates the maintenance of a credible US nuclear deterrent for the foreseeable future.

NATO allies often insist that US nuclear weapons must remain deployed in Europe to provide the necessary assurance, while Japanese officials are equally explicit that US nuclear weapons must be "on-call" in a timely fashion, but not deployed on Japanese territory. The contemporary challenge in this regard is obvious: As WMDs spread to regional rogue powers, US allies in rough neighborhoods correspondingly become increasingly concerned about the details of the US extended nuclear deterrence commitment and the forces intended to make it credible. Their various and diverse views with regard to the US nuclear forces necessary for extended deterrence and assurance will need to be integrated into US force-sizing considerations.

There is a direct connection between allied perceptions of the assurance value of US nuclear weapons for extended deterrence and nuclear nonproliferation: The degradation of US nuclear extended deterrent credibility would create new and powerful incentives for nuclear proliferation among some US friends and allies who, to date, have felt sufficiently secure under the US extended nuclear deterrent to remain nonnuclear.[24] As a 2007 report by the Department of State's International Security Advisory Board concludes:

> There is clear evidence in diplomatic channels that U.S. assurances to include the nuclear umbrella have been, and continue to be, the single most important reason many allies have foresworn nuclear weapons. This umbrella is too important to sacrifice on the basis of an unproven ideal that nuclear disarmament in the U.S. would lead to a more secure world. . . . A lessening of the U.S. nuclear umbrella could very well trigger a cascade [of nuclear proliferation] in East Asia and the Middle East.[25]

The United States can decide what priority to place on the assurance of allies and how it will proceed to support that goal, but only the allies can decide if they are assured. In the contemporary environment, available evidence suggests strongly that assurance is an important goal and that the particular characteristics for US nuclear weapons described above are critical to the assurance of key allies.

Dissuasion and Inducements

Another national goal that should be included in the measure of US strategic force adequacy is dissuasion. Dissuasion also is not new; it was articulated well as a national goal by Secretary McNamara in the 1960s and the Clinton administration's "lead and hedge" strategy was intended to help dissuade a Russian return to arms racing.[26]

Dissuasion is the "flip side" of the traditional recommendation that US strategic force choices be guided by the expectation that US restraint would induce opponents' restraint. The expectation is that US armament choices should be shaped by the goal of affecting opponents' weapons acquisition policies. With dissuasion, the contention is that in some cases the manifest capability of standing US forces or the US potential for the acquisition of strategic capabilities can discourage opponents from competition; the goal is to undercut the opponent's expected value return from arms competition to such an extent that the opponent decides against competition.

Dissuasion adds a unique temporal dimension to the measures of merit for US strategic forces and the definition of adequacy. The seeds of dissuasion must be sown in advance of the manifest appearance of a threat. To discourage opponents from taking the course of armaments competition, by definition, requires the dissuasive effect of US strategic potential when opponents are making acquisition decisions, not after the threat emerges. If dissuasion works, the feared competition never materializes. There are several possible contemporary US dissuasion goals, including dissuading

- rogue states from investing in WMD and missiles,
- the Chinese leadership from pursuing a significant buildup of strategic nuclear weapons, and
- the Russian leadership from reverting to the former Soviet goal of building up its strategic forces in pursuit of counterforce capabilities against the United States.

How and whether the character of US strategic forces can contribute to dissuasion is not self-evident, and numerous uncertainties are unavoidable in attempting to dissuade. Nevertheless, the potential for dissuasion linkages may yield to examination and considering how to dissuade opponents and potential opponents with the size and character of US strategic forces is as coherent a goal as attempting to induce an opponent's restraint by US restraint—a theme of US arms control policy for decades.

For example, the continued unbeatable survivability of US deterrent forces may be a key to discouraging Russia or China from pursuing Soviet-like extensive counterforce strategic capabilities. And, the US potential to develop, deploy, and reconstitute forces in a timely fashion may be key to being able to dissuade opponents from unwanted weapon or force deployment initiatives.

Multiple Goals, Strategic Force Sizing, and Contemporary Measures of Merit for US Strategic Forces

The measures of merit for nuclear forces must transcend the old narrow formula for determining overall requirements from deterrence goals alone. Requirements for damage limitation, assurance, and dissuasion may change, and their respective priorities can shift across time and circumstance, but they are of continuing relevance and importance in the contemporary threat environment. How could they not be included in the calculation of US strategic forces?

Given multiple goals with shifting priorities and the diversity of strategic forces that may be suited to these goals, an overarching US strategic requirement is for flexibility and resilience in the force structure and the capability to adapt planning to variable demands. There is no "point solution" in terms of US force numbers or types that can withstand time or scrutiny. Consequently, an arms control agenda that attempts to codify any point solution risks locking in a force structure that is incompatible with shifting needs.

Strategies for deterrence, assurance, dissuasion, and defense—and the calculation of force requirements to support those goals—should be informed to the extent possible by a comprehensive understanding of specific opponents and allies in order to tailor US strategies accordingly, set priorities and limit the prospects for surprise. In a dynamic strategic environment, US strategic forces should provide defensive hedges as well, to include the potential for imperfect protection against the possibility of surprising behavior and deterrence failure.

If US force sizing is to be goal-/strategy-driven—as opposed to strategies being driven by some preselected, preferred number of warheads—the calculation of strategic requirements must reflect the integration and rationalization of shifting requirements across these goals. No single definition of requirements can be adequate. There are likely to be overlapping force requirements to support the goals of deterrence, assurance, dissuasion, and defense, but no one goal is likely to suggest the same set of force requirements as another because the goals themselves are so different.

Approaching the question of strategic force sizing as the integration of requirements across multiple national goals suggests some conclusions about general principles for US strategic forces. While precise requirements and details must await the type of broad-based, comprehensive net assessment suggested above, these general principles are important starting points and can be identified.

- The most important post–Cold War deterrence-related measures of merit for US forces include the quantity, lethality, and flexibility necessary to threaten the spectrum of targets potentially important for deterrence, the resilience of the US force structure, and adaptability of deterrence planning and strategies to adjust to shifting threats and contingencies.

- The requirements for assurance must include an understanding of and integration of allied concerns. Those concerns appear to focus on the provision of US nuclear capabilities with various preferred force characteristics and locations. This points to a spectrum of possible requirements because allies judge US forces according to their own varying and unique security circumstances. Some allies appear to care deeply about the quantity, characteristics, and location of US nuclear forces. Ensuring that US strategic capabilities are seen as being at least comparable to those of Russia appears to be a basic parameter for assurance.

- The requirements for damage limitation and optimal defensive measures will also vary considerably depending on the set of threats against which US officials expect them to perform, and the desired level of effectiveness. The threats to be considered could include terrorist and rogue WMD threats that are judged to be of questionable susceptibility to deterrence. Numerous past analyses also suggest that relatively austere civil defense measures can provide the highest initial return on the dollar for protection across a broad spectrum of plausible nuclear threats.

- Given the unique time line associated with the requirements for dissuasion, they are likely to include the manifest potential of the US industrial infrastructure to dissuade well before threats materialize. The more agile and flexible the US capability to do so, the less likely the need for standing forces to carry the burden of dissuasion. To the extent that the US infrastructure is moribund, the greater is the opportunity for opponents to see the potential value in arms competition. The long-standing requirement for US force survivability could also help discourage any repeat of a Soviet-like drive by China or Russia to acquire a powerful counterforce c apability against US strategic forces.

Comprehensive US strategic force requirements may be considered the sum of these parts. The graphic below (fig. 5.1) illustrates conceptually a variety of basic measures of merit for strategic forces that the national goals discussed here suggest and that are likely to entail both overlapping and unique strategic forces requirements. The prioritization of these goals and the instruments used to advance them will change with different threat circumstances, defense budgets, and technical and political realities. But, as noted above, the goals themselves have had great continuity. Even if budgetary, technical, and political realities preclude meeting the various requirements suggested by these goals, understanding their basic strategic force requirements should help to identify force measures of merit coherently, to understand potential contradictions, trade-offs, and shortfalls and thereby help allocate wisely the resources available.

Forces with the lethality, flexibility,
quantity, and survivability to threaten a
spectrum of targets, and adaptability in
planning

Deterrence

Agile/flexible
industrial
infrastructure
and force
survivability

Dissuasion

Damage
Limitation

Optimal mix of
defenses, scaled
to designated
threats

Assurance

Nuclear and nonnuclear capabilities with a
focus on quantity, presence, visibility, speed,
discriminate effects, and threat credibility

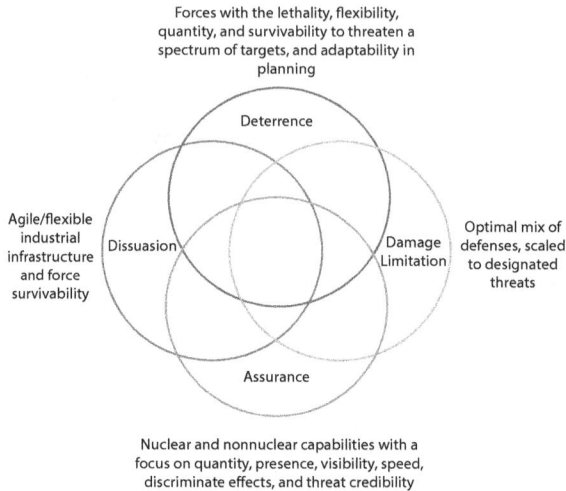

Figure 5.1. Requirements for strategic forces

In the contemporary strategic environment, it is impossible to provide high-confidence, quantitatively precise, and enduring answers to the question "How much is enough?" for deterrence. The familiar game of linking confidently some specific number of nuclear weapons to deterrence and the adequacy of US strategic forces in general remains popular, but it is unsupportable. Whether the answer is 100, 500, 1,000, or 1,500 weapons, that answer is of little value for defining deterrence requirements without the rigorous analysis of opponents and contexts described above. Even if that analysis is done rigorously, identifying the requirements for deterrence is an incomplete basis for defining the necessary parameters for US strategic forces in general. The integration of requirements across the four goals described above points to some important additional measures of merit for US strategic forces.

The numbers and types of weapon deemed necessary for deterrence are likely to be fluid, but the importance of resilience, flexibility, and survivability for deterrence and dissuasion indicates the continuing value of multiple US strategic-force platforms. The traditional nuclear triad of ICBMs, SLBMs, and heavy bombers has long been valued for the flexibility, diversity, and survivability inherent in its differing attributes and redundancy. A different mix of strategic-force platforms may provide the same benefits in the future, but the flexibility and survivability of forces provided by a diversity of strategic platforms will remain important. Those platforms should also allow some margin for uploading and downloading weapons as necessary to assure, deter, dissuade, and defend in a dynamic threat environment.

The goal of assurance provides some additional pertinent metrics for US force adequacy. For example, officials in some NATO countries have indicated that US strategic nuclear force levels should be comparable to Russia's and that US nuclear weapons must remain deployed on NATO territory. These metrics appear to have nothing to do with the possible demands of "war fighting," but are important for the psychological/political goal of allied assurance. And, as noted above, Japanese officials have indicated that US nuclear forces, while not deployed on Japanese territory, should be credible, readily available in the area, capable of discrete targeting and visible as necessary. This mix of desirable characteristics again suggests the value of a mix of US force platforms with a range of possible force loadings.

These force attributes of resilience, diversity, flexibility, and survivability, and the adaptability of US planning were compatible with the Cold War's high numbers of weapons and strategic platforms, and with continuous nuclear modernization programs. Those attributes may also be possible at lower numbers of deployed forces and platforms, but the pursuit of ever lower numbers will impose limitations on these measures of merit and call into question the viability of the US industrial infrastructure necessary to produce strategic forces. Recognition of these various force and infrastructure attributes—important for deterrence, assurance, dissuasion, and damage limitation—should contribute to how adequacy is defined for the US strategic arsenal and the US arms control agenda. If so, some helpful parameters will be injected into the ongoing discussion of "How much is enough?"

Notes

1. For example, see the explicit use of this target-based methodology linked to deterrence in Senate, *Testing and Operation Requirements for the B-2 Bomber*, 8–20. See also Seiler, *Strategic Nuclear Force Requirements and Issues*.

2. Fetter, "Nuclear Strategy and Targeting Doctrine," 57.

3. Reif, "Nuclear Weapons."

4. Davis, "The Attribution of WMD Events." See also Phillips, "Uncertain Justice for Nuclear Terror."

5. Senate, *The Continuing Threat from Weapons of Mass Destruction*; and Carus, *Bioterrorism and Biocrimes*, 20.

6. See the discussion of the extreme fluidity of contemporary developments in National Intelligence Council, *Mapping the Global Future*, 4, 18–19. See also the discussion of past rapid changes in threat conditions in Odom et al., *The Emerging Ballistic Missile Threat to the United States*, 19–21.

7. Craig and George, *Force and Statecraft*, 188.

8. Dror, "High-Intensity Aggressive Ideologies as an International Threat," 161.

9. Quoted in "Pak's N-bomb Prevented India from Attacking It after 26/11," available in Department of State, *ISN News*, 10 March 2009.

10. As concluded by Lebow and Stein, *We All Lost the Cold War*, 356.

11. See Senate, *Hearings on MX Missile Basing System*, 6–7.

12. Medalia, *"Bunker Busters": Robust Nuclear Earth Penetrator Issues, FY2005–FY2007*; and his, *"Bunker Busters": Sources of Confusion in the Robust Nuclear Earth Penetrator Debate*, 1. See also the extended discussion of this subject in Guthe, "Implications of a Dynamic Strategic Environment."

13. See the Commission on Integrated Long-Term Strategy, *Discriminate Deterrence*, 2.

14. Guthe, *Ten Continuities in U.S. Nuclear Weapons Policy, Strategy, Plans and Forces*.

15. Secretary of defense to the president, draft memorandum, 3 December 1964, 24. Document has been redacted and declassified.

16. Senate, *Hearings on Nuclear Terrorism*.

17. Ibid., 6–11.

18. Dallas, quoted in, "Study Finds U.S. Not Ready for Nuke Hit," *Washington Times*, 21 March 2007, A-3. This article quotes Dr. Dallas from Bell and Dallas, "Vulnerability of Populations and the Urban Health Care Systems to Nuclear Weapon Attack—Examples from Four American Cities."

19. Secretary of defense to the president, draft memorandum, 6 December 1963, I-21–22. Document has been redacted and declassified.

20. Carter, May, and Perry, "The Day After"; and Payne et al., *Bioterrorism and a Strategy of Concomitant Deterrence*, 78–88.

21. See Payne, *The Great American Gamble*, 43–44, 219–20.

22. See a review of the officially expressed reasons for essential equivalence in Payne, "The Schlesinger Shift: Return to Rationality."

23. Howard, "Reassurance and Deterrence."

24. See the discussion in Department of State, International Security Advisory Board, *Report on Discouraging a Cascade of Nuclear Weapons States*, 22–23.

25. Ibid., 23.

26. Secretary of defense to the president, draft memorandum, 1 November 1965, 5, 22 (document has been redacted and declassified); and secretary of defense to the president, draft memorandum, 15 January 1968, 13 (document has been redacted and declassified).

Chapter 6

Tailored Deterrence, Smart Power, and the Long-Term Challenge of Nuclear Proliferation

Jonathan Trexel

There are many strategic deterrence challenges facing the United States now and over the long term. For example, one might want to deter aggression, deter an adversary from using weapons of mass destruction (WMD) once a conflict has begun, or deter cyberspace or counterspace attacks in a crisis. But a growing challenge for the United States, one that will likely recur (possibly several times) in the coming years, is stemming nuclear weapons proliferation among potential adversaries.

When we consider the ways to support the president's emphasis on addressing nuclear nonproliferation, there is a role for strategic deterrence. But when one considers this problem, a conceptual bridge is needed to help think about such challenges with a long-term perspective. Strategic deterrence concepts provide one such bridge. My intention is to present three broad, long-term deterrence problems or scenarios as ways to think about deterrence activities and capabilities and then cull ideas for future discussion.

From a strategy perspective, some long-term context for current thinking on near-term deterrence planning and strategy is provided. The current deterrence framework, as outlined in the 2006 *Deterrence Operations Joint Operating Concept* (*DOJOC*), suggests that we build deterrence strategies responding to understandings of potential adversary perceptions. These strategies necessarily tend to be products of military planning processes characterized by near-term definitions of the problems and emphasis on hard-power capabilities and activities. However, as one proceeds over the time horizon of our understanding of emerging and distant threats and how potential adversaries might calculate regarding acquisition and/or development of nuclear weapons, the role of the military instrument likely diminishes and soft power increases in prominence.

Background

The broad idea that deterrence is about decisive influence applies to long-term and near-term deterrence problems. The primary differences between long-term and near-term deterrence concepts are of magnitude and outcomes. A short review of near-term deterrence from the *Deterrence Operations Joint Operating Concept* follows.

> Deterrence operations convince adversaries not to take actions that threaten US vital interests by means of decisive influence over their decision making. Decisive influence is achieved by credibly threatening to deny benefits and/or impose costs while encouraging restraint by convincing the actor that restraint will result in an acceptable outcome.[1]

The Deterrence Framework

The goal in near-term deterrence is to influence an actor to restrain from taking egregious action against us or our allies (fig. 6.1). We begin by understanding the actor's core decision factors: the things that matter most from a strategic perspective. Next we consider those factors within a specific scenario to assess the actor's decision calculus. This calculus is the actor's computation of the relative costs and benefits of taking specific actions and is the focus of near-term

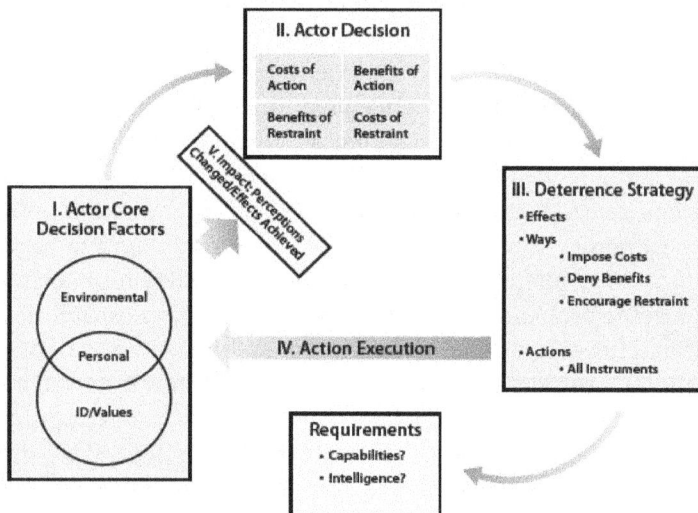

Figure 6.1. Strategic deterrence model

deterrence. Understanding the adversary's decision calculus informs deterrence strategy development including determining the desired cognitive effects on the actor and determining the means of national power to achieve those effects. Core decision factors are the objects of deterrence strategies because changes in core decision factors change an actor's decision calculus. Therefore desired cognitive effects are products of altering an actor's core decision factors. Deterrence strategy requires a cycle of assessment, strategy adjustment, and reassessment. Importantly, the hard power, or force, used to accomplish this influence can go beyond nuclear assets to include conventional and even defensive capabilities. Further, nonmilitary capabilities and activities are important to consider precisely because they matter in potential adversary decision making.

The appropriate application of power (both military and nonmilitary) to achieve a deterrence objective, taking into consideration the adversary and his decision calculus, is tailored deterrence. Unpacking an adversary's decision calculus is the essential feature in strategic deterrence strategy development and is the springboard for understanding how to tailor US strategy to deter effectively an adversary's decision to pursue a program intended to develop nuclear weapons.

Deterrence Tailoring

The features of a tailored deterrence strategy depend in part on whether the strategy is intended to deter near- or long-term threats.[2] For example, if the concern involves a state's acquisition or development of nuclear weapons, one might employ a near-term strategy that includes denying the adversary access to the various parts of the nuclear fuel cycle, while at the same time, through diplomatic means, raising the value of cooperation so as to enhance stability through economic interdependencies and treaties. A broad US government strategy might also attempt to incorporate pursuing common interests such as fighting disease, hunger, and famine and promoting education and human capital investment at the societal level, all the while threatening to impose costs for aberrant behavior upon the leadership. In contrast, a long-term strategy might be to lessen the value attributed to nuclear weapons as a means of guaranteeing security by reducing fears of external attack. Considering both near- and long-term aspects of the proliferation problem can help us understand how to sculpt a more consistent long-term US national deterrence strategy. This is accomplished by understanding the actor and how our deterrent actions might need to change should long-term efforts fail.

On Power

The United States possesses significant national power. When applied this power must be measured, timely, and decisive even in pursuit of deterrence strategies aimed at nuclear proliferation challenges. The consequences of inappropriate application of US power can include a lasting, tarnished US image in the international community, irrevocable loss of precious resources, strains of overextension, as well as deterrence failure. Conversely failing to plan and organize, to marshal, and to use US power will frustrate other national security strategies and compound adverse consequences upon us regardless of the problems at hand.

When we think of power, we often think of the acronym DIMEFIL (diplomatic, information, military, economic, financial, intelligence, and law enforcement). However, we typically do not consider applying all these elements of power in a coordinated or synchronized way toward deterrence. Economic power, for example, has many aspects and serves many purposes; it undergirds social well-being, trade, taxes, government programs, and so forth, but it can also be used to influence others through, for example, the withholding of economic benefits. Unfortunately, when we think of our nation's "deterrence" or "strategic deterrence," we usually associate such power with long-range nuclear forces.

Strategic deterrence is principally a competition of wills. In the twenty-first century, our political opponents' decision calculus will include many considerations beyond such weapons. The application of US power to achieve deterrent effects should, therefore, consider all types of power and not be limited to long-range nuclear forces. How power is applied is what distinguishes its utility as a deterrent. This is to say, the power to influence others in what matters most is not simply physical destructive power. Rather, deterrent power, in this way, can be thought of as any power marshaled specifically for deterrent effects. Deterrent power can be either hard power or soft power or a fusion of the two into what is today termed *smart power*.[3] The sum of our nation's varied strategic capabilities is tailorable. A purposeful, disciplined, collaborative, and tailored deterrence campaign development process is needed for deterrent power to achieve its desired cognitive effects. Effectively marshaling deterrent power, however, can be useful in day-to-day conditions, acute deterrent problems, and long-term strategic deterrence scenarios, such as those dealing with nuclear proliferation described below.

Smart power is known for the caution and care in which it is applied and the self-limiting objectives that guide its application. Smart power can range from positive policy attraction by others (described by some as soft power) to armed coercion and the decisive use of force (hard power), albeit within a framework of smart power. Smart power can include the powers to attract and to instill fear, governmental and nongovernmental, military and nonmilitary, kinetic and nonkinetic, as well as less tangible instruments, such as US strength of character. The smart-power concept should be attractive to US policy makers because it can be applied as the capacity to influence. It can more effectively deter our potential and immediate adversaries from egregious actions, assure our allies and friends of US commitment and resolve, develop improved relations with competitors and indifferent states to dissuade them from trends infringing on our interests, relieve fears in foreign social groups of US intentions and possibly foster good will among them, and reassure our citizens' fears.

Long-Term Deterrence Concept

Some long-term deterrence problems and strategies consider actor decisions beyond the alternatives of action or restraint described in the basic deterrence framework above. The long-term deterrence concept suggests presenting alternatives to an adversary that are aimed at abandonment of an egregious decision altogether for a more attractive favorable decision that is potentially of greater long-term value. Unlike typical near-term deterrence strategies, the long-term deterrence approach provides pathways to a totally different outcome for everyone involved. The actor is influenced away from egregious action for the indefinite future, not by restraint alone but by replacing the adversary's choice with a mutually acceptable alternative course of action (COA). So while a fundamental distinction exists in that near- and long-term deterrence options presuppose different deterrence pathways (restraint versus alternative COA), the central idea remains the same: decisive influence over an actor's decision calculus resulting in enhanced US national security.

Overview

Three broad strategies pertaining to the concept of long-term deterrence of nuclear weapons (NW) development are summarized below (fig. 6.2). These include

1. engaging in a deterrence campaign to influence an actor's decision to act or refrain over an extended period of time,

2. offering an actor an acceptable option of an entirely new alternative COA when favorable circumstances arise during an ongoing deterrence campaign, and

3. encouraging friendly relations early as a preventive measure.

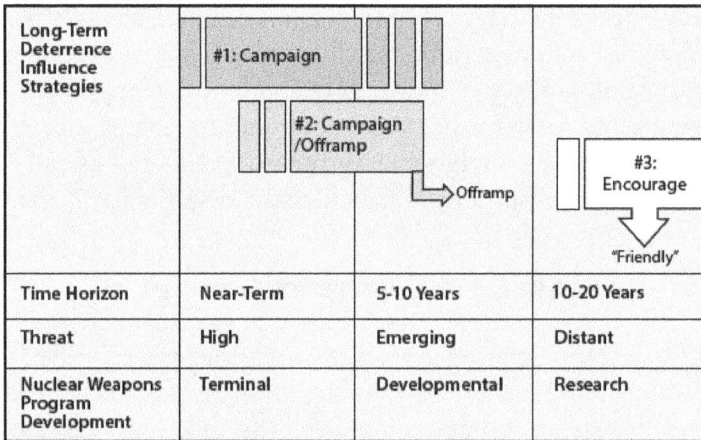

Long-Term Deterrence Influence Strategies	#1: Campaign	#2: Campaign/Offramp →Offramp	#3: Encourage →"Friendly"
Time Horizon	Near-Term	5-10 Years	10-20 Years
Threat	High	Emerging	Distant
Nuclear Weapons Program Development	Terminal	Developmental	Research

Figure 6.2. Long-term deterrence strategies

These scenarios also reflect different target core decision factors as time and circumstances change demanding from us appropriate long-term deterrence capabilities, approaches, and strategies (fig. 6.3). Each long-term deterrence strategy will be explored briefly below and also point to three broad strategy options.

1. Deter by confronting the actor, given its adversarial identity and values, thus confounding the threat and the threatening behavior indefinitely.

2. Deter by convincing the otherwise adversarial actor to be friendly, thus removing the prospects for threatening behavior by changing the nature of the threat.

3. Deter by encouraging the actor to be friendly before becoming adversarial and thus preventing the threat and threatening behavior from ever emerging.

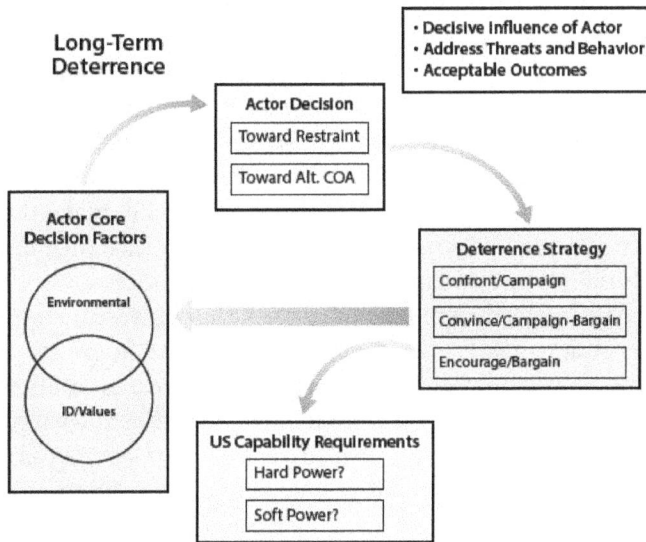

Figure 6.3. Strategy options

Historical Insights

There are several historical cases one can use for support or comparison strategies to deter potential adversaries from pursuing WMD programs. South Africa and Libya are two such cases.[4] South Africa made the decision to abandon its nuclear weapons program principally out of fear of potential expansion of Soviet influence and with it possible invasion.[5] However, factors surrounding the decline in Soviet power, internal domestic problems, and a marred international image led South Africa's leadership to see its security position enhanced without nuclear weapons. It was not the deterrence strategy of imposing external costs that mattered most, but the drastic alteration of the post–Cold War security environment that changed how South African leaders valued their nuclear weapons.

The most celebrated case of an adversarial state giving up its nuclear weapons program is the case of Libya. Libya's nuclear weapons program originated in some of the most trying years of the broader Arab-Israeli conflict and was intended in part—perhaps a large part—as a deterrent and counter to the Israeli nuclear program. The A. Q. Khan network also aided it. Libya never acquired nuclear weapons, but its leadership's decision calculus for pursuing its WMD program was changed by a combination of developments, including the loss of a significant program equipment shipment, consideration of the US invasion of Iraq, the possibility Libya could also be attacked, and overtures suggesting a significant bargain was at hand.

While Libya stood to lose the prestige of eventual nuclear status and, with it, nuclear deterrent security, Libyan leaders seem to have perceived that their nuclear program might actually make them less secure. The bargain of program abandonment in exchange for lifting economic sanctions, an end to political isolation, removal from the state sponsors of terrorism list, renewal of direct investment in Libya, and other inducements collectively served Libya's interests, particularly with regard to its security position. In the cases of both South Africa and Libya, security was understood to be better without nuclear weapons. Especially in Libya's case, security was seen as the opportunity to choose an alternative course of action and to provide its leadership with a choice with which we can all live.

Long-Term Deterrence Scenarios

There are two broad possibilities when we consider the sort of long-term deterrence that includes continuous deterrence. The first is continuous deterrence of an existing threat. The second is continuous deterrence of an emerging threat evolving over a long period of time. The existing *DOJOC* concept can be used to describe the differences between these two in terms of adversary perceptions and appropriate deterrence strategies.

Scenario 1: Continuous Campaign

Unlike other deterrence challenges, the pursuit of nuclear weapons entails a series of decisions made by the adversary over a period of several years, beginning with an initial decision to proceed with research and fuel-cycle needs and culminating with final decisions to test a nuclear device and deploy weapons. The issue of an actor pursuing nuclear weapons over several years suggests we take a broad, long-term view in order to craft and implement an effective deterrence strategy (table 6.1).

Table 6.1. Long-term deterrence strategy overview

	Continuous Campaign	Campaign Bargain	Bargain
Desired Actor Choice	Restrain	Off Ramp to Alternative COA	Alternative COA
US Strategy Approach	Confront	Convince	Encourage
Goal of Long-Term Strategy on Threat	Contain	Remove	Prevent
Threat Characteristics	Existing Threat	Emerging Threat	Distant Threat
US Power Emphasis	Hard-Soft	Soft-Hard	Soft
Strategy's Effect on Actor's Relations with the United States	Adversarial (Unchanged)	Toward Friendly	Friendly
Goal of Strategy on Actor's Value of WMD	Confound (Value Likely Remains High)	Marginalize	Eliminate

In the first scenario, an actor might contemplate taking an action we deem egregious or against our interests and, as a result, might lead us to conduct an active deterrence campaign against this threat over an extended period of time, if not indefinitely. As long as conditions remain basically unchanged, the option available to the actor associated with this situation is simply a decision to act or not act—that is, a decision to proceed with the egregious action or restrain from doing so. Examples of this scenario might include North Korea's contemplation of attacking South Korea over the past several decades or perhaps Soviet decision making relative to a nuclear attack during the Cold War period. Given the actor's historical animosity toward the United States, the US deterrence strategy in this scenario would be to confront the actor and seek to acquire and maintain continuous influence over his decision to restrain from taking hostile action and doing so indefinitely or until the threat ends. This is done by understanding the actor's decision calculus. The task then is to threaten and/or actually impose costs, deny sought-after benefits, and encourage restraint by reducing the actor's perceived costs of restraint and reinforcing the actor's perceived benefits of restraint. These actions stabilize the threat in conditions of a general deterrence, status quo environment indefinitely, hopefully leading to the adversary's eventual abandonment of the threat to the United States as he recognizes its diminishing value.

The key here is that the actor's motivations for considering pursuit of nuclear weapons are value based. Nuclear weapons would be valued as addressing the security concerns of a rogue state, which might include a relatively weak military position or significant imbalance, fears of potential internal political consequences, and vulnerability to political manipulation by other states, particularly regional antagonists or competitors. The actor's key question is, "What will happen if I do not pursue NWs?"

Years later, at the terminus of his development program, when possession is relatively close at hand, the adversary's decision calculus is likely based more on the benefits of possession, though potential costs would most likely be much higher, and his calculus might be based more on the probabilities. In this case, his key question will be, "What will happen if I *continue* to pursue?"

Evaluating a potential adversary's perceptions in pursuing nuclear weapons and formulating an appropriate deterrence strategy that applies all elements of national and international power might present several advantages for the United States, its allies, and the international community.

1. Altering political and regional security conditions that reduce the adversary's fear of attack might be considered a small investment relative to the potential costs and intended consequences of going to war later with a nuclear-armed state. Since changing conditions to be more favorable to the adversary might take a long time to accomplish, the earlier a government assesses this to be a viable strategy to deter nuclear weapons pursuit, the higher the likelihood of achieving the outcomes sought.

2. Increased use of positive political and economic power, or soft power, might improve the global image of the United States by demonstrating a willingness to explore new noncoercive measures, which may ultimately result in making threats to use

hard power more credible. Further, adversary perceptions of US military overstretch might weaken how those adversaries view US hard-power deterrent threats.

3. An effective deterrence strategy can inform, if not guide, US strategic communication strategy as we seek to promote and strengthen the US position globally.

4. Employing all instruments of national power, not simply the military instrument, can build trust and confidence in the United States and perhaps increase the viability of nonproliferation inspection regimes. This also might make partnerships on nonproliferation strategies more palatable politically.

5. The United States can assure allies of regional commitments.

6. Such a strategy will be more useful in finding coalition members previously unable or unwilling to participate in US nonproliferation initiatives because the military is the sole instrument being used.

7. The United States would make regional security dynamics more stable.

8. Most importantly, the specific proliferation problem being considered would be contained, reduced, eliminated, or even prevented because a panoply of instruments and options are in play.

Deterrence failure early (or failing to try) makes deterrence success harder at the terminal end, or near-term end, except with higher risks of military force and the potential second- and third-order effects and unforeseen consequences in the aftermath. But note that, while military threats might be decisive, they probably heighten adversary fears and reinforce his belief that he needs nuclear weapons precisely to deter US attack.

Scenario 2: Campaign Bargain

A second long-term deterrence scenario can occur during an ongoing deterrence campaign, in crisis, or when circumstances have changed so much that they might present an opportunity to offer an actor an entirely new course of action. Here, we are concerned with presenting the actor with a choice for a different future, not merely the choice to act or restrain from a hostile behavior. That is, we would seek to encourage the actor down the path of an entirely new alternative course of action that presents a different but acceptable outcome for both parties. The actor must envision an alternative future that is sufficiently secure without possessing threatening capabilities or behavior. In this scenario, deterrence activities would not be limited simply to near-term incentives, such as financial reward or avoiding financial loss, but would emphasize a long-term option that sufficiently satisfies the actor's core security concerns and in a way that satisfies our need to reduce or eliminate the hostile threats and capabilities he poses to us. The actor initially chooses to restrain from egregious behavior but, more importantly, chooses a value system no longer characterized by the United States as adversarial.

An example of this long-term deterrence scenario would be Libya's decision to reestablish friendly relations with the West and abandon its WMD program in 2003–4 rather than simply restrain from advancing it along its technological path (fig. 6.4). This long-term deterrence strategy is likely a very difficult challenge when in crisis or when the developmental threat has approached completion, especially since our efforts to deter the actor's egregious actions at this point are likely to be increasingly coercive in nature, with cost-imposition military capabilities and activities at the center of our strategy. However, as in the Libyan case, a significant regional security event that brought a large number of US combat forces to the region as part of the coalition intervention in Iraq can spur the actor to accept the choice of a long-term alternative course of action marked by a vision of a secure future and friendly relations with the United States.[6]

The 2003 attack on Iraq and the ultimate overthrow of Saddam Hussein altered Muammar Qadhafi's perceptions by convincing him he, too, faced the possibility of regime change for continuing his nuclear weapons program. Environmental change can and does occur in the international security environment, resulting in change that impacts the decision making of leaders. Such change worked to influence Qadhafi's decision to consider an alternative course of action in the form of a grand bargain to get the result the United States wanted—a long-term deterrence outcome of good relations with the West and Libya possessing no threatening, destabilizing, or nuclear capabilities. US intervention in Iraq triggered the opportunity for the bargain to be offered and accepted. Qadhafi would not have accepted the bargain until he fully understood the likely costs for continuing to pursue his nuclear weapons program.

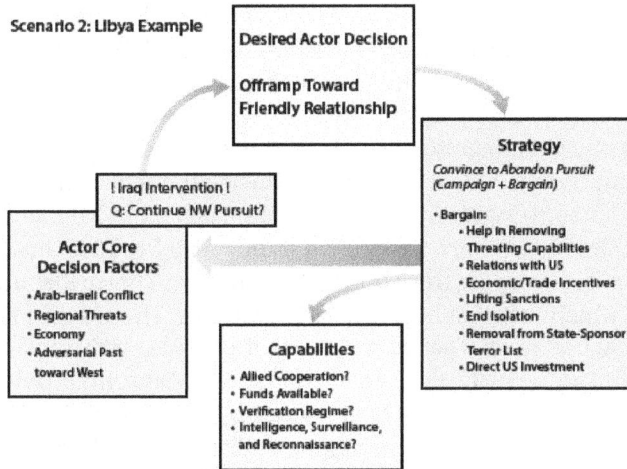

Figure 6.4. Campaigning and bargaining

Scenario 3: Bargain

The third long-term deterrence scenario considers an actor's option to change strategic course early, while any potential threat to us is but "smoke rising on the horizon." Since this threat is perceptible, yet still on the distant horizon (e.g., an actor's early decision to pursue a nuclear power capability that could transition later to a nuclear weapons capability), new opportunities present themselves for shaping the actor's perceived security environment and thereby the calculus for choosing among broad alternative courses of action. While the tools and ways available to us to influence the decision making remain the same, the actor's choice is not limited to deciding to act or restrain as described above.

Rather, the concept of long-term deterrence, while the threat is still distant, might involve presenting the actor with multiple alternative choices. However, we are seeking influence toward a choice that takes into account what we deem to be threatening capabilities or intent, even if those capabilities will take years to mature, along with the root security issues driving the actor to value those capabilities (nuclear weapons) in the first place (fig. 6.5). The difference is that we are packaging purposefully and actively a bargain early in the process of an actor's development of a capability that may be a threat to the United States in the future. Properly negotiated, this approach will encourage a potential adversary to choose a value system and a behavioral path that are not adversarial to us. As with scenario 2 above, this requires us to understand and address the root motivations in the actor's decision calculus to pursue a capability that positions him as a potential US adversary. Doing so could include taking political and economic measures that align or even integrate the actor with the United States and its allies. But it would also include removing or reducing the actor's most threatening and destabilizing military capabilities, such as WMD and related means of delivery, however rudimental they may be. Thus, his decision goes beyond restraining from pursuit to a strategic choice that involves a future in which restraint becomes an imperative. The US goal is for the actor to choose an alternative bargain that provides enduring, credible, and stabilizing security measures while at the same time reducing or eliminating his perceived costs of restraint. By doing so, the perceived value of WMD and other threatening military capabilities is reduced and ultimately eliminated.

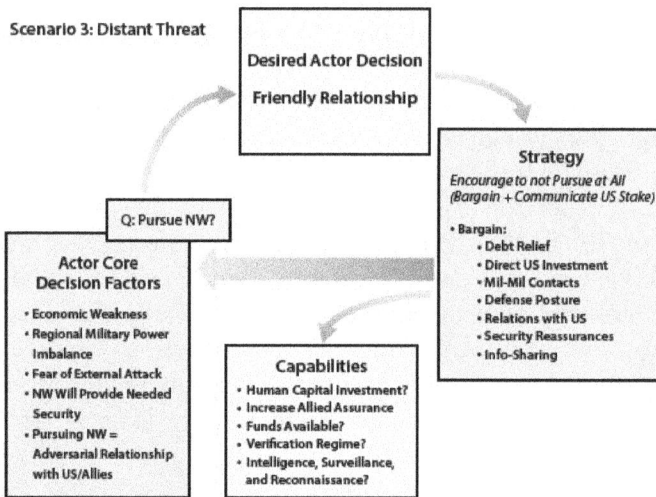

Figure 6.5. Bargaining early

When we consider this third scenario, it is difficult to identify historical cases that match the concept envisioned here as few cases can be cited when the United States acted decisively to influence a distant threat precisely in the manner outlined above. However, there are cases generally representative of the idea. Egypt, for example, explored the possibility of developing a nuclear weapons program during the 1960s and 1970s in response to various perceived threats posed by Israel, including fear of Israel's possible development of its own nuclear weapons. However, an alternative course of action involving peaceful relations with the United States and Israel was presented and eventually accepted, culminating in Egypt's 1979 peace settlement with Israel, brokered by the United States at Camp David. Additionally, Egypt's 1980 decision to ratify the Nuclear Non-Proliferation Treaty and an influx of significant US aid and other assurances likely contributed to Cairo backing away from the nuclear option. The goal of influencing Egypt away from continuing its nuclear weapons program was accomplished not merely by influencing its decision to restrain from nuclear weapons pursuit, but by crafting a long-term alternative option that amounted to a bargain that addressed its fundamental regional security concerns and other interests. Thus, scenario 3 illustrates the prevention of a threat when we can only imagine it as potential "smoke rising on the horizon" and when an actor is more amenable to US overtures. Actors like Burma (Myanmar) or Venezuela might fit into this category.

Actor Core Decision Factors

The second and third long-term deterrence scenarios emphasize actions and capabilities not simply to persuade an actor to restrain from continuing an egregious course, but to provide him a credible and durable alternative course that he perceives to enhance his security more than the course he is pursuing currently. Likewise, long-term deterrence emphasizes actions and capabilities that dispel an actor's fears of potential costs of restraint by mitigating long-term motivations pressuring the actor to follow an egregious course of action. Alleviating the actor's perceived costs of restraint intrinsically alters the actor's decision making. More importantly, it strengthens the credibility and the attractiveness of the alternative course of action he is presented.

In General

Long-term deterrence emphasizes consequences of restraint, especially the benefits of changing course, for two important reasons.

First, not many costs, especially military ones, can be imposed on an actor presenting a distant threat that will influence him to accept a positive, long-term alternative course of action. This is mainly because posing significant near-term costs regarding a threat that might never emerge will not be credible. Secondly, if one waits to threaten heavy cost imposition until the threat posed by an actor is a near-term one, such an approach will likely influence the actor only in terms of his near-term decision to act or restrain. In either case the problem is that threatening heavy costs tends to reinforce an actor's enduring security fears and thus may undergird why he values nuclear weapons (for example) in the first place.

As the Libya case demonstrated, the prospect of near-term and heavy costs upon Libya for development of a nuclear weapons capability in the aftermath of the attack on Iraq only found significant meaning in the regime's decision making when combined with a credible, durable, and beneficial alternative course of action that jettisoned nuclear weapons development and a policy of confrontation with the West. In this case, Libya's security concerns were adequately addressed, allowing Libya to accept a long-term alternative course of action characterized by less confrontational relations with the United States.[7] Libya's strategic "sea change" was, in essence, a decision to change its values made possible by political, economic, and security relational and environmental changes. This is an example of long-term deterrence succeeding under the circumstances of an ongoing deterrence campaign.

It should be noted that emphasizing the cost-imposition or benefit-denial aspects of an actor's decision making might be effective in influencing his decision to act or restrain, but doing so without addressing his consequences of restraint might not be tenable over time. This is because it reinforces the actor's fears and his policy of challenge to us and, therefore, is unlikely to incentivize the actor to a long-term alternative course of action.

In each of these long-term deterrence scenarios, an actor's decision making will include consideration of both external environmental and internal factors. Environmental factors (i.e., political, economic, military) comprise his real world of action and interaction. Internal factors (i.e., his identity, values, and fears) shape how he will interpret his environment and provide motivations for action within and upon his environment and likewise determine how environmental change might affect him internally. In long-term deterrence scenarios, however, the internal-external mix of decision factors differs, with salient aspects being how an actor would interpret alternative courses of action and, therefore, differences in the long-term deterrence strategy, actions, and capabilities we would need to marshal. This also explains why unexpected and radical changes to conditions can be destabilizing and dangerous.

In scenario 1 (a continuous campaign), environmental factors matter most, since our relationship with an actor is relatively unchanged given the latter's static identity. Given the ongoing threat he poses, our long-term deterrence actions and capabilities, therefore, will emphasize his basic calculus to act or restrain. These will also require coercive measures, including the prospects of defensive and offensive military options. But long-term deterrence strategies, as in deterring conflict on the Korean Peninsula, seek to provide stability to political, economic, and military conditions.

In scenario 2 (a campaign bargain), there is time for external factors to change significantly and perhaps affect the actor's basic calculus, possibly presenting us an opportunity for a "grand bargain" with the actor. However, we need insight into the actor's decision calculus, how it might be changing, and a preplanned "bargain" or one that can be cobbled together with little time. Here, internal and environmental factors work together to "motivate" the actor toward a new course of action where he can envision himself securely in a world in which his bilateral and regional relations are significantly altered and the value he places on WMD or other threatening military capabilities is significantly reduced.

In scenario 3 (a distant threat), the threat is in its earliest stages, and the United States might be in a position to decisively influence the actor away from further pursuit and toward acceptance of a long-term bargain. The most effective way to achieve this will likely be strategies that reduce the actor's perceptions of external or existential threats. Fostering beneficial conditions or assurances will also be needed. Reducing an actor's fears decreases his perceived benefits for pursuing nuclear weapons, while assurances will persuade the actor to find benefits of restraint attractive. However, these perceptions must seem to be enduring if we are to expect any long-term alternative option to be of value and accepted.

In Relation to US Deterrence Strategies

When an actor first considers a decision to pursue nuclear weapons, his decision calculus is likely to be dominated by perceptions of various consequences of restraint—that is, what might happen if a nuclear weapons program is not pursued. Further, they will not likely respond to threats of attack, especially a nuclear threat, as such threats will likely be perceived as premature, hence less than credible. They also might not respond to other potential costs, such as financial or economic sanctions. The thought about deterrence strategy should stretch beyond a capabilities-based approach to "tailor" our deterrence strategies not only to the diverse range of adversaries and diverse deterrence challenges facing the United States today but also with means beyond the military instrument. This is true for near-term and long-term deterrence problems. However, to do so the United States must be willing to engage adversaries with a view toward making long-term commitments and policy trade-offs. Providing alternative courses of action, or grand bargains, essentially gives the actor a package of benefits that is irresistible.

An alternative long-term deterrence strategy would shape the conditions that inform decisions to seek nuclear weapons. This is a multifaceted strategy, but one that must, of necessity, have two essential military features to influence the adversary's perceptions favorable to deterrence outcomes. Both must be addressed for a long-term deterrence strategy to be effective. First, discreet or implied threats of military costs if the adversary continues to pursue a nuclear weapons program communicate a US intention to raise the stakes if the adversary jettisons the deal and pursues the full suite of technologies, knowledge, and nuclear weapons capabilities later on. Second, the adversary's fears that drive the pursuit of nuclear weapons need to be addressed with US allies and partners. Moreover, allies and partners must be reassured about US commitments and enduring stakes in the region. Reassurance would strengthen US relationships with those states.

A US deterrence strategy aimed at influencing adversary decisions to proceed or continue with a nuclear weapons program must guard against adversary perceptions that nuclear weapons provide increased security and that the benefits of restraint are hollow. This would not only raise the specter of renewed interest in WMD in that adversary state, but risk nuclear proliferation among US friends and allies who perceived cracks in the US ability to thwart WMD development and opted to pursue them on their own. For example, it remains to be seen if Libya's commitment to refrain from pursuing nuclear weapons will endure. In recent years Libya has expressed disappointment that political and economic benefits promised by the United States and others have failed to materialize. Should Arab or Muslim states, such as Iran, continue to be denied a nuclear capability by the United States or Israel, as with Iraq and Syria, it is not difficult to imagine that Libya, coupled with new perceptions of being given a raw deal and feeling less secure for it, might decide to pursue nuclear weapons again.

Considerations

Long-term deterrence described herein is highly situation-dependent. As history demonstrates, international security circumstances can and do change, impacting relationships among actors. Former adversaries, such as Germany and Japan, became close allies of the United States as well as formidable economic and military powers. Similarly, the aftermath of the Cold War brought about significant changes among several former republics of the Soviet Union that have since become members of NATO. Moreover, as previously mentioned, Libya's relationship with the United States and Libyan participation in the international political system shifted shortly after the attack on Iraq. Generally, the point here is not to prescribe a formula for threat reduction, but to acknowledge that conditions, when they change, can afford opportunities to address long-term or long-standing threats by influencing leaders toward alternative outcomes and nonadversarial relationships. Specifically, in relation to nuclear ambitions, whether considering scenarios 2 or 3, it is important to recognize that other actors have walked away from the pursuit or possession of nuclear weapons, albeit for a variety of reasons. However, some of these reasons included bargains made possible by external actors and changes in external circumstances that were meaningful to the actor in question.[8]

Being prepared for such opportunities requires careful interagency and interallied planning. This planning must, first of all, be rooted in an in-depth study and understanding of one's potential adversaries. This planning activity certainly includes an assessment of the actor's existing capabilities, intentions, and willingness to act aggressively toward us or our allies. It also means understanding the actor's motivations for adversarial behavior. Further, this study must work diligently, some would argue with greater and more focused investment than in the past, to understand various actors and their values and the cognitive perceptions critical to their decision making. Long-term deterrence strategies would capitalize upon this knowledge and plan for opportunities to present these actors alternative courses of action to prevent threats from emerging.

The careful planning that is required, but clearly exists today in limited capacity, involves the deliberate coordination of several activities in order for long-term deterrence plans and strategies to be effective. These activities include sharing information, intelligence, and long-term deterrence studies about both state and nonstate threats; policy planning that provides more accurate risk assessments of various policy options in light of existing, emerging, and distant threats; capability assessments germane to long-term deterrence needs, including interagency capabilities that address gaps in non-military instruments of deterrence; and impact assessments of possible alternative courses of action to influence actor decision making.

It is a formidable task to organize for long-term deterrence problems, including capabilities to understand and deter various actors in order to prevent emerging and distant threats. This is particularly true since we are hardly organized to address the myriad of near- and mid-term deterrence problems that challenge us with the security complexities inherent in a post–Cold War, twenty-first-century world. Complex deterrence problems, however, are not impossible ones, and consideration for how we can and must organize to address long-term deterrence problems will also provide immediate value as we confront and deter near-term threats.

Attention to deterrence challenges and consistent calls for deterrence-related transformation have come from diverse and authoritative sources. For example, ADM Michael Mullen, as chairman of the Joint Chiefs of Staff, argued, "We need a new model of deterrence that helps us bring our own clock up to speed with the pace and the scope of the challenges of this new century. Time hack . . . now."[9] A new capability is needed that authoritatively crafts national deterrence plans to

- provide decision makers comprehensive courses of action for day-to-day, crisis, and long-term deterrence challenges;

- integrate and synchronize national power and activities for deterrence objectives;

- coordinate US government deterrence strategies with those of US allies and partners, as needed;

- expand deterrence-focused adversary analysis in support of deterrence strategies and other national-security-related plans activities; and

- provide national, interagency, and regional leaderships a common deterrence picture and tool for deterrence-oriented decision making.

A national deterrence or "strategic engagement" center, perhaps modeled on the composition and activities of the National Counterterrorism Center (NCTC), especially if combined with other influence-oriented centers (including a NATO Deterrence Center of Excellence), is one way of looking ahead to face these twenty-first-century problems. Doing so could provide a new capability in one location that would develop, integrate, and orchestrate interagency deterrence-focused planning, activities, and effectiveness assessment for our nation's leadership. A national deterrence center would have the capacity for fully integrating national intelligence information into deterrence-specific adversary assessment. This center could also review and update indicators daily for impact assessment of ongoing deterrence actions. Further, if modeled after NCTC, such a center would have the capability to be staffed for planning and cuing of courses of action for coordination, integration, and synchronization with members across the interagency as well as the DOD, the national labs, and expertise from academia and the private sector for research into capabilities, methods, and assessments, as well as allied integration for planning activities, information, and intelligence sharing. This is particularly important in today's security environment where there are threats of mutual interest to our allies, such as NATO, but also with other partners where there are other opportunities to collaborate on combined capabilities, such as integration of missile defenses that could be used to deter or cyber capabilities that could be used to deter, defend, and defeat, as well as other interagency activities such as financial sanctioning.

Conclusion

There are three basic values for considering and expanding a concept of long-term deterrence as described in this chapter. First, doing so provides a time-related context for how we currently model the near-term deterrence framework contained in the 2006 *DOJOC*, namely influencing an adversary's decision to act or restrain and doing so usually after the United States is aware of the threat. Continuing to do so, despite recognition that actors consider alternative courses of action in addition to consequences of a single decision, would be to limit future deterrence-planning options and fail to recognize how one might effectively develop influence campaigns that span several years or decades.[10]

Second, this concept is intended to illustrate that there might be times and conditions in which preferred deterrence strategies emphasize early proactive measures to head off development of threats emerging "over the horizon." This is because it might be much harder to deter later when the threatening capabilities are fully developed.

Third, concepts such as long-term deterrence scenarios can assist in crafting future experimentation, gaming, and exercises in which deterrence capabilities, activities, and situational conditions can promote better understanding of potential adversaries, threats, and strategies to address them.

Notes

1. Department of Defense, *Deterrence Operations Joint Operating Concept* (*DOJOC*), 8. US vital interests might include maintaining territorial integrity, preserving basic political sovereignty and societal integrity within the United States, preventing mass casualties among the population, securing critical US and international infrastructure assets (energy, telecommunications, water, essential services, etc.) that support economic viability, and supporting the defense of friends and allies.

2. Deterrence can be "tailored" in several ways, including use of instruments of power appropriate to the need and operations supporting, complementing, or at least being consistent with all other US national security and foreign policy strategies. These should be designed to suit one problem at a time; adversaries with specific motivations, intentions, history, culture, values, goals, and capabilities; and threats as they are understood on the time horizon (above).

3. A thorough report on smart power was provided by the Center for Strategic and International Studies Commission on Smart Power. See Cohen, Nye, and Armitage, *A Smarter, More Secure America*.

4. One could consider others, such as Sweden, or Ukraine's decision to return or destroy the nuclear weapons stockpile it inherited after the dissolution of the USSR.

5. While not a clear, long-term deterrence case within the concept presented in this chapter, South Africa's abandonment of its nuclear weapons program does illustrate how changing political, economic, and security conditions impact the value of nuclear weapons and, consequently, the willingness of leadership to accept an entirely different future and alternative course of action without possessing them.

6. For further background on how the coalition intervention influenced Libya's decision making, see Amb. Robert Joseph's book, *Countering WMD*.

7. On Libya's relations with the United States, see page 122 of Bahgat, "Proliferation of Weapons of Mass Destruction." It should be noted that Bahgat's position is that the Libya case was isolated and will not be repeated.

8. In addition to Libya, some of these include South Africa, Kazakhstan, Argentina, and Taiwan. An overview chart of nuclear proliferation since the 1940s, taken from the book *The Nuclear Express* by Thomas C. Reed and Danny B. Stillman, can be found in the *New York Times* online, http://www.nytimes.com/imagepages/2008/12/09/science/20081209_BOMB_GRAPHIC.html.

9. Gurney, "Executive Summary."

10. See the 2006 *DOJOC*, 11, 23, 25.

Chapter 7

Is a New Focus on Nuclear Weapons Research and Development Necessary?

Anne Fitzpatrick

In the past several years there has been considerable public discussion over the future of the US nuclear weapons program, a topic that raises many large-scope, high-level policy questions ranging from the future of nuclear deterrence to the possibility of eliminating nuclear devices altogether. Yet lying below these 10,000-foot-high debates are important questions about their fundamental epistemological and technical underpinnings. Some of these questions include, Is specialized knowledge of nuclear weapons eroding to the point of no return, and does this matter? Or is the knowledge instead changing markedly? And does this necessitate a new or reinvigorated focus on nuclear weapons science, research, development, and fielding? Moreover, what is—exactly—a "new" focus on weapons that is markedly different from the design and testing cycles pre-1992? Do these activities contribute significantly to deterrence in the post–Cold War environment?

To various degrees and for divergent reasons, the questions posed above have been raised and analyzed by two main public communities not affiliated with government:

1. the nongovernmental special-interest policy organizations (NGO) that generally desire to either rid the world of nuclear weapons or at least reduce their numbers and

2. a small slice of the academic community. Here it is important to note that the academic literature on the nuclear weapons enterprise as a whole falls all over the place in terms of disciplinary foci.

The US nuclear weapons enterprise—its history, scientists, technology, and culture—has been examined and interpreted by many historians as well as sociologists, anthropologists, science and technology studies (STS—the branch of academia that studies scientific activity, knowledge, and scientists themselves) experts, and communications studies specialists.[1] Some of this scholarship is well regarded in academic circles; in addition, a couple of well-researched and well-written trade histories of nuclear weapons have received international recognition.[2]

Yet within this body of scholarship only a minority of studies, particularly in the sociological and anthropological fields, delve into nuclear weapons knowledge and expertise. Sociologists Donald MacKenzie and Graham Spinardi's groundbreaking study, "Tacit Knowledge and the Uninvention of Nuclear Weapons,"[3] is the most directly relevant. They challenge the long-standing notion that technology will inevitably march forward once it is invented. Specifically, they postulate that if nuclear weapons design ceases and no special, tacit knowledge is passed on to the would-be next generation of designers, the technology may be "uninvented." The value in MacKenzie and Spinardi's piece is the credibility of the research they conducted, based largely on interviews with technical staff at Los Alamos and Lawrence Livermore National Laboratories; thus, the authors were able to integrate a great deal of firsthand accounts of what it is like to work on nuclear weapons, as opposed to approaching the topic strictly from a sociological theory perspective. Their conclusions are largely speculative about the future and are not a prescription for taking any political course of action.

In 1998 anthropologist Hugh Gusterson published a full-length book, *Nuclear Rites*, which intriguingly explores Lawrence Livermore National Laboratory as a community and analyzes how activities such as nuclear testing helped form scientists' beliefs, sense of identity, and mission.[4] Also, but to a lesser degree, Gusterson addresses knowledge loss from an outsider's point of view and leaves open the question of what roles the national laboratories should play in the future. His research, like MacKenzie and Spinardi's, relies heavily on numerous interviews with the Livermore scientific community.

The most recent among this thread of published studies focusing on knowledge in the US nuclear weapons program is cultural anthropologist Laura McNamara's chapter, "TRUTH Is Generated HERE," in a 2007 communications studies edited volume.[5] This is a provocative essay suggesting that the nuclear weapons research and development (R&D) landscape is changing in ways unforeseen by anyone. All of the above literature will be discussed more in depth later in this chapter. One of the aspects that these studies have in common is that they either explicitly raise or brush up against the subject of deterrence in relation to the process of nuclear weapons R&D, the resulting knowledge and quality of that knowledge, and what the term "new" entails in nuclear weapons research and development.

Why are there so few academic studies of knowledge generation and loss in the nuclear weapons realm that focus on the national laboratories? Part of this gap in the scholarship, of course, is due to lack of access to classified materials. The few scholars who have gained these privileges, including the author of this chapter, are limited in the depth that they can discuss the scientific and technical details of their research.[6] Also, there is some evidence that the nuclear deterrent today does not seem to sport the public popularity it once did, and arms control as a public debate does not command the attention of the average US citizen, even if our current national leadership still deems nuclear deterrence an important national policy.[7] Changes in military requirements after 1992, where nuclear weapons and their delivery systems declined to a lesser priority, have no doubt permanently altered some part of the public view of nuclear weapons and their purpose.[8] Partly because of classification barriers, as noted above, but also partly due to the antinuclear lobbyist community's unclear definition of "new" when speaking of nuclear weapons, largely missing from public discussion are

1. the nuclear weapons-related knowledge base and its evolution,

2. the nature of the nuclear weapons enterprise's evolution since the end of the Cold War, and

3. the whole spectrum of other critical defensive and offensive national security science and technology that this enterprise directly supports.

A review of these subjects is necessary for a better-informed public debate on the role of nuclear weapons and deterrence in general, especially as a serious reconsideration of current US nuclear policy is under way.[9]

Some new government-sponsored and other openly published materials have become available in the past few years to complement the small amount of academic literature, which together may begin to address the questions posed above. Several of the government-sponsored studies address knowledge loss in terms of laboratory staffing and workforce succession planning—topics that are useful to consider.[10] This material, compared with analysis of the academic portion, raises some intriguing insights into the state of the nuclear weapons enterprise, its value to national security, its resident expertise and generation of new knowledge, how we might better define a new focus on nuclear weapons R&D, and how that may contribute to current thinking on deterrence in a meaningful way.

1992 and the Standup of Stockpile Stewardship

When nuclear testing ceased in 1992, no one could predict the future for the nuclear weapons laboratories and their staff, or exactly what the size, configuration, and technology of the nuclear stockpile would look like many years down the road. To mitigate this uncertainty and to meet the Comprehensive Nuclear Test-Ban Treaty (CTBT) requirements, the Department of Energy (DOE) and the weapons laboratory managers proposed the Science Based Stockpile Stewardship Program (SBSS)—now called the Stockpile Stewardship Program (SSP).[11] The SSP embodied an ambitious plan to maintain confidence in the nuclear stockpile based on predictive capability through the construction and employment of brand new computational, experimental, and visualization tools—absent full-scale nuclear testing. The program demanded an enormous increase in laboratory capabilities: materials science, computational hardware and software, high-energy-density physics, and hydrodynamics.[12]

Nothing like this had ever been attempted before, anywhere, and naturally, a great deal of controversy over and criticism of the program emerged throughout the 1990s. In an interview in 1995, physicist Richard Garwin categorized the program as a payoff the laboratories received in return for agreeing to stop nuclear testing:

"What could they get?" Garwin said. "Sandia got the microelectronics research center, which had minimal relevance to the CTBT. Los Alamos got the Dual-Axis Radiographic Hydrodynamic Test [DARHT] facility. Livermore got the National Ignition Facility [NIF]—the white elephant eating us out of house and home. They all maintained these were essential to stockpile stewardship, which they are not."[13]

Indeed, the NIF, the DARHT, and some of the early SSP high-performance computing projects housed under the Accelerated Strategic Computing Initiative (ASCI, now renamed, Advanced Simulation and Computing Program or ASC) were more often than not over budget, behind schedule by several years, and facing some serious technical setbacks, at least until recently.[14] By 2009, the NIF and both axes of the DARHT were operational (although at the time of this writing the NIF had not yet achieved ignition),[15] the ASC modeling and simulation efforts were maturing, and several lesser-known but equally important additional sets of SSP experimental facilities' results (some examples are noted later in this chapter) had been regularly feeding into improving the collective understanding of nuclear weapons functioning and providing data for the annual assessment of the performance, safety, and reliability of the US nuclear stockpile.[16]

Today's means of certifying the US nuclear weapons stockpile is a very different process than that conducted pre-1992. Until the underground test moratorium took effect, the nuclear design laboratories engaged in a regular multiphase weapons acquisition cycle: concept studies, scientific feasibility, engineering development, production engineering, initial production, quantity production, and retirement and disassembly.[17] McNamara descriptively analyzed the pre-1992 process, which

> produced confidence in the nuclear deterrent through an iterative cycle of designing, testing, refining, and stockpiling nuclear explosives. That cycle, which structured work practices at the national laboratories for forty-seven years, was abruptly truncated in July of 1992, when Congress approved the Hatfield-Exon-Mitchell Amendment to the Energy and Water Appropriations Act. Within a few months, funding for the DOE's underground nuclear testing program evaporated, and the laboratories' core experimental program was quite literally left hanging, with massive assemblies suspended in mid-completion over the dry desert floor of the Nevada test site [NTS].[18]

The National Nuclear Security Administration (NNSA), the semi-autonomous agency that supports nuclear weapons activities within DOE, administers this program's successor, the Phase 6.X process, now. In 2001 the Department of Defense (DOD) christened the Phase 6.X process as procedural guidelines to manage the stockpile Life Extension Program (LEP) refurbishment workflow, which mimics the pre-1992 full acquisition process but only applies to life extension and refurbishment of legacy weapons.[19] Parallel to and supporting this was a whole new series of science and engineering efforts, tools, capabilities, databases, and other components within the overall SSP program. The NIF, DARHT, and ASC were among the larger of these—and part of the original proposal for a "troika of computer simulation, experiments, and previous nuclear test data that provides the complete toolbox for the assessment process," and as such have perhaps received the most public scrutiny.[20] Yet, the SSP's physical, technical, and scientific landscape today looks somewhat different than was described in 1994 by the JASON group, who at that time evaluated the program's viability and prospects for success.[21]

For one example, the 1994 JASON report on "Science Based Stockpile Stewardship" reported that the Intel Paragon chip held the world's speed record of approximately 140 Gflops.[22] Since then, commercial computational horsepower has increased exponentially and—partly as a result the nuclear weapons modeling capability and its required software—has come a long way and is projected to reach the exascale level in the next 10 years.[23]

2010 and After

Today's key SSP scientific and technical tools, facilities, and capabilities are far more numerous than the NIF, DARHT, and ASC computers and include, for example, subcritical testing performed at the Nevada Test Site U1A facility, inertial confinement fusion experiments carried out at the Sandia Z-Pinch facility, the high-explosive analysis at Pantex, and many other activities at other sites. The DOE NNSA 2011 Congressional Budget Request states,

> Over the past 15 years, the nation has made significant investment in stockpile stewardship tools and capabilities, which allow the nuclear weapons stockpile to be annually assessed and certified as safe, secure, and effective, without requiring underground nuclear tests. While challenges remain, the growing knowledge and understanding of the stockpile enabled by these tools have reached a level of maturity that not only replaces the need to conduct underground tests, but surpasses the benefits originally realized by previous testing. The data collected from hundreds of previous nuclear tests, along with continued experimental science, remain available to validate predictive simulations of weapons performance. Many of the gaps are closing—or are closed—in understanding the key physics processes, and insights into system and component aging are being realized. These insights will enable better preventative care for the stockpile.[24]

While somewhat generic, the above description is factual. Stated another way, a large portion of the day-to-day nuclear weapons work looks little like it did in the testing era. One way to summarize the difference is in the overall approach: prior to 1992, nuclear weapons experts validated nuclear tests and the loads of data collected from them with computer modeling, but now that has been essentially turned on its head. Today they validate computer simulations of weapon behavior and other phenomena with a large array of small-scale (small compared to full-scale nuclear tests) experiments. Today computational simulations indeed underpin a significant portion of nearly all nuclear weapons work, and simulation codes play a large part in the nuclear stockpile annual assessment. The result is indeed a significant knowledge and understanding gain of how nuclear weapons operate with levels of detail that were not possible in the past.

These evolutions are significant to several debates that range from the need to return to nuclear testing to how the value of this new knowledge compares to that of older, Cold War–era knowledge that may be lost as older designers retire.[25] Some government-sponsored analyses even raise concerns that the United States has let the nuclear-deterrence knowledge base erode too far to sustain an adequate national nuclear-deterrence capability and urge the reinvigoration of these skills.[26] According to a 2008 "Report of the Defense Science Board Task Force on Nuclear Deterrence Skills," the average DOE laboratory worker is old—over age 50—relative to the US workforce and some prospective employees perceive the nuclear weapons enterprise as a declining industry.[27] A recent JASON examination of the LEP program went even further, warning that US nuclear expertise was "threatened by a lack of program stability, perceived lack of mission importance, and degradation of the work environment."[28]

These are valid concerns that require and will continue to demand management and programmatic attention, but from an intellectual point of view they beg the question of how we should interpret *new* when speaking of a new focus on nuclear weapons research and development. The academic anthropologists, sociologists, and communications scholars have not addressed this particular question, while the antinuclear-weapons community remains insistent on using the term *new* within the parameters of the nuclear devices—new physics packages in warheads and/or their specific components. Yet, equally if not more important than the weapons (products) themselves is how the continual generation of new knowledge about the weapons, combined with now-established stewardship practices, may force us to rethink to some degree what is meant by "new." As for the weapons themselves, Congress has already defined *new* clearly and simply in the FY 2003 National Defense Authorization Act, section 3143: "The term 'new nuclear weapon' means a nuclear weapon that contains a pit or canned subassembly, either of which is neither (A) in the nuclear stockpile on the date of the enactment of the Act; nor (B) in production as of that date."[29]

Furthermore, the *2010 Nuclear Posture Review (NPR)* stated that "the United States will not develop new nuclear warheads [and] Life Extension Programs (LEP) will use only nuclear components based on previously tested designs, and will not support new military missions or provide for new military capabilities."[30]

Congressional verbiage, like that noted in the *NPR*, is direct and simple, yet various interpretations of this abound apparently because much of the special-interest NGO community is strictly pinned on the goal of abolishing nuclear weapons based on the argument that nuclear weapons today neither play the Cold War deterrent role they once did nor support any compelling broad set of missions.[31] An even more narrowly focused segment of this community is obsessed with the idea that the NNSA and the DOD are covertly seeking to design and build new weapons, such as the reliable replacement warhead (RRW).[32] Curiously, this group does not devote much in-depth analysis to the problem of knowledge loss and what continuing or "new" nuclear weapons work in any form means for workforce replacement and the continuity of nuclear weapons-related skills. Hans Kristensen summarizes this simply as:

The training argument depends on a combination of assumptions:

1. The country will eventually need new nuclear weapons and these will need to be sophisticated weapons requiring high levels of expertise,

2. The expertise needed for continuing stockpile maintenance is not adequate to maintain the expertise needed to design and build new weapons, and

3. The knowledge and skills needed to build new weapons cannot be written down and can only be preserved over the next two or three decades by keeping it alive in people. The truth of all of these assumptions depends in large part on choices we make about the future missions and requirements for nuclear weapons.[33]

Such analyses do not answer the question of whether or not a new focus on nuclear weapons research and development is necessary or why.[34] It goes without saying that the Cold War nuclear mission of deterring a monolithic threat is indeed no longer the same, but it has evolved into a very different set of activities and processes that needs to be taken into consideration by all who analyze the current and future role of nuclear weapons and modern-day deterrence. Getting rid of all nuclear weapons and their supporting knowledge and capabilities might indeed be an ideal, peaceful goal, but doing so would also rid us of numerous related essential national security missions for which the nuclear enterprise acts as technological backbone. LEP activities serve as a good example of the far-reaching effects of this technological backbone, have cumulatively led to some unexpected results, and may help us move beyond the critiques of the nuclear weapons enterprise merely existing to seek new warheads, dream of wild new missions for nuclear weapons, or find work for underemployed weapons scientists, as some critics would have readers believe.[35]

LEPs are not only a means of tinkering with the weapons in a manner void of any intellectual content whatsoever. In *Nuclear Rites,* Gusterson remarked, "University physicists often disparage [nuclear] weapons physics as more high-tech artisanship than science. One physics professor told me that the intellectual challenges in contemporary weapons designs were minimal: "Weapons design now is just like 'polishing turds.'"[36] Indeed some academic physicists may liken the weapons profession to an engineering practice of refining objects and making incremental improvements, but many weapons physicists argue otherwise given the complexity of what they are trying to model, which includes laborious hydrodynamics and rapidly changing densities in materials as a nuclear device operates.

Producing an improved detonator assembly, for example, may be an engineering increment and not scientifically significant, but it is the larger picture that needs to be kept in mind. LEPs are not only resulting in physical change and evolution in the stockpile over the long term, but moreover, in order to certify an LEP as successful, that process needs to match well to recorded underground test data, the current depth of understanding of how the weapons work and many ongoing nonnuclear and subcritical experiments. Doing this opens a huge scope of scientific problems that require solving. Even though nuclear weapon operation has been well studied over the past several decades, it is still not understood completely because of the complexity of the weapons, how their parts and physical phenomenon interact, and the extreme physical conditions that occur when they are fired. Getting to a more thorough understanding of these is a key basis for supporting the continuation of a no-testing regime and maintaining confidence in the stockpile.

The issue of stockpile confidence itself and how that relates to current arguments for a need to return to nuclear testing are beyond the scope of this chapter. However, the subject of nuclear testing is worth mentioning here for the purpose of discussing what testing did—and did not—do, since several of the academic scholars cited here spent a significant amount of time analyzing the social, political, and technical role(s) testing played in the Cold War. It is worth comparing a few of their key findings to more recent nuclear weapons enterprise activities.

Gusterson asserts that nuclear tests were "important for their cultural and psychological as well as their technical significance and that they have been vital not only in the production of nuclear weapons but also in the production of weapons scientists and in the social reproduction of the ideology of nuclear deterrence."[37] And towards his conclusion he argues, "The weapons scientists' sense of mastery over nuclear weapons is reinforced by participation in nuclear tests."[38] But this raises the question: Assuming this were true prior to 1992, is this still the case today? Possibly not because both policymakers' and scientists' own philosophical beliefs about nuclear deterrence are going through a great deal of reinterpretation currently—based on the immense changes in the way nuclear weapons work is rapidly changing.

Since *Nuclear Rites* was published, the process of working on nuclear weapons has evolved drastically. To his credit, in 2004 Gusterson published a collection of articles in a volume titled *People of the Bomb*, where some of the chapters served as an update to *Nuclear Rites*. In one chapter he deconstructs virtual weapons science, "referring to the increasing use of simulation and computing as the main activity that weaponeers engaged in as a successor to nuclear testing but sticks to his earlier argument in *Nuclear Rites* that nuclear tests were traditionally the ultimate means of producing knowledge and power among US nuclear weapons scientists."[39] Gusterson supported his case through several interviews with scientists who expressed doubt about the ability of simulation technologies and the overall viability of weapons work without the testing phase.[40] Although *People of the Bomb* was published in 2004, this particular chapter was written in 2001. In that piece Gusterson reported that older designers—those who have participated in nuclear testing—worried about younger colleagues placing too much confidence in the predictive ability of their computer codes and the basic principles of physics.[41]

Like Gusterson, but for different reasons, MacKenzie and Spinardi concluded in their study that testing was a critical part of nuclear weapons work—in their words part of the designers' "epistemic culture"—a way of making visible their judgment. MacKenzie and Spinardi's interviews with the then current (early 1990s) generation of designers revealed their fear that in the absence of testing, weapons certification would have to rely very heavily on explicit knowledge alone in the form of computer simulation.[42] Yet both Gusterson's and MacKenzie and Spinardi's analyses raise a generational argument. The younger, up-and-coming generation of nuclear weapons experts—those working today, about 20 years after MacKenzie and Spinardi conducted their interviews—has a great deal of faith in computational abilities and with compelling reasons. Too, anecdotal evidence suggests that some older designers are now beginning to place more faith in computation.

MacKenzie and Spinardi's main question, "If there was a sufficiently long hiatus in their [nuclear weapons] design and production (say, two generations) that tacit knowledge might indeed vanish," remains to be proven in the next decades.[43] But 20 years after the cessation of testing—and we can comfortably assume that one generation has passed the torch by now—other new forms of knowledge in the nuclear weapons programs are becoming accepted and institutionalized concurrently as some older tacit knowledge is disappearing.

This is a large and perhaps unexpected paradigm shift for the nuclear weapons research, development, test, and evaluation process. Where MacKenzie concluded that designers circa early 1990s overwhelmingly relied on the empirical testing—a physical, observable activity—part of this process as well as theoretical bases to have confidence in their work, today the high-quality images and results coming from hydrodynamic tests, advanced radiography, subcritical tests, and other small-scale experiments are supplying new empirical scientific bases that may well alter how we should debate and define nuclear deterrence.[44]

Speaking strictly in terms of the information testing provided, and without going into their political and symbolic meanings, McNamara argues, "Nuclear testing provided an epistemological basis for nuclear confidence but not in a classical statistical sense. Although tests provided a great deal of data about explosive performance, they were far too expensive and difficult to perform multiple trials for any weapon system, much less isolate and repeatedly measure a single feature of a primary or secondary."[45] Furthermore, McNamara correctly argued, "The terrain of weaponeering is simultaneously more stable and more contested than MacKenzie and Spinardi imagined," and "In working to establish new 'ways of knowing' nuclear weapons, which SSP is doing, weapons experts are redefining the very nature of nuclear confidence at a time when the role of nuclear weapons in national security is itself undergoing rapid change."[46]

Even if older, tacit knowledge is lost over time, as MacKenzie and Spinardi predict, the current and future combinations of recorded knowledge—massive amounts of nuclear weapons data is maintained in archives—and the new knowledge being generated and learned by new weaponeers are at least as important to the nuclear deterrence calculus as are the presence of the active weapons themselves. This raises the question: In the present day and into the future can we have a scientific-technical-capability-based deterrent? This may be possible. McNamara concluded, "The credibility of the nation's nuclear deterrent was rooted in the expertise of individuals with the most intimate knowledge of nuclear explosives, so that the laboratory's weapons-related judgments were as much the bedrock of nuclear deterrence as were the weapons themselves."[47]

Even during the Cold War the technical basis of the nuclear deterrent was not derived merely from the act of testing or its empirical results. It was also derived in part from the weaponeers' deep knowledge. What scientists know about nuclear weapons and related programs and how well they know these things contribute to credible deterrence in the view of US allies and enemies. If adversaries see the scientific and technical talent as credible, their products—the devices—will be viewed as credible. It is important to emphasize that one cannot simply attend graduate school to learn nuclear weapons design and development. It is a years-long, intensive, hands-on process, akin to apprenticeship, performed only within the design laboratories.

The Defense Science Board summarized these kinds of skills very well in a 2008 study:

> Nuclear deterrence expertise is uniquely demanding. It cannot be acquired overnight or on the fly. It resides in a highly classified environment mandated by law, it crosses a number of disciplines and skills, and it involves implicit as well as requires explicit knowledge. Nuclear weapons expertise is necessary to design and build nuclear weapons, to plan and operate nuclear forces, and to design defense against nuclear attack. It is also necessary to analyze and understand foreign nuclear weapons programs, devise nuclear policies and strategies,

deal with allies who depend on the American nuclear umbrella, prevent and counter nuclear proliferation, defeat nuclear terrorism, and—in the event that a nuclear detonation takes place by accident or cold, hostile intent—cope with the catastrophic consequences.[48]

Similarly, the 1994 JASON Stockpile Stewardship study enumerated several nuclear-weapons-activity spin-off benefits that support arms control and nonproliferation efforts: "Another major laboratory activity that supports stockpile stewardship both directly and indirectly is the collection of activities involving Nonproliferation, Intelligence, and Arms Control (NIAC). . . . The groups now doing this work are likely to be the only ones at either laboratory who will continue to study new weapons designs in order to understand both what is happening elsewhere and as part of the study of how to counter such weapons in the hands of others."[49]

Most of this work is, not surprisingly, highly classified and cannot be elaborated on in detail publicly, but its importance is paramount especially given its unique knowledge base that is continually accumulating. Other equally very important—and classified—fields that support nonproliferation, noted generally in the 2008 DOD study, are highly specialized nuclear forensics and nuclear device intelligence analysis and evaluation. These sets of activities rely deeply on those people in the weapons laboratories with experience in US nuclear design to evaluate the technology sophistication, rate of advancement, specific design, materials used, and other factors a foreign country might exhibit. New and fundamental scientific activities in the weapons programs are becoming applicable in these fields, and if our computational models are becoming viable and accepted by the nuclear weapons community, then we should be able to model what other nations and nonstate actors are doing if we have good intelligence.

Older methods of empirical observation of phenomena in weapons work and estimation in the weapons design and development processes are being replaced by new scientific means: For example, the Quantification of Margins and Uncertainty (QMU) methodology, an entirely new—and controversial—nuclear weapons science tool is currently coming into significant usage. QMU, based on statistical methods and high-level computational capability, calculates uncertainty when it comes to judging the active stockpile's reliability and safety.[50] Exactly how well it does that and the risk one should assign to the uncertainty factor remain to be determined, but the value and utility of computation in general, while still understandably criticized by some skeptics, is providing visual and statistical-like results on stockpile safety and reliability that has not been possible until now. Computational horsepower has improved exponentially over that available in the early 1990s, and simulations are less costly and time-consuming than testing. Computer simulation allows researchers to study anomalies in a weapon over and over, as many times as they want. This cannot be accomplished using explosive testing, and the ability to do these things directly translates into real benefits to national security endeavors in the areas noted above. That is a genuinely new focus coming out of nuclear weapons research and development that needs to be encouraged and maintained. And not only computing, but all of the activities described in the paragraphs above feed into a strong nuclear attribution capability—which itself is a deterrent.

Conclusion

Critics argue that we do not need a highly developed scientific and technical capability to support the stockpile because we do not need a sophisticated, advanced stockpile in the post–Cold War world, and that there are no new physics needs to understand nuclear weapons adequately. For example, Ivan Oelrich has argued "there is little to no technical challenge left for American and other advanced nuclear weapon states in just getting a bomb to explode and we could design bombs that do not require a complex supporting infrastructure." His argument is that the stated need to maintain scientific and technical expertise in the national laboratories rests solely on a blind desire to continue maintaining a Cold War–era mission for our current stockpile.[51]

This kind of reasoning is exactly why we must redefine what we mean by "new" with clarity and careful thought, move beyond wrangling over the semantic differences between terms such as "life extension" and "modernization," and draw into any discussions about the future of deterrence the significant paradigm shift that is occurring at our laboratories, moving us from testing-based knowledge to simulation-based knowledge dependent on validation methods. Ongoing deepening understanding of these processes does have a significant impact on national security and enriches discussion about what kind of deterrent we may want for the twenty-first century.

While few people would argue that better arms control measures and nuclear-weapons-related policies are good things, nuclear deterrence in some form is likely to remain a part of America's national security policy for the foreseeable future. Calls for an end to all nuclear weapons activities and zero nuclear weapons are good goals for an ideal world, but until we live in such a world, with no proliferators, we still need to maintain as much knowledge as we can while generating new understanding and thinking about scientific and technical means of bolstering national security and formulating what nuclear deterrence truly means in the twenty-first century.

Notes

1. For a solid, albeit dated, review of historical studies of nuclear weapons published up through 1990, see Seidel, "Books on the Bomb." Other, more recent historical studies may be found in the history of science literature. Sociological, anthropological, science and technology studies, and communications studies treatments of the nuclear weapons laboratories and their activities and people are discussed later in this chapter.

2. See Rhodes, *The Making of the Atomic Bomb*; and his, *Dark Sun: The Making of the Hydrogen Bomb*.

3. MacKenzie with Spinardi, "Tacit Knowledge and the Uninvention of Nuclear Weapons."

4. Gusterson, *Nuclear Rites*.

5. McNamara, "TRUTH Is Generated HERE."

6. For insight on conducting academic research inside the classified environment, see McNamara, "Ways of Knowing about Weapons"; and Fitzpatrick, "From Behind the Fence."

7. Kelly, "Arms Control: Where Now?"

8. Air Force Nuclear Task Force, *Reinvigorating the Air Force Nuclear Enterprise*.

9. Sanger and Shanker, "White House Is Rethinking Nuclear Policy."

10. For example, see Murdock, *The Department of Defense and the Nuclear Mission in the 21st Century*.

11. For more on the SSP program's founding, see Fitzpatrick and Oelrich, "The Stockpile Stewardship Program."

12. Ibid. *Confidence* in this context means that weapons would perform as required for military operations.

13. *Hodge and Weinberger, "A Nuclear Family Vacation."* Garwin was referring to the Sandia Microsystems and Engineering Sciences Application Facility (MESA).

14. Post, "Lessons Learned from ASCI [Accelerated Strategic Computing Initiative]," an abridged version of LA-UR-04-0388; Department of Energy (DOE), Office of Inspector General, "Introductory Letter," in *Audit Report DOE-IG-0699*; DOE, Secretary of Energy Advisory Board, *Interim Report of the National Ignition Facility Laser System Task Force*; and Government Accountability Office (GAO), *Report to the Subcommittee on Military Procurement, Committee on Armed Services, House of Representatives*.

15. DOE, "Weapons Activities: Inertial Confinement Fusion Ignition and High Yield Campaign." For more technical analysis of NIF (National Ignition Facility), see Hammer et al., *NIF Ignition*.

16. The annual assessment process is a many-months-long effort in which the nuclear weapons community examines various technical issues affecting the safety, reliability, performance, and military effectiveness of the active stockpile. Their work ultimately results in the Nuclear Weapons Council report on the assessments, accompanied by a joint letter signed by the secretaries of energy and defense and reports from the nuclear weapons laboratory directors and the US Strategic Command commander.

17. Gusterson, *Nuclear Rites*, 132–39. Gusterson provides some lengthy and informative discussion of several of these individual phases. For details on the phases see "An Agreement between the AEC and the DOD for the Development, Production, and Standardization of Atomic Weapons."

18. McNamara, "TRUTH Is Generated HERE."

19. GAO, *Nuclear Weapons*; and Nuclear Weapons Council, "Procedural Guidelines for the Phase 6.X Process."

20. Senate, *The Safety and Reliability of the U.S. Nuclear Deterrent*, 267.

21. Drell et al., *Science Based Stockpile Stewardship*. JASON is an independent group of scientists, established in 1960, which advises the US government on matters of science and technology. The group was first created to get a younger generation of scientists—that is, not the older Los Alamos and MIT Radiation Laboratory alumni—involved in advising the government. It has somewhere between 30 and 60 members.

22. Ibid., 92. *Gflops* is giga flotation-point operations per second, a measure of computer performance.

23. DOE, *FY 2011 Congressional Budget Request, National Nuclear Security Administration*, "Weapons Activities: Advanced Simulation and Computing Campaign," 125–26.

24. Ibid., "Weapons Activities: Overview," 49.

25. The DOE has made significant investment into preserving documentation and recording individuals' knowledge of all aspects of nuclear weapons research. Many DOE sites have participated; one example is the *Preserving Nuclear Weapons Information*. Lawrence Livermore Nuclear Weapons Information Project. https://www.llnl.gov/str/Lowns.html.

26. DOD, Office of the Undersecretary of Defense for Acquisition, Technology, and Logistics, *Report of the Defense Science Board Task Force on Nuclear Deterrence Skills*.

27. Ibid., 61, 25.

28. *Lifetime Extension Program (LEP) Executive Summary*, 4.

29. US House, *National Defense Authorization Act for Fiscal Year 2003*, 772.

30. DOD, *Nuclear Posture Review Report*, xiv.

31. See Oelrich, *Missions for Nuclear Weapons after the Cold War*.

32. For a recent analysis of the apparent remaining keen interest in pursuing a reliable replacement warhead (RRW), see Kristensen and Oelrich, "JASON and Replacement Warheads." In this piece, Kristensen asserts that "the quest for new weapons is not dead yet." For more on the debate over what "new" might mean in terms of weapons, see Kristensen, "Testing the No-New-Nuclear-Weapons Pledge"; and Collina, "News Analysis."

33. Kristensen and Oelrich, "JASON and Replacement Warheads."

34. It is possible that the terminology used in the LEP programs may lead observers to suspect that the door is being left open for brand new warhead development in violation of what Congress has stipulated. LEPs are complex in that they are multiyear, multi-faceted, large-scale, managed programs intended to extend the "life," or time, that a

weapon can remain safely and reliably in the stockpile without having to be replaced or removed. The NNSA does provide a public description of how LEPs are intended to function: "Not all weapons and types are the same. NNSA must develop individual life extension programs, sometimes referred to as LEPs, for each weapon type and develop specific solutions to extend the lifetime of each particular warhead or bomb. This includes identifying and correcting potential technical issues with each weapon, and then refurbishing and replacing certain components as necessary. Life extension efforts are intended to extend the lifetime of a warhead or warhead component for an additional 20 to 30 years." The paths on which LEPs are carried out are specified. NNSA defines the implementation of an LEP as one of three approaches:

1. Refurbishment (current implementation of LEP)—Very generally, individual warhead components are replaced before they degrade with components of (nearly) identical design or that meet the same 'form, fit, and function.' "

2. Warhead Component Reuse—Refers to the use of existing surplus pit and secondary components from other warhead types. Approach may permit limited warhead surety improvements and some increased margins.

3. Warhead Replacement—Some or all of the components of a warhead are replaced with modern designs that are more easily manufacturable; provide increased warhead margins; forego no-longer-available or hazardous materials; improve safety, security, and use control; and offer that potential for further overall stockpile reductions.

Normally, changes in components that result in changes to operational characteristics, safety or control features, or technical procedures are designated with a modification, or "Mod," number, which the Nuclear Weapons Council also assigns sequentially. For example, Los Alamos repackaged existing B61 Mod 7 gravity bombs into an earth-penetrating steel case designed by Sandia, resulting in the designation Mark B61 Mod 11. The first component set of a new mark is designated Mod 0, although the Mod 0 designation is usually omitted to avoid confusion if no other modifications exist.

If changes in components do not result in changes to operational characteristics and the differences are transparent to military units and other users, the changes, or alterations, are designated as an "ALT." For example, the development of new spin rocket motors for the B61 results in ALTs numbered 356, 358, and 359. Lewis, "After the Reliable Replacement Warhead."

35. The Federation of American Scientists labeled nuclear weapons activities, particularly in the context of the RRW program, as "nuclear social welfare." See Oelrich, "A Response to Congresswoman Tauscher's Article on Nonproliferation Review."

36. Gusterson, *Nuclear Rites*, 48.

37. Ibid., 132.

38. Ibid., 220.

39. See Gusterson, *People of the Bomb*, 147–64, passim, and 178.

40. Ibid., 174–75.

41. Ibid., 156.

42. MacKenzie and Spinardi, "Tacit Knowledge and the Uninvention of Nuclear Weapons," 218. Also like Gusterson, MacKenzie and Spinardi published their 1998

piece based on interviews they conducted in the early 1990s. Notably, in this chapter the authors neither prescribe any specific length of time for a design and testing hiatus nor make any moral judgments about doing so. Likewise, although the article's title is provocative, the overall piece is not a call for the elimination of nuclear weapons.

43. Ibid., 217.

44. Ibid.

45. McNamara, "TRUTH Is Generated HERE," 176.

46. Ibid., 169.

47. Ibid., 176.

48. DOD, Office of the Undersecretary of Defense for Acquisition, Technology, and Logistics, *Report of the Defense Science Board Task Force on Nuclear Deterrence Skills*, v.

49. Drell et al., *Science Based Stockpile Stewardship*, 25.

50. For more detail on Quantification of Margins and Uncertainty (QMU), see National Research Council, *Evaluation of Quantification of Margins and Uncertainties Methodology for Assessing and Certifying the Reliability of the Nuclear Stockpile*; and Helton, *Sandia Report: Conceptual and Computational Basis for the Quantification of Margins and Uncertainties*.

51. Oelrich, "Congressional Commission and Nuclear 'Requirements.'"

Chapter 8

Mathematical Foundations
of Strategic Deterrence

Edward H. Robbins, Hunter Hustus, and James A. Blackwell

Past approaches to understanding strategic deterrence are anachronistic and, for the twenty-first century, probably dangerous. As the United States attempts to lead the way to create a world without nuclear weapons, there is a critical need to understand the phenomena that comprise the central dynamics of deterrence in the twenty-first century.

During much of the latter half of the twentieth century, strategic deterrence thought was dominated by a relatively simple theory, in which the massive nuclear forces of the United States and the Soviet Union so threatened each other's destruction as to prevent either side from initiating nuclear war. Since that time the world's complexities have multiplied many times over and Russian and US strategic nuclear arsenals have shrunk, partly through unilateral actions by each side and partly through bilateral treaty obligations. Nuclear planners must now be prepared to ask, "How low can we go?" in future reductions of arsenals and how to guarantee that smaller arsenals will nevertheless preserve strategic deterrence. Simultaneously, several other nuclear nations have increased the size of, and defenses provided to, their arsenals; nuclear weapons technology has flowed to rogue states; and terrorist groups have sought to purchase and employ nuclear weapons.[1] Older methodologies and doctrines proposing defeat, deterrence, dissuasion, and assurance need no longer be valid.

This paper seeks to advance theoretical developments in strategic deterrence by laying out new mathematical foundations. We extend a 1960s model of crisis stability to establish a game-theoretic paradigm for studying a broad range of modern strategic deterrence issues. The result is a simple set of rules—though differing from past theories—through which strategic deterrence is achievable and applicable to some practical issues in modern strategic deterrence.

The authors thank our many colleagues who have stimulated and encouraged us in this work. Special thanks go to Steve Turnbull, University of Tsukuba, Japan, who contributed greatly to many of the technical details regarding equilibrium concepts and formulations that appear throughout the chapter.

Many individuals see nuclear deterrence as out of step with the exigencies of contemporary conflicts, a relic of the Cold War. They contend that those who advocate for, or practice, nuclear deterrence are impeding progress toward a world of few or no nuclear weapons. In this paper, we accept some risk of encouraging that characterization and resultant dismissive attitudes by reanalyzing classic concepts and restructuring an early Cold War game theory model.

Our views:

- Some things old are new again. Concepts created to understand Cold War deterrence dynamics are not irrelevant to twenty-first century challenges. While insufficient to provide modern understanding, they help guide us.

- Some things known are wrong. As we delve into the past to re-investigate basics, we discover that conventional wisdom and analysis that formed the bases for understanding nuclear deterrence during the Cold War were flawed. These models and associated assumptions seemed adequate only because powerful conditions overwhelmed the necessity of additional requirements that failed to be recognized. Reassessment of legacy analysis will help correct perceptions that decision makers bring to future nuclear crises.

- Game theoretic/rational economic man approaches still provide valuable insight and a useful, clean-lined framework for analysis. In the 1960s, game theory was debated as a foundation for thought on strategic deterrence.[2] For today, we believe that assuming rationality among opponents and determining consequently optimal behavior should form at least the first order of decision making.

The Ellsberg Model

The foundations of nuclear weapons technology arose during the same era that saw the early development of game theory.[3] As American and Russian nuclear arsenals grew from the 1950s through the 1970s, parallel developments in game theory extended the intellectual basis for thinking about possible employment of nuclear weapons in warfare to defeat an enemy or to deter nuclear warfare between rational opponents.[4] One of the simplest descriptions of nuclear conflict decision making between the great powers was presented as an incomplete normal-form game by Ellsberg (1961),[5] in which each side has only two possibilities available to it, namely, to wait or to strike. He presents the payoff matrix for this incomplete game as in table 8.1, where the values represent social utility payoffs to Americans and Soviets, respectively.

Table 8.1. Ellsberg's nuclear warfare incomplete game payoff matrix

United States	Soviet Union	
	Wait	Strike (p)
Wait	U_{11}, V_{11}	U_{12}, V_{21}
Strike (q)	U_{21}, V_{12}	--

Crucially, the game is incomplete in that the fourth cell contains no values. The first cell represents attained social utilities under the conditions of *no nuclear war*. To its right is a cell in which America waits but receives a Soviet first strike and, therefore, responds with a second strike. Symmetrically, beneath the original cell is a cell where America attacks (first strikes) while the Russians wait; thereafter, the Soviets retaliate in a second strike. To many people, this formulation is quite natural, for the missing fourth cell would represent the possibility of joint attacks—simultaneous strikes—and it is hard to envision what that would mean.[6]

Completing the fourth cell in this matrix and analyzing the consequences are precisely what we shall seek to accomplish in this paper. Clearly, in the face of such deep-seated objections, it will be necessary for us to justify our action.

Our choice reflects simple mathematics. Under the mixed-strategy Nash equilibrium concept upon which our investigations will primarily rely, the two players select actions based upon identical information sets without observation of their opponent's choice. Therefore, the stochastic selections occur independently of one another. By definition the probability of both players opting for attack is then the product of the probabilities of each choosing to do so. Consequently, should each player set a nonzero probability on attack, the probability of joint attack is nonzero. The fourth cell must be considered. Likewise, in our alternative of a pure-strategy Nash equilibrium, we grant each nation the choice of wait or attack. Were we not to consider the possibility that both nations choose to attack, we would inherently have to assume coordination between them—clearly, an unreasonable assumption.

But there is a more subtle rationale for considering this fourth cell. The very possibility of simultaneous strikes compels us to examine the actual behavior of the two parties, in a way that is not obvious for the other three cells. Here, each side must ponder whether it is launching an attack against an entity that is also doing so. If that is the case, then an attack on strategic nuclear forces is largely futile: ICBMs are already out of their silos, mobile ICBMs have departed their garrisons, bombers have flown from their bases, and submarines have put out to sea. Although incoming weapons have not yet wreaked their havoc, there is no point to targeting the enemy's forces. Targeting value assets, as should logically occur in a retaliatory second strike, is much more the appropriate strategy.[7] The conundrum faced by the potential attacker is which attack scheme to follow: that of a first striker, that of a second striker, or, since he really doesn't know which comparable path he is pursuing, some elements of either. Extending to the full matrix shows us that the game was previously ill formed, at least within that fourth cell. Expected social utilities that serve as payoffs are themselves components of the play of the game since the best method of attack would depend entirely upon the attacker's information set and perception of the probability of simultaneous attack.

Why do we pursue this exercise? Since the end of the Cold War there has remained the chance of a nuclear confrontation between the United States and the Russian Federation. Is it worthwhile to investigate clearer conditions under which those nations would resort to nuclear war? For many reasons, the answer is yes.

1. The conflicts of interests between the United States and Russia are not finished.

2. With this still evolving strategic relationship, it is important to understand implications of unilateral and bilateral arms control to the respective strategic defenses, concepts, and operational plans.

3. Given continuing nuclear proliferation, the model should also be applicable to any pair of nuclear-armed adversaries and to

certain cases of extended deterrence where a nuclear-armed state provides assurances to allies and partners.

4. To whatever extent the model fails with regard to *irrational players* such as rogue states or violent extremist organizations, it might suggest further lines of research.

5. The decreasing size of US and Russian arsenals and nuclear proliferation have led to the possibility of nuclear warfare being fought by coalitions of states—our model might contribute to understanding strategic deterrence in possibilities involving more than two nuclear-armed states.

Section 2 contains our conceptualization of how to fill Ellsberg's empty fourth cell. Because we consider strategic behavior within each of the possible sets of actions, our normal-form payoff matrix involves each element depending on the information known to each player. Since we assume social utility, we can also assume that decision making is governed by expectations. This affords wider analytical boundaries. As so frequently happens with simple 2x2 matrix games, we are able to conclude linearity, so that optima can only be attained at endpoints—that is, when the probability of a party attacking is either zero or one. Thus, our model finally devolves to a true matrix game.

Sections 3 and 4 are investigations into possible equilibria in pure or mixed strategies. Because of the simplicity of the game formulation, decision makers' optimal choices are dictated by comparatively straightforward inequality conditions. While the mathematics is simple, the implications prove to be profound. The mathematical conditions derived in Section 4 must be met through force-structure and policy decisions that can be achieved in the real world. Section 5 demonstrates—in the context of our model—why Cold War requirements for strategic deterrence proved adequate even though they were conceptually incorrect. But it also shows that treaties, declines in nuclear arsenals, and nuclear weapons proliferation probably have already brought about the collapse of the Cold War form of misspecified equilibrium. Our model identifies conditions needed to prevent nuclear war. Section 6 addresses force-structure and policy issues. We propose survivability guaranteeing efficacy of a second strike as a principle to guide force-structure decisions. However, we do not investigate methods to achieve survivability. We do examine targeting concepts for both a first strike and second strike that might reinforce stability. And we explore a stabilizing role for ballistic missile defense. We close the paper by providing a summary in Section 7.

Revision of the Ellsberg Model

Because we seek a firm foundation for strategic deterrence research into modern problems, we chose to depart from the Soviet Union versus United States focus of the Ellsberg research. We continued the tradition of two states in potential conflict, although we believe that some of the methods are extendible to multiplayer games.[8] Thus, our two states of interest are "Q" and "X," which might be Israel and Iran, China and India, North Korea and Japan (assuming Japan might begin a nuclear weapons program—assurances of the US nuclear umbrella not withstanding), or a host of other combinations. How to extend this two-player game to multiple players is not directly addressed—but is being examined in subsequent research.

The preceding section's limitations of literal application of the Ellsberg model led us to alter the depiction of the game and propose the two-by-two matrix game presented in table 8.2.

Table 8.2. Altered model (payoff matrix) of two-player nuclear war

	X Waits $(1 - p^X)$	X first strikes (p^X)
Q Waits $(1 - p^Q)$	U_N^Q, U_N^X	U_2^Q, U_1^X
Q first strikes (p^Q)	U_1^Q, U_2^X	U_S^Q, U_S^X

Labeling within the matrix should be relatively clear. The superscript represents which nation's social utility is being calculated. In every cell of the payoff matrix, we first report nation Q's expected social utility. The subscript represents the cell, together with the corresponding conditions: "N" stands for "no nuclear war" and is symmetric between the two nations, "S" stands for "simultaneous attack" and is also symmetric, although in the opposite way, and "1" represents "first strike," inevitably paired with "2" representing "second strike." This game formulation repairs several problems identified above with the Ellsberg model.

Possible Modern Pairings of Nations Pursuing Nuclear War

No longer does our focus lie solely on the United States and Russia. While those could prove to be the adversaries, other pairings are just as valid: Pakistan and India, Israel and Iran, or India and China.

Filling in the Fourth Cell of the Matrix

The lower right quadrant of the matrix in table 8.2 presents the missing fourth event of simultaneous strikes. Does *simultaneous strike* mean launch on warning? No, it does not. *Launch on warning* is one variant of a second strike.[9]

Alternative versions of a second strike are likely to involve absorbing the first strike from the opponent and—after some form of delay—carrying out a full-bore retaliatory strike against that opponent. Ellsberg has separately dealt with second strike social utility payoffs in his analysis, and we shall follow his lead. That is where to look for expected payoffs through carrying out a "launch on warning" or other forms of second strike.

What then is simultaneous strike from our perspective? From a mathematician's eye, it is a needed element, in order to make the payoff matrix symmetric and coherent. Suppose only that each possibility of first strike constitutes an event that could occur with positive probability.

$$p^X > 0 \ \text{ and } p^Q > 0 \qquad\qquad 2.1.$$

This seems a natural possibility given Ellsberg's model. Then,

$$p^{X \text{ and } Q} = p^X \times p^Q > 0 \qquad\qquad 2.2.$$

Conclusion 2.2 is inevitable provided the decisions reflected in inequalities 2.1 are selected independently. And this is precisely the condition that we require to justify creation of the fourth cell in the matrix. If it is a possibility, it is necessary to account for it. Ellsberg does not do so in his matrix (table 8.3).

Table 8.3. Ellsberg's incomplete game restated in our context and notation

Nation Q's Decision	Nation X's Decision	
	Wait (w.p. $1 - p^X$)	Attack (w.p. p^X)
Wait (w.p. $1 - p^Q$)	U_N^Q, U_N^X	U_2^Q, U_1^X
Attack (w.p. p^Q)	U_1^Q, U_2^X	--

However, he then carries out calculations for wait versus attack decisions such as the following:

$$(1 - p^Q) \ U_N{}^X \ + \ p^Q \ U_2{}^X \ > \ U_1{}^X \qquad 2.3.$$

One way of interpreting this calculation is that Ellsberg is stating that, in deciding whether to carry out a first strike, each player can ignore whether the opponent is also planning a first strike. In a second interpretation, what he is doing is treating the missing cell as if the actual matrix took the form of table 8.4.

Table 8.4. Tacit formulation of Ellsberg's game in our context/notation

Nation Q's Decision	Nation X's Decision	
	Wait (w.p. 1- p^X)	Attack (w.p. p^X)
Wait (w.p. 1- p^Q)	$U_N{}^Q$, $U_N{}^X$	$U_2{}^Q$, $U_1{}^X$
Attack (w.p. p^Q)	$U_1{}^Q$, $U_2{}^X$	$U_1{}^Q$, $U_1{}^X$

Since the previous computation is reconstituted as:

$$(1-p^Q) \ U_N{}^X + p^Q \ U_2{}^X \ > \ (1-p^Q) \ U_1{}^X + p^Q \ U_1{}^X$$
$$= \ U_1{}^X \qquad 2.4.$$

Note that this second matrix constitutes a restriction on our more general matrix in table 8.2, in which we allow for general values to the simultaneous strike payoffs. Ellsberg's more restrictive form demands

$$U_S{}^Q \equiv U_1{}^Q \quad \text{and} \quad U_S{}^X \equiv U_1{}^X \qquad 2.5.$$

There are many reasons to reject the restrictive form. To whatever extent each side is targeting strategic nuclear forces in their intended first strike, the most critical idea is that they will miss the opponent's simultaneously launched assets. Ex ante rationality dictates that the simultaneous striker must devote some of his attacking assets to the value assets of his opponent.[10] Thus, the combined attacks

- miss the opponent's nuclear forces, and
- hit the opponent's value assets.

It is hard to guess whether the stated equalities in 2.5 should be replaced by inequalities in one direction or the other.

Put simply and bluntly, our form of the matrix—i.e., one including simultaneous strike social utilities that may differ from first strike social utilities—is more general and unquestionably more reasonable.

But there is another lesson from this approach. A player carrying out a first strike cannot know in advance whether he will turn out to be a true first striker or, instead, a simultaneous striker. His targeting must be the same. That is, his ex post realized social utility must depend upon how he has altered his attack/defense plans.

We are not done here. For the player who chooses to wait, social utility will be influenced by his choices for establishing defense—even down to the level of local-time decisions regarding civil defense.[11] All of these conditionalities are assumed built into the elements presented in our payoff matrix in table 8.2; that is, each potential payoff represents the result of much analysis of optimal attack, optimal defense, exceptional planning for economic and social recovery, etc.

Implicit Computation of Social Utilities

As with Ellsberg, we do not offer further indications for the computation of social utilities.[12] Our analysis will focus upon inequalities in attained values of expected social utility. Therefore, relative magnitudes of social utilities will come to the fore in our interpretive analysis, rather than exact values. Practical methods to attain strategic deterrence will seek solutions interior to regions. We actively reject exact boundary solutions because of their inherent "knife-edge" nature with strategic nuclear war occurring with only infinitesimal changes to any proposed equilibrium solution or to minor errors in conducting assessments.

In furtherance of this concept of avoidance of the details of computing social utilities, let us add the following commentary. It is highly likely, whatever the selected functional form, that form will to exhibit much smoothness because calculating expectations, which requires Riemann-Stieltjes integration with respect to probability distributions, typically smoothes overall solutions. Therefore, absent nuclear war in previous periods of analysis, moderate changes in the underlying state of the world should generate, for each type of social utility $\blacksquare = N, 1, 2, S$:

$$U_{\blacksquare}^{Q}(new) \approx U_{\blacksquare}^{Q}(old) + \sum_{j=1}^{J} \frac{\partial U_{\blacksquare}^{Q}(old)}{\partial j} \qquad 2.6.$$

That is, we can approximate the new social utility as the previously calculated social utility plus the first total derivative with respect to various changes in the components of that derived social utility. Later in the paper, we shall impose our *deep interiority criterion*. We seek to achieve strategic deterrence. When we establish conditions under which *no nuclear war* proves to be the optimal bilateral solution to the game, we demand that the players jointly find themselves nowhere near any boundary at which they might optimally switch to some alternative solution. Our goal is to establish strategic deterrence as the unambiguous mutual choice of both parties and to avoid the possibility that war occurs, for example, through misspecification of the incentives of one nation or the other. Under this restriction, approximate equality 2.6 can be employed to argue that—without significant changes to underlying values of factors determining social utility—we should remain deeply interior to the region in which not carrying out a first strike is optimal.

Implications of the New Model—
Nash Equilibrium in Pure Strategies

Direct comparisons within the payoff matrix presented in table 8.2 allow us to specify four different Nash equilibria in pure strategies that correspond to the four cells in that matrix. To examine how these work, let us emphasize the cell that generates greatest social desirability—that in which no nuclear war breaks out and mutual strategic deterrence holds. That is the upper left-hand cell.

For Nash equilibrium in pure strategies, we maintain that (1) holding nation X's behavior fixed, nation Q has no incentive to move to a first strike; and (2) holding nation Q's behavior fixed, X likewise has no incentive to move to a first strike. Under the conditional for (1), we lie in the first action/payoff column of the matrix (i.e., nation X waits). And for Q to remain in the upper left-hand cell, that nation prefers the social utility of that cell to what it they would obtain if it they were to move to the lower left-hand cell in a first strike. That requirement is simple, namely, $U_N^Q \geq U_I^Q$. Because of the symmetry of the problem, X is playing in the first action/payoff row of the matrix and must simply prefer not to move from the upper left-hand cell to the upper right-hand cell. The requirement is entirely analogous to what was required for nation Q, namely, $U_N^X \geq U_I^X$. In short, we can describe the first possible equilibrium in pure strategies as

Pure Strategy Equilibrium (PSE) 1—mutual strategic deterrence where neither side carries out a first strike:

$$(p^Q, \ p^X) = (0, \ 0), \tag{3.1a,}$$

characterized by the conditions:

$$U_N^Q \geq U_I^Q \ \text{ and } \ U_N^X \geq U_I^X \tag{3.2a.}$$

Among the various equilibria available for consideration, PSE 1 will be of greatest natural interest to us, for it corresponds to the condition in which strategic deterrence mutually occurs; neither side is motivated to carry out a first strike. The characterization conditions are symmetric. For each player, if the opponent has no intent of attacking, it is also better not to attack.

Three other equilibria in pure strategies arise through analogous argument:

PSE 2—nation Q carries out first strike while nation X chooses to wait:

$$(p^Q, \ p^X) = (1, \ 0) \tag{3.1b,}$$

characterized by the conditions:

$$U_N^Q \ < \ U_I^Q \ \text{ and } \ U_2^X \geq U_S^X \tag{3.2b.}$$

PSE 3—nation X carries out first strike, while nation Q chooses to wait:

$$(p^Q, \ p^X) = (0, \ 1) \tag{3.1c,}$$

characterized by:

$$U_2^Q \ \geq \ U_S^Q \ \text{ and } \ U_N^X \ < \ U_I^X \tag{3.2c,}$$

and PSE 4–both sides simultaneously carry out first strikes:

$$(p^Q, \ p^X) = (1, \ 1) \tag{3.1d,}$$

characterized by the conditions:

$$U_2{}^Q \; < \; U_S{}^Q \;\; \text{and} \;\; U_2{}^X \; < \; U_S{}^X \hspace{4cm} \text{3.2d.}$$

Possibility PSE 2 also piques our interest. It tells us something crucial to understanding strategic deterrence—the strategic deterrence of nation X is no guarantee of nation Q's strategic deterrence. Despite its own good intentions, nation Q is not deterred by the mere fact that nation X does not intend to attack. Stronger conditions are required, and it is possible that nation X might seek to avoid nuclear war, while nation Q initiates it. The model would be incomplete to assume that, if nation X wants no nuclear war, nation Q will agree. Later, we shall take up the task of interpreting the criteria presented in expression 3.2a and how they relate to traditional thinking concerning strategic deterrence.

Putting equilibrium PSE 3 into practical terms, it corresponds to the greatest traditional concern among US strategists, namely, that the Russians, nation X, will wish to carry out a first strike and that American, nation Q, forces will choose only to retaliate with a second strike.[13] It is, perhaps, more than a bit odd that it technically dualizes equilibrium PSE 2, seemingly easily dismissed in traditional American thinking about strategic deterrence. They are two sides of the same coin. Conditions for seeking/avoiding first-strike attacks are merely flipped from one nation to the other.[14]

In contrast, PSE 4 serves as the dual of our mutual strategic deterrence equilibrium. Here, both players are motivated to carry out a first strike and do so simultaneously. Note, however, that these decisions are taken because each nation finds that choice optimal from the perspective of societal payoffs, not from observation of the opponent's launch. Retaliation for a first strike—that might be associated with "launch on warning"—falls into the categories PSE2 and PSE 3.

Summarizing our conclusions to this point, all four explicit equilibria in pure strategies seem possible when specific conditions justify them, but obviously all of those conditions cannot be valid at the same time. One nation can choose to attack or to wait, while its opponent can choose to attack or to wait. Simultaneous first strikes are not inevitable. Rather, the governing principles deriving from differing Nash equilibria in pure strategies are the conditions 3.2a–d.

Implications of the New Model—Nash Equilibrium in Mixed Strategies

To generalize these considerations to mixed strategy equilibria we must lay out a pair of decision criteria for the Q and X players. Each seeks to maximize his or her expected payoff given a probability distribution assessment for the other. The optimization criteria can thus be expressed as computed expected social utilities with the opponent's distributional choice assumed to be established while one's own choice is optimized.

First, Q optimization—for a set value[15] $p^X \in (0,1)$, choose p^Q so as to maximize:

$$E\{Payoff \text{ to } Q|\ p^x\}$$

$$= \Pr\{Q \text{ Waits}|\ p^x\}\ E\ \{Payoff \text{ to } Q|Q \text{ Waits, } p^x\}$$

$$+ \Pr\{Q \text{ Attacks}|\ p^x\}\ E\ \{Payoff \text{ to } Q|Q \text{ Attacks, } p^x\}$$

There is nothing surprising going on to this point in the analysis. We are merely expanding conditionally upon whether player Q chooses to wait or to carry out an attack.

$$= (1 - p^Q)\ \{(1 - p^x)\ U_N{}^Q + p^x\ U_2{}^Q\}$$

$$+ p^Q\ \{(1 - p^x)\ U_1{}^Q + p^x\ U_S{}^Q\}$$

At the next stage, some surprises occur. The conditional expectation collapses. Why? Quantity p^X is "in the mind's eye" of player Q, rather than being an absolute quantity. That is, it is a probability assessment made by player Q. So we have simplified. He will choose a probability contingent upon that set so as to optimize his expected social utility.

$$= \{(1 - p^X)\ U_N^Q + p^X\ U_2^Q\}$$

$$+ p^Q\ \{(1 - p^X)\ (U_1^Q - U_N^Q) + p^X\ (U_S^Q - U_2^Q)\} \qquad \text{4.1a.}$$

Note, of course, that the first expression in the final result for 4.1a is constant—given the assumption of fixed behavior for the opponent. Therefore, we find that optimization depends only on the second component. Furthermore, the overall expression is purely linear in the choice of optimal probability choice p^Q, where the slope is the multiplier term inside curly brackets.

The situation is as depicted in figure 8.1, where we find either a rising line (attack, i.e., carry out first strike) or falling line (wait). The third possibility is perfect indifference among choices for the probability for nation Q's attack; therefore, only two realistic possibilities discussed above arise. Given the choice of nation X for their probability of carrying out a first strike, Q will necessarily respond with either $p^Q = 0$ or $p^Q = 1$. That is, they will turn to a pure strategy, with certainty either to carry out a first strike or to wait.

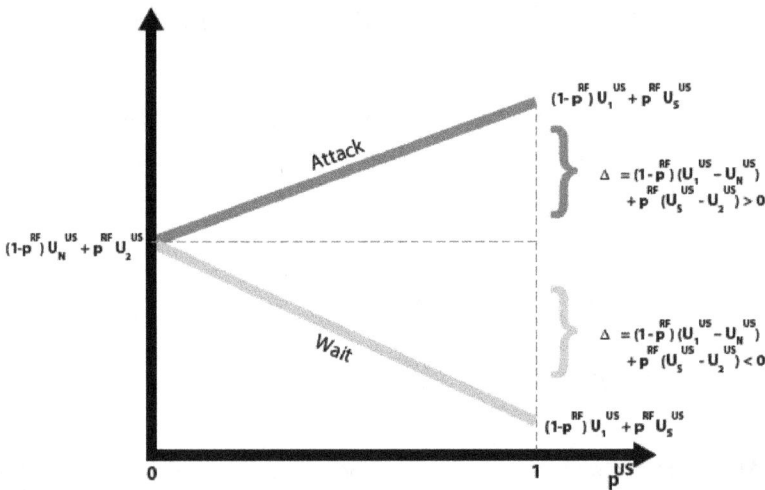

Figure 8.1. Depiction of optimization of the linear function for first strike

Second, Nation X optimization—or fixed[16] $p^Q \in (0,1)$, nation X must be expected to choose p^X so as to maximize:

$E\{Payoff$ to $X|\ p^Q\}$

$= \Pr\{X\ Waits|\ p^Q\}\ E\ \{Payoff$ to $X|X\ Waits,\ p^Q\}$

$\quad + \Pr\{X\ Attacks|\ p^Q\}\ E\ \{Payoff$ to $X|X\ Attacks,\ p^Q\}$

$= (1 - p^X)\ \{(1 - p^Q)\ U_N^X + p^Q\ U_2^X\}$

$\qquad + p^X\ \{(1 - p^Q)\ U_1^X + p^Q\ U_S^X\}$

$= \{(1 - p^Q)\ U_N^X + p^Q\ U_2^X\}$

$+ p^X\ \{(1 - p^Q)\ (U_1^X - U_N^X) + p^Q\ (U_S^X - U_2^X)\}$ \hfill 4.1b.

Analysis of this expression is entirely analogous to that of 4.1a. The expression is linear in the choice of the probability of conducting a first-strike attack. The solution must lie at $p^X = 0$ or at $p^X = 1$, depending upon the sign of the slope multiplier.

We can now use the inevitability of pure strategy equilibrium to extend the characterization of the equilibria identified in the preceding section. We have the following result.

Theorem 4.1. Strong Characterization of Mixed Equilibria (i.e., Sufficient Conditions)

$$
(p^Q,\ p^X) = \begin{cases}
(0, 0) & \text{if } U_1^Q \leq U_N^Q \ \text{ and } \ U_S^Q \leq U_2^Q \\
& \text{and } U_1^X \leq U_N^X \ \text{ and } \ U_S^X \leq U_2^X \\[8pt]
(0, 1) & \text{if } U_1^Q \leq U_N^Q \ \text{ and } \ U_S^Q \leq U_2^Q \\
& \text{and } U_1^X > U_N^X \ \text{ and } \ U_S^X > U_2^X \\[8pt]
(1, 0) & \text{if } U_1^Q > U_N^Q \ \text{ and } \ U_S^Q > U_2^Q \\
& \text{and } U_1^X \leq U_N^X \ \text{ and } \ U_S^X \leq U_2^X \\[8pt]
(1, 1) & \text{if } U_1^Q > U_N^Q \ \text{ and } \ U_S^Q > U_2^Q \\
& \text{and } U_1^X > U_N^X \ \text{ and } \ U_S^X > U_2^X
\end{cases}
$$
\hfill 4.2.

On the right-hand side of equation 4.2, each possible conclusion is associated with two pairs of conditions. The first pair guarantees the sign of the slope in the decision making 4.1a for nation Q, and the second pair guarantees the sign of the slope for nation X's decision making 4.1b—QED.

We have called Theorem 4.1 a "strong characterization" because the conditions compel the sign of the slope. Clearly, these conditions can prove to be overkill requirements, since each slope's sign being positive or negative can be fulfilled if only one element from each pair holds. The strong characterization is sufficient but need not be necessary. We can establish it through the following alternative.

Theorem 4.2. Weak Characterization of Mixed Equilibria (i.e., Necessary Conditions)

$$(p^Q,\ p^X) = \begin{cases} (0,0) \text{ only if } [U_1^Q \leq U_N^Q \text{ or } U_S^Q \leq U_2^Q] \\ \quad\quad\quad\ \text{and } [U_1^X \leq U_N^X \text{ or } U_S^X \leq U_2^X] \\[6pt] (0,1) \text{ only if } [U_1^Q \leq U_N^Q \text{ or } U_S^Q \leq U_2^Q] \\ \quad\quad\quad\ \text{and } [U_1^X > U_N^X \text{ or } U_S^X > U_2^X] \\[6pt] (1,0) \text{ only if } [U_1^Q > U_N^Q \text{ or } U_S^Q > U_2^Q] \\ \quad\quad\quad\ \text{and } [U_1^X \leq U_N^X \text{ or } U_S^X \leq U_2^X] \\[6pt] (1,1) \text{ only if } [U_1^Q > U_N^Q \text{ or } U_S^Q > U_2^Q] \\ \quad\quad\quad\ \text{and } [U_1^X > U_N^X \text{ or } U_S^X > U_2^X] \end{cases} \quad 4.3.$$

Of course, it is possible that—if one condition from a pair holds but the other does not—the slope parameter could take the sign opposite to that desired for a particular outcome of probability pair. Then, the desired conclusion would not follow. That is, the conditions stated in equation 4.3 are necessary but not sufficient to guide us to a solution.

Another interpretation of Theorem 4.1 comes in terms of war or peace—in terms of the success or failure of strategic deterrence. Peace and strategic deterrence are characterized by $(p^Q,\ p^X) = (0,\ 0)$. So we can pull out those results from the theorem:

Corollary 4.3. Characterizations of Peace/Strategic Deterrence

1. Sufficient conditions for nation Q not to carry out a first strike are:

$$U_N{}^Q - U_1{}^Q \geq 0 \geq U_S{}^Q - U_2{}^Q \qquad \text{4.4a.}$$

2. A necessary condition for nation Q not to carry out a first strike is that either the left-hand side or right-hand side inequality in 4.4a hold.

3. Sufficient conditions for nation X not to carry out a first strike are:

$$U_N{}^X - U_1{}^X \geq 0 \geq U_S{}^X - U_2{}^X \qquad \text{4.4b.}$$

4. A necessary condition for nation X not to carry out a first strike is that either the left-hand side or right-hand side inequality in 4.4b hold.

5. Sufficient conditions for no strategic nuclear war to break out are 4.4a and 4.4b.

6. Necessary conditions for no strategic nuclear war to break out are that at least one inequality from each of 4.4a and 4.4b hold.

Extending, we can use Corollary 4.3 to define sufficient or necessary conditions to determine the behavior of each nation in going to war.

Corollary 4.4. Characterizations of War/Failure of Strategic Deterrence

1. Sufficient conditions for nation Q to carry out a first strike are the violation of both inequalities from 4.4a.

2. A necessary condition for nation Q to carry out a first strike is the violation of least one of the inequalities in 4.4a.

3. Sufficient conditions for nation X to carry out a first strike are the violation of both inequalities from 4.4b.

4. A necessary condition for nation X to carry out a first strike is the violation of at least one of the inequalities in 4.4b.

5. Sufficient conditions for a strategic nuclear war are 1 or 3 from this corollary.

6. Necessary conditions for a strategic nuclear war are 2 or 4 from this corollary.

It is also possible to take Corollary 4.3 in a different direction by interweaving it with pure strategy equilibrium results that we investigated in the previous section. Once we have conditions strong enough to guarantee that one side will wait rather than pursue a first strike, it suffices for the other side to use that information in its own decision making via 3.2a.

Corollary 4.5. "Slightly Weaker Characterization of Peace/Strategic Deterrence"

1. Sufficient conditions for no strategic nuclear war to break out are 4.4a and
$$U_N{}^X \geq U_1{}^X \qquad\qquad 4.5a.$$

2. Alternative sufficient conditions for no strategic nuclear war to break out are 4.4b and $\quad U_N{}^Q \geq U_1{}^Q \qquad\qquad$ 4.5b.

Analysis of Relationships to Traditional Concepts of Strategic Deterrence

Up to this point we have

- noted comparable modeling in the existing research literature, criticized certain details of that modeling, and altered it;

- investigated implications of the new model for Nash equilibrium in pure strategies (for each party to carry out first strike or wait);

- investigated implications of the new model for Nash equilibrium in mixed strategies with probabilities stated over choice to first strike or to wait;

- and concluded that the most critical derived inequalities constitute sufficient conditions or necessary conditions to eliminate the possibility of nuclear war.

We now wish to relate these conclusions to some of the fundamental/traditional concepts of strategic deterrence: mutually assured destruction (MAD), second-strike capability (SSC), and crisis stability/first-strike stability (CS/FSS).

To achieve these goals requires us to specify the older concepts in terms of the elements of our model. On one hand, that is difficult and might lead to some argument. On the other, we are thereby "operationalizing" these alternative concepts in terms of our own variables. We leave open to others who might disagree the opportunity to conduct alternative operationalizations and to investigate the consequences.

MAD contends that, no matter what other outcomes are examined,[17] payoffs to each party are far, far worse than from no war at all.
In the context of our model, for player Q, this renders three constraints:

$$U_N^Q \gg U_1^Q \qquad\qquad 5.1a.$$

The social utility incurred for nation Q when neither side launches a first strike is far greater than (expressed by the symbol "$\gg$") the social utility the nation attains when only nation Q (but not nation X) launches a first strike:

$$U_N^Q \gg U_2^Q \qquad\qquad 5.1b$$

and

$$U_N^Q \gg U_S^Q \qquad\qquad 5.1c.$$

For nation X, MAD requires that the very best results are obtainable when no nuclear war occurs. Thus, we have the symmetric requirements:

$$U_N^X \gg U_1^X \qquad\qquad 5.2a,$$

$$U_N^X \gg U_2^X \qquad\qquad 5.2b,$$

and

$$U_N^X \gg U_S^X \qquad\qquad 5.2c.$$

SSC is a more modern concept that seems more commonly advocated by many of our colleagues as wholly sufficient to sustain strategic nuclear deterrence.[18] Here, the focus concentrates on the ability to retaliate, to respond to an initial attack. In terms of the elements of our model, this merely requires a strict subset of the requirements stated above for MAD, namely, 5.1a, nation Q is far worse off as a first-striker than under no nuclear war, and 5.2a, likewise for nation X.[19]

Thus, there is much overlap in our operationalization of the two concepts. In fact, as we see it, MAD is a strict subset of SSC—in having requirements that are more restrictive. Put otherwise, MAD is a sufficient condition for SSC, and SSC is a necessary condition for MAD as well. However, because MAD requires the additional conditions 5.1b, 5.1c, 5.2b, and 5.2c beyond those required for SSC, MAD is typically much more demanding a condition than is SSC. Clearly, the concepts are not equivalent, and the conditions under which SSC holds are typically more general than are the conditions that generate MAD.

None of the conditions 5.1b, 5.1c, 5.2b, or 5.2c ever appeared among any of our necessary or sufficient conditions to prevent or to induce a nuclear war. We must regard them as irrelevant to our investigation.

In contrast, it is where MAD and SSC coincide, namely in the conditions specific to SSC, that we relate to our earlier results. In fact, 5.1a and 5.2a stand as strong forms of the joint inequalities 3.2a that served as necessary and sufficient conditions for PSE 1 in which no nuclear war occurred. Likewise, they serve as strong forms of some of the alternative inequalities appearing in 4.3 that governed the behavior of the counterparties to no first strike in theorem 4.2.

But why should we bother with inequalities that are hugely satisfied, when even weak inequality would prove satisfactory? To understand this problem, it is undoubtedly best to return to expressions 4.1a and 4.1b, which served as the genesis of all of our necessary or sufficient conditions to prevent a nuclear war from breaking out. By enforcing 5.1a and 5.2a, we are likely to enforce that the signs of the slopes in 4.1a and 4.1b are both negative—unless, of course, $p^X \approx 1$ or $p^Q \approx 1$.

Let us here speculate that this conclusion held between America (A) and the Soviet Union/the Russian Federation (RF) for the many decades of the Cold War and in its aftermath. That is, we speculate that, even when positive, the quantities $U_S^A - U_2^A$ and $U_S^{RF} - U_2^{RF}$ were both of a comparatively tiny magnitude when compared to $U_N^A - U_1^A$ and $U_N^{RF} - U_1^{RF}$. Consequently, the 4.1a and 4.1b precursors to our sufficient conditions presented in Theorem 4.1 would have been fulfilled, and no nuclear war would have broken out (consistent with institutional evidence).

However, conditions have changed motivated by considerations not directly related to maintaining nuclear stability such as

- reducing the total number of nuclear weapons,

- limiting flexibility in force-structure decisions,

- eliminating certain classes of weapons,

- dropping inventories of back-up warheads and weapons,

- choosing not to test or to modernize nuclear weapons systems, and

- reducing capabilities of defense against nuclear weaponry.

We may no longer be able to guarantee that

$$U_N^Q - U_1^Q \gg U_S^Q - U_2^Q \qquad \text{5.3a.}$$

and

$$U_N^X - U_1^X \gg U_S^X - U_2^X \qquad \text{5.3b.}$$

This may erode optimality of the mutual decisions not to initiate a nuclear war in mutual assurance of the ability to carry out a first strike.

Less is not just less; less is different—between the two peer adversaries, shrinking the number of warheads in parallel does not retain the inherent nature of strategic deterrence. In fact, it alters the environment and the decision calculus each side will apply within that environment. Thus, one effect of smaller strategic nuclear arsenals is crucial—strategic deterrence may fail. We need to exert significant intellectual efforts to assure that with smaller arsenals, especially, this conclusion is not met so nuclear war will never occur. The second effect is quite a bit subtler. As we perform these analyses, we must be prepared to do so in a sophisticated manner because the essential nature of the problem is likely to have changed.

With this possible weakening of a previously self-enforcing peace, it is necessary, instead, to ask how to enforce strict negativity of the slope parameters in 4.1a and 4.1b into the future, irrespective of the selections of p^Q and p^X. That is how the conditions provided in theorems 4.1 and 4.2 and their Corollaries 4.3 and 4.4 enlighten us. Earlier, we declared that conditions 5.1a–c and 5.2a–c define MAD and conditions 5.1a and 6.2a define SSC. All of those conditions were embedded within the basic data of the model. None relied upon assessments of probabilities over behavior by the counterparties.

In making an assessment of what FSS means in the context of our model, we shall rely upon the same sort of restriction. Therefore, we define FSS, respectively, for nation Q and for nation X, to be inequalities 4.4a and 4.4b. Each pair is sufficient to guarantee that the specific nation governed by those inequalities will find it to be a dominant strategy not to carry out a first strike. According to Corollary 4.5, it is easy to see that mutual FSS is somewhat more than is needed to fulfill either of the sufficient conditions found in Corollary 4.3. That is, mutual FSS is amply sufficient for no nuclear war.

Nevertheless, it might be difficult to enforce this standard without turning to the "overkill" requirements imposed in traditional analyses—only when we have strong solutions, as in the following extensions to 4.3a–b, will we feel comfort that strategic deterrence is actually in place:

$$U_N^Q - U_1^Q \gg 0 \gg U_S^Q - U_2^Q \qquad\qquad \text{5.4a}$$

and

$$U_N^X - U_1^X \gg 0 \gg U_S^X - U_2^X, \qquad\qquad \text{5.4b.}$$

These we can refer to as strong mutual FSS.

In our modern world of success in reducing arsenal sizes, strong mutual FSS becomes our analytical standard of choice to achieve strategic nuclear deterrence. Modern strategic deterrence requires us to turn toward more stringent standards that induce nations not to carry out a first strike rather than merely to be fearful of the consequences of retaliation. In order to attain this higher standard, it is necessary to examine explicit policy options that will save us from nuclear war.

Practical Methods for Achieving Strategic Deterrence

Cold War methods run counter to modern purposes. In the earlier era we could rely upon the adequacy of 5.1a and 5.2a. Nuclear powers now need to achieve 5.4a and 5.4b. To this point in the paper, we have demonstrated "Why?" The remaining question is "How?" In this section we suggest a number of propositions for further refinement and analysis through hypothesis testing and empirical solution. We do not propose any particular insight below as strategic policy or practice until the proper analyses can be conducted.

The left-hand-side inequalities in 5.4a and 5.4b merely reiterate SSC and, by extension, stand as components of MAD. Therefore, we need to ask, "what were the underpinnings of those conditions?" And how can we reinforce them in contemporary and future situations—as arsenals decline through continuing treaty obligations and through unilateral actions? The essence of our answer is that the first striker must be made much worse off carrying out a first strike and receiving a retaliatory second strike than if no nuclear attacks occurred. A sequence of conditions is necessary for this conclusion.

1. The attacked nation possesses forces that display "survivability." A sufficient portion of the attacked nation's total force will live beyond the initial onslaught as to be able to threaten the assets of the first striker.

2. The attacked nation possesses weaponry among its survivable forces that can influence an attacker's calculation of social utility.

3. The attacked nation possesses an effective plan for retaliation. Targeting empty silos is undoubtedly inadequate; SSC must focus on punishing the first striker to be able to deter.

4. The attacked nation possesses a perceived willingness to retaliate across a spectrum of attacks.

All of those statements must be credible to achieve modern strategic nuclear deterrence.

How do we guarantee the fulfillment of right-hand side inequalities in 5.4a and 5.4b? That is none too easy. We seek to establish heuristic conditions under which a nation is far better off retaliating in a second strike rather than carrying out a simultaneous first strike. Perhaps we could invoke some sort of social or legal justification—"we believe that we are justified in retaliating to an attack, rather than carrying out a first strike or a simultaneous strike with our opponent." It is doubtful whether such "feelings based" analysis would justify choices to attack or to seek to avoid war.

Let us consider the conditions of responding to an unprovoked attack, targeting in first and second strikes, and defense against first and second strikes.

Effective Response to Unprovoked Attack

For "waiting" to be optimal, when the other side might attack, each side must possess the ability to respond to such an attack. Therefore, each side must continue to maintain its strategic assets—unilateral strategic disarmament is unacceptable—and those assets must display survivability. This need not be a property of individual systems but rather the portfolio of strategic weapons systems put into place.

- As an example of system-wide survivability, think of two critical components of the traditional US triad: intercontinental ballistic missiles (ICBM) and submarine launched ballistic missiles (SSBN). Many analysts contend that the latter are survivable, while the former are not. However, SSBN survivability is actually ensured by the missile fields serving as a sink for the massive numbers of nuclear weapons that a comparably nuclear-armed opponent would need to employ in an attack on ICBMs. The opponent's weapons therefore do not remain available to hunt for submarines at sea. In short, survivability of the response force arises through interaction capabilities provided through joint forces.

- Additional examples of generating survivability include deploying mobile ICBMs, hardening ICBM silos, and dispersing aircraft. Typically, survivability is enhanced simply by diversifying strategic nuclear forces among asset classes so as to complicate the attacker's problem.

Differential Targeting in First and Second Strikes

A nation that chooses to pursue a first strike is likely to try to destroy the strategic nuclear forces of its opponent––to conduct primarily a force-on-force strike. That is a rational position, for it tries to minimize the adversary's response capability. Nevertheless, it exposes the initial attacker to devastating retaliation by surviving assets. Because the first striker has used his nuclear warfare assets,[20] a retaliatory attack will naturally target the *value* assets of the first striker rather than empty silos, mobile ICBM garrisons, bomber bases, and submarine bases. This interpretation greatly helps to reinforce the no-nuclear-war equilibrium. Any societal gain from the first striker's destroying much of the strategic nuclear warfare capabilities of the opponent will be far outweighed by societal losses from a counterattack on the first striker's cities, their populations, and economically productive assets, even with arsenal sizes smaller than needed for assured destruction.

Differential Defense against First and Second Strikes

It is reasonable for each nation to establish conditions inducing and supporting differential targeting by its opponent (i.e., first strike force-on-force; second strike force-on-value).[21]

- Provide knowledge regarding some of the nuclear forces—but not enough to aid targeting of the intended survivable elements of the force.

- Provide protection aimed at guarding the security of second strike assets. Limit ballistic missile defenses (BMD) to value assets such as cities. Provide interceptors to deter bomber strikes on cities.

- Do not use BMD or interceptors to protect general strategic nuclear forces—other than those intended to fall into the survivable category.[22]

The preceding thoughts suggest that the following alternatives offer methods to control the problem of the second set of inequalities.

- Target military facilities with any first strike. Try to make it clear to the opponent that this is the intent and practice. Try to negotiate arms control treaties that reinforce this form of targeting.

- Allow military facilities to be targetable for a first strike. Make known the locations of ICBM silos, bomber bases, and SSBN bases. Do not strongly defend those facilities from nuclear attacks.

- To whatever extent possible, protect nonnuclear forces from strategic strikes. Provide interceptors to eliminate bomber strikes on cities. Keep their bases primarily coastal or along major rivers where the greatest cities are located. Introduce ballistic missile defense to protect nonmilitary assets such as cities.

- Retain survivable strategic nuclear forces that can retaliate during a second strike. This requirement might be quite problematic. Some nations seem to have no truly survivable strategic nuclear assets. This situation is exceptionally volatile, as such states must remain constantly ready to "use or lose" their nuclear deterrent.

- Finally, it is important to develop credible mechanisms for implementation of this policy, so that it cannot be quickly undone during the course of wartime.

Many of these methods will be seen as ugly components of strategic nuclear war, and they are precisely intended to be. When a player is forced to move to a second strike scenario, she or he should be willing to do so and prepared to make that strike as painful as possible for the initial attacker. Doing so reinforces the no-nuclear-war equilibrium.

Summary

It is perhaps peculiar that this document seems to have produced fairly clean-lined mathematical foundations in an area of theory that has been held in dispute for three generations. Undoubtedly, part of this clarity derives from the simplicity of Ellsberg's model and our extension of it. We encourage researchers to investigate more elaborate models to determine the extent to which these conclusions remain or collapse in more complex modern settings. We can summarize the most important of these results as guaranteeing no first strike provided that

- each side would prefer no nuclear war to being the unique initiator of such a war, and

- each side would prefer to carry out a second strike in retaliation for a first strike against it than to be the joint initiator of such a war.

These conditions can be encouraged, if not determined, through appropriate choices of forces, military policies, and societal organization. That is, it is often possible to deter strategic nuclear war between nations.

As we move to the modern era of post–Cold War nuclear war threats, we find that crisis stability/first-strike stability moves to the forefront as the concept for strategic deterrence. CS/FSS is codified in the two conditions identified in the preceding paragraph.

Our interpretation of mutually assured destruction and second strike capability might have proven adequate to deter nuclear war in the era of huge nuclear stockpiles and massive investment in weapons delivery systems. That is because they strongly fulfill our first requirement, namely, preference for no nuclear war over being a first striker. Limitations arising from ongoing and future strategic arms reduction treaties make those conditions insufficient to achieve strategic deterrence in the twenty-first century, which has brought the crisis stability/first-strike stability requirements to the fore.

Notes

1. Compare Department of Defense, *Nuclear Posture Review Report*.
2. See, for instance, Wohlstetter, "Sin and Games in America."
3. Neumann and Morgenstern, *Theory of Games and Economic Behavior*.

4. See, for example, Kahn, *On Thermonuclear War*; Schelling, *Strategy of Conflict*; and Schelling, *Arms and Influence*. For an exceptional history of theories of strategic deterrence, see Delpech, *Nuclear Deterrence in the 21st Century*.

5. Ellsberg, "The Crude Analysis of Strategy Choices."

6. A narrower application, and indicative of approaches when arsenal sizes were high, is the formulation by Kent, Thaler, and their colleagues, who focus on an equivalent single-shot game whose payoffs are replaced by "costs," presumably to the strategic forces that are targeted in an attack. Compare Kent, DeValt, and Thaler, *Calculus of First-Strike Stability*; Kent and Thaler, *First-Strike Stability*; and Kent and Thaler, *First-Strike Stability and Strategic Defenses*. Because our analysis agrees with Ellsberg in identifying social utility as the appropriate payoff and in using a normal form matrix to structure those payoffs, we do not further investigate these alternatives and similar work.

7. Brodie, *The Anatomy of Deterrence*, 20 and following. However, Brodie recognized that this policy, while being ex ante optimal in deterring "nuclear total war," might not be ex post rational. For example, a second strike against cities and other value assets would be likely to incur a third strike against comparable assets of the second striker. Thus, such a response might be forgone. In fact, Delpech, *Nuclear Deterrence*, 40, notes that Secretary of Defense McNamara tried unsuccessfully to get the Soviets to agree to a mutual policy of "city avoidance."

8. Likewise, some readers might find themselves put off by the fact that we limit attention to completion of Ellsberg's single-shot game, rather than to show how behavior evolves with time. In an unpublished appendix, the authors demonstrate that the values appearing in table 8.2 are consistent as a single-shot roll-up for an otherwise infinite-period game.

9. Frankly, for many paired states, it may be regarded as a dangerous variant. False interpretations of signals could lead to the conclusion that a nation is under attack and should launch its weaponry in a "use it or lose it" scenario. Because of the danger of false positive measurements, the United States has sought to forbid launch on warning. The Russians, possessing less sophisticated detection and interpretation systems, have nonetheless accepted the possibility of launch on warning. Nevertheless, there have been several historical examples in which the Russians faced the possibility of incoming weaponry but chose not to counterlaunch. For other nations whose nuclear-armed adversaries lie on or near their borders, the idea of "launch on warning" is not within the realm of physical capability.

10. Each side may target the opponent's nuclear forces that create unintended destruction of value assets. Alternatively, a target considered by an attacker to be a component of the nuclear forces might be considered by the attacked as a value asset. Likewise, opponents may have different perceptions as to whether nuclear employments to create a high-altitude electromagnetic pulse are nuclear attacks.

11. Compare the discussions of civil defense and its consequences for anticipated deaths in the population and for destruction of economically productive assets in Kahn, lecture 1, "The Nature and Feasibility of Thermonuclear War"; and chapter 2, "Will the Survivors Envy the Dead?" in his *On Thermonuclear War*.

12. Defining and analyzing how actors would determine social utility is external to the analysis within this paper.

13. Indeed, there is evidence that for quite some time into the Cold War, Soviet doctrine called for a nuclear-war-winning approach. See, for example, Wohlstetter, *The Delicate Balance of Terror*; or Battilega, "Soviet Views of Nuclear Warfare."

14. Keep in mind that the payoffs will not be mirror-image because they are wholly dependent on the social utility calculation by each state.

15. Note that the calculations are valid across the open interval $p^x \in (0,1)$. At the boundaries of that interval, we return to conditions of pure strategy equilibrium (PSE) for the X player, which were tacitly investigated in the preceding section. To make the examination complete, in this footnote we consider the pure strategies for the X player, while allowing player Q to indulge in mixed strategy equilibrium. For $p^x = 0$, choose p^Q so as to maximize:

$$E\{Payoff \quad to \quad Q| \quad p^x = 0\}$$

$$= \quad Pr\{Q \quad Waits| \quad p^x = 0\} \; E\{Payoff \quad to \quad Q|Q \quad Waits, \quad p^x = 0\}$$

$$+ \quad Pr\{Q \quad Attacks| \quad p^x = 0\} \; E\{Payoff \quad to \quad Q|Q \quad Attacks, \quad p^x = 0\}$$

$$= \quad (1 - p^Q)\, U_N{}^Q \quad + \quad p^Q\, U_1{}^Q$$

$$= \quad U_N{}^Q + p^Q \{U_1{}^Q - U_N{}^Q\} \qquad\qquad 4.1a1.$$

Because of linearity in p^Q, this expression is necessarily maximized at either $p^Q = 0$ (and we have player Q's payoff for pure strategy equilibrium PSE 1, or at $p^Q = 1$ (and we have his payoff for PSE 2). Similarly, for $p^x = 1$, choose p^Q so as to maximize:

$$E\{Payoff \quad to \quad Q| \; p^x = 1\}$$

$$= \quad Pr\{Q \quad Waits| \quad p^x = 0\} \; E\{Payoff \quad to \quad Q|Q \quad Waits, \quad p^x = 1\}$$

$$+ \quad Pr\{Q \quad Attacks| \quad p^x = 0\} \; E\{Payoff \quad to \quad Q|Q \quad Attacks, \quad p^x = 1\}$$

$$= \quad (1 - p^Q)\, U_2{}^Q \quad + \quad p^Q\, U_S{}^Q$$

$$= \quad U_2{}^Q + p^Q \{U_S{}^Q - U_2{}^Q\} \qquad\qquad 4.1a2.$$

Once again, we encounter linearity in p^Q, so that this expression is necessarily maximized at either $p^Q = 0$ and we have player Q's payoff for pure PSE 3 or at $p^Q = 1$ and we have his payoff for PSE 4.

16. Analogously to the earlier footnote, the problem simplifies if we lie at either boundary of the valid region for probability assessments. The solutions will prove, once again, to be linear in the assignment of p^x. And the payoffs to the X player will correspond to those of PSEs 1 through 4, respectively.

17. Although mutually assured destruction appears to hold a prominent position in contemporary thinking about Cold War strategic deterrence, Delpech, *Nuclear Deterrence*, 35, contends to the contrary that it only came into vogue about 1964 and

even then was rejected as an acronym by Secretary of Defense Robert McNamara, who thought it to be insane as a concept, and rejected as a policy by Albert Wohlstetter, who found it a feeble justification for mass murder. Wohlstetter, "How Much Is Enough?"

18. Global Zero U.S. Nuclear Policy Commission, *Modernizing U.S. Nuclear Strategy*, 7–8.

19. While conditions 4.5a and 4.5b are necessary, we are distrustful of such conditions as they may be ambiguously implemented. The deep interiority we seek comes by satisfying conditions 5.1a and 5.1b.

20. Our extension of the Ellsberg model continues the assumption of a single-strike capability for each opponent. Thus, there is no opportunity to shoot first at some assets while holding back part of the force. This simplicity induces our ability to generate clean-lined policy implications.

21. We even anticipate that this might occur jointly. Conditions can be established through treaty negotiations and reinforced through observation provided in the treaty and compelled through treaty penalties.

22. This may be one of the first arguments to contend that ballistic missile defense and other strategic defenses can be stabilizing rather than destabilizing. These recommendations provide for differential usage of strategic defenses that lie outside of contemporary policy and are novel.

SECTION 3

New Approaches To

Conventional Deterrence

Chapter 9

Deterring Rogues

Modeling the Intent of Revolutionary State Actors

Gary Schaub Jr.

How should policy makers approach divining the intentions of revolutionary adversaries who may take actions that the United States wishes to deter? Revolutionary states are those that "consider the international order or the manner of legitimizing it oppressive. . . . The distinguishing feature of a revolutionary power is not that it feels threatened . . . but that nothing can reassure it."[1] Such states aim to revise substantially the status quo, challenging those they perceive to threaten or oppress them, perhaps to the point of trying to overthrow the international order and reconstitute it along principles other than that of the sovereign state system.[2] Many have considered the Soviet Union and Iran as revolutionary states. How have their intentions been gauged? What policies have been proposed to deter them from their messianic missions?

The United States has addressed both states with a policy of deterrence in the service of containment. Although deterrence formed the core mission of the US military throughout the Cold War,[3] a great deal of deterrence theory and planning took place in a strategic and political vacuum based upon presumptions about the motives of Soviet and other adversaries. Capabilities analysis married to worst-case scenarios of what they could accomplish indicated adversary intent. Most believed that the success of deterrence in general or in any particular case was a function of American capabilities and willingness to use them in the event that deterrence failed. Whether something other than a reset of the relationship would happen if deterrence succeeded and the adversary's intent was frustrated was rarely considered.

From a theoretical standpoint, deterrence links a demand that the adversary refrain from undertaking a particular action to a threat to use force if it does not comply. Deterrence places the adversary in a situation in which it has a choice of complying inaction or risking the implementation of the deterrer's threatened sanction. How the adversary generates expectations about the consequences of its alternatives—the relative importance of these considerations and how they are combined to yield an estimate of consequences—has been the subject of wide and varied speculation.[4] These expectations are distilled into expected value calculations. Expected value calculations require that the costs and benefits of an outcome be discounted by the probability of its occurrence ([benefits − costs] x probability) and that the expected value of possible outcomes stemming from a single course of action be summed. In deterrence, the adversary compares the expected value of compliance and defiance. For a deterrence attempt to be successful, the deterrer's threatened sanction must reduce the expected value of defiance to the degree that it is less than the expected value of compliance. The deterrer can do that by threatening to reduce the benefits of defiance or increase its costs. The former would constitute a denial threat while the latter would be a threat of punishment. And because the adversary will discount these threats by its assessment of the likelihood that the deterrer will implement them, the deterrer must convey these threats credibly.[5]

The *Deterrence Operations Joint Operating Concept* (*DOJOC*), a product of US Strategic Command and US Joint Forces Command, adopts this framework and, doing so, has improved the official conception of deterrence markedly.[6] It defines "deterrence operations [as those that] convince adversaries not to take actions that threaten US vital interests by means of decisive influence over their decision making. Decisive influence is achieved by credibly threatening to deny benefits and/or impose costs [if the undesirable action is taken], while encouraging restraint by convincing the actor that restraint will result in an acceptable outcome."[7] The *DOJOC* thus takes an active view of deterrence operations: Achieving decisive influence over an adversary's decision making requires deliberate action on the part of a joint force commander or other American policy makers. Such deterrence operations can include force projection, the deployment of active and passive defenses, global strike (nuclear, conventional, and nonkinetic), and strategic communication.[8]

The key to knowing when to practice deterrence is determining an actor's intent. Patrick Morgan notes, "The intentions of opponents are notoriously difficult to fathom."[9] This seems to be especially the case for revolutionary-oriented state actors. How do joint force commanders, those who populate the staffs of the US government, and the elites upon whom they rely for subject-matter expertise determine adversary intent? Is there doctrinal guidance that military staffs rely upon to perform this key task? Are certain patterns of thought or interpretive lenses commonly employed by officers, civilian policy makers, or scholars? How have adversary intentions been discerned in key episodes in the past? Finally, how can the process of intent determination be improved?

There is little doctrinal guidance for determining adversary intent. What exists is contained in Joint Publication (JP) 2-0, *Joint Intelligence*.[10] This doctrine manual contains superficially useful sections, such as "Intelligence and the Levels of War," "Intelligence and the Range of Military Operations," "Prediction—(Accept the Risk of Predicting Adversary Intentions)," and "Intelligence Support during the Deterrence Phase." Unfortunately, most of these sections are not helpful. Beyond exhorting "intelligence professionals" to "go beyond the identification of capabilities" and take the risk of predicting adversary intent and basing such forecasts on "solid analysis," JP 2-0 is not particularly helpful in guiding such analysis.[11] Indeed, by indicating that such "an intelligence product . . . usually reflects enemy capabilities and vulnerabilities," the authors of this doctrine indirectly encourage substitution of capability analysis for intent analysis.[12] While capabilities do suggest some general directions of intent—why invest in a particular capability if you are not going to use it?—they utterly fail to answer questions of the conditions under which such capabilities would be used. The military intelligence process, at the tactical or operational level of war, does not address these political issues.

Interpreting Intent: Two Frameworks

If joint military doctrine is not a helpful guide in determining adversary intent, how can operators structure this problem to solve it? Intelligence analysts operate in a complex environment and they, like human beings more generally, are unable to process all of the innumerable stimuli that they encounter. In this context, Roberta Wohlstetter usefully distinguished "between signals and noise. By the *signal* of an action is meant a sign, a clue, a piece of evidence that points to the action or to an adversary's intention to undertake it, and by *noise* is meant the background of irrelevant or inconsistent signals, signs pointing in the wrong directions, that tend always to obscure the signs pointing in the right way."[13] What Wohlstetter left unsaid was that noise and signals do not come clearly marked for the analysts as they sift through mountains of information. Rather, the analyst determines what is signal and what is noise.

This is a difficult task. Analysts suffer the same cognitive limits as everyone else, and therefore necessarily deal with "a dramatically simplified model of the buzzing, blooming confusion that constitutes the real world."[14] These simplified models of reality focus attention toward certain pieces of information and away from most others, and generally represent the "most significant chains of causes and consequences" as "short and simple."[15] These models allow analysts to discriminate between signals and noise. However, many models may adequately fit the data, and it is up to the analyst to determine which best explains the adversary's intent.[16]

American scholars and policy makers have been apt to apply one of two models to comprehend the intentions of other international actors, be they regular states or revolutionary states. The first is the strategic intent model and the second is the internal logic model.

Each model posits that the actor is purposive: that it seeks to achieve a particular goal with each action. When working retrospectively, this presumption risks making either framework tautological, as "an imaginative analyst can construct an account of value-maximizing choice for any action or set of actions."[17] Tautology can be escaped, however, with the presumption that the preferences against which alternatives are considered are relatively stable. This allows an analyst to erect a set of principles that appear to guide the actor's choices over time and across domains. These principles provide generic preferences for particular actors and allow some degree of operationalization of the model. They can be derived from "(1) propensities or personality traits or psychological tendencies of the nation or government, (2) values shared by the nation or government [or organization], or (3) special principles of action [that] change the 'goals' or narrow the 'alternatives' and 'consequences' considered."[18]

The strategic intent and internal logic models differ with regard to the problems that they believe an actor is attempting to solve by taking actions in the interstate arena. The strategic intent model presumes that the actor is solving an external problem while the internal logic model presumes that it is solving an internal one.

The Strategic Intent Model

The strategic intent model presumes that state actors direct their behavior toward achieving political goals vis-à-vis external actors. It presumes that they desire to influence the decisions, behavior, and/or attitudes of these other actors and that they have chosen the most effective means available to them, as delimited by their capabilities and tendencies, to achieve this end. Whether they do so via coercion, inducement, or persuasion,[19] using whatever power resources they have available, matters not. What does matter is that the impact on the external actor is of paramount concern to the adversary.

Thus the key variables determining the adversary's intent to act are the costs of undertaking the action, the benefits that would accrue from successful action, and the costs and benefits of not acting. The strategic intent model is vague with regard to what factors determine costs and benefits of these two courses of action. Lawrence Freedman has argued that the costs of undertaking the action can be bifurcated into those costs associated with implementing the choice and those associated with enforcing it after the fact.[20] The benefits of undertaking the action have not been given as much attention as the costs but would be composed of material benefits accrued, intangible benefits—including prestige and reputation, among others—and the new opportunities made possible by successful conclusion of the action. The costs of inaction, or "restraint" in the parlance of the *DOJOC*, can be broken down into the international and domestic costs of foregoing action, including suffering the unwanted reactions of opponents in the near and far term, and the negative reactions of domestic audiences. The benefits of inaction or restraint have not been well considered in the literature either, but would include desirable international and domestic reactions—such as praise for being reasonable or a deescalation of tensions, or tangible benefits provided by those who did not favor action. Despite the obvious utility that considering domestic reactions to the choice made by the adversary's leadership, the strategic intent model generally focuses upon externally generated costs and benefits.[21]

The Internal Logic Model

The internal logic model, on the other hand, presumes that actors are directing their activities inward, enhancing their support or the cohesion of the group, and that actions directed toward other actors—

be they states or otherwise—are judged primarily by their internal effects rather than their external effects. Hence international political behavior is primarily a consequence of domestic (or internal) politics and may be more incidental than intended. "The idea that political elites often embark on adventurous foreign policies or even resort to war in order to distract popular attention away from internal social or economic problems and consolidate their own domestic political support is an old theme in the literature on international politics," notes Jack Levy.[22] Ned Lebow argues that states with weakening political systems, weakening political leaders, or elites engaged in a competition for power may "resort to the time-honored technique of attempting to offset discontent at home by diplomatic success abroad."[23] While success vis-à-vis external actors would certainly be welcomed, the cohesion within the group and support for the leadership generated by conflict abroad is the primary purpose of such actions.

The key variables within this framework are the internal or domestic groups whose support is required to allow the leadership to continue in office. After these have been identified, the relative ability of these groups to influence the leadership by providing benefits such as continued support or imposing costs such as removing leaders from power, how these audiences view the merits of the action to be undertaken (or not), and the relative ability of the leadership to substitute the support of one group for another must be assessed.[24] Thus the internal logic framework requires substantial knowledge of the adversary beyond the leadership and its preferences, especially the leaders' domestic political situation. A great deal of work has addressed the propensities of certain types of regimes to engage in external behavior to ameliorate internal dissension or promote internal cohesion in democratic states particularly.[25] The manner of interpretation and use of deterrent threats with internal needs-driven external behavior has received attention from scholars such as Ned Lebow and Janice Stein, but their insights were not incorporated into the corpus of deterrence theory—to the detriment of our knowledge.[26]

This has been reflected in how analysts have inferred adversary intent. American policy makers, scholars, and analysts have relied upon these two frameworks of rational action to infer the intent of adversaries. They clearly direct attention toward different aspects of the adversary's makeup, its capabilities, and particularly the hierarchy of its goals. Unsurprisingly, they often provide contradictory prescriptions with regard to how to approach an adversary and what to do to influence its behavior. Two short examples of each model in action should make their differences clear.

Sources of Soviet Conduct

During the Cold War there was a grand debate between those who used the strategic intent model and those who used the internal logic model to infer Soviet behavior. Those who utilized the strategic intent model can be divided into those who saw Soviet motivations as an attempt to obtain security in an insecure environment and those who saw the Soviet Union (USSR) as an opportunistic yet traditional great power.

Strategic Intent

The first group saw the USSR operating in an environment in which it had real enemies and "a compulsion to overinsure against potential threats."[27] Soviet leaders inherited traditional Russian insecurities deriving from the lack of geographic barriers to invasions and a history of many such invasions married to "a politically xenophobic Communist ideology that interpreted the external world as implacable to the Socialist state."[28] In this conception, the Soviets were seen as overreacting to the influences of their environment and the behavior of external actors. George Kennan put it thusly: "What is called 'Soviet behavior' is, in far higher degree than seems to be realized in Washington, a reaction by the leaders of that country to the manner in which we ourselves treat them."[29] These analysts therefore argued that American actions should bear in mind Soviet sensitivities and that Washington should pursue policies that avoided unnecessary provocation. Indeed, they saw in this room for cooperation between the superpowers on the basis of overcoming common threats to their security, particularly those caused by the existence of nuclear weapons. Hence they advocated arms control to enhance strategic stability, nonproliferation efforts to halt the further spread of nuclear weapons, and greater transparency in the form of cooperative security arrangements—all designed to reassure the Soviets that their environment was less dangerous than they perceived and therefore influence its behavior.[30]

A related strategic view accepted that the Soviet Union received an inheritance from Tsarist Russia, particularly its self-image as a great power. According to Henry Kissinger, "Soviet policy is also, of course, the inheritor of an ancient tradition of Russian nationalism. Over centuries the strange Russian empire has seeped outward . . . across endless plains where no geographical obstacle except distance set[s] a limit to human ambition, inundating what resisted, absorbing what yielded."[31] Its continued outward drive manifested itself in the Cold War era in traditional great-power fashion as continued consolidation of the empire, the control over the buffer states of Eastern Europe, preventing encirclement by hostile states, and reshaping the rules of the international system to its liking.[32] In essence, those who held this view saw the mellowing of Bolshevik ideological fervor and decreasingly reluctant acceptance of the Soviet Union's role in the established international system. But they did not infer that Soviet intentions were benign.

This conception emphasized the opportunistic nature of Soviet forays abroad. In his famous article, "The Sources of Soviet Conduct," Kennan argued that Soviet "political action is a fluid stream which moves constantly, wherever it is permitted to move, toward a given goal. Its main concern is to make sure that it has filled every nook and cranny available to it in the basin of world power."[33] Kissinger agreed that "Soviet strategy [is] essentially one of ruthless opportunism."[34]

In both variants of the strategic intent conception of Soviet motive, the Soviet leadership was composed of clearheaded and rational people operating in an environment where their behavior was determined by the expected value of available courses of action. They were therefore viewed as amenable to influence from external actors—amenable in the sense that they were not implacable or insensitive to the consequences of their actions deriving from the reactions of others. For this reason Kennan prescribed, "That the main element of any US policy toward the Soviet Union must be that of a long-term, patient but firm and vigilant containment of Russian expansive tendencies."[35] Kissinger likewise counseled, "To foreclose Soviet opportunities is thus the essence of the West's responsibility. It is up to us to define the limits of Soviet aims."[36]

This view became the basis for deterrence theory as it developed in the Cold War. The Soviet leaders might desire to take advantage of every opportunity to increase their security, material power, and/or political influence, but American strategists believed that they would not risk war with the United States to obtain these goals. They held this belief for two reasons. First, they knew that Soviet leaders—Stalin in particular—could count, and America's military and economic

preponderance was obvious to all. Therefore, the Soviets would ultimately content themselves with consolidating that which they already
had to avoid overt conflict with the United States. Second, communist ideology would reinforce this tendency. "The Kremlin is under
no ideological compulsion to accomplish its purposes in a hurry,"
argued Kennan. "It can be patient. It has no right to risk the existing
achievements of the revolution for the sake of vain baubles of the
future."[37] The Soviets believed that time was on their side and that
tactical withdrawals were not indicative of a strategic retreat. Indeed,
Kennan continued, "The Kremlin has no compunction about retreat-
ing in the face of superior force. . . . If it finds unassailable barriers in
its path, it accepts these philosophically and accommodates itself to
them."[38] Successful deterrence would depend upon this peculiar Soviet
trait. As Bernard Brodie put it, "The saving grace of the Soviet philosophy so far as international relations are concerned is that, unlike
the Nazi ideology, it incorporates within itself no time schedule. . . . The
Soviet attitude appears to be much more opportunistic. The Soviets
may be unshakably convinced that ultimately there must be war. . . . What
we can do, however, is to persuade them each time the question arises
that 'The time is not yet!' "[39]

Internal Logic

Those who saw Soviet behavior through the prism of the internal
logic model also began their analyses with George Kennan, but discounted the ability of external influences to affect Soviet calculations.
In this view, dealing with internal solidarity was

> one of the most basic of the compulsions which came to act upon the Soviet
> regime: since capitalism no longer existed in Russia and since it could not be
> admitted that there could be serious or widespread opposition to the Kremlin
> springing spontaneously from the liberated masses under its authority, it be-
> came necessary to justify the retention of the dictatorship by stressing the
> menace of capitalism abroad.
>
> . . . [T]he stress laid in Moscow on the menace confronting Soviet society from
> the world outside its borders is founded not in the realities of foreign antago-
> nism but in the necessity of explaining away the maintenance of dictatorial
> authority at home.[40]

Analysts such as Richard Pipes, Colin Gray, and William Odom
continued this line of argument in the late 1970s and early 1980s.[41]
Their analyses suggested a characterization of "endemic militarism"

in the Soviet system of governance and that it was "as central to Soviet communism as the pursuit of profit is to societies with market-oriented economies."[42] Thus they saw the use of force abroad as a good in itself, one that enhanced the identity of the Soviet state. "According to this view," wrote Douglas Seay, "the Soviet iteration of an implacable foreign threat results not from paranoia or from fear of invasion but rather from the regime's self-interest, a foreign threat being an indispensable element in the regimentation of Soviet society."[43] Indeed, this posture had "the additional benefit of helping to legitimize an otherwise illegitimate regime."[44]

The internal logic view of Soviet conduct implied that there was a fundamental impediment to changing their behavior. They could not be influenced on a case-by-case basis through coercive strategies, such as deterrence, or induced through acts of goodwill, or persuaded through diplomacy. Given that the sources of Soviet conduct were internal and endemic, only physical barriers to Soviet action would affect them. Only if they became physically unable to achieve their goals would they refrain from acting. Analysts who held this view argued strenuously for national missile defense as an alternative to an inherently unreliable deterrent,[45] against strategic nuclear arms control, and were opposed to détente.

These analysts did believe that it was possible for the United States to achieve its objectives vis-à-vis the Soviet Union—once it collapsed. Kennan had argued that the internal contradictions of the Soviet system and the unbearable strain that it would place on its population could result in a collapse of the Soviet system. "Soviet Russia might be changed overnight from one of the strongest to one of the most pitiable of national societies," he argued.[46] But those who emphasized the internal logic of the Soviet system as the motivator behind its policies saw such a collapse as perhaps the only way to affect Soviet behavior. Pipes, for instance, argued, "The Soviet Union will be a partner in peace only when it makes peace with its own people. Only then will the danger of nuclear war recede."[47]

Clearly, there were substantial differences in the views and prescriptions of analysts who utilized the strategic intent model to infer Soviet intentions and those who used the internal logic model. These views helped shape the debates of US foreign policy, particularly after the Vietnam War, and continue to have echoes today. Some of these are evident in the debate about the intentions of Iran's leaders.

The Islamic Republic of Iran

There has been a similar debate between those who use the strategic intent model and those who use the internal logic model to infer Iranian behavior. Most analysts who use the strategic intent model locate the drivers of Iran's foreign policy in a sense of insecurity among its leaders, a sense of national and cultural pride, and a sense of mission. In this view Iran is an opportunistic heir to the ancient Persian Empire, surrounded by unfriendly neighbors, and motivated by an ideological zeal to achieve regional hegemony if not export its revolution.

Strategic Intent

Many analysts that use the strategic intent model recognize that Iran is located in a region in which it is in many ways an outsider. "A Persian, Shiite nation struggling in an Arab, Sunni Middle East, Iran has always lived with the fear of being surrounded by foes."[48] Its recent history has seen the intervention of external powers in its internal affairs, from the British and American support of the coup that overthrew Prime Minister Mohammed Mosaddeq and installed Reza Pahlavi as shah in 1953 to the diplomatic and economic sanctions leveled against it in the aftermath of the 1979 revolution. The US military presence in the region, from its continuous naval presence in the Persian Gulf to its forces in the Arab monarchies after Operation Desert Storm and in Afghanistan and Iraq after the invasions of 2001 and 2003, has further isolated and contained Iran. And, of course, Saddam Hussein's Iraq attacked Iran in 1980.

Analysts with this view see Iran's foreign policy as primarily driven by the insecurities of its situation but do not see its policies as benign; rather they have the flavor of a revolutionary power that desires to make its environs more congenial. Early in its history, at least through the tenure of Ayatollah Khomeini, "[t]he Islamic Republic of Iran [was] a self-professed revolutionary state . . . [that] rejected the status quo and deliberately incited regional instability. . . . Its revisionism was related to status, not land."[49] It combined a pride in its cultural heritage with a sense of aggrievement to form a positive international "manifest destiny" for itself.[50] "To this sense of nationalism and historical grievances, the mullahs added an Islamist dimension. Ayatollah Khomeini bequeathed his country an ideology that divided the world between the oppressed and the oppressors. The Islamic Republic was to be a vanguard state leading the subjugated masses toward freedom and justice. . . . The old balance between ideology and pragmatism has yielded to one defined by power politics and religious fervor."[51]

Along these lines Barry Posen argued, "It is reasonable to expect that revolutionary Iran, like Iran under the shah, has pretensions to regional hegemony."[52] Michael Eisenstadt contended, "Iran is not pursuing nuclear weapons just to enhance its ability to deal with perceived threats. There are other powerful motives at work here, including the regime's drive for self-reliance and its desire to transform Iran into a regional power."[53] Others see this balance a bit differently, with Kenneth Timmerman arguing that a "nuclear-ready Iran will not stop at violently suppressing domestic dissent, but will actively seek ways of lashing out at what it sees as the sources of that dissent: the United States and Israel."[54] Michael Ledeen goes further, arguing that "the mullahs do not share our dreams; they dream of our destruction. . . . Western civilization will be consigned to the garbage heap of history by the twelfth Imam. . . . These are dreams of global conquest and domination."[55] Thus these analysts see a wide prism of possible Iranian behavior that can be pragmatic, opportunistic, or aggressive—but all expect it to be expansionist and motivated by the value of the stakes sought.

This strategic narrative sees the Iranian leadership as rational, acting upon their estimates of the costs and benefits of various courses of action, be they strategic or tactical. These leaders can therefore be influenced by the actions of external actors such as the United States. As Kenneth Pollack puts it, "Our goal should be to present the Iranians with two different paths. If they choose to go down the path of confrontation—stubbornly clinging to their nuclear program, their support for terrorism, and their violent opposition to a Middle East Peace—then at each step they will be hit with progressively more painful consequences. If they choose the path of cooperation—by giving up those same patterns of behavior—then at each step they will be rewarded with progressively more advantageous benefits."[56]

Where analysts using the strategic intent model differ is their assessment of the risk attitudes among Iranian leaders. Some see Iranian leaders as risk-neutral or even risk-averse. Pollack argues,

> Iran's behavior over the past fifteen years suggests that it can probably be deterred from taking the most harmful offensive actions even after it has acquired nuclear weapons. . . . In fact, all of the reporting . . . indicates that they want nuclear weapons to deter an American—or, to a lesser extent, Israeli or Iraqi—attack. Nor does the current Iranian leadership have a history of reck-

less behavior. . . . None of this makes it certain that Iran could be deterred once it acquired nuclear weapons, but all of it indicates that there is a strong basis for believing it could be.[57]

Posen agrees, arguing, "The strategy of deterrence and containment has worked for the United States before; there is no reason why it cannot work again. . . . In a confrontation with the United States, Iran could run risks of complete destruction, and it cannot threaten the United States with comparable damage."[58] And Eisenstadt emphasizes,

> Because Shi'i religious doctrine exalts the suffering and martyrdom of the faithful, and because religion plays a central role in the official ideology of the Islamic Republic, Iran is sometimes portrayed as an 'undeterrable' state driven by the absolute imperatives of religion, rather than by the pragmatic concerns of statecraft. . . . However, the perception of Iran as an irrational, undeterrable state with a high pain threshold is wrong. Iranian decision-makers are generally not inclined to rash action. Within the context of a relatively activist foreign and defence policy, they have generally sought to minimize risk.[59]

On the other hand, some see Iran's leaders as risk-acceptant or even reckless. Barry Rubin argues, "Tehran may not be suicidal, but it is prone to risk taking, and as a highly ideological regime that profoundly misunderstands the West, it is likely to miscalculate in ways that could lead to war. . . . Iran's regime is the farthest thing from a rational state that the United States has confronted since Nazi Germany."[60] Analysts from the Heritage Foundation concur:

> The United States' unrivalled military power would be a powerful deterrent against an Iranian direct nuclear attack, but relying on the threat of massive retaliation could be risky. The Iranian hard-liners could miscalculate and misperceive; they are profoundly ignorant about the outside world and have shown a tendency to gamble recklessly. They frequently proclaim their conviction that the United States would not or could not attack them. In addition, there are legitimate questions about whether Ahmadinejad, who reportedly harbors apocalyptic religious beliefs regarding the return of the Mahdi, or others in the Iranian regime like him[,] would have the same cost-benefit calculus about a nuclear war that other leaders would have.[61]

Internal Logic

Although the complex and factional nature of Iranian decision making is widely noted, those who offer an internal logic analysis of Iranian motives are few. In general, those of this view hold that the Iranian government uses foreign conflict to enhance domestic unity and support for the regime and their policies. "The empirical record

seems to suggest that public dissatisfaction has led to the regime ex-
acerbating tensions with the U.S. to distract the population's attentions
from domestic political problems and demonstrate [Ahmadinejad's]
revolutionary credentials," argues Graeme Davies.[62] Shahram Chubin
writes,

> For self-proclaimed revolutionary regimes like Iran, foreign policy is an expres-
> sion of its values and a validation of its struggle. Hence, there is an intimate con-
> nection between domestic legitimization and foreign policy conduct. Foreign
> policy and foreign threats are routinely invoked to control domestic politics. . . .
> Foreign policy, therefore, is at once an extension of domestic politics, an expres-
> sion of the regime's identity, and a barometer of its intentions. . . . Regime survival,
> equated with [the hard-liner's] primacy, depends upon embattlement.[63]

The authors of a recent RAND study agree, albeit within an elite-
centric frame of reference, arguing, "Leadership factions frequently
wield foreign policy issues as tools to outmaneuver their rivals and
form tactical alliances that will aid their domestic standing. . . . The
actual issues debated are secondary to the larger prizes of patronage,
power, and privilege."[64]

The internal logic view of Iranian conduct leads to the conclusion
that its leaders are not particularly amenable to external influence.
They are difficult to coerce, induce, or persuade to change their behavior—
be it with regard to their nuclear program, their sponsorship of terrorist organizations throughout the region, or their conflict with Israel.
The legitimacy of the regime—founded on "a transnational mission
of redeeming the Middle East for the forces of righteousness" and being "a vanguard state leasing the subjugated masses toward freedom
and justice"—deprives their leaders of the political space necessary to
comply with Western, especially American, demands.[65] "The influence of powerful hard-line minorities in each country [Iran and the
United States] and a number of outstanding disputes that push domestic political buttons have held back efforts at conciliation."[66] Indeed, as Pollack put it, "The backing of the United States has generally
proven to be the kiss of death for Iranian leaders. Khatami himself is
the best proof of this: his effort to reach out to the United States early
in his presidency was a serious mistake that convinced the hardliners
that he opposed the fundamental principles of the revolution upon
which their legitimacy was based."[67]

Surprisingly, however, few of these analysts offer prescriptions that
derive from the internal logic framework. Pollack, for instance, treats
Iran as a unitary actor when proposing a three-tiered approach of

offering a grand bargain, then using carrots and sticks if that fails, and finally preparing to contain Iran indefinitely.[68] So does Ray Takeyh in offering his strategy of engagement.[69] Eisenstadt, on the other hand, argued for a deterrence-by-denial strategy that "depriv[es] Iran of the resources it could have otherwise used for a military buildup" because "regime factionalism . . . could make it difficult to establish a stable deterrent relationship with a nuclear Iran."[70] And the RAND team of Wehrey et al. proposes "essentially reversing the traditional good cop/bad cop roles" of the United States and its allies, and letting the Russians and Chinese lead multilateral coercive efforts, so as to deprive Iranian factions the unifying force of a continuous American or European threat. Unlike prescriptions based upon the domestic needs of Soviet leaders, this literature eschews regime change, externally assisted, or not, as the best way of dealing with leaders preoccupied by their own domestic travails.[71]

Prescriptive Problems

The strategic intent model and the internal logic model of adversary intent produce very different pictures of what motivates adversaries. Do they desire to influence external actors to achieve a political outcome vis-à-vis that actor? Or do they desire to bolster their domestic solidarity in the face of centrifugal forces? Is the outcome of the action that we wish to deter of primary or secondary importance to the adversary? Making this determination is important when deciding whether to attempt to deter the adversary's actions or to take another approach, such as preemptive brute force or actions to increase or decrease the adversary's feelings of insecurity.

Deterrence is a strategy to pursue when one judges that the primary motivation of the adversary's intended action is strategic goals. Given direction toward external actors in such situations, identification of the adversary's goal is a matter of routine. Focusing deterrent demands toward that objective—"don't do *that*"—places the adversary in a decision situation in which it can either comply with what has been demanded of it or defy those demands and risk the implementation of the deterrer's threatened sanction. As the *Deterrence Operations Joint Operating Concept* rightly suggests, denying the adversary's leadership the potential benefits of the actions that it intends to take or imposing costs that reduce the net utility of the action are the two ideal ways of reducing the likelihood that the adversary will choose to act.[72] The objective of this deterrent threat is to reduce the expected value of "doing that" to a point that the consequences of compliance are of greater value. The *DOJOC* explains, "Adversaries weigh the perceived benefits and costs of a given course of action *in the context of* their perceived consequences of restraint or inaction. Thus deterrence can fail even when the adversary perceives the costs of acting as outweighing the benefits of acting if he believes the costs of inaction are even higher still."[73] (emphasis in the original) When the adversary is basing his choice upon these considerations, the correctly targeted deterrence has a chance of success.

Deterrence may not be the strategy to pursue if the adversary's external behavior is for enhancing internal cohesion or the power of the leadership. Providing overt signs of an external threat is precisely the outcome desired by the adversary's leadership. A threat from an external actor allows them to take actions to increase their support, silence moderates or critics, mobilize resources that might otherwise be unavailable, and provides the opportunity to forge or reinforce common in-group identities. The achievement of these goals requires the deterrer to provide the missing ingredient: its hostile reaction. If the deterrer falls into the trap, then the adversary has the means it needs to achieve its goal of increased cohesion. If the deterrer refrains from reacting, then the adversary may still capitalize on the lack of a reaction to motivate support for strong leadership. Yet this is less likely than action-provoking hostility as people are less motivated to act to seize opportunities than they are to avoid potential losses.[74]

Deterring Adversaries Motivated by Internal Logic

If the adversary's motivation is internal logic, is it really a no-win situation for the deterrer? Is deterrence a nonstarter? Are there alternatives to issuing an immediate deterrent threat directed against their intended external action or doing nothing and letting the adversary's provocation pass unanswered? There are a number of options.

First, one can still attempt to deter the adversary directly through passive measures that deny it the opportunity to carry out its intended action and also deny it the visible indicators of hostility that it seeks to engender. There are a number of means to do this. One denial measure is to harden soft targets—for example, police stations—through passive point defenses. This makes it less likely that spectacular successes can be had against these targets, and given their passivity—barriers, reinforced concrete, or even ballistic missile defenses (provided that they are well beyond the ability of the adversary to observe)—they deprive the deterrer of the ability to overreact and justify the adversary's actions.[75] Passive area defenses can also be used to deny the adversary the interaction that it needs with the deterrer to achieve its internal goals. Possibilities in this realm include measures such as the fence that Israel has erected around Palestinian areas, which has decreased suicide attacks substantially since its completion,[76] or diplomatic isolation such as that imposed upon the People's Republic of China, Cuba, or Iran after their revolutions. A potential drawback to passive area defenses is that they themselves might become symbols of implacable and unyielding hostility that the adversary can use repeatedly to rally its domestic constituents.[77]

Second, one can attempt to deter the adversary indirectly—by directing the deterrent threat toward the members of the group the leadership is attempting to bolster or recruit. The adversary's external challenge is designed to attract these followers, and a deterrent threat directed toward the group's members and potential members may cleave them away by highlighting personal over group interests.[78] All groups engaged in conflict that are attempting to recruit or retain members ask these people to put aside their personal interests for the benefit of the group cause, even though their individual contributions will be marginal (in most cases, suicide terrorism is designed to overcome this recruitment challenge). As LichBach notes "Thus rebels confront the possibility of disastrous private costs and uncertain public benefits. . . . Unless the collective action problem is somehow overcome, rational people will never rebel—rebellions, that is, require irrationality."[79] Israel has pursued a policy of deterring group members by threatening to destroy the family homes of young Palestinians who were involved in attacks.[80] Aerial surveillance capabilities, such as that of the Predator remotely piloted vehicle, have been key to operationalizing this strategy. Such an option would be an attempt to deny the adversary leadership the domestic benefits of its intended action by threatening to punish individual members of the group.

Third, one can pursue a similar goal but through inducements to members of the adversary's constituency rather than through coercion. Counterinsurgency (COIN) strategies, such as those discussed in FM 3-24, *Counterinsurgency*, work on this principle: "The real battle is for civilian support for, or acquiescence to, the counterinsurgents and host nation government. The population waits to be convinced. Who will help them more, hurt them less, stay the longest, [and] earn their trust?"[81] Indeed, the "Anbar Awakening" in Iraq is quite a vivid example of using inducements to cleave potential supporters away from an adversary—in this case, al-Qaeda in Iraq.[82]

Fourth, one can attempt to "encourage adversary restraint," as the *DOJOC* puts it, by "try[ing] to communicate . . . benign intentions . . . to reduce the fear, misunderstanding, and insecurity that are often responsible for unintended escalation to war."[83] Engaging in such persuasion is an alternative to influence through coercion or inducement. It involves altering the considerations for evaluating compliance and defiance. The persuader does not promise or threaten action, but convinces the adversary to see the situation in such a way that he realizes it is in his own interests to act a certain way. This can be done by highlighting—without altering—costs or benefits related to complying with or defying the persuader's demands or by offering new alternatives that allow the adversary to achieve his goals in ways that do not harm the persuader's interests. These persuasion strategies treat the definition of the problem facing the adversary—in this case increasing cohesion, recruitment, or retention of members—as given or settled. Another avenue of persuasion requires understanding the basis upon which the target frames the issue and shifting it.[84] Persuasion is generally seen as a fruitless option, particularly when dealing with an adversary with internally generated primary concerns or has revolutionary orientations.

Fifth, one can forego influence altogether and use brute force against the adversary to prevent it from undertaking action.[85] This can take the form of disarming the adversary to deny it the capability to pursue the action that it intends or decapitating the adversary to disrupt its ability to act. Either action risks increasing the cohesion of adversaries by justifying their hostility toward the deterrer and/or creating a martyr of the leadership. Decapitation of the leadership could also disrupt the internal cohesion of the adversary to some degree.[86]

The Internal Constituencies

Overall, if it is determined that an adversary decision maker is motivated by the internal logic of his group's situation, deterrence may work—but not in the manner prescribed in the *DOJOC*. Rather, deterrent demands and other influence attempts should be directed at the primary objectives of the adversary in these situations: the internal constituencies whose support the leadership hopes to rally by its external actions. Clearly, actions should also be taken to mitigate the impact of those actions as well, since nothing fails like failure. But it should be borne in mind that mere signals of hostility directed toward the group (or nation) as a whole in an attempt to deter the unwanted action could provide the adversary leader precisely what he or she wants: an external enemy that his or her people can oppose in unity.

Conclusion

How should policy makers approach divining the intentions of revolutionary rogues who may take actions that the United States wishes to deter? Although deterrence formed the core mission of the US military throughout the Cold War, adversary intent was based upon capabilities analysis married to worst-case scenarios of what they could accomplish. Whether deterrence would succeed in general or in any particular case was likewise inferred to be a function of American capabilities and willingness to use them in the event that deterrence failed. The consequences that would befall the adversary if deterrence succeeded in frustrating its objectives were rarely considered.

The *DOJOC* rectified a basic problem in previous deterrence thinking by recognizing that an adversary has a choice between complying with a demand to refrain from action and defying that demand—and that the adversary will consider the expected value of each of these options. No longer is "restraint" considered an option that is outside the deterrence calculus for the adversary or the deterrer. This has opened significant doors to making the deterrence planning and assessment processes used by the US military, from Strategic Command to the regional combatant commands, much more sophisticated and, hopefully, effective.

Getting the basic framework correct has led to the next issue: determining how much the adversary desires to undertake particular actions, those that the United States would prefer that it not undertake, and others that might provide less offensive alternatives. This requires assessing adversary intent. Regrettably, there is no set process or framework for undertaking this necessary analysis. The United States merely exhorts intelligence analysts to "take risks" to "predict" adversary intent. Intelligence officers, uniformed and civilian, view the production of such analyses as more of an art than a science without specific methodology—leaving intelligence analysts to develop their own methods to produce their analytic products.[87] Hoping that particular analysts in key positions are da Vincis or Michelangelos is simply unacceptable. Military staffs excel at planning and use set processes to yield acceptable and improvable products. There is a need to establish methodologies for inferring adversary intent on a continuous basis so that a usable product is available to assist in routine planning or in the event of a crisis.

Such a process should begin with a skeleton framework that focuses on producing at least two narratives of adversary behavior: a strategic intent model and an internal logic model. The strategic intent narrative would build a case that the adversary was intending to act to achieve external goals. It should begin with an overview of the adversary's grand strategy: the goals that its leadership has traditionally sought, the goals sought by its current leadership, the environment in which it finds itself and how it facilitates or hinders pursuit of those goals, and the capabilities in its possession to overcome these obstacles and take advantage of situations as they arise. The narrative should also locate the adversary's potential actions in its strategic culture and operational procedures to identify indicators and warnings providing information about intent as events unfold.

The internal logic narrative would build a similar case to explain what the adversary might intend to do, but its focus would be on the internal or domestic imperatives and constraints facing the adversary's leadership. Such a narrative would begin by identifying the structure of the leadership, those who hold those positions, and their relations to one another. It would also identify various internal constituencies upon whom the leadership is dependent or responsible, in particular those who are in a position to sanction or reward those leaders given their behavior. Finally, it would attempt to identify the internal problem that the adversary leaders would attempt to solve by acting externally. As with the strategic intent model, there is need for indicator and warning systems keyed to the reactions of these domestic constituencies to provide information that can confirm or invalidate hypotheses about the adversary's intent as events unfold.

As discussed in the preceding sections, these two frameworks have provided the bases for rival interpretations of adversary behavior from that of the Soviet Union during the Cold War to Iran today.

They have also provided alternative prescriptions for American behavior. Their explicit use would allow debate and discussion in the intent assessment process that could inform a commander or political leader about the issues, foreign and domestic, that are pressing on the adversary's leadership and thereby provide his planning staff the basis for recommending whether deterrence or some other strategy is wise in the present circumstances, and also provide a basis upon which to assess the likelihood of success. Prescribing at least two frameworks, rather than a single consolidated one, would highlight the biases inherent in each framework and those introduced by the analysts themselves, mitigating the dangers of groupthink.[88] This would greatly enhance the ability of commanders to determine when deterrence is wise and necessary and how best to implement it.

Notes

1. Kissinger, *A World Restored*, 2.

2. See Kissinger, *Nuclear Weapons and Foreign Policy*, 316–24; Morgenthau, *Politics among Nations*, 57–67; Gilpin, *War and Change in World Politics*; Schweller, "Bandwagoning for Profit"; Schweller, "Neorealism's Status Quo Bias"; and Snyder, "The U.S. and Third World Revolutionary States."

3. Indeed, as Bernard Brodie famously put it, "Thus far the chief purpose of our military establishment has been to win wars. From now on its chief purpose must be to avert them. It can have almost no other useful purpose." Brodie, "Implications for Military Policy," 76.

4. See, for example, Kaufmann, "The Requirements of Deterrence"; George and Smoke, *Deterrence in American Foreign Policy*; and Huth and Russett, "What Makes Deterrence Work?"

5. See Press, *Calculating Credibility*, for a discussion of the constituents of credibility.

6. Previous official conceptions of deterrence have been underdeveloped. Joint Publication (JP) 1-02, *Department of Defense Dictionary of Military and Associated Terms*, defines deterrence as "the prevention from action by fear of the consequences. Deterrence is a state of mind brought about by the existence of a credible threat of unacceptable counter action." This definition does not specify the relationship between "fear" and reasoned consideration of consequences, the nature of the "credible threat of unacceptable counter action," nor its origin. It also reflects and encourages considering deterrence only in the nuclear context. As late as January 2007, the US Air Force, for example, subsumed deterrence under nuclear operations. Air Force Doctrine Document (AFDD) 1-2, *Air Force Glossary*, 11 January 2007, 58, only mentions deterrence in its definition of "mutual assured destruction."

7. Department of Defense (DOD), *Deterrence Operations Joint Operating Concept*, 3 (hereafter cited as *DOJOC*).

8. *DOJOC*, 6.

9. Morgan, *Deterrence Now*, 39.

10. JP 2-0, *Joint Intelligence*.

11. JP 2-0, *Joint Intelligence*, 22 June 2007, IV-13.

12. Ibid., II-9–II-10.

13. Wohlstetter, "Cuba and Pearl Harbor," 691.

14. Simon, *Administrative Behavior*, xxix.

15. Ibid., xxx.

16. Any framework that simplifies reality will not be neutral. It will bias the decision maker's observations and inferences. It will therefore result in at least some misperceptions. See Jervis, *Perception and Misperception in International Politics*. Although Jervis and others make the case that misperceptions inherently undermine the quality of decision making, this is not necessarily the case, as argued by Levy, "Misperception and the Causes of War"; Grigerenzer and Goldstein, "Reasoning the Fast and Frugal Way"; and Goldgeier and Tetlock, "Psychology and International Relations Theory," 4.

17. Allison, *Essence of Decision: Explaining the Cuban Missile Crisis*, 35.

18. Ibid., 36–37.

19. For the relations between these forms of influence, see DOD, *Strategic Communication Joint Integrating Concept*, 101–3.

20. Freedman, "Strategic Coercion," xx.

21. The lack of domestic-level independent variables is considered in Schaub, "Deterrence, Compellence, and Rational Decision Making."

22. Levy, "The Diversionary Theory of War," 259.

23. Lebow, *Between Peace and War*, 66–69.

24. For an overly abstract discussion of these variables, see Bueno de Mesquita, Smith, Siverson, and Morrow, *The Logic of Political Survival*.

25. For a recent study, see Bulé, "Congress, Presidential Approval, and U.S. Dispute Initiation."

26. Rather, their work is seen as providing an alternative to deterrence theory. See Lebow and Stein, "Beyond Deterrence"; Lebow and Stein, "Rational Deterrence Theory"; Huth and Russett, "Testing Deterrence Theory"; and Lebow and Stein, "Deterrence."

27. Seay, "What are the Soviets' Objectives in their Foreign, Military, and Arms Control Policies?" 71.

28. Ibid., 72.

29. Kennan, "Toward Peace on Two Fronts," 378.

30. Warnke, "Apes on a Treadmill"; and Seay, "What Are the Soviets' Objectives?" 76–87.

31. Kissinger, *White House Years*, 118. "The result is a foreign policy free to fill every vacuum, to exploit every opportunity, to act out the implications of its doctrine. Policy is constrained principally by calculations of objective conditions." Ibid., 117.

32. Simes, "Assessing Soviet National Security Strategy."

33. Kennan, "Sources of Soviet Conduct," 861.

34. Kissinger, *White House Years*, 119.

35. Kennan, "Sources of Soviet Conduct," 861.

36. Kissinger, *White House Years*, 119.

37. Kennan, "Sources of Soviet Conduct," 860–61.

38. Ibid., 861. Here Kennan was elaborating on Lenin's dictum: If one encounters steel, withdraw; but if one finds mush, push on (paraphrased).

39. Brodie, "The Atom Bomb as Policy Maker," 23. Also see Garthoff, *Soviet Military Doctrine*, 11; and Kaufmann, "Limited Warfare," 103.

40. Kennan, "Sources of Soviet Conduct," 856–57.

41. See Pipes, "Militarism and the Soviet State"; Pipes, *Survival is Not Enough*; Gray, "SALT II"; Gray, *Missiles against War*; and Odom, "Whither the Soviet Union?"

42. Seay, "What Are the Soviets' Objectives?" 54; and Pipes, "Militarism and the Soviet State," 1.

43. Seay, "What Are the Soviets' Objectives?" 55.

44. Ibid.

45. "Both Nitze and Gray have in mind using the perceived advantages of the Strategic Defense Initiative to push the Soviet Union toward a reformulation of deterrence, from an offense-based mutually assured destruction to a deterrence based upon defensive systems." Seay, "What Are the Soviets' Objectives?" 69–70.

46. Kennan, "Sources of Soviet Conduct," 868, 866.

47. Pipes, *Survival Is not Enough*, 278.

48. Takeyh, *Guardians of the Revolution*, 1–2. Also see Posen, *A Nuclear-Armed Iran*, 9; and Giles, "The Crucible of Radical Islam," 146.

49. Byman, Chubin, Ehteshami, and Green, *Iran's Security Policy in the Post-Revolutionary Era*, 8. Also see Eisenstadt, "Living with a Nuclear Iran?" 125.

50. Giles, "Crucible of Radical Islam," 146.

51. Takeyh, *Guardians of the Revolution*, 2, 6. Also see Wehrey et al., *Dangerous but Not Omnipotent*, 9.

52. Posen, *Nuclear-Armed Iran*, 8.

53. Eisenstadt, "Living with a Nuclear Iran?" 129.

54. Timmerman, "The Day after Iran Gets the Bomb," 121.

55. Ledeen, *The Iranian Time Bomb*, 24–25.

56. Pollack, *The Persian Puzzle*, 406.

57. Ibid., 384–85.

58. Posen, *Nuclear-Armed Iran*, 24.

59. Eisenstadt, "Living with a Nuclear Iran?" 134–35. Also see Eisenstadt, "Deter and Contain."

60. Rubin, "The Containment Conundrum," 164.

61. Berman et al., "Iran's Nuclear Threat," 2.

62. Davies, "Inside Out or Outside In," 213. It should be noted that Davies' analysis of dyadic event data from 1990–2004 "suggests that the Iranians tend not to engage in diversionary hostility; rather they encapsulate their problems and avoid confrontation with the United States. The model indicates that the greater the level of domestic conflict within Iran the more cooperative the Iranians become toward the United States." Ibid., 220, 221–22.

63. Chubin, "The Iranian Nuclear Riddle after June 12," 165.

64. Wehrey et al., *Dangerous but not Omnipotent*, 22. Also see Eisenstadt, "Living with a Nuclear Iran?" 131.

65. Takeyh, *Guardians of the Revolution*, 2.

66. Amuzegar, "Iran's Crumbling Revolution," 45.

67. Pollack, *Persian Puzzle*, 388.

68. Ibid., 400–416. "If the Iranians can ever get over their psychological and political hurdles regarding the United States, the Grand Bargain would be the best way to handle our mutual problems," he begins.

69. Takeyh, *Guardians of the Revolution*, 261–65.

70. Eisenstadt, "Living with a Nuclear Iran?" 142, 136.

71. Those who do advocate regime change, such as Timmerman and Ledeen, base their analyses upon the strategic intent model and posit extreme goals for Iran.

72. *DOJOC*, 26–27.

73. Ibid., 21.

74. On the differential weighting of gains and losses generally, see Kahneman, Knetsch, and Thaler, "Anomalies." For an application to the domestic costs of conflict, see Nincic, "Loss Aversion and the Domestic Context of Military Intervention."

75. This is an application of Schelling's art of the commitment. See Schelling, *The Strategy of Conflict*.

76. Byman, "Do Targeted Killings Work?" 96, 105–6.

77. Kalman, "Israeli Fence Puts 'Cage' on Villagers."

78. See Tolbert, *Crony Attack: Strategic Attack's Silver Bullet?*; and Lichbach, *Rebel's Dilemma*. On the other hand, Jerrold Post argues that "Once in the group, though, the power of group dynamics is immense, continually confirming the power of the group's organizing ideology and reinforcing the member's dedication to the cause." Post, "Deterrence in an Age of Asymmetric Rivals," 171.

79. Lichbach, *Rebel's Dilemma*, 7.

80. "Israeli officials said that the destruction of an Arab home with dynamite or bulldozers was a rare, deliberate, and highly publicized event, designed to serve as an effective deterrent to adults who might permit or encourage illegal acts by younger members of their families." Carter, *Palestine: Peace, Not Apartheid*, 123. Israel stopped this policy in February 2005 after it was challenged domestically by human rights groups. "Israel to Destroy Attacker's Home," *BBC News*.

81. Sewall, "Introduction to the University of Chicago Press Edition," xxv.

82. A nice account can be found in Ricks, *The Gamble*, 61–72. For an analysis see Koloski and Kolasheski, "Thickening the Lines."

83. Lebow and Stein, "Beyond Deterrence," 40.

84. There are generally three such bases: consequentialism, authority, or principles. *Consequentialism* is the easiest basis within which to operate as the adversary is considering outcomes, and these are all potential as opposed to actual. They can therefore be altered by shifting the type of problem to be solved, and hence the solution set from which it is appropriate to consider options. *Authority-based* frames are more difficult to affect because they are given to the adversary by another party, one to which the adversary has previously ceded decision authority. Thus a better target for the influence attempt is that entity. But another approach here is to provide the adversary with another authority to which it has previously ceded the decision, one that conflicts with the current authority frame, and make the case that it should switch. Finally, frames based upon *principle* are likewise difficult to affect, although the mechanism is similar: find a principle to which the adversary adheres and make the case that it applies more than the principle that provided the basis for defiance.

85. Jones and Libicki find that only 7 percent of terrorist groups that "ended" in their sample of 268 such groups were defeated by military force. "Militaries tended to be most effective when used against terrorist groups engaged in an insurgency in which the groups were large, well armed, and well organized. Insurgent groups have been among the most capable and lethal terrorist groups, and military force has usually been a neces-

sary component in such cases. Against most terrorist groups, however, military force is usually too blunt an instrument." Jones and Libicki, *How Terrorist Groups End*, xiii–xiv.

86. Langdon, Sarapu, and Wells, "Targeting the Leadership of Terrorist and Insurgent Movements," found that killing the leader of a nonstate movement led to the disbanding or moderation of the movement in 61 percent of the cases that they examined.

87. Personal interviews with author.

88. For more on motivated and unmotivated biases see Jervis, *Perception and Misperception in International Politics*. On groupthink see Janis, *Groupthink*; and Turner and Pratkanis, "Theoretical Perspectives on Groupthink." Alexander L. George prescribes multiple assessments and other process fixes to this dilemma in "The Case for Multiple Advocacy in Making Foreign Policy," as does Hart in "Preventing Groupthink Revisited."

Chapter 10

Deterring Nonstate Actors

Adam Lowther

In the aftermath of World War II, the United States took center stage in an international system dramatically different from the one that existed a decade earlier. As the Cold War took shape in the late 1940s, the United States played the protagonist to a Soviet Union seeking to export communism around the world. One school of thought regarding US foreign policy holds that Americans traditionally prefer to remain aloof from international politics.[1] In the twentieth century US policy makers repeatedly departed from this perspective—in both world wars, the Korean War, and in taking the lead to form the United Nations and the North Atlantic Treaty Organization—to pursue and protect the country's interests. As the expansionist ideology of the Soviet Union threatened to overwhelm the free world during the Cold War, American policy makers—armed with the atom bomb—developed a grand strategy for containing the Soviet Union that ultimately succeeded.[2]

Among the most important of these early strategies was deterrence. In the early years of the Cold War, the Eisenhower administration's New Look policy focused on deterring the Soviet Union by threatening to launch a massive nuclear strike in response to conventional or nuclear aggression.[3] Although deterrence and nuclear weapons need not be coupled, they became inextricably linked for more than a half century.

As the Cold War came to an end after nearly a half century, deterrence fell by the wayside as the United States sought to take advantage of the peace dividend that was the fruit of victory.[4] In the 1990s a strategy of globalization and a policy of engagement with the world supplemented deterrence. No longer did the United States simply seek to prevent the spread of communism. It also sought to assist the former Eastern Bloc countries as they attempted to develop market economies and democratic institutions. This approach to the world saw the United States take on policing the world, as it made the world safe for democracy by addressing threats to international order.[5]

Lasting less than a decade, the relative tranquility of America's "hege-monic moment" was shattered by the attacks of 11 September 2001. Although the United States was well aware of al-Qaeda's desire to strike a painful blow, as the amorphous organization attempted on at least five previous occasions, the use of commercial aircraft as mis-siles to strike the US homeland caught the nation off guard.[6] Where America's previous responses to al-Qaeda attacks were largely ineffec-tive, a new president and an enraged public would bring the full might of the American military to bear in Afghanistan and anywhere else al-Qaeda and its affiliates might seek refuge. The "global war on terror" had begun.[7]

Within the United States, this new approach to terrorism signaled a dramatic shift in the balance of power within the international rela-tions liberalism school of thought. Throughout the 1990s a war of words filled the pages of Beltway publications as the two factions—economic globalists and neoconservatives—fought for supremacy.[8] Advocates of economic globalization came to dominate public policy and succeeded in keeping their ideological competitors from ascend-ing to power in the federal bureaucracy. This changed with the 2000 election and the victory of neoconservatism. Where economic global-ists sought to remake world order through the largely peaceful develop-ment of social-market democracy and international institutions, neoconservatives believed in the utility of force to achieve similar objectives.[9] Preemption and a concerted effort to impose democracy in strategic regions became the underlying initiatives of the post–9/11 Bush administration.[10] Conspicuously absent from any position of prominence in the debate were the realists, who had dominated foreign policy decision making throughout the Cold War, but this, too, would eventually change.

On 7 October 2001, the United States invaded Afghanistan. Early success has been followed by a persistent and growing Taliban insur-gency. Thus, few were surprised when former NATO commander in Afghanistan Gen Stanley McChrystal wrote of the urgent need for more troops to secure victory. US operations in Iraq turned out very differently and appeared to indicate the emergence of a stable govern-ment. Some analysts are concerned, however, that opponents of the regime are biding their time as the Americans withdraw forces from the country.[11] Only time will tell if Iraq was a victory.

Whatever the outcome of these two conflicts may eventually be, they had a profound effect on the 2008 US presidential election. After eight years of conflict, war fatigue was apparent during the campaign—Americans wanted change. That change came in the form of Senator Barack Obama (D-IL) and a Democrat majority in both houses of Congress. With his election as president, it became clear that US foreign policy would take a new approach. It was from that milieu that an emphasis on deterrence reemerged. It did so, however, in a much different world from the one in which it once held sway. Rather than facing a peer competitor in a bipolar international system, the primary security challenges the United States appears to confront in a post–9/11 security environment come in the form of nonstate actors.

Although post–World War II deterrence strategy was designed to deter a Soviet nuclear attack, today's scholars and policy makers are asking if deterrence can be applied against the nation's current adversaries.[12] This chapter seeks to examine that possibility by addressing five central questions:

1. What is deterrence?

2. What is a nonstate actor?

3. Do nonstate actors pose a threat to the United States?

4. Is it possible to deter a nonstate actor?

5. How do you deter nonstate actors?

What Is Deterrence?

According to Joint Publication 1-02, *Department of Defense Dictionary of Military and Associated Terms*, deterrence is "the prevention from action by fear of the consequences. Deterrence is a state of mind brought about by the existence of a credible threat of unacceptable counteraction." By design, deterrence aims to achieve a specific psychological effect, which causes an adversary to alter potential behavior. Since deterrence is comprised of two components—capability and credibility—its success or failure is based on the ability of A to convince B that altering the status quo presents risks that outweigh potential benefits.

Although deterrence and nuclear weapons have been closely linked for a half century, the concept of deterrence is far older than its modern understanding. Human history is replete with examples of individuals, tribes, empires, and states using deterrence to dissuade adversaries from taking an undesired action.[13] One familiar example is worth noting. After the Congress of Vienna (1814–15), Great Britain served as the balancer in Europe by ensuring that neither a Franco–Russian alliance nor the German states and Austria–Hungary were able to dominate the continent. By siding with the weaker alliance, Britain sought to deter the stronger.[14] This is only one of many examples of deterrence at work. As historians will certainly note, the Concert of Europe ultimately failed with the outbreak of World War I—after nearly a century of relative stability on the continent. Like all approaches to foreign policy, deterrence does not guarantee permanent peace. The relevant point is that deterrence may be applied against actors at any level of analysis (individual, domestic, or international).

One recent effort to revitalize deterrence is the US Strategic Command's (STRATCOM) *Deterrence Operations Joint Operating Concept* (*DOJOC*), which clearly illustrates that the US military is not "stuck in a Cold War mind-set."[15] The *DOJOC* is a clear sign that STRATCOM and the DOD understand the changing nature of the strategic environment and the need to evolve deterrence strategy. The document exemplifies the collaboration taking place between academia and the military as the two work together to develop a broader approach to nuclear and conventional deterrence in a world that is no longer dominated by the bipolar competition of the United States and the Soviet Union. In attempting to develop an approach to deterrence that incorporates the range of conventional and nuclear threats, the authors of the *DOJOC* have undertaken a very difficult task.

The Deterrence Spectrum

While somewhat different than the approach used in the *DOJOC*, one way of conceptualizing deterrence is to think of it as a continuous spectrum with three components (fig. 10.1). At one end is deterrence by dissuasion.[16] At the other end is deterrence by threat.[17] In the middle is deterrence by denial.[18] Moving from left to right increases the level of action by the state seeking to deter an ally or adversary. The specific design of a deterrence strategy will depend on the value of the interest at stake and the capabilities of both A and B. Because the target of deterrence may be either an ally or adversary, a hostile relationship is not required.

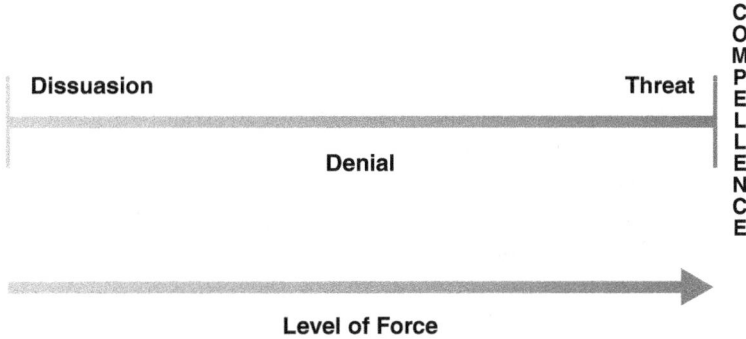

Figure 10.1. Deterrence model

Deterrence by Dissuasion

The most passive component of deterrence, deterrence by dissuasion can take a number of forms, such as efforts to influence target-nation public opinion, public diplomacy, or propaganda, or the offer of a benefit for maintaining the status quo. Dissuasive efforts are notably different from deterrence by threat because they do incorporate the threat of violence or punitive action.[19]

Deterrence by Denial

Deterrence by denial seeks to deny the target a desired objective through largely defensive measures. By increasing the risks a target must accept to achieve an objective while also reducing the probability of success, it may be possible to deter a target effectively. Denial can take a number of forms as well. Effective policing, passenger and cargo screening, intelligence gathering, and "no fly" and watch lists are all among the means of deterrence by denial.[20]

Deterrence by Threat

The overt use of a specific threat can range from the low (targeted strike) to the high (invasion) end of conflict.[21] Threats can also incorporate punitive measures, including diplomatic and economic sanctions. For the threat to be effective, it must pose greater costs on the target than the reward for altering the status quo. Credibility is the key if deterrence by threat is to work.[22] Empty threats only serve to undermine deterrence. Once a threat is issued, its issuer must be prepared to carry it out.

Any or all three components of deterrence can be combined at any time. There is no requirement that a deterrence strategy begin with dissuasion and progress to a threat. The interests at stake, the actor's objectives—seeking to deter—and the available means for deterrence play vital roles in determining the design of a strategy. The greater the interest at stake, the more likely deterrence by threat will play a role in a deterrence strategy.

In the event that deterrence fails, reversing the new status quo may require applying punitive measures against the target. *Compellence*, as this strategy is called, attempts to force a return to the previous status quo. If effective, the credibility of future deterrence may increase. Thus, deterrence and compellence can work as a feedback loop where the effectiveness of one increases or decreases the need and effectiveness of the other.

What Is a Nonstate Actor?

When major European powers agreed to the Peace of Westphalia (1648) ending the Thirty Years' War, the modern nation-state was born.[23] In the years since the nation-state came to dominate the international system, states have never been its only actors. Super-empowered individuals, private organizations, religious movements, transnational ethnic groups, and economic interests have long exerted influence in international relations. While the term *nonstate actor* is generally associated with the likes of al-Qaeda and other terrorist groups, the term is not limited to these groups. The International Committee of the Red Cross, established in 1863, is one example of a nonstate actor founded to provide medical aid to wounded soldiers—very different from the negative stereotype. Modern violent Islamic fundamentalists are not even unique in their role as a negative example of a nonstate actor.[24] In the half-century between 1881 and 1914 left-wing revolutionary anarchists assassinated a number of world leaders and prominent citizens in their efforts to spark social revolution.[25] They, too, were nonstate actors.

Modern nonstate actors fall into two categories—peaceful and violent.[26] Peaceful nonstate actors are the most numerous. They include international nongovernmental organizations, international religious organizations, multinational corporations, super-empowered individuals, and transnational diaspora groups. Violent nonstate actors include international criminal organizations, terrorist networks, and insurgent groups.[27] Because the former operate within the bounds of national and international law, they need not be deterred. The latter, however, flaunt national and international laws and are a focus of deterrence. Violent nonstate actors are divided into the three groups mentioned above because the composition, objectives, and tactics of each often differ.

International Criminal Organizations

International criminal organizations include a variety of groups.[28] The Mexican and Colombian drug cartels, for example, grow, process, and export illegal drugs. The majority of cartel members are young men who view the drug trade as their best opportunity for material success. When governments interfere with their enterprise, violence frequently results. Currently, Mexican cartels present a real challenge to Mexico's government in its border states.[29]

The Italian, Japanese, and Russian mafias engage in the distribution of drugs, arms trafficking, prostitution, human trafficking, and other illegal activities. They, too, are composed largely of young men who desire greater economic success through criminal enterprise. With few exceptions, the various criminal organizations have shown a reluctance to challenge national governments directly. However, their methods and their products weaken societies at both the production and distribution ends of the supply chain.

Terrorist Groups

In *How Terrorist Groups End*, Seth Jones and Martin Libicki suggest that terrorist groups can be divided into four types: left-wing (Marxist-Leninist, animal rights, environmental, anarchical, and anti-globalization), right-wing (neo-Nazi and neo-fascist), nationalist (Hamas, Hezbollah, Irish Republican Army, Kurdistan Workers Party, and Tamil Tigers, etc.), and religious (al-Qaeda and Jemaah Islamiyah, etc.).[30] While each focuses on violence against civilians to achieve political objectives, each group's motivation and desired end state vary. As Jones and Libicki note, the end state sought by a group largely determines its probability of success. The more limited the objectives, the higher the likelihood of achieving them. For example, the Irish Republican Army (IRA), a nationalist group, was able to negotiate a political settlement with the British government through *Sin Fein* because IRA objectives were finite and both parties were willing to negotiate. On the other hand, al-Qaeda seeks to topple the governments of the Middle East to restore the Islamic Caliphate.[31] Neither al-Qaeda nor the governments of the region are willing to negotiate. Thus, reaching some sort of accommodation is unlikely.

Modern history suggests that types of terrorism often wax and wane.[32] As mentioned earlier, the first episode of terrorism in the modern era began late in the nineteenth century with assassinations by left-wing anarchists. By espousing an ideology in opposition to ordered society, anarchists proved difficult to organize. Thus, their efforts to destroy society ultimately ended with the onset of World War I.

The dramatic change in the international system brought about by World War II led to a second episode of terrorism. As European colonialism collapsed in the postwar years, nationalist groups turned to terrorism to garner independence for their nation or ethnic group. Some achieved their objectives in a few years; others did not and they continue to exist. By the 1960s, left-wing terrorism was on the rise again as Marxist-Leninist groups used terrorist tactics to spur revolution around the globe, often with the support of the Soviet Union. The Red Brigades (Italy), the Red Army Faction (Germany), and the Weather Underground (USA) all struck domestic targets between 1960 and 1990. Like their left-wing predecessors, they too failed.[33] Today, religious terrorism directly challenges international order. Led by imams preaching a violent interpretation of Salafism, al-Qaeda and its affiliates are responsible for the deadliest period of terrorism in history.[34] While they are unlikely to achieve victory, these groups are proving to be resilient.

Insurgent Groups

Separating insurgents and terrorists into distinct categories is a common practice, but it is a somewhat arbitrary distinction.[35] Both terrorists and insurgents seek to alter the status quo, but terrorists, by virtue of their weakness, are defined by the tactic they employ. Insurgents, on the other hand, are defined by their objectives. As David Galula wrote, perceived grievances drive insurgents into "challenging a *local* ruling power controlling the existing administration, police, and armed forces." Galula adds, "An insurgency is a *protracted struggle* conducted methodically, step by step, in order to attain specific inter-mediate objectives leading finally to the overthrow of the existing order."[36] Insurgents engage in revolutionary warfare, but their violence focuses primarily on the military, police, and government supporters. While insurgents may use terrorism on specific occasions, as Mao Zedong recognized, the people are the center of gravity for insurgents and counterinsurgents alike, and their support is the key to victory.[37]

Perhaps because insurgents actively engage in attempts to seize and hold territory and to replace an existing regime, they are accorded a status above terrorists, but they often vary only in their capabilities. Both terrorists and insurgents are fundamentally dissatisfied with the existing order and are willing to use violence to alter it.[38]

Do Nonstate Actors Pose a Threat to the United States?

To understand the threat nonstate actors pose to the United States, it is helpful to have first a firm grasp of the United States' national interest. Figure 10.2 shows one way to view the nation's interests.[39]

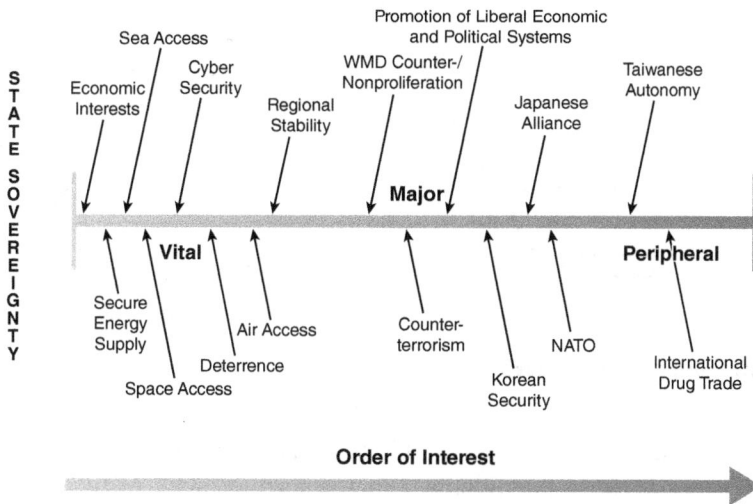

Figure 10.2. National interests

Moving from left to right, interests move from vital to peripheral— declining in importance. Vital interests are most important to the nation and are of sufficient importance that the United States will go to war to protect them.[40] Major interests will not precipitate the large-scale use of military force, but a threat to them can lead to limited use of military force. Diplomatic coercion and economic sanctions are, however, much more common. Peripheral interests do not directly affect state sovereignty (survival) or economic interests. In many instances they are associated with the cultural and moral preferences and norms of the nation and its citizenry but are not of significant importance to the United States to solicit more than a negligible response to their violation.

Historically, violent nonstate actors have not presented existential threats to the United States. This is to say they can only pose limited risks to the vital interests of the nation and have yet to threaten its survival.[41] As figure 10.3 illustrates, nonstate actors are likely the most numerous threat, but also the least dangerous of any potential adversaries.

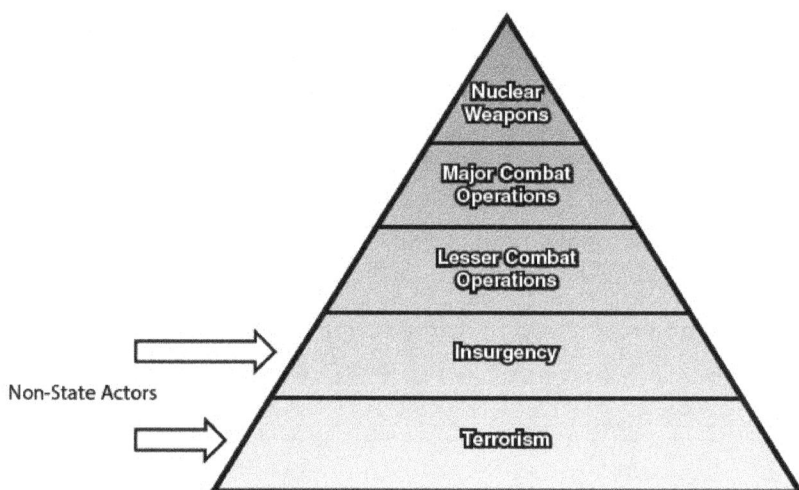

Nuclear Weapons

Major Combat Operations

Lesser Combat Operations

Insurgency

Non-State Actors

Terrorism

Figure 10.3. Conflict pyramid

Violent nonstate actors are capable of posing threats to the major and peripheral interests of the United States and they may one day prove much more formidable. But the current state of technology (even with cyberterrorism) and the structure of the international system do not provide nonstate actors with the means to challenge the United States' sovereignty or vital interests directly.[42]

As the attacks of 9/11 illustrate, the United States is susceptible to terrorist attack. On that day, almost 3,000 civilians were killed and over $1 trillion worth of damage was inflicted.[43] Since the invasion of Afghanistan, more than 900 Americans have given their lives in Operation Enduring Freedom. In Iraq more than 4,000 Americans have died fighting an insurgency that, until 2011, proved difficult to defeat.[44]

The fiscal cost of both wars exceeds $1 trillion and continues to rise.[45] While the ultimate outcome in Afghanistan and Iraq is yet to be determined, it is clear that the cost of defeating nonstate actors in both countries is significant. Thus, nonstate actors clearly pose a risk to the United States, but fortunately, that risk is limited.

Can Violent Nonstate Actors Be Deterred?

Providing an answer to this question is as complex and varied as the actors the United States seeks to deter. According to terrorism experts Paul Davis and Brian Michael Jenkins:

> Although causing a member of al-Qaeda to change his stripes may be out of the question, deterring individuals from attacking individual targets is not. To the contrary, the empirical record shows that even hardened terrorists dislike operational risks and may be deterred by uncertainty and risk. A foot soldier may willingly give his life in a suicide mission, and organizations may be quite willing to sacrifice such pawns, but mission success is very important and leaders are in some ways risk-averse.[46]

With three distinct types of violent nonstate actors (international criminal organizations, terrorist groups, and insurgents), the motivations, objectives, and grievances of each make it difficult to develop a standard approach to deterrence. Thinking about deterrence in terms that were appropriate during the Cold War offers limited utility for today. Three examples illustrate the differences in deterring a nonstate actor and a Cold War–era nation-state. First, unlike states, nonstate actors do not exercise sovereignty over a given territory—in fact, they often seek to undermine state credibility by attacking the state's ability to exercise sovereign control over its territory.[47] Because the sovereign territory of a nation-state is more easily held at risk, it is possible to threaten that control and deter a nation. This is a key difficulty in the relationship between states and nonstate actors; often nonstate actors can deter states more effectively than states can deter their nonstate adversaries. Second, nonstate actors lack clearly identifiable centers of gravity that can be readily targeted.[48] For a nation-state, the capital, military forces, or political leadership usually function as the centers of gravity. Third, nonstate actors exist to change the status quo, unlike nation-states.[49] States have an inherent desire to protect that which they already possess, which makes them susceptible to coercion should they desire a change in the status quo. These and other differences between nonstate actors and nation-states make deterrence of violent nonstate actors a far more complex and difficult task today.

If deterrence is understood as operating along the spectrum proposed—with deterrence by dissuasion, denial, and threat available for application—it may be possible to devise a deterrence strategy that is effective in deterring some, if not all, violent nonstate actors. As in economics, there is a diminishing marginal utility for deterrence efforts.[50] Although it may be possible to deter every threat by putting a border patrol agent along every inch of the US border, turning every American home into a fortress, or conducting a complete background investigation of every person entering the United States, such efforts would be cost prohibitive. Absolute certainty is not possible when attempting to deter nonstate actors. Thus, it is imperative that any deterrence strategy provide the greatest level of deterrence at the lowest possible cost.

Some nonstate actors, such as al-Qaeda, are less likely to be deterred permanently.[51] With objectives that offer little room for negotiation or addressing specific grievances, there are virtually no options but destruction of the group.

Developing a detailed understanding of each nonstate actor's motivations, objectives, and desired end state is necessary to determine the efficacy of a deterrence strategy.[52] Simply dismissing a terrorist group as a gang of bloodthirsty killers—and therefore not susceptible to deterrence—may play well with an angry public, but it ignores what may be legitimate grievances that can be redressed with varying degrees of effort. Nonstate actors should not be dismissed because of the tactics (terrorism, assassination, ambush) they use. This is neither helpful in determining the most effective ways of deterring them nor in designing a strategy for their defeat.

How Do You Deter Violent Nonstate Actors?

Developing an effective deterrence strategy presents no easy task with a readily apparent solution. The simple application of force is insufficient to coerce deterrence targets into maintaining the status quo. Success requires far more than in decades past, but it is possible in some if not every instance.

Know Your Enemy

As previously mentioned, before an effective deterrence strategy can be developed, it is necessary to understand the conditions that gave rise to the criminal organization, terrorist group, or insurgency. Understanding the cultural, economic, historical, and political conditions of the nation in which a nonstate actor develops provides a clear sense of the potential appeal, strength, and longevity of the group or organization. It also enables the strategist to design a set of policies that effectively apply dissuasion, denial, and threat at each of the three levels of analysis (individual, domestic, and international). As figure 10.4 shows, a multipronged approach to deterrence may be most appropriate. But in order to develop such an approach, a thorough knowledge of an adversary and his environment is an essential criterion for success.

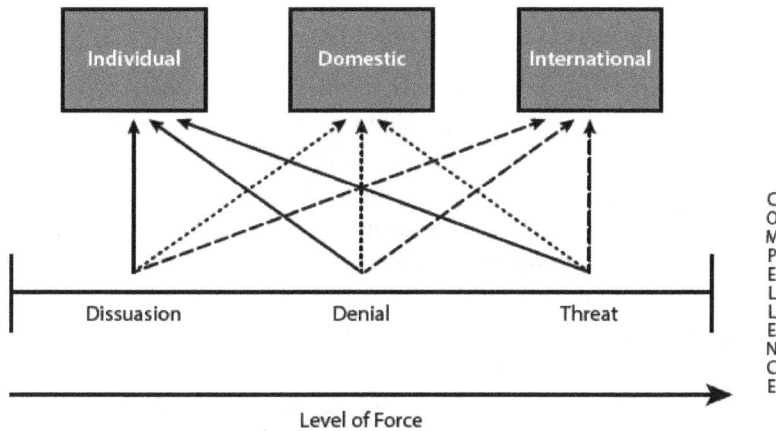

Figure 10.4. Nonstate actor deterrence model

While suggesting "know thy enemy" may appear so fundamental to any deterrence effort that it need not be said, the United States does not have a history of developing an in-depth understanding of its adversaries—Iraq and Afghanistan are cases in point. Instead, American leaders have long relied on the nation's economic and military power to overwhelm any potential adversary. When engaging with nonstate actors, this approach is less successful because this is the very strength that they are actively seeking to challenge.

Violent nonstate actors, particularly those that pose a threat over an extended period of time, are most often found in states with nondemocratic regimes, low levels of economic development, constrained upward mobility, and restrictions on human rights.[53] Rarely do they arise in states with the most oppressive regimes—North Korea, for instance. Instead, they develop and thrive in countries where the citizenry often have legitimate grievances against the government and where bright and well-educated young people experience what Ted Robert Gurr calls "relative deprivation."[54] According to Gurr, citizens rebel because they perceive that their absolute condition should be better than it is, not because it is unacceptable. This state of affairs can give rise to all three types of violent nonstate actors.

For a deterrence strategy to work, specific policies must be developed that target the individual group member, the nation, and society giving rise to a group, and the international system in which nonstate actors operate. A multilayered approach to deterrence offers the greatest chance for success.

Recommendations at the Individual Level

The design of a deterrence-by-dissuasion approach can take a number of forms. First, the United States could wage an active propaganda campaign targeting those most likely to join criminal organizations, insurgencies, or terrorist groups.[55] In most instances the United States is not directly responsible for the deprivation facing many around the globe, but it does a poor job of selling American ideals and efforts to improve lives around the world, leaving millions with an incorrect impression of the United States. Second, the US could actively support and assist those individuals and groups actively challenging the ideologies espoused by many nonstate actors.[56] The imams, for example, who do not support a violent global jihad, are, in many cases, an effective tool in preventing potential members from joining a terrorist group. Third, the United States could sponsor alternative organizations that provide an outlet for disaffected individuals to express their concerns, turn to for support, and find alternatives to violence. As Marc Sageman notes, those who join the jihad tend to be new to a foreign country, lonely, unhappy in their current circumstances, and susceptible to influence.[57] Providing alternative organizations to radical mosques can prevent the conversion of many to the terrorists' cause.

Deterrence by denial can also take a number of forms. First, effective security measures at airports, border crossings, and seaports act as an active defense that may deter some seeking to carry out terrorist attacks.[58] As the probability of a successful attack decreases, the probability of successful deterrence increases. For terrorists, a failed attack is worse than no attack at all. Second, potential targets should be hardened. A passive defense may be sufficient to convince an attacker that success is unlikely. Third, effective intelligence gathering, policing, and forensic investigation may be successful in convincing individual group members that they will be denied the anonymity they seek.

Deterrence by threat is undoubtedly what Americans are most familiar with, but current efforts have not proven as effective as desired. As Audrey Kurth Cronin notes, targeted assassination and related approaches to addressing terrorism may have some deterrent value, but they are difficult for democratic leaders and societies to accept as a legitimate means of deterring violent nonstate actors.[59] However, the threat of violence can have a positive effect, but only if backed by a credible ability to target that which a violent nonstate actor values most and seeks to prevent its harm. While violent nonstate actors use what Moises Naim calls "the five wars of globalization"—illegal trade in drugs, arms, intellectual property, people, and money—to further their causes, current government efforts to control these adversaries are having only limited effect.[60] Although a number of cases exist where governments used massive repression and violence in an attempt to eradicate terrorist organizations—some successfully—the indiscriminant use of violence often leads to pyrrhic victories.[61]

Instead, the threatened use of violence should be precisely targeted at that which individual violent nonstate actors hold dear. Developing the ability to devise such an approach requires an intimate knowledge of the individuals comprising terrorist networks or organizations. Again, the threat of violence and its ultimate use is not the only approach to deterring and defeating violent nonstate actors. They are parts of an integrated strategy that layers a variety of policies designed to prevent terrorism and other acts of violence.

While the threat of massive retaliation must always remain an option to underscore deterrence credibility and eradicate criminals, insurgents, and terrorists, states will stand a better chance in the competition against violent nonstate actors if they have a robust tool kit that applies an array of options to the deterrence calculus.

Recommendations at the Domestic Level

Because nonstate actors are dissatisfied with the status quo in a world dominated by nation-states, focusing deterrence at the state or society levels is as important, if not more so, as directing it at the individual. Much counterinsurgency literature describes "the people" as the center of gravity.[62] Win the support of the people, and the insurgency can be defeated. While accomplishing this feat is no easy task, it plays an important role in defeating criminal organizations and terrorist groups as well.

Deterrence by dissuasion offers the opportunity to apply a number of policies directed at political leaders and societies. First, the United States should work with foreign leaders to address the possible legitimate grievances of some nonstate actors.[63] While political leaders in the nondemocratic nations from which most terrorist and insurgent groups develop will not accede to free and fair elections, it is possible for American policy makers to use the considerable leverage of the United States to promote economic and human rights reforms. This is a desirable option because it has the potential to reduce or eliminate the grievances that give rise to violent nonstate actors and the opportunity to show the United States in a positive light. As the civil war in Libya illustrates, American leaders are apt to interpret the United States' interests very broadly, which can lead to intervention when a nation experiences internal instability. Thus, encouraging national leaders to address grievances well before terrorist groups and insurgencies develop stands to limit more invasive American involvement around the world.

Second, and related, a more effective societywide use of pro-American propaganda could dramatically improve the United States' image around the world.[64] Such efforts were highly successful during the Cold War and may be successful in the present security context. Since the end of the Cold War, organizations such as the Voice of America have been largely ineffectual in promoting a generally positive view of the United States. It is time to mobilize national capabilities to combat poisonous ideologies as was done against communism during the Cold War. This can be done with relatively limited fiscal resources, while repeating significant gains.

Third, the president and the secretary of state could take a more active role in discouraging allies—those with large populations of discontented citizens—from using state-controlled media to blame domestic ills on the United States, which is rarely responsible.[65] This practice is more than a half-century old in the Middle East. Authoritarian regimes employ this method of obfuscation in order to turn the ire of their people away from the regime's failures. In many instances, the regimes that are guilty of this practice are allies or friends of the United States.

Deterrence by denial can also play an important role at the domestic level. Illiberal regimes are susceptible to a denial of economic benefits tied to reform.[66] Again, eliminating the grievances that give rise to nonstate violence and lead segments of society to support them is necessary. The United States can also provide many states the training and support necessary to create honest and effective police forces—a common problem in many countries.[67] Denying nonstate actors anonymity through successful local policing may be sufficient to defeat them. Additionally, the United States can deny allies the military aid they often receive. American troops play a key role in assisting, funding, and training local military forces as part of ongoing foreign internal defense (known as FID) programs. Loss of US assistance might force these regimes to address the grievances of nonstate actors or face a serious challenge to the regime.[68]

Deterrence by threat may be the most effective way to apply domestic pressure. American forces can assist local forces in presenting a clear military threat to insurgent or terrorist groups.[69] The United States can also encourage political leaders—in susceptible countries—to place significant resources and time into addressing their internal problems by clearly communicating that the United States will not respect territorial sovereignty when hunting down those who have attacked the American people. The United States can also make it clear that it will hold governments accountable for the acts of their citizens.[70] For example, Saudi Arabia turned a blind eye to Wahhabi jihadists as long as terrorism was directed externally. Only when the kingdom became a target did the king act. Other "allies" are undertaking similar, and unacceptable, approaches. Thus, a change in approach by the United States could go a long way in deterring violent nonstate actors.

Recommendations at the International Level

Because nonstate actors are not recognized participants in the international system, it is more difficult to design deterrence policies at this level. However three specific policies can assist in deterring these groups. First, the international community, led by the United States, can bring significant weight to bear in creating a broad cultural rejection of the tactics used by violent nonstate actors.[71] If the international community could, for example, reach consensus on a definition of terrorism, it may be possible to create a broader dissuasive effect that filters down to the societal and individual levels. As examples such as the Irish Republican Army (IRA) and al-Qaeda illustrate, significant funding and support for local activities comes from international sources.[72] Thus, developing a consensus on what is and is not acceptable behavior has the potential to assist in eliminating these sources of support.

Second, improved intelligence gathering and greater cooperation across national intelligence agencies can significantly contribute to denying potential criminals and terrorists the ability to travel internationally, to launder illicit funds, and to communicate with other members and supporters around the globe.[73] Interagency and multinational cooperation does occur, but there is certainly room for improvement. However, the case of PFC Bradley Manning and Wikileaks has undermined efforts to promote openness among the federal government's information and intelligence-gathering organizations, making this recommendation more difficult than before.[74]

Third, the United States could shift to a policy of offshore balancing in much of the world. As Robert Pape notes in his work on suicide terrorism, groups within countries where American forces are present perceive the presence of American troops in the Middle East and elsewhere as a threat to the "homeland." Pape suggests that moving US forces offshore will likely reduce the perceived threat. Thus, a reduction in terrorism and insurgent activity may occur as a result.[75]

Conclusion

Developing an effective deterrence strategy for today's adversaries is more complex and difficult than at any time in American history. The range of adversaries confronting the United States is staggering. Developing tailored approaches to deterring our adversaries may provide the United States with a more effective solution to the challenges facing the nation. Addressing common misconceptions in a variety of areas will enable the United States to develop a clearer picture of the threats facing the American people and assist in developing workable approaches to protecting the nation's interests.

In some instances, deterrence will prove effective. In others, it will not. Neither political leaders nor the American people should expect deterrence to work in every case in which it is applied. Deterrence can never be the sole strategy of the United States. It must work in conjunction with other strategies designed to accomplish national objectives through alternative means. Through the layered approach suggested, the United States may have a greater probability of succeeding in ongoing efforts to defend the country and its interests.

Notes

1. Doenecke, "American Isolationism, 1939–1941"; Astore, "The New American Isolationism"; and Patterson, et al., *American Foreign Relations*, 133–135.

2. Gaddis, *Strategies of Containment*, 53–96.

3. Ibid., 162–96.

4. Nichols, *Eve of Destruction*, 46–52.

5. Stiglitz, *Globalization and Its Discontents*, 3–22.

6. Falk and Morgenstern, *Suicide Terror*, 275.

7. Belasco, *The Cost of Afghanistan, Iraq and Other Global War on Terror Operations since 9/11*.

8. The debate between these two perspectives was, and is, seen regularly in publications such as the *Weekly Standard*, the *Nation*, the *New York Times,* the *National Interest*, the *New Republic, Blueprint Magazine, Foreign Affairs*, and the *Atlantic Monthly*. Perhaps the most well-known neoliberal is Harvard University professor and former Clinton administration assistant secretary of defense for international security affairs Joseph Nye. During the George W. Bush administration, neoconservatives such as William Kristol, Robert Kagan, Paul Wolfowitz, and Douglas Feith rose to prominence. See Ehrman, *The Rise of Neoconservatism*.

9. Kristol, "The Neoconservative Persuasion"; and Vaisse, *Neoconservatism*, 110–47.

10. Miller, "Explaining Changes in U.S. Grand Strategy."

11. "Al Maliki Defiant in Face of Regime's Opponents," *Arizona Daily Star*.

12. See Lebovic, *Deterring International Terrorism and Rogue States*.

13. Naroll, Bullough, and Naroll, *Military Deterrence in History*.

14. Sheehan, *The Balance of Power: History & Theory*, 122–45.

15. US Strategic Command, *Deterrence Operations Joint Operating Concept*.

16. Roberts, "Deterrence and WMD Terrorism," 275.

17. Payne, *Deterrence in the Second Nuclear Age*, 129–32.

18. Jackson, Frelinger, Lostumbo, and Button, *Evaluating Novel Threats to the Homeland*, 95.

19. Luttwak, *Strategy*, 225–32; and Kugler, "Dissuasion as a Strategic Concept."

20. Pape, "Coercion and Military Strategy"; and Byman and Waxman, *Dynamics of Coercion*, 50–56, 80–91.

21. Brodie, *Strategy in the Missile Age*, 264–304.

22. Kahn, *On Thermonuclear War*, 26–35.

23. White, *Nation, State, and Territory*, 121–40.

24. An Ismaili terrorist movement was established by Hassan-i-Sabbah, ca. 1080. These people were known derisively as "Hasishin" or "users of hashish." This is where the modern word "assassin" and the words for "murder" in some other languages come from. These assassins were called "Fida'i" meaning "self-sacrificing agents." The point here is that Muslim terrorism is indeed ancient.

25. Ward, *Anarchism*.

26. Mulaj, *Violent Non-state Actors*, 1–27; and Peters, Koechlin, Förster, and Fenner Zinkernagel, *Non-State Actors as Standard Setters*.

27. Naim, "Five Wars of Globalization."

28. Richards, *Transnational Criminal Organizations, Cybercrime, and Money Laundering*, 2–20.

29. Mainwaring, *A Contemporary Challenge to State Sovereignty*, 23–33.

30. Jones and Libicki, *How Terrorist Groups End*, 15.

31. Blanchard, *Al-Qaeda*.

32. Carr, *Lessons of Terror*, 161–165.

33. Jones and Libicki, *How Terrorist Groups End*, 25–29, 35–43.

34. Nance, *An End to Al Qaeda*, 134–36; and Rabasa, et al., *Beyond al Qaeda*, 35–36.

35. Shultz and Dew, *Insurgents, Terrorists, and Militias*, 17–37.

36. Galula, *Counterinsurgency Warfare*, 1–2. Emphasis is in the original.

37. Mao, *On Guerilla Warfare*, 41.

38. See Snow, *Uncivil Wars*, 3–24; and Jenkins, *Unconquerable Nation*, 74–76.

39. The *National Security Strategy* (NSS) describes the nation's "enduring national interests" as

- Security: The security of the United States, its citizens, and US allies and partners.
- Prosperity: A strong innovative and growing US economy in an open international economic system that promotes opportunity and prosperity.
- Values: Respect for universal values at home and around the world.
- International Order: An international order advanced by US leadership that promotes peace, security, and opportunity through stronger cooperation to meet global challenges.

The *NSS* is overly generic in its description of national interests, failing to describe interests that are readily translatable into policy. *National Security Strategy*, 17.

40. For a detailed explanation of the vital, major, and peripheral categorization used above, see Snow and Drew, *Making Twenty-First-Century Strategy*, 31–1.

41. Coolsaet, *Jihadi Terrorism and the Radicalization Challenge in Europe*, 19; and Lesser, Hoffman, Arquilla, Ronfeldt, and Zanini, *Countering the New Terrorism*, 3.

42. Hoffman, *Inside Terrorism*, 229–56.

43. Biddle, *American Grand Strategy after 9/11*, 20.

44. Fischer, *U.S. Military Casualty Statistics*, 5.

45. Belasco, *The Cost of Iraq, Afghanistan, and Other Global War on Terror Operations since 9/11*.

46. Davis and Jenkins, *Deterrence and Influence in Counterterrorism*, xii.

47. Hoffman, *Inside Terrorism*, 229–56.

48. Steed, *Piercing the Fog of War*, 251.

49. Gareau, *State Terrorism and the United States*, 14–15.

50. The law of diminishing marginal utility holds that as a person increases consumption of a product, while keeping consumption of other products constant, there is a decline in the marginal utility of consuming each additional unit of that product.

51. Geltzer, *US Counterterrorism Strategy and al-Qaeda*, 43–65.

52. Davis and Jenkins, *Deterrence and Influence in Counterterrorism*, 9–28.

53. Jones and Libicki, *How Terrorist Groups End*, 3–4.

54. Gurr, *Why Men Rebel*.

55. Mainwaring, *Deterrence in the 21st Century*, 87–88.

56. See Ismail, *Rethinking Islamist Politics*.

57. Sageman, *Understanding Terror Networks*, 99–136.

58. Lebovic, *Deterring International Terrorism and Rogue States*, 147–76.

59. Cronin, *How Terrorism Ends*, 25.

60. Naim, "The Five Wars of Globalization," 35–36.

61. Cronin, *How Terrorism Ends*, 141–44.

62. See Forest, ed., *Countering Terrorism and Insurgency in the 21st Century*, 38.

63. Moghadam, *The Roots of Terrorism*, 45–65.

64. Forest, *Countering Terrorism and Insurgency in the 21st Century*, 394; and Altheide, *Terrorism and the Politics of Fear*, 87–132.

65. Snow, *Information War*, 130–32.

66. Wilkinson, *Terrorism versus Democracy*, 49–58.

67. Pickering, McCulloch, and Wright-Neville, *Counter-terrorism Policing*, Ch. 4, 71–88.

68. Ucko, *The New Counterinsurgency Era*, 88–90.

69. Ganor, *Counter-Terrorism Puzzle*, 63–96.

70. Lebovic, *Deterring International Terrorism and Rogue States*, 104–76.

71. Omilecheva, *Counterterrorism Policies in Central Asia*, 8–10.

72. Johannes and Marc, "Aftermath: Investigation and Mobilization: Irish Nationalists May Feel US's Funding Squeeze"; and Lichtblau, "Threats and Responses."

73. Schaffer, "Detecting Terrorist Financing through Financial Intelligence."

74. Gould, "Pfc. Faces 22 New Charges in Wikileaks Case."

75. Pape, "Suicide Terrorism and Democracy."

Chapter 11

Space Strategic Deterrence

Achieving Space Superiority

Dale Hayden

Today, America's preeminence in space is being challenged. The United States relies more heavily on space than any other nation. However, that reliance has also created a vulnerability—presenting an attractive target for potential adversaries. The nation's vulnerabilities in space are most apparent in the area of assured access to space—a national priority. Presently, the United States has limited ability to protect its space assets or to deny the actions of others in space, which has made "space superiority" only a concept and not an operational reality. Except for direct strikes against launch sites, the United States lacks any true capability to deny another nation's access to space.

Before going further into the discussion of strategic space deterrence, it might be helpful to understand more about the medium and how the United States has arrived at its current reliance upon space assets. Operational space exists in principally near-, low-, and high-Earth orbit. By international treaty, space begins at 65,000 feet. It extends upward in all directions from the earth's surface, and it is a global common. Near-Earth orbit begins at 65,000 feet—a little over 12 miles up, low-Earth orbit ranges from approximately 100 to 1,240 miles, and high-Earth orbit generally means geostationary orbit, approximately 22,240 miles up. Near-Earth has eddies and wind currents and is capable of sustaining high-altitude balloons. Low-Earth orbit is where most satellites and the *International Space Station* operate, and high-Earth orbit, or geostationary orbit, is where the capability exists to position a satellite over a specific area on Earth and keep it there.

Why Is Space Important?

Today, no one questions the importance of space operations as an integral part of American national strategy. During the Cold War, the space race represented not only national pride, but national security as well. In the 1960s Vice President Lyndon B. Johnson stated, "One can predict with confidence that failure to master space means being second best in every aspect, in the crucial arena of our Cold War world. In the eyes of the world first in space means first, period; second in space is second in everything."[1] In the past 15 years reliance on space has grown geometrically. Global Positioning System (GPS) receivers are commonplace in many of today's vehicles. Commercial banking is dependent upon satellite communications, and both land-based and satellite cable television receivers rely upon space-based assets. Military reliance is no less dramatic. From intelligence, surveillance, and reconnaissance (ISR) to targeting, satellites provide a technological infrastructure that enables today's precision strike and superiority of the battlespace. But our increased reliance on space capabilities has turned advantages into vulnerabilities and likely targets for potential adversaries. Thus, deterrence becomes paramount in the defense of critical national assets.

Directly related to the missions of deterrence and denial, in 1984 and 1985 the United States tested antisatellite (ASAT) technology, going so far as to launch interceptor missiles from an F-15 toward points in space on four separate occasions. Finally in September 1985, an interceptor missile was launched against an actual target, destroying a gamma ray spectroscopy satellite, *Solwind* P78-1. Congress refused to fund further testing of this technology in 1988, in part due to technical difficulties and in part due to cost growth. In February 2008 the Missile Defense Agency successfully destroyed a failing ISR satellite by firing an interceptor from the Navy's ballistic missile defense cruiser USS *Lake Erie*, using targeting data from the US Air Force. This, however, was not supposed to be an ASAT demonstration. The demonstrated capability was intended for suborbital warheads, objects below the lower limits of low-Earth orbit. Further complicating the issue is the question of how the United States distinguishes an antisatellite weapons launch from any other launch.

During the past 40 years, space exploration under direct governmental control has moved to public and private exploitation; space has become a medium not that different from the land, sea, or air. Gordon Adams, director of Security Policy Studies at George Washington University, puts it this way: "Space is no longer a frontier, used and occupied solely by governments. From an environment in which only governments operated, largely for exploration and military purposes, space has rapidly filled with assets used for intelligence and military operations to civilian communications, to observation and commerce. Today, more launches are dedicated to commercial purposes than to military ones."[2] The numbers support his views. In the year 2010, the commercial space industry generated over $189 billion in worldwide revenue.[3] The largest share of this commercial market was in space products and services, such as the use of satellites to deliver telephone, television, radio, data communications, remote sensing data, and government services, accounting for 37 percent of total commercial space revenues in 2010.[4]

Today, space exploration has even wider connotations. The European Union asserts, "Space systems are strategic assets demonstrating Europe's independence and readiness to assume global responsibilities. The strategic mission of the European Space Policy, jointly developed by the European Commission and the ESA [European Space Agency], is based on the peaceful exploitation of outer space."[5]

As in Europe, space asset usage has become a commonplace occurrence for the average American over the past 50 years. An example is our blind acceptance of the technology of television. When we turn on the TV, we simply expect the picture and sound to be there; no one speaks with awe about how the video and audio waves appear. Many of us will start our day by driving to work in an auto with a graphic display depicting our present location and directing us across town to a predetermined destination. We can gas up using a credit card and then remove money from our account using an automated bank teller machine in a different bank in another part of the country. We will think nothing about the technological wizardry, but these transactions—location, directions, and link to credit card and banking accounts—are all made possible by instantaneous access to multiple satellite constellations, something we all take for granted.

These and other satellite systems can provide navigation for civilian airliners, identify underground water in sub-Saharan Africa, and mark the destruction of the Amazon rain forests, in addition to numerous other everyday services we have all come to expect from a modern society. The failure of a single satellite in May 1998 disabled 80 percent of the pagers in the United States, cable and broadcast transmissions, credit card authorization networks, and corporate communication systems. If the GPS—a multisatellite constellation originally designed for military navigational assistance—were to fail, economic growth, transportation safety, homeland security, and critical national infrastructure in the United States would be put at risk.[6] Space, therefore, whether we realize it or not, plays an increasingly important role in everyday life.

The evolution of space from a frontier to an operating environment serving numerous customers raised a new set of issues for American policy makers. Recognizing the importance of space to US national interests, Congress chartered a review of national security space activities. Released in May 2001, *The Report of the Commission to Assess United States National Security, Space Management and Organization*, better known as the "Space Commission Report," concluded that the security and economic well-being of the United States and its allies and friends depend on the nation's ability to operate successfully in space. To be able to technologically and operationally contribute to peace and stability in a distinctly different but still dangerous and complex global environment, the United States needs to remain at the forefront in space, as we have in the air, on land, and at sea. Further, it must deter others from taking hostile actions against US space assets. Specifically, the United States must have the capability to use space as an integral part of its ability to manage crises, deter conflicts, and, if deterrence fails, prevail in conflict.[7]

Not surprisingly, military reliance on space is no less dramatic than that of today's American public. Satellites provide the technological infrastructure that enables today's precision strike and superiority of the battlespace. The military has long understood the significance of space, recognizing it as the ultimate "high ground" for military operations. Space provides the opportunity for surveillance without the issues of overflight and instantaneous communications capability that enables command and control of forces across the globe. Secretary of the Air Force Dr. James G. Roche stated, "Space capabilities in today's world are no longer 'nice to have,' they've become indispensable at the strategic, operational and tactical levels of war."[8] A decade ago, Peter B. Teets, undersecretary of the Air Force, director of the National Reconnaissance Office, and the senior Department of Defense (DOD) space official, emphasized the critical nature space plays: "I think the recent military conflict [Afghanistan] has shown us, without a doubt, how important the use of space is to national security and military operations."[9]

Gen Norton Schwartz, Air Force chief of staff, stated as recently as 2012,

Even with extraordinary budget pressures, we are protecting—and in some cases, even increasing—investments in our top acquisition priorities, including space systems that we deem critical to Joint war-fighting requirements. In fact, space acquisitions represent 21 percent of all Air Force investment spending, and include 4 of our 10 largest procurement programs: Space-Based Infrared, Global Positioning System–III, and Advanced Extremely-High Frequency systems, and the Evolved Expendable Launch Vehicle.[10]

How Did We Get to Where We Are Now? The Evolution of US National Space Policy

While it may be simplistic to state that it all began with a single launch—it all began with the Soviet Union's *Sputnik* launch in 1957, which made the USSR the first space-faring nation. That launch shook the United States like nothing since the opening days of the Korean War. How could anyone but US scientists have the necessary background with which to accomplish such a feat? The Eisenhower administration moved rapidly to determine a direction for America's space effort and created the National Aeronautics and Space Administration (NASA) on 1 October 1958, which dictated the civilian route of the US entry into space. During this same period, the US Air Force moved quickly to stake its claim to military operational interests. Gen Thomas D. White issued the first Air Force space doctrine on 29 November 1957, which included the ideas that space power would someday prove as dominant in combat as the Air Force believed that airpower already was and that the Air Force should have operational control over all forces within this medium.[11]

Today, civilian-operated NASA controls manned space flight and space exploration, while the DOD directs the nation's military space efforts, with the Army, Navy, and Air Force operating separate organizations responsible for space application within their services. Following the Space Commission Report in May 2001, DOD identified the Air Force as the military's executive agent of space, reporting to the undersecretary of the Air Force.[12] Within the Air Force, Air Force Space Command serves as the "space corps" discussed in the commission's report, with cradle-to-grave responsibility for space systems acquisition and operations.[13] Further streamlining the administrative function of space within DOD, effective 1 October 2002, United States Strategic Command assumed control of military space as the nation's unified command.

One significant change since the earliest days of the US space program is the current state of cooperation between NASA and the military. Through much of US space history, NASA and the military competed for resources, which is understandable with space being an extension of Cold War expectations. During the post–Cold War era, the paradigm changed, culminating in May 2002, when Congress directed the secretary of the Air Force to continue the growing cooperative relationship with NASA and explore the possibility of a joint development project for future space lift that could meet each organization's requirements.[14] One outgrowth of this new direction was the Air Force's XB-37B, an orbital test vehicle, which was an unmanned vehicle capable of multiple launch and recovery while sustaining low-Earth orbit for months at a time.

Just as the US national security strategy evolved and adapted to a changing international environment, so did space policy. During the Cold War it reflected the struggle between East and West. According to Matthew J. Mowthorpe, author of *US Military Approach to Space during the Cold War*, American administrations generally viewed space as a "sanctuary" during the early period of the Cold War—that is, not to be used for military purposes and to remain free from weapons. Space could then provide strategic stability by providing surveillance of missile launches and increasing the survivability of retaliatory strategic forces.[15] During the 1980s, the Reagan administration shifted US policy from viewing space as a surveillance medium to exploring the feasibility of using space for strategic defense.[16] The announcement of the Strategic Defense Initiative in March 1983, coupled with the *Challenger* disaster in January 1986, led to a revised US space policy in January 1988 that set up four new pillars for space: deterring or defending against enemy attack, assured US space access, negating hostile space systems, and enhancing operations of United States and allied forces.[17]

The Reagan administration's policy shift implied for the first time that space was not a pristine environment, but like land, sea, and air, simply another arena for military operations. As the first post–Cold War statement of national space policy, the 1996 National Space Policy continued this trend and announced, "Access to and use of space is central for preserving peace and protecting US national security as well as civil and commercial interests."[18] Completing the transition in national space policy, President Clinton's secretary of defense, William Cohen, wrote in a letter to his service secretaries and senior military personnel, "Space is a medium like the land, sea, and air within which military activities will be conducted to achieve US national security objectives."[19]

Recognizing the increasing importance of space, the *National Security Strategy* (*NSS*) of December 1999 declared for the first time that the "unimpeded access to and use of space is essential for protecting U.S. national security."[20] The congressionally chartered "Space Commission" completed the current evolution of US space policy when it reached five unanimous conclusions in its report:

> First, the present extent of U. S. dependence on space, the rapid pace at which this dependence is increasing, and the vulnerability it creates all demand that U. S. national security space interests be recognized as a top national security priority. . . . Second, the U. S. government—in particular, the Department of Defense and the Intelligence Community—is not yet arranged or focused to meet the national security space needs of the twenty-first century. . . . Third, U. S. national security space programs are vital to peace and stability. . . . Fourth, we know from history that every medium—air, land, and sea—has seen conflict; reality indicates that space will be no different. Given this virtual certainty, the US must develop the means both to deter and to defend against hostile acts in U. S. and from space. . . . Finally, investment in science and technology resources—not just facilities, but people—is essential if the U.S. is to remain the world's leading space-faring nation.[21]

The Bush administration's *National Security Strategy* of September 2002 remained consistent with the policy transition begun during the Reagan administration. The 2002 Bush NSS addressed space in the post–9/11 environment:

> Before the war in Afghanistan, that area [space] was low on the list of major planning contingencies. Yet, in a very short time, we had to operate across the length and breadth of that remote nation, using every branch of the armed forces. We must prepare for more such deployments by developing assets such as advanced remote sensing, long-range precision strike capabilities, and transformed maneuver and expeditionary forces. This broad portfolio of military capabilities must also include the ability to defend the homeland, conduct information operations, ensure U. S. access to distant theaters, and protect critical U. S. infrastructure and assets in outer space.[22]

Recognizing a need to update the 1996 US space policy to reflect both the post–Cold War and post–9/11 situations, on 28 June 2002, President Bush directed the National Security Council to chair a review of US space policy and report back during 2003.[23] The destruction of the shuttle *Columbia* during reentry on 1 February 2003 caused an almost three-year delay in the report. On 31 August 2006,

President Bush signed off on the new space policy—a document that superseded the September 1996 version of the directive. The new policy supported not only a Moon, Mars, and beyond exploration agenda, but also responded to a post–9/11 world of terrorist actions, such as the need for intelligence gathering internal and external to the United States. The directive recognized that "space has become a place that is increasingly used by a host of nations, consortia, businesses, and entrepreneurs. . . . In this new century, those who effectively utilize space will enjoy added prosperity and security and will hold a substantial advantage over those who do not."[24]

In 2010 Pres. Barack Obama's administration announced it would shift spending from government projects (e.g., the decision to cancel NASA's Constellation manned spaceflight program) and rely more heavily upon commercial endeavors like those of SpaceX. Marking a potentially dramatic change in American space policy in the second decade of the twenty-first century, the United States appears poised to place greater emphasis on private companies, rather than relying heavily upon government-developed programs.[25]

Who Are the Players and Why Are They Important?

Throughout most of the Cold War, the United States and the Soviet Union were the only nations with the industrial infrastructure and political will to break the bounds of Earth. Today, in addition to the European Space Agency consortium, no less than seven countries have space-launch capability.[26]

Furthermore, space activities are moving away from government operation and are increasingly becoming commercially oriented. The proliferation of space activities broadens the threat. The US industrial base finds new invigorated competition, potentially driving the few remaining American companies abroad to remain competitive, while directly challenging the decades-old US space preeminence. The US dependence on space further highlights its vulnerability. Today, any nation with adequate funding can purchase capability for almost any purpose. This dramatically changes the dynamic from the Cold–War era.

A decade ago Charles V. Pena of the Cato Institute described space as it relates to national security as being shaped and influenced more by the future of commercial space activities rather than international military competition.[27] We have seen this emerge where commercial ventures continue to rise to fill the demand for low-cost, reliable lift. However, full comprehension of the challenge requires an appreciation of the evolution of the early twenty-first century environment.

During the 1990s, the United States, Europe, China, and Russia developed proven commercial launch capabilities. Orbital Sciences Corporation of Dulles, Virginia, launched a Department of Defense satellite aboard an air-launched Pegasus rocket in 1990. It became the first privately developed space launch vehicle and launch bought by the government on a commercial basis.[28]

The European Space Agency's family of Ariane vehicles has been the chief US competitor in the international launch market. Ariane vehicles have dominated the market, launching 55 percent of all commercial payloads between 1990 and 1995, China's Long-March vehicle captured 9 percent, and the United States, 36 percent.[29] Russia entered the commercial launch market through a consortium with Lockheed Martin, called International Launch Services, while offering other independent commercial launch services at the same time. India, Israel, Japan, and Australia round out the list of countries with proven space-launch capabilities and, with the exception of Japan, have yet to offer international commercial services. This reality has provided a significant opening for such privately owned companies as SpaceX and Orbital to enter the marketplace. The new reality is even recognized by NASA administrator Charles Bolden in remarks articulating the future for United States manned spaceflight, where he sees a growing role for commercial space effort, particularly in low-Earth orbit.[30]

As we are seeing, the future space exploitation may not be restricted primarily to governments and multinational corporations but may follow the proliferation pattern exhibited by aviation. One such example is an attempt to emulate the aviation industry of the early 1920s when private organizations offered monetary rewards in an attempt to spur technological development. In the spirit of Charles Lindbergh and his winning the race for the first solo flight across the Atlantic, a group of St. Louis, Missouri–based business leaders started the X-Prize in 1996 to promote private space travel. In all, 21 teams from six countries—Argentina, Canada, Romania, Russia, United Kingdom, and the United States—joined the competition for the $10 million prize to be the first amateur team that builds and flies a manned craft into space.[31] On 29 September and 4 October 2004, *SpaceShipOne* broke the 100-kilometer mark (62.5 miles), the internationally recognized boundary of space. A public company, Virgin

Galactic, is now poised to ferry paying customers into suborbital flight out of a New Mexico spaceport.

Amateur unmanned programs have proliferated as capabilities increase and cost decreases. Virgin Galactic successfully demonstrated the way for a number of privately owned efforts, to include Civilian Space eXploration Team, Interorbital Systems, and Starchaser Industries, just to name a few. By 2010, Elon Musk's company, SpaceX, successfully launched light- and medium-lift vehicles in Falcon 1 and Falcon 9. Attempting to shape space launch through the public sector, both the Falcon 1 and 9 significantly reduce cost and are designed to undercut their rivals (Boeing and Lockheed Martin) by a factor of 10.[32] In December 2008 NASA selected SpaceX to resupply the *International Space Station* during the hiatus of US manned flight following the last space shuttle mission in July 2011.[33]

For the immediate future, space remains the purview, principally, of nation-states, despite great commercial and private involvement. Space exploration reflects national pride and represents strategic national interests. Henry Kissinger, President Nixon's secretary of state, noted that the "international system of the twenty-first century will contain at least six major powers—the United States, Europe, China, Japan, Russia, and probably India."[34] These also happen to be the nations most capable of independent projection into space for both the present and the near term. Each has highly capable industrial infrastructures and possesses the will to expend scarce resources to support space-faring goals. None yet has the ability to directly threaten US dominance in space. But an accurate picture requires one to look at capabilities and future intent. Before determining what impact they may have on future US policy—and ultimately deterrence—the state of play in each power should be reviewed. Russia, inheritor of much of the Soviet Union's Cold War space heritage, is a logical place to begin.

Russia

Today, the Russian space program faces many daunting challenges, with shortfalls in financing being blamed for a series of failures and placing in question the continuing relationship with NASA.[35] Much change has occurred since the "fall of the wall," and the dissolution of the Soviet Union. While the Russian government inherited vast capabilities, it also inherited significant challenges from its Soviet predecessor. The Russian Federal Space Agency or Roscosmos and the Russian Space Forces, both founded in 1992, were given the initial responsibility for maintaining a diverse constellation of approximately 170 operational spacecraft and the industry behind them.[36] In December 2011, Russia transitioned satellite and Plesetsk Cosmodrome operations to the Russian Aerospace Defence Forces. Administrative changes have not slowed criticism of a program that some 50 years ago placed the first satellite in space.

Yuri Koptev, Roscosmos director, concluded that the steady decline of Moscow's space program meant it was only capable of providing services to others—no longer capable of independent major mission launch. The Russian space budget has shrunk to one-nineteenth of what it was in 1989. Mr. Koptev remarked at a conference on space research in December 2002, "Our NASA colleagues are terrified by the fact that their budget amounts to $15 billion a year, but Russia's space budget totals $309 million." He added that India spends nearly $530 million annually on space research.[37]

Underfunding not only affects the Russian space effort, but its infrastructure as well. A May 2001 fire at Serpukhov, 150 miles from Moscow, severely damaged Russian command and control capabilities, while in May 2002 a roof collapsed at the Baikonur Cosmodrome, killing six workers and damaging the Buran shuttle spacecraft, the only one of three built to have flown in space. The Soviets initiated the Buran project in 1976 in response to the US shuttle program but abandoned it after the fall of the Soviet Union.[38]

Further hampering the Russian space effort is the location of its main launch site at the Baikonur Cosmodrome in the now independent Republic of Kazakhstan, in the former Soviet Central Asia. Moscow leases the facility from its neighbor but has been trying to shift launches to its own Plesetsk Cosmodrome, which represents yet another funding challenge.[39]

The increased revenue generated by Russian oil fields is, for now, providing the financial wherewithal for a resurgent Russia. Russia retains a robust launch capability, able to place objects in both near-Earth and deep-space orbits. Its Soyuz rocket, the backbone of Russia's space operations, traces its origins to the rocket that sent the first man, Yuri Gagarin of the Soviet Union, into space in 1961. It remains highly reliable and has experienced only one failure within the past 11 years. Following NASA's ending of the space shuttle program in 2011, Russia's launch capability represents the only viable lifeline to the *International Space Station* for the foreseeable future. While the past presents a proud heritage for the Russian space program and the present displays hope, the future may not be as bright.

China

Another Cold War adversary and potential competitor is the People's Republic of China, which has made significant advances toward reaching its goals as a space-faring nation. It launched its first satellite on 24 April 1970 and possesses a robust family of boosters called Long March. Launching from three sites—Jiuquan, Xichang, and Taiyuan—it has established an integrated command and control network capable of directing satellites in both near-Earth and geostationary orbit, the largest models being three tons.[40]

Taking its first steps toward reaching manned space flight on 20 November 1999, China launched an unmanned experimental spacecraft and then recovered it the next day.[41] The *China Business Times*, a Chinese government-run publication, noted the military implications for the space flight, as well. It quoted a Chinese military expert as stating the same low-power propulsion technology used to adjust a spacecraft's orbit could also be used to alter the path of offensive missiles, helping them evade proposed US antimissile defense systems.[42]

Luan Enjie, administrator of the China National Space Agency, proclaimed at the 4 October 2000 Third United Nations Conference on the Exploration and Peaceful Uses of Outer Space, "The development and application level of the space technology has become an important indicator of a nation's comprehensive strength. Sustained development and application of the space technology has been the important topic of every country dedicated to its own development." He went on to state that "China will actively and pragmatically implement a comprehensive multilayer and multiform strategy of international cooperation and exchange in space technology according to the market demands of space science, space technology and space application. The new century is a century for Chinese space industry to develop continuously."[43]

China's Tenth Five-Year Plan, published in December 2001, gave more details of its space goals and articulated a new generation of boosters with greater thrust, higher reliability, and lower cost. It also described aspirations for a manned space program that could potentially lead to lunar and deep space exploration.[44]

China became the third country with a successful manned space program by sending an astronaut into space aboard Shenzhou 5 on 15 October 2003 for more than 21 hours. Since then, China has turned its focus to extraterrestrial exploration beginning with the Moon. The first Chinese Lunar Exploration Program unmanned lunar orbiter, *Chang'e* 1, was successfully launched on 24 October 2007, making China the fifth nation in the world to master this technology. Further demonstrating advanced capabilities, the Chinese government has placed a space station in low-Earth orbit, successfully carrying out docking and undocking maneuvers,[45] something only two other nations have successfully accomplished. Attempting to avoid public missteps of both the US and Russian space programs, China's manned space program goals remain simultaneously guarded and deliberate.

China, however, faces many challenges in the near future. To date, it appears to be effectively transforming itself from a command economy to a more capitalist model. A new moneyed elite is emerging, and entrepreneurs were welcomed for the first time at a Chinese Communist Party Congress in November 2002, yet vast areas within China remain unaffected by the economic boom of the first part of the twenty-first century. Furthermore, officials are struggling with the question of how to reform the party while retaining control of the government, something few one-party systems have ever accomplished. While there is no guarantee of China reaching its full potential, underestimating China would be foolhardy. China sees itself as a future world player to be taken seriously.

Japan

Long in the shadow of shared US space technology, Japan is beginning to strike an independent path. The National Space Development Agency (NASDA), established in 1969 to oversee most of Japan's space effort, witnessed its first satellite launch in 1970. Over the next two decades, Japan based its booster program on shared US technology, but during the 1980s, it began developing a domestically designed booster to take advantage of the growing commercial market and to increase its flexibility.[46]

While Japan was poised to enter the competitive commercial market with its domestically produced H-2 booster, Japan experienced failure after failure and eventually canceled the H-2 program in 1999.[47] In August 2001, Japan successfully launched its H-2A booster, which ended six major setbacks in seven years, restoring much of Japan's sapped morale. The Japanese vision for space development was based upon NASDA doctrine: (1) establishing a strong foundation for the future of Japanese space development programs; (2) involvement in developing new and innovative space technologies and systems; and (3) promoting international cooperation programs by sharing philosophical ideas behind the future of space development. Because of this direction, Japan has placed higher priority on four areas: construction of a global Earth observation system, promotion of advanced space science and unmanned lunar exploration, an in-orbit laboratory, and development and operation of new space program infrastructures.

The Japanese space program continues to evolve and since 2003 has been guided by the Japanese Aerospace Exploration Agency (JAXA). Formed from three previously existing organizations, the Institute of Space and Astronautical Science, the National Aerospace Laboratory of Japan, and NASDA, JAXA is responsible for research, technological development, and satellite launch. The new Japanese space goals are articulated in JAXA 2025, but even there the challenges Japan faces are evident.[48] Phrases such as "establish space transportation system," "revive aircraft manufacturing," and "establish indigenous technologies for human space activities," foreshadow the difficult path ahead.[49]

Looking toward space exploration and exploitation, Japan is moving further into the marketplace on an almost two-decade quest to compete in the world's commercial satellite-launch business.[50] While this was built on the success of the Japanese economy at the close of the twentieth century, the intervening decades have not been kind. Presently, Japanese space expenditures hover around $4 billion annually.[51] Nevertheless, despite lofty goals and aspirations, the Japanese space program faces significant challenges. In addition to financial issues, a significant limiting factor for Japan will probably be human capital, as the Japanese cadre of scientists and engineers that constitute the space workforce diminish further in the face of demographic challenges. The estimated space workforce for Japan today is roughly 6,500 workers, in comparison to China's 50,000. One virtue of the small satellite development efforts in Japan is that spreading this work into universities and other institutions helps to cultivate younger engineering and scientific talents.[52]

Further complicating finances, Hughes satellite manufacturing pulled out of a contract with Japan to launch 10 of its satellites on the

H-2A, and other clients seem reluctant to risk their satellites on this still unproven rocket when other, more established launch vehicles are available.[53] In addition, the commercial launch business is becoming more competitive, with Russian and Chinese launch systems, not to mention SpaceX, providing viable launch alternatives at a competitive price. An editorial in the *Yomiuri Shinbun* newspaper expressed early public concerns about the Japanese space program in light of Japanese involvement in the *International Space Station* and the economic stagnation of the Japanese economy over the past decade. Labeling the national goal for space as "unclear mission creep," the editorial concluded with these questions: "How much money is needed for space development? What can be done when? Or, what cannot be done? Is the final goal a practical space manned flight? Or is it just a fundamental technological experiment?"[54] A decade later these concerns continue, fuelled by the global economic downturn that began in 2007, questions both the Japanese government and its people must eventually answer.

European Space Agency

The most immediate commercial competitor to the United States space effort is the European Space Agency (ESA), a consortium of European nations representing 19 member states: Austria, Belgium, the Czech Republic, Denmark, Finland, France, Germany, Greece, Ireland, Italy, Luxembourg, the Netherlands, Norway, Portugal, Spain, Sweden, Switzerland, and the United Kingdom. Canada takes part in some projects under a cooperation agreement. Romania signed its accession agreement with ESA on 20 January 2011 and became the 19th member state in December 2011. Hungary, Poland, Estonia, and Slovenia are European Cooperating States. Other countries have signed cooperation agreements with ESA. The European Union and ESA are independent of each other, but they interact in evolving European space programs and policy.[55]

ESA's charter is to "provide for and to promote for exclusively peaceful purposes, cooperation among European States in space research and technology and their space applications, with a view to their being used for scientific purposes and operational space applications systems."[56] While individual members retain some autonomy and nations such as the United Kingdom (UK) and Germany have expressed space goals, the true might of the European space effort is expressed through ESA. Though not a subsidiary of the European Union (EU), the EU and ESA do cooperate closely.

Late in 2000 the EU Research Council and the ESA Ministerial Council met and outlined a new European space strategy. Edelgard Bulmahn, Germany's federal minister of education and research, described the strategy as "aimed at providing Europe with its own access to space."[57] The strategy detailed three lines of action: strengthen the foundations of space activities, enhance scientific knowledge, and reap the benefits for society and seize markets opportunities.[58] According to the ESA, the first line of action encompasses broadening space technology and guaranteeing access to space through a family of launch vehicles. The second sees Europe continuing to pursue cutting-edge technology, while the third has the objectives of seizing market opportunities and meeting new societal demands.[59] Whereas lines one and two have significant international implications, with the Ariane family of rockets proving quite reliable and competitive on the commercial market, in line three the Europeans see their greatest promise. The European Space Agency puts the case directly: "The challenge is to ensure that Europe can take a fair share of the global market and related jobs."[60]

In a highly competitive market and with an eye toward peaceful space exploitation, where might Europe be headed? In a 1999 article in *The Parliamentary Monitor Magazine*, Ian Taylor, a member of the UK Parliament, observed that economic challenges are "transforming the space industry, with larger, leaner suppliers emerging in both the United States and Europe." In an attempt to define what role Europe might play in space, he went on to say, "Perhaps we [Europeans] could challenge the US dominance by backing dedicated niche applications," such as better, smaller, and cheaper satellites.[61] The November 2000 report to the ESA director general (commonly referred to as the "Wise Men Report") asserted, "Without a clear space component, the evolution towards the [European Security and Defense Policy] will be incomplete."[62]

European leaders see space as an arena that must be actively engaged. Europe is moving ahead with *Galileo*, a civilian satellite navigation program comparable to the US GPS constellation. Per the ESA to the European Parliament, "*Galileo* is one of the Union's flagship programmes and the first satellite navigation system in the world designed for civilian use. It will enable the Union to remain independent in a time when reliance on global navigation systems continues to grow."[63]

The European Union and ESA have both the political drive and the technological ability to implement their goals; the problematic area is funding. By 2012 the ESA budget had reached between $4 and $5 billion annually, slightly more than the Japanese space budget.[64] The challenge facing the ESA is the successful articulation of goals to an ever-stressed international consortium of independent states. Despite funding limitations and competing national priorities, Europe remains a fierce competitor within the aerospace arena.

The Rest

The remaining space-faring nations include India, Australia, Israel, and potentially North Korea and Iran. Each has demonstrated space-access capabilities to varying degrees of success. Looking at their accomplishments and aspirations shows that the future model for international development in space will be proliferation rather than retrenchment.

India. India entered the fellowship of space-faring nations on 15 October 1994, with the successful launch of its polar satellite launch vehicle PSLV-D2 rocket with an 804kg *Indian Remote Sensing*-P2 satellite. The focus of India's space program is in the arena of weather, surveillance, and communications, particularly in light of increased tensions with its Pakistani neighbors. The Indian launch program remains active, with its seventh successful flight of its indigenous PSLV in September 2002, which placed its first dedicated weather satellite in orbit.[65] India reached further in 2008 when it launched *Chandrayaan*-1, an unmanned lunar orbiter on a two-year mission to explore the Moon.[66]

Australia. Australia has a long history of involvement in space flight, mostly through their cooperation in US and British launches from their Woomera launch site. Australia has on numerous occasions attempted to join the space-faring nations independent of its old allies. The latest attempt occurred in 1999, when SpaceLift Australia Ltd signed an agreement with Russia to launch payloads less than 800 kilograms into low-Earth orbit. The agreement remains only a stated goal at this time, as the company has yet to meet its planned test launch of 2001.[67] Australia continues to await independent launch capability without a clear path to obtain it. This agreement opened avenues for continued partnering between the two nations. Alexei Korostelev of the Russian space agency Roskosomos stated, "Australian organizations may also participate in other

Russian scientific programs, such as putting Australian materials processing equipment on board the Russian segment of the *International Space Station*."[68]

Israel. Israel's space program also has a long history, dating back to 1961 with the launch of its first solid fueled minirocket. Desiring greater independence and self-reliance following the 1986 *Challenger* accident, Israel felt compelled to develop an indigenous space capability, and on 19 September 1988 launched its first domestically constructed satellite.[69] Since 1988 Israel has continued domestic satellite launches from its Palmachim site, though it also relies upon US and ESA launch support for surveillance and communications capabilities.

North Korea. North Korea announced on 4 September 1998 that four days earlier it had placed its first satellite into orbit aboard a Taepodong, or Kwangmyongsong-1, rocket.[70] Again, on 5 April 2009, the North Korean government publically declared the successful launch of a satellite aboard a Kwangmyongsong-2 rocket. While international debate immediately erupted concerning the success and intent of both launches, North Korea certainly exhibited both ICBM and space launch intent, if short of full capability. Shortly after new North Korean leader Kim Jong-un came to power, a spectacular failure of a rocket meant to put a satellite into orbit was more than a $1 billion humiliation.[71] Despite its failures, the attempts, coupled with an open admission of a continued nuclear research with open testing, mark North Korea as a challenge, if not a direct threat, to US policy makers in the areas of both international relations and space development.

Iran. On 4 February 2008 Iran successfully launched the two-staged, all-liquid propellant suborbital rocket Kavoshgar-1 (Explorer-1) on a maiden suborbital test flight from Shahroud, its newly inaugurated domestic space-launch complex. Since then, Iranian state television reported that Iran's first "domestically" made satellite, the *Omid* (Persian meaning "Hope"), had been successfully launched into low-Earth orbit by a domestically produced Safir-2 rocket on 2 February 2009. The operation was made to coincide with the 30th anniversary of the Iranian revolution. Almost immediately following the launch, US leadership expressed concern about an overlap between the technology used to launch satellites and the technology necessary for making advanced ballistic missiles. Acting State Department representative Robert Wood said in a statement: "Iran's development of a space launch vehicle (SLV) capable of putting a satellite into orbit establishes the technical basis from which Iran could develop long-range ballistic missile systems. Many of the technological building blocks involved in SLVs are the same as those required to develop long-range ballistic missiles."[72]

Iran has also expressed an interest in manned space flight, publically declaring that it would place an Iranian in orbit aboard its own spacecraft by 2021. Scientific research on this program has already begun as Iran considers a manned space program, much like its nuclear program, vital in its technological race. While reality may be different, as with North Korea, the expressed intent and some demonstrated capabilities present a challenge for their neighbors, as well as for US policy makers.

This brief review of space-faring nations points to a future where space capability represents not just a nation's pride, but also its strategic interests. US policy makers face many uncertainties, though possibly none is more daunting than intent and direction of international space development. Due to the increased activity over the past decades, the question remains whether the United States should be concerned, and if so, what is the best approach to protect its own national interests? The old paradigm of a single adversary is long past. Definitions like *enemy* or even *adversary* may be obsolete, particularly in an era when cooperation and competition live side by side. The loss of a bipolar military environment, rather than simplifying deterrence, has added significant complexity to the equation.

The Threat: Some Considerations Complicating Deterrence

Every nation with space-faring capability or such aspirations openly advertises its peaceful intentions for space. There is open cooperation on the *International Space Station* and among the United States, Canada, Japan, Russia, the EU, and the ESA. Furthermore, international agreements and treaties discourage weapons in space. But to appreciate fully the impact of increased international development in space, it is necessary to widen the concept of threat. *Threat* need not be simply defined as militarily based; policy makers must expand the concept to include economic development, because underlying the openly peaceful aspirations for space that are universally expressed are the realistic expressions concerning national security and self interests.

Three areas that provide some indication of the threat are competition, proliferation, and surveillance.

Competition

Today's space race is active and highly competitive. The European Space Agency's Ariane, China's Long March, Russia's Soyuz, and the Japanese H-2A boosters have all been proven highly reliable, and American industry is positioning for the future with continued successful launches of the Delta IV and Atlas V boosters, and most recently Falcon 1 and Falcon 9. However, launch competition is only one challenge facing the United States. A greater concern to policy makers might well be competition in areas they consider safe, specifically the high technology sector. The ESA has openly expressed the goal of improving its market share in a number of areas, including the civilian navigational satellite market through the program entitled *Galileo*. The outcome of the first partnership between ESA and the European Commission, the 30-satellite *Galileo* navigation system is designed to provide high-quality positioning, navigation, and timing services to users across the whole world as a civil-controlled service offering guaranteed continuity of coverage.[73] Referring to *Galileo* in a January 2002 statement, Claudio Mastracci, ESA's director of application programs, said, "The stakes here [with *Galileo*] are commercial. The technical issues can be worked out between us [the United States and Europe] without much difficulty. They are not a problem."[74] French president Jacques Chirac's comments on the situation can be interpreted from an economic as well as a political perspective when he suggested the failure to go ahead with *Galileo* would have resulted in Europe becoming a "vassal" of the United States.[75]

In light of potential commercial competition, policy makers must address the state of health of the American space industry. Space infrastructure and support industries, such as satellite manufacturing, now account for the second-largest component of the commercial space sector, reaching 32 percent of global space activity by 2010.[76] Total global and total US space sales have continued to increase, mostly in services. However, the US share of the global market has decreased. For example, the US share of satellite manufacturing decreased 20 percent for all commercial communication satellite (COMMSAT) sales and 10 percent for geosynchronous Earth orbit (GEO) COMMSATs between 1999 and 2007.[77] Defense funding, domestic nondefense services, and ground equipment dominated US space industry sales. Export sales, though, represented less than 10 percent of total US company revenues annually from 2003 to 2006.[78] Then the question is, Is the US space commercial sector healthy enough to sustain competition from European consortiums that have proven quite capable and competitive?

Proliferation: The Greatest Threat to Deterrence

Beyond the challenge exhibited by direct competition, the United States must face the specter of technological proliferation, further complicating the deterrence equation. Commercial space-launch enterprises have produced some unexpected consequences for US national space policy. Following a Chinese Long March-2E vehicle failure in January 1995 with a Hughes Space and Communications satellite payload onboard, China and Hughes immediately commissioned an independent review to determine the cause of the failure. The US State Department concluded in its analysis of the review that "Hughes assistance directly supported the Chinese space program in the areas of anomaly analysis/accident investigation, telemetry analysis, coupled loads analysis, hardware design and manufacturing, testing, and weather analysis. Moreover, the assistance provided by Hughes is likely to improve the standing of the Chinese in the commercial launch market, as they make improvements in spacelift reliability and performance."[79] The report went on to predict, "The long-term effect of increased reliability will be to improve the rate of successful deployment of Chinese satellites and, in turn, to facilitate China's access to space for commercial and military programs."[80] China has not had a failure of its Long March family of vehicles since the assistance from Hughes.

History has proven technology is extremely difficult to contain, with proliferation appearing as the natural order of things. Accordingly, America is faced with enhanced Chinese space-lift capabilities, increased commercial launch competition, and the potential transfer of technology from the civilian to a more hostile military sector. Policy makers must rapidly determine the most appropriate response to deter potential hostile actions in space, particularly when faced with technological proliferation driven by almost universal access to the Internet and ready entrée by the international community to American colleges and universities.

Intelligence, Surveillance, and Reconnaissance

Beyond the arena of increased ISR threat posed by nation-states, US policy makers must also concern themselves with commercially available imagery. Over the past decade, numerous companies have begun providing high-resolution satellite imagery to those willing to purchase their product. One example is the SPOT Image Corporation of France that has been commercially offering high-resolution imagery since the early 1990s. SPOT provides Earth observation products for such diverse applications as agriculture, cartography, cadastral mapping, environmental studies, urban planning, telecommunications, surveillance, forestry, land-use/land-cover mapping, natural hazard assessments, flood risk management, oil and gas exploration, geology, and civil engineering.[81]

The concern over commercially available imagery became so great during the 2002 Afghanistan campaign that the US National Imagery and Mapping Agency purchased exclusive rights to pictures taken of the war zone by Space Imaging's *IKONOS* satellite, which has one-meter black and white resolution and four-meter color resolution. According to Charles Pena of the Cato Institute, this "buy to deny" policy is an example that demonstrates the importance of and demand for commercial space assets.[82] While such arrangements augment government-owned resources, they also preclude others from obtaining like intelligence data. Commercial imagery is rapidly improving, with less than one-meter resolution available. Further, as providing commercial imagery becomes more profitable, new companies will certainly be enticed to enter the marketplace. For the United States, will "buy to deny" continue to be a successful deterrence strategy to restrict space access? If not, what might be an alternative?

Space Defense in Depth: A Viable Deterrence Strategy

As more nations field systems, to include such technologies as anti-satellites and ground-based jammers and lasers, space superiority cannot be assured. Space control, a concept little different from that of air and potentially cyberspace control, is problematic. The United States does not have the ability to either protect its space assets or deter the actions of others in space. As more nations field space systems, space superiority becomes an illusion. The challenge is to establish a strategy that furthers US national interests and creates a realistic space control architecture. Existing US vulnerabilities in space could drive a strategy that would lead to space weaponization. For years space professionals have discussed the potentiality of weapons in space. The imagination of science fiction depicted in such television series as *Star Trek* and movies like *Star Wars* excites the imagination of the possible. To many, space weaponization seems inevitable. As weapons moved from land to sea to air, logically, space seems the next domain. The United States could potentially spark a space arms race by placing weapons in space.

A less volatile, less expensive, and potentially more successful strategy to deter hostile actions and obtain space superiority would be to use the entire spectrum of diplomatic, information, military, and economic capabilities to develop a *defense-in-depth* construct for US space operations. By a multilayered approach, the space defense in depth takes advantage of the nation's strength. Not knowing what asset to attack to reach the US space center of gravity places the adversary in a defensive position. This might also be known as the "make my day" approach. By instilling doubt in the adversary's decision-making process, the United States forces any foe to face the question Clint Eastwood posed in his movie *Dirty Harry*: "You've got to ask yourself one question: 'Do I feel lucky?' Well, do ya punk?"[83]

Space defense in depth should not begin with a military solution. It starts with the United States taking the lead in engaging the international community to the fullest extent in creating a system of protocols and relationships that encourages beneficial and benign behavior in space. Through economic and technical cooperation, nations become interdependent and much less likely to act against their own interests. America already partners widely with the international community in space operations. The United States is engaged with Russia, Japan, Canada, Brazil, the EU, and ESA in the *International Space Station*. Russia, China, and the ESA have launched satellites for United States–based corporations. Further, the United States and Europe are cooperating to avoid frequency overlap in the deployment of *Galileo*, a European version of GPS. The hope is that through economic and technical cooperation nations become interdependent and less likely to act against their own interests.

Partnering also lays the foundation for international negotiation, regulation, and governance by the rule of law, powerful concepts appreciated by our allies. Currently, the United States is party to a series of international regulations across land, sea, air, and space. A new round of international agreements could call for eliminating all weapons in space, which many nations may well find attractive. Precedents exist to regulate space activity through international negotiation and regulation. Following a successful US space-based nuclear weapons test during the early 1960s, the international arena—with US support—moved to ban such weapons in space.

Such an opportunity exists in relation to ASAT weapons. One side effect of the successful Chinese ASAT launch in 2007 was a massive debris field that extends from less than 125 miles to more than 2,292 miles—this range encompasses much of low-Earth orbit. Nicholas Johnson, NASA's chief scientist for orbital debris, stated that "this satellite breakup represents the most prolific and serious fragmentation in the course of 50 years of space operations."[84] The resulting clutter will affect all nations, including the Chinese, who desire to place satellites in low-Earth orbit. However, as the Chinese discovered with their ASAT launch, unintended consequences often outweigh the advantage.

Through global partnering, or rather building partnership capacity, the United States could also gain access to more economical lift. Nations like Brazil offer the potential for modern launch facilities where decreased lift is required to place an object in orbit. Further, combining on-site fabrication facilities for satellites and lifters could reduce cost and enhance responsiveness. The United States will continue to need its continental–United States launch ranges, such as Vandenberg Air Force Base and Kennedy Space Center, particularly for sensitive payloads, but it must move to a lower-cost, more-capable alternative for routine lift.

Pres. Ronald Reagan once said, "Trust, but verify." In space this is problematic, for without situational awareness it is difficult to do either. While deterrence is not directly connected to knowing where the aggressor lies, it is certainly enhanced when the deterrer possesses that information. The United States must be prepared to act unilaterally when required to ensure space control and deter hostile activities. Unilateral action, however, requires enhanced situational awareness. Currently, adversaries could alter a satellite's orbit by a few degrees, and requisitions may take days or weeks. Additionally, microsatellites are becoming an increasing reality, and the United States has little or no ability to track objects that small. Many of our land-based radar systems were originally designed for ICBM early warning, not objects in low-Earth or geosynchronous orbit.

The Air Force has taken positive steps to correct the deficiency with the launch of the *Pathfinder*, the first space-based surveillance system, in an attempt to improve space situational awareness of geosynchronous orbit. However, the Air Force must also field a capability designed to detect objects in low-Earth orbit and integrate space, ground, and maritime systems into a coherent detection architecture. Only with a robust system observing both low- and high-Earth orbits will the United States be able to provide comprehensive space situational awareness—an essential element for ensuring true space superiority.

Another essential element to space control, and ultimately space superiority, is guaranteed access to the domain. The Air Force has a rich history of being involved in the nation's race to space. However, it does not have a record of responsive launch. Special handling requirements for lift vehicles and satellites require months, or years, of planning for any on-time launch. Space systems must become more responsive *and* less vulnerable to meet the war fighter's needs as warfare continues to evolve. DOD has long relied upon large, expensive satellite systems to meet its needs. However, the launch of the Defense Satellite Communication System (DSCS) follow on, the Wideband Global System (WGS), is an example of this good-news-and-bad-news story. While each WGS satellite is more capable than the entire constellation of nine DSCS satellites, the planned six-satellite WGS constellation increases US space vulnerabilities by placing greater reliance on a reduced number of satellites.

Operationally Responsive Space: A Necessary Concept for Deterrence

Operationally responsive space (ORS), while not a cure-all, must become an element of US national space policy. Over the years the term *ORS* has become synonymous with what in one era was termed "cheap sat," systems less capable and potentially less effective than the current family of space assets. Under Secretary of the Air Force Peter B. Teets defined ORS in a much broader sense when he identified it as a means "to create a more responsive, reliable, and affordable lift family capable of fulfilling both current and future launch requirements, and the corresponding responsive and affordable satellites."[85]

Spacelift is possibly the most critical element of space control. Without the ability to place satellites in orbit, the United States regresses to the 1950s—totally reliant upon air breathing and terrestrial-based capabilities. The primary space launch vehicles in use by the US Air Force today are known as the evolved expendable launch vehicle (EELV)—Boeing's Delta IV family and Lockheed Martin's Atlas V family, launched under the joint United Launch Alliance venture. These two lift families are designed to be the primary medium and heavy lifters well into the next decade. Becoming operational in 2002 and at about $100 million per vehicle, EELV was designed to standardize and improve space launch operability, reduce the government's traditional involvement in launch processing, and save a projected $6 billion in launch costs between 2002 and 2020.

In 2006 a congressionally mandated National Security Space Launch Requirements Panel addressing DOD lift concluded that "ample evidence suggests that these rockets [Delta IV and Atlas V] can meet the NSS [National Security Strategy] launch needs of the United States through 2020 (the end of the [panel's] study period), barring the emergence of payload requirements that exceed their design lift capability." The report noted, however, that the two launch families were "largely uncompetitive in today's commercial market," and that because ORS concepts were in the formative stages, "it was premature to specify launcher requirements."[86] The Air Force objective must be to achieve lower cost with responsiveness marked by days and weeks rather than months and years. Less expensive lifters and satellites that are also operationally responsive must become commonplace in the Air Force inventory.

To further mitigate vulnerability in space and enhance deterrence capabilities, the United States must establish greater resiliency in its satellite constellations. Accordingly, deterrence need not be through offensive actions alone. It can be dramatically enhanced by robust, resilient defensive capabilities. This can be accomplished by numerous means, some of which include networking a larger number of satellites, having spares on orbit, and/or being able to replace lost assets rapidly. The basic idea is to eliminate any incentive for an adversary to destroy US space-based assets. If an adversary neutralizes one or more satellites, the nation could recover through networking potentially less complex satellites together, as is done today with computers.

Additionally, operational capability can be enhanced through re-sponsive launch and the ability to reconstitute capabilities rapidly.

The US Air Force has a rich history of being involved in the nation's space efforts. However, it does not have a record of responsive launch. Special handling requirements for the lift vehicle and the satellites dictate months of planning for an on-time launch. Responsive launch has traditionally been viewed in months rather than days or weeks. Further, the space operations process remains mired in a slow, highly expensive acquisition cycle. A stressed national budget will eventu-ally drive a new paradigm for space operations. Smaller, less expen-sive lifters and satellites must become commonplace. The nation will always require large and correspondingly more expensive satellites, especially in geostationary orbit. However, a mix of both systems is needed to increase capability and simultaneously reduce vulnerability.

Space systems must become more responsive and less vulnerable at the same time. The Air Force is moving in the right direction with the Minotaur IV, a modified Peacekeeper ICBM, which reduces cost with a smaller lifter for smaller payloads. Additionally, Congress has appropriated funds for continued research and development of ORS systems. With the nation depending to even a greater degree on com-mercial industry, partnering will be necessary to reach the goal set by Secretary Teets. Commercial companies like SpaceX and Virgin Galactic may hold the key to rapid and reliable space access, particularly if costs can be driven to single digits when compared to over $30 mil-lion per Minotaur.

The US Air Force has for decades attempted to improve its space acquisition process. Historically, it was common for a 10- to 15-year period to occur from system requirement to launch. Reducing the acquisition cycle reduces US vulnerabilities, enhances deterrence through resiliency, and allows for greater use of current technologies while avoiding the potential for launching satellites designed a de-cade earlier. Space systems acquisition lives with the heritage of ex-ploring the new frontier. US satellites have been essentially one of a kind, handmade marvels that often push the technological envelope. Cost overruns in the space-based infrared system (SBIRS) and the cancellation of the space radar program point to an obvious conclu-sion that Congress has little confidence in the Air Force's ability to acquire and field new space systems. It may take a decade or longer to right the ship, so the programs the Air Force fields in the future must come in on time, on budget, and on message—the Air Force cannot overpromise. Accordingly, the next major space program must be well conceived, ruthlessly managed, and delivered as promised.

Space systems have long fallen prey to the approach that the enemy of good is not just better but best. Stability must be the watchword for all future space systems, ensuring the right people are in charge of and associated with the programs they manage over longer periods and stability within the requirements process—just say no to the C model when you need the system sooner and the A version will do. Spiral development is a strategy long used in aircraft acquisition where production of A, B, and C variants are commonplace. The military industrial complex provides exceptional capabilities, and it is often difficult for the Air Force to say no to enhancements when offered up by industry. Stability when combined with standardization, from the bus to the subsystems, can make a significant impact on reducing cost and potentially shorten production times.

Conclusion

Deterrence is seldom a simple proposition. The US nuclear deterrence strategy of mutually assured destruction took decades to mature. A comparable deterrence strategy for space will also likely take decades. In the interim, the United States enjoys a significant amount of freedom of action in space. As with air superiority, which the United States has enjoyed since the Korean Conflict, the nation can never take space superiority for granted. The approach of defense in depth offers a way ahead, a strategy that the nation, and more specifically the Department of Defense, can implement, even in a resource-constrained environment. It is not a panacea, nor does it pretend to satisfy those who would call for immediate weaponization of space. What the strategy attempts to do is to provide an alternative that protects US vital national interests, is less costly, garners international support, and at minimum, slows the march toward a weapons race in space. Reasonable men may disagree, but only the most foolhardy would discount the concept and ignore its potential benefits.

Notes

1. Cited from McDougall, *Heavens and the Earth*, 320.
2. Gordon Adams, quoted in Nardon, *Satellite Imagery Control*, 3.

3. *The Space Report*, 6.

4. Ibid.

5. European Commission, *Space*.

6. Government Accountability Office (GAO), *House Subcommittee on National Security and Foreign Affairs,* 1.

7. *Report of the Commission to Assess United States National Security, Space Management and Organization,* 9.

8. Elliott, "SECAF: Space Forces Have Become Indispensable."

9. Elliott, "Partnership Will Guide Military, Civilian Space Activities."

10. Schwartz, "National Security Space and the Air Force."

11. Mowthorpe, "The United States Approach to Military Space during the Cold War."

12. Davidson, Letter.

13. *Report of the Commission to Assess United States National Security,* chap. 6, 80.

14. "National Defense Authorization Act for FY 2003 Report."

15. Mowthorpe, "United States Approach to Military," 11.

16. Ibid., 4.

17. "Presidential Directive on National Space Policy."

18. National Space Technology Council, "Fact Sheet."

19. Department of Defense Directive 3100.10, *Space Policy*.

20. *National Security Strategy for a New Century*, 25.

21. *Report of the Commission to Assess United States National Security,* chap. 7, 99–100.

22. *National Security Strategy of the United States of America*, 29–30.

23. "National Space Policy Review."

24. Office of Science and Technology, "Fact Sheet."

25. Chang, "Obama Calls for End to NASA's Moon Program."

26. Nations with space-faring capability: United States, Russia, China, Japan, India, Australia, Iran, and Israel. The first three have exhibited manned space capabilities. Added to this list of nations would be the European Space Agency, with France, Germany, and Great Britain in the lead.

27. Pena, "US Commercial Space Programs," 10.

28. Myers and Ball, "Space Transportation."

29. Ibid.

30. Bolden, "NASA Administrator Bolden Defends Future Manned Space Flight Program."

31. Stenger, "Armadillo, Romanians Join $10 Million Space Race."

32. Siemens PLM Software, "Case Study," 15.

33. "Dragon Overview," Space Exploration Technologies Corporation.

34. Huntington, *Clash of Civilizations*, 28.

35. Moskowitz, "Are Russian's Recent Space Woes a Sign of Larger Problems?"

36. Federation of American Scientists (FAS) Space Policy Project (SPP), "Russian and Soviet Space Agencies."

37. "Top Official Deplores Decline of Russian Space Program," *Sydney Morning Herald*.

38. "Bodies Found in Cosmodrome Debris," *BBC News*.

39. FAS SPP, "Baikonur Cosmodrome."

40. Information Office of the State Council, People's Republic of China (IOSC, PRC), "China's Space Activities."

41. IOSC, PRC, "The Day of Carrier Space Flight of China is not Far Off."

42. Windrem and Boyle, "China Space Shot Has Military Implications."

43. Luan, "Chinese Space Undertakings toward the 21st Century."

44. IOSC, PRC, "Development of China's Aerospace Industry."

45. Jones, "China's Space Program Accelerates."

46. National Aeronautics Space Development Association, "To a New Phase of Japanese Rocket Development."

47. "Japanese Rocket Blasts Off," *BBC News.*

48. Japan Aerospace Exploration Agency, "JAXA Vision."

49. Ibid.

50. Dawson, "Japan Launches Space Cargo Push."

51. Wilkinson, "Japan's Evolving Space Program."

52. Ibid.

53. Whitehouse, "Japan's Uncertain Space Future."

54. Chino, "Need for Japanese Manned Spacecraft."

55. European Space Agency (ESA), "New Member States."

56. ESA, "ESA's Purpose."

57. Likanen, "Aerospace and the Evolution of Europe."

58. ESA, "ESA and the European Union."

59. Ibid.

60. ESA, "Shaping the Future of Europe."

61. Taylor, "A Competitive Space."

62. Bildt, Peyrelevade, and Spath, *Towards a Space Agency*, 9.

63. Commission to the Council, *Toward a Space Strategy*, 4.

64. ESA, "Funding."

65. "India Launches Its First Weather Satellite," *CNN.com.*

66. Somini Sengupta, "India Launches Unmanned Orbiter."

67. "Spacelift: Spacelift Australia," *SpaceDaily.*

68. "Russia and Australia," *SpatialSource.com.*

69. Israeli Space Agency, "Israel Space Agency History."

70. James Martin Center for Nonproliferation Studies, *CNS Resources on North Korea's Ballistic Missile Program.*

71. Choe and Sanger, "Rocket Failure."

72. Lake, "Iran's Space Launch Turns Clock Back."

73. ESA, "*Galileo* IOV" (In-Orbit Validation).

74. de Selding, "Europeans Blame US Government," 6.

75. Logsdon, "A Security Space Capability for Europe?"

76. *The Space Report*, 6.

77. Department of the Air Force, *Defense Industrial Base*, xi.

78. Ibid.

79. Department of State (DOS) Memorandum, subject: Review of APSTAR II/ Long March 2E Failure Investigation Data, 18 December 1998, In *Report of The United States House of Representatives Select Committee on U.S. National Security and Military/Commercial Concerns*, 76.

80. Ibid.

81. SPOT Image Corporation, website.

82. Pena, "US Commercial Space Programs," 10.

83. Fink and Fink, *Dirty Harry*.

84. David, "China's Anti-Satellite Test," 2.

85. "Congressional Hearing Testimony for the Under Secretary of the Air Force the Honorable Peter B. Teets."

86. McCartney et al., *National Security Space Launch Report*, xv–xvi, 42.

Chapter 12

Unmanned Air Systems and Deterrence

James D. Perry

This chapter examines the role of unmanned air systems (UAS)* in deterrence and argues that potential adversaries will increasingly adopt "antiaccess" strategies in order to deter the United States from projecting power within their geographic regions. If the United States can overcome these antiaccess strategies, then such strategies no longer have any deterrent value. Furthermore, the US ability to project power, to deny the adversary military victory, and to hold his most valuable assets at risk would likely exert a strong deterrent effect. This chapter argues that UASs are the most efficient way—in some cases, the only way—to overcome antiaccess challenges, and thus should have a significant deterrent effect if they are acquired in sufficient numbers. Also the ways in which UASs provide deterrent effects that are *qualitatively* different from manned airborne platforms, rather than simply providing "more of the same" due to greater endurance are examined. Lastly, the pros and cons of UASs in "strategic deterrence" (i.e., nuclear delivery) and the role of UASs in deterring terrorists and insurgent movements are briefly considered.

Classic deterrence theory holds that deterrence results from effective threats of punishment or denial. "Deterrence through punishment" entails a threat to inflict unacceptable damage on something an adversary values. "Deterrence through denial" involves an effort to convince an enemy that an attack will fail or only succeed at unacceptable cost. Both types of deterrence require accurate knowledge of the adversary—what it values, its capabilities and intentions, and its willingness to take risks and accept costs in order to achieve a particular objective. Both types of deterrence require the United States to communicate threats to the adversary in a timely and credible manner. The historical record contains numerous examples of the Unite States failing to understand what its enemies value (and do not value), to

---

*The Air Force uses the terms *remotely piloted vehicle* and *remotely piloted aircraft* to refer to unmanned systems.

appreciate the costs and risks that adversaries are prepared to accept, and to communicate threats effectively. Therefore, the United States should plan for deterrence to fail from time to time, and should prepare to defeat its adversaries rather than simply punish them after the fact. Of course, preparations to defeat the adversary are required in any case to make the threat of "deterrence through denial" credible.

Deterrence and the Antiaccess Threat

For the past 12 years, the Defense Department has described the antiaccess threat as a major challenge to American power projection, particularly in Asia. The 1997 National Defense Panel observed that the ability to project power is the "cornerstone of America's continued military preeminence," and that "much of our power projection capability depends on sustained access to regions of concern."[1]

Using the threat of punitive strikes, perhaps involving weapons of mass destruction (WMD), adversaries could coerce US allies into refusing access to forward ports and bases. Adversaries could also attack forward ports and bases with WMDs, cruise missiles, or ballistic missiles to deny access.[2] The 2001 *Quadrennial Defense Review* (QDR) emphasized the need to "overcome anti-access or area-denial threats," and set as a critical goal for the Defense Department "projecting and sustaining US forces in distant anti-access or area-denial environments and defeating anti-access and area-denial threats."[3] The 2006 QDR noted the Defense Department's continued efforts to "mitigate antiaccess threats and offset potential political coercion designed to limit US access to any region," and repeatedly emphasized the need for the capability to operate "at great distances into denied areas."[4]

Adversaries understand the central importance of airpower to American military operations, and thus particularly strive to reduce the effectiveness of US joint air forces. As US airpower principally consists of relatively short-ranged aircraft, one objective of an anti-access strategy is to deny these aircraft the use of the bases they need to operate. To this end, an enemy could employ ballistic and cruise missiles with precision guidance and submunitions.[5] An enemy could also attack theater airbases with WMDs, terrorists, or special operations forces.[6] To deny access to sea-based airpower, an adversary could employ antiship ballistic missiles, or launch antiship cruise missiles from air, surface, and subsurface platforms. An adversary could also employ advanced submarines, surface vessels, and sea mines. Larger adversaries would have integrated air defense systems that would include so-called "triple-digit SAMs" and advanced fighter aircraft with long-range air-to-air missiles. Nonstealthy platforms could penetrate enemy airspace only with great difficulty in the face of such defenses.

Any US aircraft that did penetrate enemy defenses would face a severe problem with mobile targets. Many of an adversary's missile launchers would be mobile to complicate tracking and targeting, and long-range missile systems and space-denial capabilities would be located deep within the enemy homeland beyond the reach of manned tactical aircraft.[7] Adversary command and control, fielded military forces, and possibly irregular forces would constitute another large set of mobile or nonpreplanned targets.

A large, powerful adversary would probably have a "dense" antiaccess network consisting of many of the above capabilities deployed in large numbers.[8] Lesser powers, however, could develop a meaningful antiaccess capability relatively cheaply even without a major power sponsor. In the 1990s, the Defense Science Board estimated that

> potential US regional adversaries spending on the order of only $15–20 billion over a decade in the global marketplace could develop robust theater-denial/disruption capabilities. These include conventional anti-naval forces (e.g., ultra-quiet diesel submarines, advanced anti-ship cruise missiles, and sophisticated sea mines); theater-range ballistic and land-attack cruise missiles (with the latter expected to be available in the thousands, and, increasingly, with low-observable characteristics); and nuclear, chemical and biological weapons.[9]

Notably, combat against relatively primitive opponents in Iraq and Afghanistan required US joint air forces to find and track a large number of mobile targets, such as insurgents and foreign volunteers intermingled with the civilian population. This difficult challenge continues today.

Antiaccess strategies have a political as well as military dimension. For example, in Operations Enduring Freedom and Iraqi Freedom the access constraints were almost entirely political in nature. Neighboring countries either denied the US access outright or severely restricted what US forces could and could not do from their territory and airspace. Basing options in Central Asia were difficult to exploit because the region was remote and the infrastructure was not well developed.[10]

The fundamental purpose of an antiaccess strategy is deterrence. Potential adversaries seek to convince the United States that in the event of conflict, they can defeat US intervention and inflict unacceptable losses on critical national assets such as aircraft carriers and advanced combat aircraft. Adversaries hope that this prospect of denial and punishment will deter the United States from intervening in disputes within their spheres of influence and that America's regional allies will be politically neutralized or may even join our adversary's side. An adversary would then enjoy freedom of political and military action wherever the United States was unable to operate. Clearly, if the United States can project power effectively without suffering excessive losses, then an adversary's antiaccess capabilities no longer have any deterrent value. Moreover, the American ability to project power, to deny an adversary military victory, and to hold its most valuable assets at risk would likely exert a strong deterrent effect on an adversary. Therefore, if UASs provide an efficient way to overcome antiaccess challenges, they should have a significant deterrent effect if they are acquired in adequate numbers.

Antiaccess strategies have multiple dimensions and overcoming them will require a multidimensional approach that includes air, surface, and subsurface elements. However, this paper focuses on the air dimension. What attributes do airborne platforms need in order to defeat antiaccess strategies? In general, they require long organic (unrefueled) range, organic sensing/targeting, deep weapons magazines, and broadband, all-aspect low observability (stealth). The 2006 *QDR* describes these attributes as follows:

> Joint air capabilities must be reoriented to favor, where appropriate, systems that have far greater range and persistence; larger and more flexible payloads for surveillance or strike; and the ability to penetrate and sustain operations in denied areas. The future force will place a premium on capabilities that are responsive and survivable. It will be able to destroy moving targets in all weather conditions, exploit nontraditional intelligence, and conduct next-generation electronic warfare. Joint air forces will be capable of rapidly and simultaneously locating and attacking thousands of fixed and mobile targets at global ranges. The future force will exploit stealth and advanced electronic warfare capabilities when and where they are needed.[11]

If an adversary can deny the United States access to airbases within a certain distance of its territory, but US aircraft have sufficient range to operate effectively from beyond that distance, then the adversary's antiaccess strategy is defeated. Long organic range combined with aerial refueling capability permits aircraft to refuel from tankers orbiting beyond the range of enemy air defenses, penetrate deep into enemy territory, and persist long enough to find and attack mobile targets.[12] One analyst notes that current tactical aircraft cannot attack targets "much deeper inside defended airspace than 500–750nm [nautical miles]," but "a number of potential adversaries could locate key facilities deeper inside their borders than 500–750nm."[13] The same analyst advocates the acquisition of aircraft with an unrefueled combat radius of 3,000 nm. Very likely, 1,500 nm should be considered the minimum acceptable unrefueled combat radius needed to deny the sanctuary of strategic depth to a continent-sized adversary or even a lesser adversary located far from friendly bases.[14] An aircraft with shorter range would be inadequate if close-in basing were denied through some combination of geography, diplomatic pressure, and enemy military capability. Long organic range, of course, also increases persistence at depth—the amount of time an aircraft can spend on station over the area of interest—and reduces the burden on the tanker force.

Airborne platforms not only need the range to reach the target area, but also need the "multi-INT" sensor capability, a combination of communications intelligence, electronic intelligence, moving target indication radar, and electro-optic/infrared sensors on a single aircraft, to identify and track mobile or emergent targets. To reduce communications requirements and compress the kill chain, the aircraft should ideally have the onboard capability to process sensor information and generate targeting solutions.[15] Networking allows the aircraft to benefit from, and contribute to, joint battlespace awareness. Organic targeting capability compensates when enemy action disrupts communications links, as a competent enemy will certainly attempt to do.

A deep weapons magazine ensures that the aircraft can remain on station longer before needing to return to base to rearm. Analysts have noted the evolving trend towards payload fractionation.[16] Precision guidance enables aircraft to carry a larger number of smaller weapons per sortie, rather than the smaller number of larger weapons that aircraft typically carried in the unguided weapons era. One implication of this trend is that aircraft can be smaller, possibly cheaper, and stealthier than was previously the case. Ultimately, airborne directed-energy weapons may provide deep magazines with a lower life-cycle cost and a smaller, simpler logistics tail than conventional munitions.

Low observability is essential for survivability in high-threat, anti-access environments.[17] In order to survive, aircraft must break the air-defense kill chain at some point during detection, tracking, and engagement. Common strategies involve some form of concealment, suppression, or destruction of enemy air defenses and electronic warfare and other countermeasures. Low observability seeks to reduce the range at which early warning and fire control radars can detect the aircraft, track it, and guide a surface-to-air missile (SAM) or air-to-air missile interceptor. This allows the aircraft to escape engagement altogether, to destroy SAM sites and radars from outside SAM engagement range, or to destroy enemy fighters before they can launch their missiles. Stealth aircraft have thus far generally flown carefully preplanned routes to execute strikes against fixed targets. During such missions, the aircraft seeks to ingress and egress as rapidly as possible and does not attempt to persist in enemy airspace. An effort to persist in enemy airspace to find, track, and engage mobile targets is a far more difficult problem, requiring an organic, in-flight capability to replan the optimally survivable route in real time in response to evolving threats while still completing the mission. From the standpoint of aircraft design, aircraft that do not intend to persist in enemy airspace or go deep inland may be optimized for low observability from certain aspects—most importantly, the front—but need not be optimized in all aspects.[18] An aircraft whose radar signature is reduced from the frontal aspect can succeed against less dense threat environments through such tactics as flying around anticipated radar coverage areas. However, in heavily defended airspace with overlapping radar coverage, aircraft unavoidably expose their nonstealthy side and rear aspects to enemy radars. They are thereby detected and engaged.[19] Persistent operations at depth and in heavily defended airspace demand minimizing observability from all aspects and in all radio frequency threat bands.[20] This design reduces the number of total air-defense engagements and allows the aircraft to follow a route that enables it rapidly to detect, track, and kill time-sensitive targets. True broadband, all-aspect low observability requires a tailless flying wing design, and most optimally, an unmanned design, since a cockpit compromises stealth.[21] Subsonic aircraft are generally better suited to persistent operations than supersonic aircraft. Supersonic flight greatly increases an aircraft's infrared signature, compromising stealth. It also significantly increases an aircraft's weight and fuel consumption, decreasing persistence.

Why do unmanned, tailless aircraft combine the above attributes more effectively than manned platforms? As already noted, unmanned aircraft will have an advantage in low observability relative to manned aircraft, but the most important advantage of unmanned systems is persistence. The persistence advantage of unmanned systems emerges from the limitations that human physiology imposes on manned aircraft. Generally speaking, single-seat aircraft pilots cannot sustain operations in a combat environment for more than about five hours before fatigue levels rise and aircraft are forced to return to base.[22] In addition, pilots are limited in the number of hours they can fly per month due to the effects of cumulative fatigue.[23] These factors create a range limit beyond which manned fighter-sized aircraft simply cannot operate effectively due to human physiology; one analyst puts this limit at 1,000 to 1,500 nm.[24] On the other hand, unmanned aircraft are not subject to these limitations, and thus have a superior ability to generate the persistent coverage needed to find and attack mobile targets at long range. If an adversary denied the United States access to bases within 1,500 nm of its territory, then unmanned air systems able to generate persistent coverage from outside this range might be the best way to overcome this antiaccess challenge. Other methods such as submarine-launched cruise missiles or conventional ballistic missiles might be contemplated, but how would these weapons be targeted? Most likely, in combination with space-based sensors, UASs would provide targeting data to enable these weapons to strike mobile targets. If the UAS is in the target area anyway, why not simply arm the UASs? Cruise and ballistic missiles are much more expensive than bombs dropped from UASs, and they have time-of-flight issues that bombs from an on-station UAS do not.[25]

To illustrate the persistence advantage of unmanned over manned aircraft, let us compare two aircraft that are otherwise identical, except one is unmanned and the other is manned (Table 12.1). Both are low observable tailless designs, and both can be refueled in flight. Each cruises at 460 knots true airspeed (ktas) and has an unrefueled range of 3,000 nm. Assume that the sustained combat endurance of the manned aircraft is 10 hours, owing chiefly to human physiological constraints.[26] Assume that the refueled system endurance of the unmanned aircraft is 50 hours, limited primarily by the expenditure of consumables and equipment with periodic maintenance requirements[27] and that aerial refueling is available and requires 30 minutes per refueling.

Table 12.1. Manned and unmanned endurance

	Notional Manned Aircraft	Notional Unmanned Aircraft
Organic Range (nm)	3,000	3,000
Cruise Speed (ktas)	460	460
Aircrew Max Combat Endurance (hours)	10	50

Now let us take three scenarios: a short-range scenario with aircraft based 600 nm from their targets, a medium-range scenario with aircraft based 1,200 nm from their targets, and a long-range scenario with aircraft based 2,000 nm from their targets. Aircraft refuel at a tanker safe line (TSL) 200 nm from the target area in the first scenario, TSL is 300 nm from the target area in the second scenario, and TSL 600 nm is from the target area in the final scenario. How many hours on combat station per sortie does each aircraft generate in each scenario (Table 12.2)?

Table 12.2. Hours on station per sortie for manned and unmanned aircraft at a given range

	Short Range (600 nm with 200 nm tanker standoff)	Medium Range (1,200 nm with 300 nm tanker standoff)	Long Range (2,000 nm with 600 nm tanker standoff)
Unmanned Aircraft	37.3	29.4	21.5
Manned Aircraft	5.3	3.8	0.3

The dramatic difference in time on-station is because the manned aircraft usually can make only one ingress from the TSL before the aircrew endurance limit forces the aircraft to return to base. In contrast, the unmanned aircraft can perform multiple ingress/egress cycles from the TSL before the overall mission endurance limit forces the aircraft to return to base.

Another measure of effectiveness is how many persistent orbits a given force of aircraft can generate. A persistent orbit is defined as one aircraft constantly on station at a given distance from base. Using the same aircraft as above, and using the same scenarios, how many persistent orbits can a force of 100 manned aircraft generate? And a force of 100 unmanned aircraft (Table 12.3)?

Table 12.3. Number of persistent orbits a force of 100 aircraft generates at a given range

	Short Range (600 nm with 200 nm tanker standoff)	Medium Range (1,200 nm with 300 nm tanker standoff)	Long Range (2,000 nm with 600 nm tanker standoff)
Unmanned Aircraft	55	46.7	33
Manned Aircraft	23	15.5	1.25

Clearly, UASs are vastly more efficient at generating the persistent coverage at long range necessary to find and attack mobile targets. The unmanned force puts more than twice as many aircraft on station as the manned force in the short-range scenario and more than 20 times as many aircraft on station as the manned force in the long-range scenario. Looked at another way, the number of aircraft required to generate a persistent orbit increases much more steeply for manned aircraft than for unmanned aircraft at the given ranges. This efficiency translates into a smaller force size needed to sustain the same number of aircraft on station. The Defense Department either could spend less money on an unmanned force while maintaining the same military capability as a manned force, or could achieve far greater military capability for the same amount of money with an unmanned force relative to a manned force.

Unmanned air systems have a superior capability to overcome anti-access strategies and thus present an adversary with a credible prospect that the United States could defeat any aggression and reverse any gains the aggressor had made. In principle, this should deter a rational adversary from undertaking an aggressive act, at least insofar as aerial weapons could defeat an attack. UASs may also have deterrent effects that emerge from the mere fact that they are unmanned. If adversaries perceive that the United States can act against them without risking the capture or death of aircrew, or political embarrassment, then US airpower may be more "usable" and have a greater deterrent effect when unmanned rather than manned aircraft are employed.

Moving beyond deterrence, the Defense Department has argued that American strategic forces must not merely deter and defeat potential aggressors, but must assure allies and dissuade potential competitors from initiating military competition with the United States.[28] To this end, the *Nuclear Posture Review* recommended the acquisition of nonnuclear strategic strike forces to complement US nuclear forces. A full discussion of assurance and dissuasion is beyond the scope of this chapter. However, one should note that antiaccess strategies, if not countered, over time would increasingly convince America's allies that America could not protect them because American forces could not operate effectively from regional bases and waters in the event of conflict. A force of stealthy, refuelable UASs able to operate effectively from extended ranges would provide a powerful and credible means to assure allies in peacetime that the United States could protect them in the event of war.

Dissuasion strategies seek to increase the perceived costs and decrease the perceived benefits of competing militarily with America.[29] Stealthy, long-range UASs provide a means to conduct persistent surveillance and high-volume strikes against all classes of targets, even at extended range.[30] Therefore, they enhance the military component of dissuasion because they diminish the perceived benefits of acquiring threatening military capabilities.[31] The 2006 QDR states that "to dissuade major and emerging powers from developing capabilities that could threaten regional stability, to deter conflict, and to defeat aggression should deterrence fail," the United States needs the capability to "mitigate anti-access threats and offset potential political coercion designed to limit US access to any region."[32] To this end, the United States requires "persistent surveillance, including systems that can penetrate and loiter in denied or contested areas" and "prompt and high-volume global strike to deter aggression or coercion."[33] Stealthy, refuelable unmanned combat air vehicles clearly provide such capabilities and can mitigate antiaccess threats. In sum, a force of UASs able to overcome antiaccess threats and to deter and defeat an adversary would also be highly effective at assuring America's allies and dissuading adversaries from competing with the United States.

UASs and Nuclear Deterrence

The self-evident need to recapitalize the nation's aging nuclear weapons and delivery systems raises the question of whether some, or all, of the air-breathing component of the triad should be unmanned. The case for nuclear-armed UASs depends to a great degree on what one assumes about the nature of nuclear deterrence, defense, and warfare in the "Second Nuclear Age"; that is, whether nuclear weapons will be "usable" in certain scenarios. For example, one analyst advocates acquiring a stealthy, manned bomber in case it is necessary to conduct limited nuclear strikes "against authoritarian regimes with small atomic arsenals and less than intercontinental reach."[34] If we choose to build a new nuclear-capable bomber, the unmanned option should not be rejected out of hand, because the arguments that a nuclear-capable bomber *must* be manned are weak. The most plausible role for UASs in nuclear operations, however, is not to deliver nuclear weapons, but to provide intelligence, surveillance, reconnaissance, and targeting for other nuclear delivery systems, such as ballistic missiles.[35] UASs can also conduct conventional precision strikes on enemy strategic systems and provide a launch platform for boost-phase ballistic missile defense interceptors.

The United States has operated "unmanned" nuclear systems for a long time, in the form of intercontinental and submarine launched ballistic missiles (ICBM and SLBM) and cruise missiles, but a nuclear-capable UAS would still have to surmount strong cultural and psychological resistance. The chief difference between a UAS and a cruise missile in flight is that in the past, cruise missiles operated autonomously after launch, and could not land after launch, while UASs accepted operator control and direction, and could land after launch. The trend in cruise missiles, however, is increasingly to permit operator intervention and dynamic retasking in order to engage mobile targets. In effect, the cruise missile becomes an air-launched UAS controlled from the launch platform. The Air Force, if it developed a successor to the AGM-129, could require the new missile to accept in-flight retasking from the launch platform. If so, the resulting missile would differ from a stealthy UAS only in that it would not have the ability to land, though this, too, could be incorporated if desired in order to recover the weapon if it is not used.

The safe recovery of a nuclear-armed unmanned aircraft would be a concern, but unmanned bombers need only fly with nuclear weapons aboard during a fully generated alert. Such alerts were exceedingly rare events even during the Cold War. UASs would not need to fly training flights with nuclear weapons on board;[36] one advantage of unmanned aircraft is that operator training can occur almost entirely through simulation, reducing the costs and risks of flying the aircraft itself for training purposes.

While "low end" UASs historically have been crash-prone, there is no technical reason that UASs cannot have a level of reliability equal to manned systems, and in fact UAS reliability is already approaching manned levels.[37] Smaller UASs are more crash-prone because they are cheap and disposable by design, but a nuclear-capable UAS would be designed to the highest levels of reliability. Even a nonnuclear-capable unmanned bomber would require extremely high levels of reliability, and the same technology path would assure the reliability of an unmanned nuclear-capable bomber.[38]

Nuclear-capable UASs would unquestionably require secure, reliable, and survivable communications. This requirement is not, however, specific to unmanned aircraft. Any communications system secure, reliable, and survivable enough for manned aircraft to conduct nuclear operations should be secure, reliable, and survivable enough for unmanned aircraft too. Some analysts argue that manned bombers are preferable to unmanned aircraft or ballistic missiles "because they permit more time for second thoughts or last-minute changes of the President's mind."[39] The thought of the president making decisions on this timescale and micromanaging a nuclear operation up to the moment of weapons release scarcely seems plausible. Nevertheless, if we assume that a communications system exists that can recall a manned bomber up to the very moment of weapons release, then that same system could also recall an unmanned aircraft in the same circumstances. (Either the communications system can support nuclear micromanagement, or it cannot!) A manned bomber on a nuclear mission that lost connectivity would either attack the preplanned target or return to base without using its weapon. An unmanned bomber could certainly be programmed to perform the same tasks (attack preplanned targets or return to base) in the same situation. Moreover, the "recall" capability simply reduces the amount of time in which no recall is possible from the 15- to 30-minute transit time of a ballistic missile to the minute or two it takes for a bomb to detonate after it leaves an aircraft. Providing the president with an extra 13 to 28 minutes of "dither time" is not a compelling reason for the nation to spend tens of billions of dollars on a new bomber, whether it is manned or unmanned.

If we assume that the cultural and communications issues are surmounted, what utility would an unmanned nuclear-capable bomber enjoy versus major powers and lesser adversaries? With respect to major powers, the Air Force states that SIOP, for Single Integrated Operational Plan, missions—for example, nuclear operations against a major power after deterrence has failed—"usually strike fixed, high-value targets."[40] In such a scenario, presidential micromanagement of individual aircraft is hardly possible, and the ability to recall aircraft is essentially irrelevant, if not actually harmful. (The ability to recall a nuclear attack after it is launched undermines deterrence because the possibility that you can change your mind allows the enemy to think you might actually do so.) An unmanned aircraft could certainly be programmed to attack specific, previously identified fixed targets with nuclear weapons just as a manned bomber could. UASs would provide the critical persistent surveillance needed to find enemy mobile ballistic missiles, but attacking such targets would not necessarily require arming the UAS with nuclear weapons. The UAS could attack with conventional munitions or cue an attack from a manned nuclear-armed bomber. An unmanned bomber would force the adversary to devote considerable effort to air defense; but manned bombers, cruise missiles, and even unmanned nonnuclear-capable aircraft also achieve this effect.

Against regional adversaries most strategic target classes would require conventional attack. Those that required nuclear attack, such as hardened, deeply buried facilities, would generally not be mobile or time-critical. Nuclear-armed UASs would only be useful against the very small number of targets that were mobile, not vulnerable to conventional munitions, important enough to require nuclear attack, and urgent enough to require immediate attack with nuclear gravity bombs rather than waiting 15 to 30 minutes for a ballistic missile warhead to arrive. The only mission that likely qualifies is preemption of a nuclear missile or certain other classes of WMD attacks, and arguably conventional precision strike may even suffice for this mission. Such conventional strikes would destroy the delivery systems, even if they did not destroy the weapon itself. A 2009 Defense Science Board study considered a scenario in which a regional power with a limited number of ICBMs threatened to strike the United States or one of its allies. The study argued that conventional SLBM and cruise missile attacks could defeat this threat and noted that stealthy cruise missiles offered "both penetrability without detection and hard target disruption capability." Curiously, this study did not focus on UASs as strike platforms in any detail, even though time-critical conventional strike is what stealthy UASs do best. The study did, however, recommend, "USD (ATL) [that is Under Secretary of Defense for Acquisition, Technology and Logistics], with support from the Air Force and DARPA, perform a study to evaluate the relative performance, cost and risk for a next generation remote, time critical, conventional strike capability based on loitering or penetrating unmanned air breathing weapons."[41]

UASs could support a largely, if not entirely, nonnuclear damage-limitation strategy in order to deter or defeat nuclear-armed regional adversaries with relatively limited geographic territories and missile arsenals. This would be consistent with the 2002 Nuclear Posture Review's goals of employing advanced conventional strike capabilities to assure allies and dissuade, deter, and defeat adversaries:

> Systems capable of striking a wide range of targets throughout an adversary's territory may dissuade a potential adversary from pursuing threatening capabilities. . . .

> Defenses can make it more arduous and costly for an adversary to compete militarily with or wage war against the United States. The demonstration of a range of technologies and systems for missile defense can have a dissuasive effect on potential adversaries. The problem of countering missile defenses, especially defensive systems with multiple layers, presents a potential adversary with the prospect of a difficult, time-consuming and expensive undertaking. . . .

> [Missile] defense of U.S. territory and power projection forces, including U.S forces abroad, combined with the certainty of U.S. ability to strike in response, can bring into better balance U.S. stakes and risks in a regional confrontation and thus reinforce the credibility of U.S. guarantees designed to deter attacks on allies and friends. . . .

> Composed of both non-nuclear systems and nuclear weapons, the strike element of the New Triad can provide greater flexibility in the design and conduct of military campaigns to defeat opponents decisively. Non-nuclear strike capabilities may be particularly useful to limit collateral damage and conflict escalation.[42]

The 2010 *Nuclear Posture Review* notes the importance of "strengthening regional deterrence while reducing the role and numbers of nuclear weapons."[43] Conventionally armed UASs acquired in sufficient numbers would support a strategy of strengthening the nonnuclear elements of regional security, particularly because they would be "capable of fighting limited and large-scale conflicts in anti-access environments," which the report considers critical to credible deterrence.[44] Conventionally armed UASs would also support two of the "key initiatives" for strengthening regional deterrence mentioned in the report:

> Develop non-nuclear prompt global strike capabilities. These capabilities may be particularly valuable for the defeat of time-urgent regional threats.

> Develop and deploy, over the next decade, more effective capabilities for real-time intelligence, surveillance, and reconnaissance capabilities.[45]

On the whole very little additional operational utility or deterrent effect appears to emerge from making an unmanned bomber nuclear-capable. I have argued that, contrary to the opinions of some authors, a nuclear-capable UAS could conduct limited nuclear strikes against authoritarian regimes with small WMD arsenals if that capability was desired. However, this scenario is not terribly plausible or likely to occur, and thus the need for *any* kind of aircraft, manned or unmanned, to fill this specific capability gap is highly questionable. The Air Force probably should not pursue the option of a nuclear-capable UAS, especially given that cruise missiles remain a relatively cheap, accurate, difficult-to-defend against, and politically accepted air-breathing nuclear threat. Nonnuclear-capable UASs are best employed to support all types of strategic strikes by providing persistent surveillance to cue other systems, including nuclear delivery systems, and conventional precision attacks. The shortfall in penetrating, persistent surveillance, and high-volume global strike capability amply justifies the development of a stealthy, unmanned bomber, and making this bomber nuclear-capable would only generate political controversy that would delay its development.[46] Even an unmanned bomber that could not deliver nuclear weapons should, however, be hardened for operations in nuclear environments in order to prevent adversaries from using electromagnetic pulse attacks to defeat the system.[47]

UASs and the Deterrence of Nonstate Actors

Whether or not UASs can "deter" people from joining an insurgency or terrorist group remains an open question. The question of deterring terrorism is larger than simply deterring terrorist groups themselves. If one could not deter terrorist "frontline" leaders or fighters directly, one might nevertheless seek to apply the principles of deterrence to the "less motivated" elements of the terrorist network, such as financiers, state sponsors, or the supporting population.[48] Broadly speaking, while there is no technological "quick fix" to the problems of terrorism and insurgency, unmanned aircraft could provide the persistent surveillance and attack capability needed as part of any comprehensive strategy to counter these nonstate challenges.

Some analysts argue that forcing the enemy to risk his life to fight machines, with no hope of killing a human enemy in return, and covering the battlespace with seemingly omnipresent UASs that can strike without warning, demoralizes the enemy, and deters people from joining an insurgency.[49] Others claim that the enemy regards the employment of UASs with contempt, because UASs show that the United States is afraid to put its soldiers in harm's way.[50] In a recent controversy over the ongoing "drone war" in Pakistan and Afghanistan, some observers contended that the employment of UASs was positively counterproductive, because the unmanned strikes generated outrage and provoked people to join the insurgency.[51] Former CIA Director, Gen Michael Hayden, took a contrary view:

> By making a safe haven feel less safe, we keep al-Qaeda guessing. We make them doubt their allies, question their methods, their plans, even their priorities. Most importantly, we force them to spend more time and resources on self-preservation. And that distracts them, at least partially and at least for a time, from laying the groundwork for the next attack.[52]

His successor, Leon Panetta, argued that UAS strikes were not only "very effective" but were also "the only game in town in terms of confronting or trying to disrupt the al-Qaeda leadership."[53] This is inarguably true, and thus UAS strikes will likely continue because they are the "least bad" option, whether or not they deter people from joining al-Qaeda or encourage them to do so.

One author argues that the United States should form, in conjunction with partner nations, a global counterterrorism network to deter and defeat terrorist groups. Over time,

> This network will become so expansive and dense that transnational terrorist groups will no longer be able to operate effectively. The underlying goal is to increase dramatically the anticipated costs of conducting terrorist acts, convincing would-be terrorists that the probability of successfully orchestrating a major plot is very low, while punishment would be painful, swift, and certain. In theory, by influencing the cost-benefit calculus associated with terrorists, the [network] will deter terrorists from acting—and in the event deterrence fails, it will effectively disrupt terrorist plots before they are hatched.[54]

The backbone of such a network would be human intelligence. Nevertheless, the 2006 QDR notes that "persistent surveillance to find and precisely target enemy capabilities in denied areas" and "prompt global strike to attack fleeting enemy targets rapidly" are critical capabilities for defeating terrorist networks.[55] Unmanned combat air systems provide these capabilities and complement manned aircraft and troops on the ground. For example, Predator UASs watched terrorist leader Abu Musab al-Zarqawi for 600 hours before an F-16 attack killed him.[56] The United States should therefore increase the capability and capacity of its fleet of UASs employed in irregular warfare. The United States needs not only nonstealthy, "low end," and relatively short-legged UASs such as the Predator and Reaper, but also stealthy UASs suitable for operations in denied areas:

> A major capability shortfall of the proposed hunter-killer fleet is that neither the Predator nor the Reaper is stealthy. For conducting surveillance and, in some cases, strike missions in denied areas (e.g., Iran) and sensitive areas (e.g., countries with which the United States is not at war, and which possess modern air surveillance systems), it would be highly desirable to have a stealthy, long-endurance [unmanned combat air systems]. While this is admittedly a niche capability in the war against transnational terrorist groups, it could be a critical one in many plausible contingencies. As air defense systems proliferate and become more capable over the course of the coming decade, the need for stealthy [unmanned combat air systems] will grow more pressing. This requirement, moreover, overlaps with the need to develop and field a stealthy, persistent surveillance-strike capability to hedge against the rise of China as a military competitor.[57]

Stealthy, long-range UASs could have a particularly important role in preventing states and terrorist groups from acquiring or using WMDs. States seeking to acquire WMDs might not have the anti-access capabilities described earlier in this paper, but still might have sufficiently capable air defenses to deny their airspace to nonstealthy airborne platforms. Moreover, the United States might be reluctant to risk the death or capture of aircrews in order to conduct surveillance of such a state's WMD programs on a routine basis. Stealthy UASs could provide a means to "detect, identify, locate, tag and track key WMD assets and development infrastructure in hostile or denied areas and to interdict WMD, their delivery systems, and related materials in transit" without risking aircrew loss.[58] Stealthy UASs could also support special operations forces in their efforts to collect intelligence on WMD programs, interdict WMD movements, and "render safe" loose weapons or materials.[59] Similar considerations would prevail if a time-critical target (such as a terrorist meeting or a terrorist team with WMD) emerged on the territory "neutral" state. In such scenarios, stealthy UASs would provide persistent, covert surveillance and attack capability that could support other forms of strategic strike or execute strikes themselves.[60]

Conclusion

Stealthy, long-range UASs offer a cost-effective means to provide the persistent surveillance and attack needed to find and attack mobile targets at long range in the face of enemy antiaccess capabilities. The ability of stealthy, long-range UASs to counter antiaccess strategies should deter rational adversaries and dissuade them from acquiring threatening military capabilities. Furthermore, such UASs should help to assure America's regional allies that we can protect them in the event of conflict. Stealthy, long-range UASs can contribute to nuclear deterrence principally by providing targeting information to other strike systems, though UASs could also conduct conventional strikes against enemy strategic systems and defend against enemy ballistic missile launches with air-launched interceptors. UASs can provide persistent surveillance and attack capability that may deter terrorists and insurgents from acting, and defeat them if they do. Of course, UASs are not a "stand-alone" solution to the problems of terrorism and insurgency, but must be part of a comprehensive strategy for the defeat of these nonstate challenges.

Notes

1. National Defense Panel, *Transforming Defense*, 12–13.
2. Ibid.
3. Office of the Secretary of Defense (OSD), *Quadrennial Defense Review (QDR) Report*, 30 September 2001, 30.
4. OSD, *QDR Report*, 6 February 2006, 30–31, 34, 45.
5. Stillion and Orletsky, *Airbase Vulnerability to Conventional Cruise-Missile and Ballistic-Missile Attacks*.
6. Chandler, *Tomorrow's War*, discusses WMD attacks on theater ports and airbases. Regarding ground attacks on airbases, see Vick, *Snakes in the Eagle's Nest*.
7. OSD, *QDR Report*, 30 September 2001, 31.
8. For example, OSD, *Military Power of the People's Republic of China*, 2009, 20–25.
9. Department of Defense (DOD), *Final Report of the Defense Science Board* [DSB], 25.
10. See Lambeth, *Air Power against Terror*, for a discussion of political constraints on access during Operation Enduring Freedom.
11. OSD, *QDR Report*, 6 February 2006, 45.
12. The ability to refuel in flight is critical to achieving the full persistence benefits of the unmanned revolution. Achieving long organic range *without* aerial refueling capability requires a much larger aircraft that is more expensive and—in the case of naval unmanned aircraft—is not carrier-suitable. Aerial refueling of an unmanned aircraft with a short organic range would still be useful, but the tankers would have to fly

closer to enemy territory, and would thus be more vulnerable. More importantly, the unmanned aircraft's ability to persist over enemy territory would be reduced.

13. Watts, *Moving Forward on Long-Range Strike*, 21.

14. Xinjiang, the point on Earth farthest from any ocean, is about 1,500 nm from the nearest ocean.

15. The "kill chain" is the colloquial term for the process used to prosecute "dynamic" targets (i.e., targets outside the normal tasking cycle). The kill chain has six phases: find, fix, track, target, engage, and assess (F2T2EA). See Air Force Doctrine Document 3-60, *Targeting*, 49.

16. Watts, *Long-Range Strike*, 68–70.

17. Grant, *The Radar Game*, is the basis for this discussion of stealth.

18. Ibid., 31. These aircraft have what Grant calls the "Pacman" or "Bowtie" signature.

19. See the discussion in ibid., 40–46.

20. Ibid., 30. These aircraft have the closest real-world approximation to what Grant calls the "Fuzzball" signature. See also Grant's discussion of survivability in heavily defended airspace, ibid., 40–42.

21. Cockpits are transparent to radar energy and are filled with radar-reflecting surfaces like the ejection seat and the pilot's helmet. Cockpits thus greatly increase the radar signature of an aircraft, and mitigating this problem is a critical issue in stealth aircraft design. See Richardson, *Stealth Warplanes*, 38–39. While the F-117, B-2, F-22, and other manned platforms are stealthy, unmanned platforms of equivalent size and shape to these aircraft, but without a cockpit, would be much stealthier than the manned version. This was understood even in the late 1970s. See Rich, *Skunk Works*, 65.

22. Bowie, *The Anti-Access Threat and Theater Air Bases*, 11–13.

23. Ibid., 14.

24. Ibid., 15. Keep in mind that manned aircraft would have to be based far closer to the target area to conduct persistent operations against mobile targets than they would to conduct "in and out" strikes on fixed targets.

25. Cruise missiles are about 100 times more expensive than direct-attack munitions like JDAM. Watts, *Long-Range Strike*, 71.

26. Ten hours is a very generous assumption. See Bowie, *The Anti-Access Threat and Theater Air Bases*, 11–13, for a good discussion of this point.

27. This number was arbitrarily selected and is conservative. Other complex variables have been simplified, such as mission planning and management, mission survivability, and mission availability. No crew ratio limits are assumed for manned aircraft, and maintenance turnaround time is two hours for both types of aircraft.

28. DOD, *Findings of the Nuclear Posture Review*, 9 January 2002, slide 12.

29. See OSD, *QDR Report*, 6 February 2006, 27–32; and Krepinevich and Martinage, *Dissuasion Strategy*, viii–x.

30. In principle, a sufficiently large land-based UAS could carry penetrating weapons capable of defeating even hardened and deeply buried targets.

31. See Krepinevich and Martinage, *Dissuasion Strategy*, 39–40.

32. OSD, *QDR Report*, 6 February 2006, 30.

33. Ibid., 31.

34. Watts, *Case for Long-Range Strike*, 44.

35. As noted above, due to the time-of-flight problem armed UASs are a superior alternative to ballistic missiles for prompt *conventional* strikes against mobile targets.

Time-of-flight is a less compelling argument against ballistic missiles for *nuclear* strikes. A mobile target is unlikely to get outside the envelope of lethal nuclear effects before the ballistic missile warhead arrives. More importantly, nuclear strikes are most likely to be directed against fixed targets, and against such targets the 15–30 minute time-of-flight of a ballistic missile is probably acceptable.

36. A study of accidents involving US nuclear weapons from 1950 to 1980 notes that most accidents occurred during logistic/ferry missions and during the airborne alerts that were discontinued in 1968. Hypothetical nuclear-armed UAS need not fly such missions. See DOD, "Narrative Studies of Accidents Involving U.S. Nuclear Weapons, 1950–1980."

37. DOD, *FY2009–2034 Unmanned Systems Integrated Roadmap*, 92–93. See also OSD, *Unmanned Aircraft Systems Roadmap*, appendices F and H.

38. The 2005 *UAS Roadmap* shows that UAS cost is linearly related to weight. If deemed desirable, an unmanned nonnuclear bomber would be large, and thus would not be cheap. This point is often lost on those who think UAS should be "cheap" simply because small, disposable UAS are relatively inexpensive. An unmanned bomber would have to be sufficiently reliable to preserve an asset bought in limited numbers and used for critical missions. OSD, *Unmanned Aircraft Systems Roadmap*, 57.

39. Watts, *Case for Long-Range Strike*, 49.

40. Secretary of the Air Force, *US Air Force White Paper on Long Range Bombers*, 17.

41. DSB, *Time Critical Conventional Strike from Strategic Standoff*, 5–6, 81–84.

42. "Nuclear Posture Review Report [Reconstructed]. The cover page states: "Excerpts of the Nuclear Posture Review Report were first made available at http://www.global security.org/wmd/library/policy/dod/npr htm. In order to better illustrate the structure of the report and how much of it that remains classified, this reconstruction reinstates the leaked excerpts to their respective pages. Reconstruction by Hans M. Kristensen, Director Nuclear Information Project, Federation of American Scientists."

43. DOD, *Nuclear Posture Review Report*, April 2010, 32.

44. Ibid., 33.

45. Ibid., 34.

46. One DSB study noted, "Using persistent surveillance and strike to deny sanctuary is a key objective of US forces. Current and planned forces cannot achieve this in the presence of modern air defenses. A near-term approach for achieving persistent surveillance/strike throughout moderately defended battlespace is to develop and deploy a family of stealthy, refuelable, subsonic, unmanned, global surveillance/strike systems (UGSSS)." UGSSS would have a 6,000-nm range, advanced stealth, aerial refueling capability for 100-hour sorties, multi-INT sensors, and a 20,000-pound payload. In the author's view, the case for such a system remains strong. DSB, *Future Strategic Strike Forces*, 5-12, 5-13.

47. On electromagnetic pulse, see the web site of the Commission to Assess the Threat to the United States from Electromagnetic Pulse.

48. Trager and Zagorcheva, "Deterring Terrorism: It Can Be Done." In particular, states that sponsor or host terrorists have assets that airpower can hold at risk. Deterrence should, in principle, function against these states.

49. Hsu, "Real Soldiers Love Their Robot Brethren."

50. Mazzetti, "The Downside of Letting Robots Do the Bombing."

51. Kilcullen and Exum, "Death from Above." Also Coll, "In Search of Success."

52. Schifrin, "US Drone Strikes with Deadly Accuracy."

53. "US Airstrikes in Pakistan Called 'Very Effective,'" *CNN*.

54. Martinage, *Special Operations Forces*, 27. See also Olson, "The Terror Threat," 8–9.

55. OSD, *QDR Report*, 6 February 2006, 23–24. The 2010 QDR noted the "invaluable" role of long-dwell UAS for counterinsurgency and counterterrorism, and called for an expansion of such systems. OSD, *QDR Report*, 12 February 2010, 22.

56. Bowman, "Predator Pilots Engage in Remote Control Combat."

57. Martinage, *Dissuasion Strategy*, 70, 77–78. A "moderately stealthy" UAS, the RQ-170, has operated in Afghanistan, though its precise role is unclear. Fulghum and Sweetman, "Stealth over Afghanistan."

58. OSD, *QDR Report*, 6 February 2006, 34. Also ibid., 35. "Preventing state or nonstate actors from acquiring or using WMD highlights the need for . . . persistent surveillance over wide areas to locate WMD capabilities or hostile forces." UAS excel at providing persistent surveillance over wide areas.

59. Martinage, *Dissuasion Strategy*, xiii, 37–38.

60. These scenarios are described in DSB, *Time Critical Conventional Strike from Strategic Standoff*, 69–80.

Abbreviations

AFRI	Air Force Research Institute
ASAT	antisatellite
BCP	business continuity planning
BW	biological weapons
CITS	Combat Information Transport System
COA	course of action
COIN	counterinsurgency
COMMSAT	communication satellite
COOP	continuity of operations planning
CSIS	Center for Strategic and International Studies
DOD	Department of Defense
DOJOC	DOD *Deterrence Operations Joint Operating Concept*
DSCS	Defense Satellite Communication System
EELV	expendable launch vehicle
ESA	European Space Agency
EU	European Union
F2T2EA	kill chain phases: find, fix, track, target, engage, and assess
GAO	Government Accountability Office
GEO	geosynchronous Earth orbit
GIG	Global Information Grid
GPS	Global Positioning System
ICBM	intercontinental ballistic missile
ISR	intelligence, surveillance, and reconnaissance
IT	information technology
JAXA	Japanese Aerospace Exploration Agency
JFC	joint force commander
ktas	knots true airspeed
MEF	mission-essential functions
MOPP	mission-oriented protective posture
NASA	National Aeronautics and Space Administration
NASDA	National Space Development Agency (Japan)
NCTC	National Counterterrorism Center
NGO	nongovernmental organizations
nm	nautical miles
NSS	*National Security Strategy*

NW	nuclear weapons
ORC	operationally responsive cyberspace
ORS	operationally responsive space
OSD	Office of the Secretary of Defense
QDR	*Quadrennial Defense Review*
RDT&E	research, development, test, and evaluation
RPA	remotely piloted aircraft
RRSC	Rapid Response Space Center
SAB	Air Force Scientific Advisory Board
SAM	surface-to-air missile
SLBM	submarine launched ballistic missiles
SLV	space launch vehicle
TSL	tanker safe line
UGSSS	unmanned, global surveillance/strike systems
UK	United Kingdom
USCYBERCOM	US Cyber Command
USSR	Soviet Union
USSTRATCOM	US Strategic Command
WGS	Wideband Global System
WMD	weapons of mass destruction

Bibliography

Adler, Emanuel, and Michael Barnett, eds. *Security Communities*. Cambridge, UK: Cambridge University Press, 1998.

"An Agreement between the AEC [Atomic Energy Commission] and the DOD [Department of Defense] for the Development, Production, and Standardization of Atomic Weapons," 21 March 1953.

Air Force Doctrine Document 1-2. *Air Force Glossary*, 11 January 2007.

Air Force Doctrine Document 3-60. *Targeting*, 8 June 2006.

Air Force Nuclear Task Force. *Reinvigorating the Air Force Nuclear Enterprise*. Washington, DC: Headquarters USAF, 24 October 2008.

Air Force Research Laboratory. *Proactive and Predictive Cyber Indications and Warnings (P2CIW)*. AFRL-IF-RS-TR-2006-226. July 2006.

——.Information Directorate. *Integrated Cyber Defense and Support Technologies*. BAA-08-08-RIKA. 14 October 2008. https://www.fbo.gov/index?s=opportunity&mode=form&id=e72854d6e3c1a044038563ef1e0fdfa6&tab=core&tabmode=list&=.

——. Rome Research Site. "Polymorphic Cyber Defense—Active Repositioning in Cyberspace." Award notice, 13 March 2009. https://www.fbo.gov/spg/USAF/AFMC/AFRLRRS/Awards/FA875009C0051.html.

"Airpower in Operation Desert Storm." *Air Force Fact Sheets*. http://usmilitary.about.com/library/milinfo/affacts/blairpowerinoperationdesertstorm.htm.

Alberts, David S. *Defensive Information Warfare*. Washington, DC: National Defense University Press, 1996.

Allison, Graham T. *Essence of Decision: Explaining the Cuban Missile Crisis*. Boston: Little, Brown, and Co., 1971.

"Al Maliki Defiant in Face of Regime's Opponents." *Arizona Daily Star*, 13 March 2011. http://azstarnet.com/news/world/article_2c6247ac-573d-54d7-8fbb-aa5567a88841.html.

Altheide, David. *Terrorism and the Politics of Fear*. Lanham, MD: AltaMira Press, 2006.

Amuzegar, Jahangir. "Iran's Crumbling Revolution." *Foreign Affairs* 82, no. 1 (January/February 2003): 44–57.

Angell, Norman. *The Great Illusion*. New York and London: G. P. Putnam's Sons, 1913.

Astore, William. "The New American Isolationism." *Nation*, 1 November 2010. http://www.thenation.com/article/155725/new-american-isolationism.

Augustine. *City of God*. Translated by H. Bettenson. New York: Penguin Books, 1972.

Bahgat, Gawdat. "Proliferation of Weapons of Mass Destruction: The Case of Libya." *International Relations* 22, no. 1 (March 2008): 105–26.

Battilega, John A. "Soviet Views of Nuclear Warfare: The Post-Cold War Interviews." In *Getting MAD: Nuclear Mutual Assured Destruction, Its Origins and Practice*, edited by Henry D. Sokolski, 151–164. Carlisle Barracks, PA: Strategic Studies Institute (SSI), US Army War College, November 2004. http://www.strategicstudiesinstitute.army.mil/pdf files/PUB585.pdf.

Beeker, Kevin R., Robert F. Mills, and Michael R. Grimaila. "Applying Deterrence in Cyberspace." *IO* [*International Organization*] *Journal*, February 2010, 21–27. http://www.crows.org/images/stories/IO _Journal_1st_QTR_2010.pdf?phpMyAdmin=8fb0f1471e1062f3cc 758f323e70b775.

Belasco, Amy. *The Cost of Afghanistan, Iraq and Other Global War on Terror Operations since 9/11*. Washington, DC: Congressional Research Service, 2009.

Bell, William C., and Cham Dallas. "Vulnerability of Populations and the Urban Health Care Systems to Nuclear Weapon Attack—Examples from Four American Cities." *International Journal of Health Geographics* 6, no. 5 (28 February 2007). http://www.ij-healthgeographics .com/contents/6/1/5.

Berman, Iian I., Kenneth Katzman, and James Phillips. "Iran's Nuclear Threat: The Day After." Heritage Foundation Special Report no. 53, 4 June 2009. http://www.heritage.org/events/2009/06/irans-nuclear -threat-the-day-after.

Biddle, Stephen. *American Grand Strategy after 9/11: An Assessment*. Carlisle, PA: Army War College, 2005.

Bildt, Carl, Jean Peyrelevade, and Lothar Spath. *Towards a Space Agency for the European Union, Report to the ESA Director General*, November 2000, 9. http://esamultimedia.esa.int/docs/annex2_wisemen .pdf.

Blackwill, Robert D., and Jeffrey W. Legro. "Constraining Ground Force Exercises of NATO and the Warsaw Pact." *International Security* 13, no. 3 (Winter 1989/90): 68–98.

Blanchard, Christopher. *Al Qaeda: Statements and Evolving Ideology.* Washington, DC: Congressional Research Service, 2007.

"Bodies Found in Cosmodrome Debris." *BBC News,* 13 May 2002. http://news.bbc.co.uk/2/hi/europe/1983638.stm.

Bolden, Charles. "NASA Administrator Bolden Defends Future Manned Space Flight Program." *Orlando Sentinel,* 1 July 2011. http://blogs.orlandosentinel.com/news_space_thewritestuff/2011/07/nasa-administrator-bolden-defends-future-manned-space-flight-plans.html.

Bowie, Christopher J. *The Anti-Access Threat and Theater Air Bases.* Washington, DC: Center for Strategic and Budgetary Assessments (CSBA), 2002.

Bowman, Tom. "Predator Pilots Engage in Remote Control Combat." *National Public Radio,* 4 September 2007. http://www.npr.org/templates/story/story.php?storyId=14162045.

Brodie, Bernard. *The Anatomy of Deterrence.* RM-2218. Santa Monica, CA: RAND Corporation, 23 July 1958.

———. "The Atom Bomb as Policy Maker." *Foreign Affairs* 27, no. 1 (October 1948): 17–33.

———. "Implications for Military Policy." In *The Absolute Weapon: Atomic Power and World Order,* edited by Bernard Brodie, 70–110. New York: Harcourt, Brace and Co., 1946.

———. *Strategy in the Missile Age.* Princeton, NJ: Princeton University Press, 1959.

Bueno de Mesquita, Bruce, Alastair Smith, Randolph M. Siverson, and James D. Morrow. *The Logic of Political Survival.* Cambridge, MA: MIT Press, 2003.

Bulé, David J. "Congress, Presidential Approval, and U.S. Dispute Initiation." *Foreign Policy Analysis* 4, no. 4 (October 2008): 349–70.

Burki, Shireen. "Ceding the Ideological Battlefield to Al Qaeda: The Absence of an Effective U.S. Information Warfare Strategy." *Comparative Strategy* 28, no. 4 (September/October 2009): 349–66.

Byman, Daniel. "Do Targeted Killings Work?" *Foreign Affairs* 85, no. 2 (March/April 2006): 96, 105–6.

Byman, Daniel, and Matthew Waxman. *The Dynamics of Coercion: American Foreign Policy and the Limits of Military Might.* Cambridge, UK: Cambridge University Press, 2002.

Byman, Daniel, Shahram Chubin, Anoushiravan Ehteshami, and Jerrold Green. *Iran's Security Policy in the Post-Revolutionary Era.* Santa Monica, CA: RAND Corporation, 2001.

Caldwell, Christopher. *Reflections on the Revolution in Europe: Immigration, Islam, and the West*. New York: Doubleday, 2009.

Campbell, Kurt M., Robert J. Einhorn, and Mitchell Reiss, eds. *The Nuclear Tipping Point: Why States Reconsider Their Nuclear Choices*. Washington, DC: Brookings Institution Press, 2004.

Carr, Caleb. *The Lessons of Terror*. New York: Random House, 2003.

Carter, Ashton, Michael May, and William Perry. "The Day After: Action Following a Nuclear Blast in a U.S. City." *Washington Quarterly* 30, no. 4 (Autumn 2007): 23–27.

Carter, Jimmy. *Palestine: Peace, Not Apartheid*. New York: Simon & Schuster, 2006.

Carus, W. Seth. *Bioterrorism and Biocrimes: The Illicit Use of Biological Agents since 1900*. Washington, DC: National Defense University, 2001.

Castel, Charles-Irénée, abbe de Saint-Pierre. *A Project for Settling an Everlasting Peace in Europe*. 1714. Reprint, Farmington Hills, MI: Gale ECCO, 2010.

Center for Strategic and International Studies (CSIS). *Securing Cyberspace for the 44th Presidency*. Washington, DC: CSIS, December 2008. http://www.carlisle.army.mil/DIME/documents/CSISCyber%20Report%20Final.pdf.

Chandler, Robert W. *Tomorrow's War, Today's Decisions*. McLean, VA: Amcoda Press, 1996.

Chang, Kenneth. "Obama Calls for End to NASA's Moon Program." *New York Times*, 1 February 2010. http://www.nytimes.com/2010/02/02/science/02nasa.html.

Chilton, Kevin P. "Cyberspace Leadership: Toward New Culture, Conduct, and Capabilities." *Air & Space Power Journal* 23, no. 3 (Fall 2009): 5–10. http://www.airpower.au.af.mil/airchronicles/apj/apj09/fal09/chilton.html.

Chino, Keiko. "Need for Japanese Manned Spacecraft Suddenly Argued." *The Yomiuri Shinbun*, 23 January 2002. http://www.planetary.or.jp/en/colum/20020123.html.

Choe, Sang-Hun, and David E. Sanger. "Rocket Failure May Be Test of North Korean Leader's Power." *New York Times.com*, 13 April 2012. http://www.nytimes.com/2012/04/14/world/asia/international-condemnation-follows-north-koreas-failed-rocket-launch.html?nl=todaysheadlines&emc=edit_th_20120414&pagewanted=all.

Chubin, Shahram. "The Iranian Nuclear Riddle after June 12." *Washington Quarterly* 33, no. 1 (January 2010): 163–72.

Cohen, Craig, Joseph S. Nye Jr., and Richard L. Armitage. *A Smarter, More Secure America*. Washington, DC: CSIS, 2007. http://csis .org/publication/smarter-more-secure-america.

Coll, Steve. "In Search of Success." *New Yorker*, 25 May 2009.

Collina, Tom Z. "News Analysis: What Is a 'New' Nuclear Weapon?" *Arms Control Today*, April 2010. http://www.armscontrol.org /act/2010_04/NewsAnalysis.

The Commission on Integrated Long-Term Strategy. *Discriminate Deterrence*. Washington, DC: US Government Printing Office (GPO), 1988.

The Commission to Assess the Threat to the United States from Electromagnetic Pulse (EMP) Attack website. http://www.empcom mission.org/.

The Commission to the Council, the European Parliament, the European Economic, and Social Committee of the Regions. *Toward a Space Strategy for the European Union That Benefits Its Citizens*, 4 April 2011. http://ec.europa.eu/enterprise/policies/space/files/policy /comm_native_com_2011_0152_6_communication_en.pdf.

"Congressional Hearing Testimony for the Under Secretary of the Air Force the Honorable Peter B. Teets." National Reconnaissance Office, 25 February 2004. *http://www.nro.gov/news/testimony/2004/2004-02 .pdf.*

Coolsaet, Rik. *Jihadi Terrorism and the Radicalization Challenge in Europe*. Burlington, VT: Ashgate, 2008.

Copeland, Dale C. *The Origins of Major War*. Ithaca, NY: Cornell University Press, 2000.

Craig, Gordon, and Alexander George. *Force and Statecraft: Diplomatic Problems of Our Time*, 3rd ed. New York: Oxford University Press, 1995.

Creveld, Martin van. *The Culture of War*. New York: Ballantine Books, 2008.

———. *The Rise and Decline of the State*. Cambridge, UK: Cambridge University Press, 1999.

Cronin, Audrey Kurth. *How Terrorism Ends*. Princeton, NJ: Princeton University Press, 2011.

Darwin, Charles. *The Origin of Species*. 1859. Reprint, New York: New American Library, 1958.

David, Leonard. "China's Anti-Satellite Test: Worrisome Debris Cloud Circles Earth." *SPACE.com*, February 2007. http://www .space.com/news/070202_china_spacedebris.html.

Davidson, William A., administrative assistant to the Secretary of the Air Force. Letter, subject: Organizational Stand-Up of Executive Agent for Space, 12 April 2002.

Davies, Graeme A. M. "Inside Out or Outside In: Domestic and International Factors Affecting Iranian Foreign Policy towards the United States 1990–2004." *Foreign Policy Analysis* 4, no. 3 (July 2008): 209–25.

Davis, Jay C. "The Attribution of WMD Events." *Journal of Homeland Security*, April 2003. http://www.homelandsecurity.org/journal/Articles/Davis.html.

Davis, Paul, and Brian Michael Jenkins. *Deterrence and Influence in Counter-Terrorism*. Santa Monica, CA: RAND Corporation, 2002.

Dawson, Chester. "Japan Launches Space Cargo Push." *Wall Street Journal*, 17 May 2012. http://online.wsj.com/article/SB10001424052702303879604577409933903286576.html.

The Defense Science Board (DSB). *Challenges to Military Operations in Support of US Interests*. Vol. 2, *Main Report*. Washington, DC: DOD, December 2008.

———. *Future Strategic Strike Forces*, February 2004. http://www.fas.org/irp/agency/dod/dsb/fssf.pdf.

———. *Time Critical Conventional Strike from Strategic Standoff*, March 2009. http://www.acq.osd.mil/dsb/reports/ADA498403.pdf.

Delpech, Thérèse. *Nuclear Deterrence in the 21st Century: Lessons from the Cold War for a New Era of Strategic Piracy*. Santa Monica, CA: RAND Corporation, 2012.

Department of Defense. *Annual Report to Congress: Military and Security Developments Involving the People's Republic of China*. Washington, DC: DOD, 2010. http://www.defense.gov/pubs/pdfs/2010_CMPR_Final.pdf.

———. *Deterrence Operations Joint Operating Concept*, Version 2.0. Washington, DC: DOD, December 2006. http://www.dtic.mil/futurejointwarfare/concepts/do_joc_v20.doc.

———. *Final Report of the Defense Science Board Task Force on Globalization and Security*, December 1999. http://handle.dtic.mil/100.2/ADA371887.

———. *Findings of the Nuclear Posture Review*, 9 January 2002. http://www.defenselink.mil/dodcmsshare/briefingslide/120/020109-D-6570C-001.pdf.

———. *FY2009-2034 Unmanned Systems Integrated Roadmap*, 6 April 2009. http://www.acq.osd.mil/psa/docs/UMSIntegratedRoadmap2009.pdf.

——. "Narrative Studies of Accidents Involving U.S. Nuclear Weapons, 1950-1980." http://www.dod.mil/pubs/foi/operation_and_plans/NuclearChemicalBiologicalMatters/635.pdf.

——. *Nuclear Posture Review Report*, April 2010. http://www.defense.gov/npr/docs/2010%20Nuclear%20Posture%20Review%20Report.pdf.

——. *Strategic Communication Joint Integrating Concept*, v. 0.5. Washington, DC: DOD, 25 April 2008·

——. *Unmanned Aircraft Systems Roadmap 2005–2030*, 4 August 2005. http://www.fas.org/irp/program/collect/uav_roadmap2005.pdf.

——. Office of the Undersecretary of Defense for Acquisition, Technology, and Logistics. *Report of the Defense Science Board Task Force on Nuclear Deterrence Skills*. Washington DC: DOD, September 2008. http://www.defense.gov/npr/docs/DSB%20Nuclear%20Deterrence%20Skills%20Chiles.pdf.

Department of Defense Directive 3020.40. *DOD Policy and Responsibility for Critical Infrastructure*, 14 January 2010.

Department of Defense Directive 3100.10. *Space Policy*, 9 July 1999. http://www.fas.org/spp/military/docops/defense/d310010p.htm.

Department of Energy (DOE). *FY [Fiscal Year] 2011 Congressional Budget Request, National Nuclear Security Administration*. "Weapons Activities: Advanced Simulation and Computing Campaign." http://fire.pppl.gov/fy11_doe_nnsa_details.pdf.

——. *FY 2011 Congressional Budget Request, National Nuclear Security Administration*. "Weapons Activities: Overview." http://fire.pppl.gov/fy11_doe_nnsa_details.pdf.

——. "Weapons Activities: Inertial Confinement Fusion Ignition and High Yield Campaign." http://fire.pppl.gov/fy11_doe_nnsa_details.pdf and http://fire.pppl.gov/fy11_doe_icf_details.pdf.

——. "Weapons Activities: Overview." http://fire.pppl.gov/fy11_doe_nnsa_details.pdf.

——. Office of Inspector General. *Audit Report DOE-IG-0699: The Los Alamos National Laboratory Hydrodynamic Test Program*. "Introductory Letter," 16 September 2005.

——. Secretary of Energy Advisory Board. *Interim Report of the National Ignition Facility Laser System Task Force*. Washington, DC: DOE, 10 January 2000. https://www.nrdc.org/nuclear/nif/seab0110.pdf.

Department of Homeland Security. *National Infrastructure Protection Plan: Partnering to Enhance Protection and Resiliency*, 2009. http://www.dhs.gov/xlibrary/assets/NIPP_Plan.pdf.

Department of State, International Security Advisory Board. *Report on Discouraging a Cascade of Nuclear Weapons States*. Washington, DC: Department of State, 19 October 2007.

Department of the Air Force. *Defense Industrial Base Assessment: U.S. Space Industry, Final Report*. Dayton, OH: 31 August 2007. http://www.bis.doc.gov/defenseindustrialbaseprograms/osies/defmarket researchrpts/exportcontrolfinalreport08-31-07master_3—bis-net-link-version—101707-receipt-from-afrl.pdf.

Deutsch, Karl W., Sidney A. Burrell, Robert A. Kann Jr., and Maurice Lee. *Political Community and the North Atlantic Area: International Organization in the Light of Historical Experience*. Princeton, NJ: Princeton University Press, 1957.

Doenecke, Justus. "American Isolationism, 1939–1941." *Journal of Libertarian Studies* 6, nos. 3–4 (Summer/Fall 1982), 201–17.

"Dragon Overview." Space Exploration Technologies Corporation. http://www.spacex.com/dragon.php.

Drell, S., et al. *Science Based Stockpile Stewardship*. JSR-94-345. Mclean, VA: JASON Project, MITRE Corporation, November 1994. http://www.fas.org/irp/agency/dod/jason/sbss.pdf.

Dror, Yehezkel. "High-Intensity Aggressive Ideologies as an International Threat." *Jerusalem Journal of International Relations* 9, no. 1 (March 1987): 153–72.

Dutter, Lee, and Ofira Seliktar. "To Martyr or Not to Martyr: Jihad Is the Question, What Policy Is the Answer?" *Studies in Conflict and Terrorism* 30, no. 5 (May 2007): 429–43.

Ehrman, John. *The Rise of Neoconservatism*. New Haven, CT: Yale University Press, 1995.

Eisenstadt, Michael. "Deter and Contain: Dealing with a Nuclear Iran." In *Getting Ready for a Nuclear-Ready Iran*, edited by Henry Sokolski and Patrick Lawson, 225–56. Carlisle, PA: SSI, US Army War College, October 2005. http://www.strategicstudiesinstitute.army.mil/pdffiles/PUB629.pdf.

———. "Living with a Nuclear Iran?" *Survival* 41, no. 3 (Autumn 1999): 124–48. http://www.washingtoninstitute.org/policy-analysis/view/living-with-a-nuclear-iran.

Elliott, TSgt Scott. "Partnership Will Guide Military, Civilian Space Activities." *Air Force News Link*, 17 October 2002, 13. http://www.af.mil/news/Oct2002/101702364.shtml.

——. "SECAF: Space Forces Have Become Indispensable." *Air Force News Link*, 24 September 2002. http://www.af.mil/news /Sep2002/92402411 .shtml.

Ellsberg, Daniel. "The Crude Analysis of Strategy Choices." *American Economic Review* 51, no. 2 (May 1961): 472–78.

European Commission. *Space, European Space Policy*, 28 June 2012. http://ec.europa.eu/enterprise/policies/space/esp/index_en.htm.

European Space Agency (ESA). "ESA and the European Union Adopt a Common Strategy for Space." ESA press release, 16 November 2000. http://www.esa.int/export/csaCP/Pr_74_2000_p_EN.html.

——. "ESA's Purpose." http://www.esa.int/SPECIALS/About_ESA /SEMSN26LARE_0.html.

——. "Funding." 10 January 2012. http://www.esa.int/esaMI/About _ESA/SEMNQ4FVL2F_0.html.

——. "Galileo IOV [In-Orbit Validation]," 29 June 2012. http://www .esa.int/SPECIALS/Galileo_IOV/SEMNDEITPQG_0.html.

——. "New Member States." http://www.esa.int/SPECIALS/About _ESA/SEMP936LARE_0.html.

——. "Shaping the Future of Europe in Space: Which Programmes, Which Needs?" ESA press release, 21 April 1999. http://www.esa .int/export/csaCP/Pr_6_1999_i_EN.html.

Falk, Ophir, and Henry Morgenstern. *Suicide Terror: Understanding and Confronting the Threat*. New York: Wiley, 2009.

Federation of American Scientists Space Policy Project. "Baikonur Cosmodrome." In *World Space Guide*. http://www.fas.org/spp /guide/russia/facility/baikonur.htm.

——. "Russian and Soviet Space Agencies." In *World Space Guide*. http://www.fas.org/spp/guide/russia/agency/index.html.

Fetter, Steve. "Nuclear Strategy and Targeting Doctrine." In *The Nuclear Turning Point*, edited by Harold A. Feiveson, 45–59. Washington, DC: Brookings Institution Press, 1999.

Fink, Harry J., and Rita M. Fink. *Dirty Harry*. Screenplay, 1971.

Fischer, Hannah. *U.S. Military Casualty Statistics: Operation New Dawn, Operation Iraqi Freedom, and Operation Enduring Freedom*. Washington, DC: Congressional Research Service, 2010.

Fitzpatrick, A., and I. Oelrich. "The Stockpile Stewardship Program: Fifteen Years On." *FAS [Federation of American Scientists] Occasional Paper*, April 2007. http://www.fas.org/2007/nuke/Stock pile_Stewardship_Paper.pdf.

Fitzpatrick, Anne. "From Behind the Fence: Threading the Labyrinths of Classified Historical Research." In *The Historiography of Contemporary Science, Technology, and Medicine: Writing Recent Science*, edited by Ronald E. Doel and Thomas Soderqvist, 67–80. New York: Routledge, 2006.

Forest, James, ed. *Countering Terrorism and Insurgency in the 21st Century*. Westport, CT: Praeger, 2007.

Frederick, Lorina A. "Deterrence and Space-Based Missile Defense." *Air & Space Power Journal* 23, no. 3 (Fall 2009): 107–18. http://www.airpower.au.af.mil/airchronicles/apj/apj09/fal09/frederick.html.

Freedman, Lawrence. *Deterrence*. Cambridge, UK: Polity Press, 2004.

———. *The Evolution of Nuclear Strategy*. New York: St. Martin's Press, 1989.

———. "Strategic Coercion." In *Strategic Coercion: Concepts and Cases*, edited by Lawrence Freedman, 15–36 New York: Oxford University Press, 1998.

Fukuyama, Francis. *The End of History and the Last Man*. New York: Avon Books, 1992.

Fulghum, David A., and Bill Sweetman. "Stealth over Afghanistan." *Aviation Week and Space Technology*, 14 December 2009, 26–31.

Gaddis, John Lewis. *Strategies of Containment*. Oxford, UK: Oxford University Press, 2005.

———. "Toward the Post–Cold War World." *Foreign Affairs* 70, no. 2 (Spring 1991): 102–22.

Galula, David. *Counterinsurgency Warfare*. Westport, CT: Praeger Security International, 2006.

Ganor, Boaz. *The Counter-Terrorism Puzzle*. Piscataway, NJ: Transaction Publishers, 2005.

Gareau, Frederick. *State Terrorism and the United States*. Atlanta, GA: Clarity Press, 2004.

Garthoff, Raymond L. *Soviet Military Doctrine*. New York: Free Press, 1953.

Gates, Robert. *Quadrennial Defense Review Report*. Washington, DC: DOD, 2010.

Geipel, Gary. "Urban Terrorists in Continental Europe after 1970: Implications for Deterrence and Defeat of Violent Nonstate Actors." *Comparative Strategy* 26, no. 5 (October 2007): 439–67.

Geltzer, Joshua Alexander. *US Counterterrorism Strategy and al Qaeda*. New York: Routledge, 2010.

George, Alexander L. "The Case for Multiple Advocacy in Making Foreign Policy." *American Political Science Review* 66, no. 3 (September 1972): 751–85.

———. "The Need for Influence Theory and Actor-Specific Behavioral Models of Adversaries." *Comparative Strategy* 22, no. 5 (December 2003): 463–87.

George, Alexander, and Richard Smoke. *Deterrence in American Foreign Policy: Theory and Practice*. New York: Columbia University Press, 1974.

Gerecht, Reuel Marc. "Mirror-Imaging the Mullahs: Our Islamic Interlocutors." *World Affairs* 170, no. 3 (Winter 2008): 91–100.

Gibbon, Edward. *The Decline and Fall of the Roman Empire*. 1776. Reprint, London: Penguin Press, 1994.

Giles, Gregory F. "The Crucible of Radical Islam: Iran's Leaders and Strategic Culture." In *Know Thy Enemy: Profiles of Adversary Leaders and Their Strategic Cultures*, edited by Barry R. Schneider and Jerrold M. Post, 141–62. 2nd ed. Maxwell AFB, AL: USAF Counterproliferation Center, July 2003. http://www.au.af.mil/au/awc/awcgate/cpc-pubs/know_thy_enemy/giles.pdf.

Gilpin, Robert. *Global Political Economy: Understanding the International Economic Order*. Princeton, NJ: Princeton University Press, 2001.

———. *War and Change in World Politics*. Cambridge, UK: Cambridge University Press, 1981.

Global Zero U.S. Nuclear Policy Commission. *Modernizing U.S. Nuclear Strategy*. http://www.ndr.de/info/programm/sendungen/streitkraefte_und_strategien/globalzeroreport101.pdf.

Goldgeier, J. M., and P. E. Tetlock. "Psychology and International Relations Theory." *Annual Review of Political Science* 4, no. 1 (1 June 2003): 67–92.

Gould, Joe. "Pfc. Faces 22 New Charges in Wikileaks Case." *Army Times* 71, no. 35 (14 March 2011): 28.

Government Accountability Office (GAO). *House Subcommittee on National Security and Foreign Affairs, Committee on Oversight and Government Reform, Testimony of Cristina T. Chaplain, Director Acquisition and Sourcing Management, Global Positioning System: Significant Challenges in Sustaining and Upgrading Widely Used Capabilities*. GAO-09-670T. Washington, DC: GAO, 7 May 2009. http://www.gao.gov/new.items/d09670t.pdf.

————. *Internet Infrastructure—Challenges in Developing a Public/Private Recovery Plan.* GAO-06-1100T, 13 September 2006.

————. *Nuclear Weapons: Status of Planning for Stockpile Life Extension.* GAO-02-146R, 7 December 2001. http://www.gao.gov/new .items/d02146r.pdf.

————. *Report to the Subcommittee on Military Procurement, Committee on Armed Services, House of Representatives: National Ignition Facility: Management and Oversight Failures Caused Major Cost Overruns and Schedule Delays,* 8 August 2000. http://www.gao.gov/new .items/rc00271.pdf.

Grant, Rebecca. *The Radar Game.* Arlington, VA: IRIS Research, 1998.

Gray, Colin S. "SALT II: The Real Debate." *Policy Review* 10 (Fall 1979): 7–22.

————. *Missiles against War: The ICBM Debate Today.* Fairfax, VA: National Institute for Public Policy, 1985.

Grigerenzer, Gerd, and Daniel G. Goldstein. "Reasoning the Fast and Frugal Way: Models of Bounded Rationality." *Psychological Review* 103, no. 4 (1996): 650–69.

Gurney, D. H. "Executive Summary." *Joint Force Quarterly* 51 (4th Quarter 2008): 5–7. http://www.ndu.edu/press/lib/pdf/jfq-51/JFQ -51.pdf.

Gurr, Ted Robert. *Why Men Rebel.* Princeton, NJ: Princeton University Press, 1970.

Gusterson, Hugh. *Nuclear Rites: A Weapons Laboratory at the End of the Cold War.* Berkeley: University of California Press, 1998.

————. *People of the Bomb: Portraits of America's Nuclear Complex.* Minneapolis: University of Minnesota Press, 2004.

Guthe, Kurt. "Implications of a Dynamic Strategic Environment." In *Rationale and Requirements for U.S. Nuclear Weapons and Arms Control,* vol. 2, edited by Keith Payne et al., 64–69. Fairfax, VA: National Institute for Public Policy, 2001.

————. *Ten Continuities in U.S. Nuclear Weapons Policy, Strategy, Plans and Forces.* Fairfax, VA: National Institute for Public Policy, 2008.

Hale, Brian, Michael Grimaila, Robert Mills, Michael Haas, and Phillip Maynard. "Communicating Potential Mission Impact Using Shared Mission Representations." *Proceedings of the 2010 International Conference on Information Warfare and Security,* Wright-Patterson AFB, OH, 8–9 April 2010, 120–27.

Hammer, David A., Lars Bildsten, et al. *NIF Ignition*. JSR-05-340. Mclean, VA: JASON Program, MITRE Corporation, 29 June 2005. http://www.fas.org/irp/agency/dod/jason/nif.pdf.

Harknett, Richard J. "To Deter or Not to Deter, That Is the Cyber Dilemma." Paper presented at AFEI [Association for Enterprise Information] Strategic Cyber Deterrence Conference, Washington, DC, 1–2 November 2007.

Hart, Paul. "Preventing Groupthink Revisited: Evaluating and Reforming Groups in Government." *Organizational Behavior and Human Decision Processes* 73, nos. 2/3 (February/March 1998): 306–26.

Hays, Lt Col Peter L. *United States Military Space: Into the Twenty-First Century*. USAF INSS Occasional Paper 42. US Air Force Academy, CO: USAF Institute for National Security Studies, September 2002.

Hegel, Georg W. F. *The Philosophy of History*, translated by J. Sibree. New York: Dover, 1953.

Helton, Jon C. *Sandia Report: Conceptual and Computational Basis for the Quantification of Margins and Uncertainties*, SAND2009-3055. Sandia National Laboratories, June 2009. http://energy.sandia.gov/wp/wp-content/gallery/uploads/Uncertainty.pdf.

Herz, John H. "Idealist Internationalism and Security Dilemma." *World Politics* 2 (1950): 157–80.

Hines, John G., Ellis M. Mishulovich, and John F. Shulle. *Soviet Intentions 1965–1985*. McLean, VA: BDM Federal, 1995.

Hirschman, Albert O. *The Passions and the Interests: Political Arguments for Capitalism before Its Triumph*. Princeton, NJ: Princeton University Press, 1977.

Hobbes, Thomas. *Leviathan*. 1651. Reprint, Oxford: Oxford University Press, 2008.

Hodge, Nathan, and Sharon Weinberger. "A Nuclear Family Vacation." *Slate*, 13 July 2005. http://slate.msn.com/id/2122382/entry/2122493/.

Hoffman, Bruce. "A Counterterrorism Strategy for the Obama Administration." *Terrorism and Political Violence* 21, no. 3 (July 2009): 359–77.

———. *Inside Terrorism*. New York: Columbia University Press, 2006.

Holmes, Erik. "Lab to Build Special Order Satellites in Days." *Air Force Times*, 20 February 2009. http://www.airforcetimes.com/news/2009/02/af_satellites_space_022009/.

Holmes, Oliver Wendell, Jr. "The Soldier's Faith." Address to the graduating class of Harvard University on Memorial Day. Cambridge, MA, 30 May 1895. http://people.virginia.edu/~mmd5f/holmesfa.htm.

House. *Hearings on Cyber Security: Beyond the Maginot Line before the House Science Committee.* 107th Cong., 1st sess., 2001. http://www.nae.edu/News/SpeechesandRemarks/CyberSecurity BeyondtheMaginotLine.aspx. (Statement of William A. Wulf.)

———. *National Defense Authorization Act for Fiscal Year 2003.* 107th Cong., 2nd sess., 2002, H. R. 107.

Howard, Michael. "Reassurance and Deterrence." *Foreign Affairs* 61, no. 2 (Winter 1982/1983): 309–24.

Hsu, Jeremy. "Real Soldiers Love Their Robot Brethren." *LiveScience,* 21 May 2009. http://www.livescience.com/5432-real-soldiers-love -robot-brethren.html.

Hume, David. *Essays Moral, Political, and Literary.* 1742. Reprint, Indianapolis, IN: Liberty, 1987.

Hunt, Carl, Jeffrey R. Bowes, and Doug Gardner. "Net Force Maneuver." In *Proceedings of the 2005 IEEE [Institute of Electrical and Electronics Engineers] Workshop on Information Assurance and Security.* West Point, NY: US Military Academy, 2005, 419–23.

Huntington, Samuel P. *The Clash of Civilizations and the Remaking of World Order.* New York: Simon & Schuster, 1996.

———. "No Exit: The Errors of Endism." *National Interest* 17 (Fall 1989): 3–11.

———. "Why International Primacy Matters." *International Security* 17, no. 4 (Spring 1993): 71–82.

Huth, Paul, and Bruce Russett. "Testing Deterrence Theory: Rigor Makes A Difference." *World Politics* 42, no. 4 (July 1990): 466–501.

———. "What Makes Deterrence Work? Cases from 1900 to 1980." *World Politics* 36, no. 4 (July 1984): 496–526.

Hyten, Col John E. "A Sea of Peace or a Theater of War? Dealing with the Inevitable Conflict in Space." *Air & Space Power Journal* 16, no. 3 (Fall 2002): 78–92.

"India Launches Its First Weather Satellite." *CNN.com.* 12 September 2002. http://www.cnn.com/2002/TECH/space/09/12/india.satellite .reut/index.html.

Information Office of the State Council, People's Republic of China. "China's Space Activities," 22 November 2000. http://www.fas .org/spp/guide/china/wp112200.html.

———. "The Day of Carrier Space Flight of China Is Not Far Off," 21 November 1999. http://www.cnsa.gov.cn/news/20021112002e.htm.

———. "Development of China's Aerospace Industry during the 10th Five Year Plan." 12 March 2001. http://www.fas.org/spp/guide/china/bjb031201.html.

Ismail, Salwa. *Rethinking Islamist Politics: Culture, the State and Islamism.* London: I. B. Taurus, 2006.

"Israel to Destroy Attacker's Home." *BBC News*, 4 July 2008. http://news.bbc.co.uk/go/pr/fr/-/2/hi/middle_east/7490212.stm.

Israeli Space Agency. "Israel Space Agency History: ISA Foundation and the Israeli Space Age." http://www.geocities.com/CapeCanaveral/5150/isahist.htm.

Jabbour, Kamal. "The Science and Technology of Cyber Operations." *High Frontier* 5, no. 3 (May 2009): 11–15.

Jackson, Brian, David R. Frelinger, Michael J. Lostumbo, and Robert W. Button. *Evaluating Novel Threats to the Homeland.* Santa Monica, CA: RAND Corporation, 2008.

James Martin Center for Nonproliferation Studies, Monterey Institute of International Studies. *CNS Resources on North Korea's Ballistic Missile Program: The 31 August 1998 North Korean Satellite Launch: Factsheet.* http://cns.miis.edu/archive/country_north_korea/factsht.htm.

Janis, Irving L. *Groupthink: Psychological Studies of Policy Decisions and Fiascoes.* Boston: Houghton Mifflin, 1982.

Japan Aerospace Exploration Agency. "JAXA Vision-JAXA 2025." http://www.jaxa.jp/about/2025/index_e.html.

"Japanese Rocket Blasts Off." *BBC News*, 29 August 2001. http://news.bbc.co.uk/2/hi/science/nature/1514468.htm.

Jenkins, Brian Michael. *American Foreign Policy in a New Era.* New York: Routledge, 2005.

———. *Unconquerable Nation: Knowing Our Enemy, Strengthening Ourselves.* Santa Monica, CA: RAND Corporation, 2006.

Jervis, Robert. *American Foreign Policy in a New Era.* New York: Routledge, 2005.

———. *The Illogic of American Nuclear Strategy.* Ithaca, NY: Cornell University Press, 1984.

———. *Perception and Misperception in International Politics.* Princeton, NJ: Princeton University Press, 1976.

Jervis, Robert, Ned Lebow, and Janice Gross Stein. *Psychology and Deterrence.* Baltimore: Johns Hopkins University Press, 1985.

Johannes, Laura, and Marc Champion. "Aftermath: Investigation and Mobilization: Irish Nationalists May Feel US's Funding Squeeze." *Wall Street Journal*, 27 September 2001, A.9.

Joint Publication 1-02. *Dictionary of Military and Associated Terms*, 12 April 2001 (as amended through 19 August 2009).

Joint Publication 2-0. *Joint Intelligence*, 22 June 2007.

Jones, Morris. "China's Space Program Accelerates." *SpaceDaily*, 29 June 2012. http://www.spacedaily.com/reports/Chinas_Space_Program _Accelerates_999.html.

Jones, Seth G., and Martin C. Libicki. *How Terrorist Groups End: Lessons for Countering al Qa'ida*. Santa Monica, CA: RAND Corporation, 2008.

Joseph, Robert. *Countering WMD: The Libyan Experience*. Fairfax, VA: National Institute Press, 2009.

Judt, Tony. *Postwar: A History of Europe since* 1945. New York: Penguin Press, 2005.

Kahn, Herman. *On Thermonuclear War*. New Brunswick, NJ: Transaction, 1960.

Kahneman, Daniel, Jack L. Knetsch, and Richard H. Thaler. "Anomalies: The Endowment Effect, Loss Aversion, and Status Quo Bias." *Journal of Economic Perspectives* 5, no. 1 (Winter 1991): 193–206.

Kalantari, Behrooz. "Herbert A. Simon on Making Decisions: Enduring Insights and Bounded Rationality." *Journal of Management History* 16, no. 4 (September 2010): 509–20.

Kalman, Matthew. "Israeli Fence Puts 'Cage' on Villagers: More Palestinians Scrambling to Keep Barrier from Going up." *San Francisco Chronicle*, 9 March 2004. http://www.sfgate.com/cgi-bin /article.cgi?file=/chronicle/archive/2004/03/09/MNGIP5H0IL1 .DTL.

Kant, Immanuel. *Perpetual Peace: A Philosophical Essay*. Translated by M. Campbell Smith. London: George Allen and Unwin, 1917. http://oll.libertyfund.org/title/357.

Kaplan, Fred. *The Wizards of Armageddon*. New York: Simon & Schuster, 1983.

Kaufmann, William W. *The Evolution of Deterrence 1945–1958*. Santa Monica, CA: RAND Corporation, 1958.

———. "Limited Warfare." In *Military Policy and National Security*, edited by William W. Kaufmann, 102–36. Port Washington, NY: Kennikat Press, 1956.

———. "The Requirements of Deterrence." In *Military Policy and National Security*, edited by William W. Kaufmann, 12–38. Port Washington, NY: Kennikat Press, 1956.

Keegan, John. *A History of Warfare*. New York: Alfred A. Knopf, 1993.

Keeley, Lawrence H. *War before Civilization: The Myth of the Peaceful Savage*. Oxford: Oxford University Press, 1996.

Kelly, Henry. "Arms Control: Where Now?" *FAS Public Interest Report* 55, no. 1 (January/February 2002). http://www.fas.org/faspir/2002/v55n1/control.htm.

Kennan, George F. "The Sources of Soviet Conduct." *Foreign Affairs* 65, no. 4 (Spring 1987): 852–68.

———. "Toward Peace on Two Fronts." *Christianity and Crisis,* 13 December 1982, 398–402.

Kennedy, Paul. *The Rise and Fall of the Great Powers*. New York: Vintage Books, 1987.

Kent, Glenn A., and David E. Thaler. *First-Strike Stability: A Methodology for Evaluating Strategic Forces*. R-3765-AF. Santa Monica, CA: RAND Corporation, August 1989.

———. *First-Strike Stability and Strategic Defenses: Part II of a Methodology for Evaluating Strategic Forces*. R-3918-AF. Santa Monica, CA: RAND Corporation, October 1990.

Kent, Glenn A., Randall J. DeValt, and David E. Thaler. *A Calculus of First-Strike Stability (A Criterion for Evaluating Strategic Forces)*. N-2526-AF. Santa Monica, CA: RAND Corporation, June 1988.

Kershaw, Ian. *Fateful Choices: Ten Decisions That Changed the World, 1940–1941*. New York: Penguin Press, 2007.

Khaldun, Ibn., *The Muqaddimah: An Introduction to History*. Translated by F. Rosenthal. Princeton, NJ: Princeton University Press, 1967.

Kilcullen, David, and Andrew Exum., "Death from Above, Outrage from Below." *The New York Times*, 17 May 2009, WK.13.

Kissinger, Henry A.. *Nuclear Weapons and Foreign Policy*. New York: Harper & Brothers, 1957.

———. *White House Years*. Boston: Little, Brown, and Co., 1979.

———. *A World Restored: The Politics of Conservatism in a Revolutionary Age*. New York: Grossett and Dunlap, 1964.

Koloski, Andrew W., and John S. Kolasheski. "Thickening the Lines: Sons of Iraq, A Combat Multiplier." *Military Review* 89, no. 1 (January/February 2009): 41–53.

Korb, Lawrence J., Alex Rothman, and Laura Conley. "Defensible Budget Cuts." Center for American Progress, 13 April 2011. http://www.americanprogress.org/issues/2011/04/korb_obama.html.

Krepinevich, Andrew F., and Robert C. Martinage. *Dissuasion Strategy*. Washington, DC: CSBA, 2008.

Kristensen, Hans. "Testing the No-New-Nuclear-Weapons Pledge." *FAS Security Blog*, 9 March 2010. http://www.fas.org/blog/ssp/2010/03/newnukes.php#more-2784.

Kristensen, Hans, and Ivan Oelrich. "JASON and Replacement Warheads." *FAS Strategic Security Blog*, 20 November 2009. http://www.fas.org/blog/ssp/2009/11/jason.php#more-2256.

Kristol, Irving. "The Neoconservative Persuasion." *On the Issues*, September 2003, 1–3.

Kugler, Richard. "Dissuasion as a Strategic Concept." *Strategic Forum* 196 (December 2002): 1–8.

Lake, Eli. "Iran's Space Launch Turns Clock Back." *Washington Times*, 25 Jun 2009. http://www.washingtontimes.com/news/2009/feb/04/iran-hails-30-year-old-regime-50-year-old-space-te/.

Lambeth, Benjamin S. *Air Power against Terror*. Santa Monica, CA: RAND Corporation, 2005.

Landry, Brett J. L., and M. Scott Koger. "Dispelling 10 Common Disaster Recovery Myths: Lessons Learned from Hurricane Katrina and Other Disasters." *ACM [Association for Computing Machinery] Journal on Educational Resources in Computing* 6, no. 4 (December 2006): 1–14. http://doi.acm.org/10.1145/1248453.1248459.

Langdon, Lisa, Alexander J. Sarapu, and Matthew Wells. "Targeting the Leadership of Terrorist and Insurgent Movements: Historical Lessons for Contemporary Policy Makers." *Journal of Public and International Affairs*, 15 (Spring 2004): 59–78.

Lawrence, Bruce, ed. *Message to the World: The Statements of Osama bin Laden*. New York: Verso Press, 2005.

Lebovic, James. *Deterring International Terrorism and Rogue States*. New York: Routledge, 2007.

Lebow, Richard Ned. *Between Peace and War: The Nature of International Crisis*. Baltimore: Johns Hopkins University Press, 1981.

Lebow, Richard Ned, and Janice Gross Stein. "Beyond Deterrence." *Journal of Social Issues* 43, no. 4 (1987): 5–71.

——. "Deterrence: The Elusive Dependent Variable." *World Politics* 42, no. 3 (April 1990): 336–69.

——. "Rational Deterrence Theory: I Think, Therefore I Deter." *World Politics* 41, no. 2 (January 1989): 143–69.

——. *We All Lost the Cold War*. Princeton, NJ: Princeton University Press, 1994.

Ledeen, Michael A. *The Iranian Time Bomb: The Mullah Zealots' Quest for Destruction*. New York: St. Martin's Press, 2007.

Lee Kuan Yew. *From Third World to First—The Singapore Story: 1965–2000*. New York: Harper Collins, 2000.

Lesser, Ian, Bruce Hoffman, John Arquilla, David Ronfeldt, and Michele Zanini. *Countering the New Terrorism*. Santa Monica, CA: RAND Corporation, 1999.

Levy, Jack S. "The Diversionary Theory of War: A Critique." In *The Handbook of War Studies*, edited by Manus I. Midlarsky, 259–88. Boston: Unwin Hyman, 1989.

——. "Misperception and the Causes of War: Theoretical Linkages and Analytical Problems." *World Politics* 36, no. 1 (October 1983): 76–99.

Levy, Jack S., and William R. Thompson. *Causes of War*. Chichester, UK: Wiley Blackwell, 2010.

Lewis, Jeffrey. "After the Reliable Replacement Warhead: What's Next for the U.S. Nuclear Arsenal?" *Arms Control Today*, December 2008. http://www.armscontrol.org/print/3463.

Liberman, Peter. *Does Conquest Pay? The Exploitation of Occupied Industrial Societies*. Princeton, NJ: Princeton University Press, 1996.

Libicki, Martin C. "Deterrence in Cyberspace." *High Frontier* 5, no. 3 (May 2009): 11–15.

Lichbach, Mark Irving. *The Rebel's Dilemma*. Ann Arbor: University of Michigan Press, 1998.

Lichtblau, Eric. "U.S. Indicts Head of Islamic Charity in al Qaeda Financing." *New York Times*, 10 October 2002, A.1.

Lifetime Extension Program (LEP). JSR-09-334E. Mclean, VA: MITRE Corporation, JASON Program office, 9 September 2009.

Likanen, Erkki. "Aerospace and the Evolution of Europe." European Union press release, 4 October 2002. http:europa.eu.int/rapid/start/cgi/guesten.ksh?p_action.gettxt=gt&doc=SPEECH/02/456.

Lindley, Dan, and Ryan Schildkraut. "Is War Rational? The Extent of Miscalculation and Misperception as Causes of War." In *Conference Papers—International Studies Association*. Tucson, AZ: International Studies Association, 2006.

Logsdon, John M. "A Security Space Capability for Europe? Implications for US Policy." Remarks. Symposium on the occasion of the 40th anniversary of the French Space Agency CNES [Centre national d'études spatiales], Washington, DC, Space Policy Institute, Elliott School of International Affairs, George Washington University, 18 December 2001.

Lowry, John. "An Initial Foray into Understanding Adversary Planning and Courses of Action." In *DARPA Information Survivability Conference and Exposition II, 2001 (DISCEX'01) Proceedings*, Vol. 1, June 2001, 123–33. http://www.bbn.com/resources/pdf/Adversary _CoA.pdf.

Luan Enjie. "Chinese Space Undertakings toward the 21st Century." *World Space Week News*, 4 October 2000. http://www.cnsa/gov .cn/wsw/read-news_e.asp?mc=News&tmjz=24&xsyh=01.

Luttwak, Edward. *Strategy: The Logic of War and Peace*. Cambridge, MA: Belknap Press, 2003.

Machiavelli, Niccolo. *The Discourses*, translated by L. J. Walker. London: Penguin Books, 1970.

MacKenzie, Donald, with Graham Spinardi. "Tacit Knowledge and the Uninvention of Nuclear Weapons." In *Knowing Machines: Essays on Technical Change*, edited by Donald MacKenzie, 215–60. Cambridge, MA: MIT Press, 1998.

Mainwaring, Max. *A Contemporary Challenge to State Sovereignty: Gangs and Other Illicit Transnational Criminal Organizations in Central America, El Salvador, Mexico, Jamaica, and Brazil*. Carlisle, PA: SSI, US Army War College, 2007.

———. *Deterrence in the 21st Century*. New York: Frank Cass, 2001.

Mandeville, Bernard. *The Fable of the Bees and Other Writings*. 1705. Reprint, Indianapolis, IN: Hackett, 1997.

Mao Tse-tung. *On Guerilla Warfare*. Translated by Samuel Griffith II. Urbana, IL: University of Illinois Press, 1961.

Marine Corps Doctrinal Publication 1. *Warfighting*, 1997.

Martinage, Robert. *Special Operations Forces: Future Challenges and Opportunities*. Washington, DC: CSBA, 2008.

Mazetti, Mark. "The Downside of Letting Robots Do the Bombing." *New York Times*, 21 March 2009. http://www.nytimes.com/2009/03/22 /weekinreview/15MAZZETTI.html.

McCartney, Forrest, et al. *National Security Space Launch Report*. Santa Monica: RAND Corporation, 2006. http://www.rand.org/content /dam/rand/pubs/monographs/2006/RAND_MG503.pdf.

McDougall, Walter A. *The Heavens and the Earth: A Political History of the Space Age*. Baltimore: Johns Hopkins University Press, 1997.

McNamara, Laura A. "TRUTH Is Generated HERE: Knowledge Loss and the Production of Nuclear Confidence in the Post-Cold War Era." In *Nuclear Legacies: Communication, Controversy, and the US Nuclear Weapons Complex*, edited by Bryan C. Taylor, William J. Kinsella, Stephen P. Depoe, Maribeth S. Metzler, Jennifer Duffield Hamilton, Jason N. Krupar, Laura A. McNamara, Eric L. Morgan, Jay Mullen, and Tarla Rai Peterson, 167–98. New York: Lexington Books, 2007.

———. "Ways of Knowing about Weapons: The Cold War's End at the Los Alamos National Laboratory." PhD diss., University of New Mexico, May 2001.

Meade, Walter Russell. "The Bush Administration and the New World Order." *World Policy Journal* 8, no. 3 (Summer 1991): 375–420.

Mearsheimer, John J. *The Tragedy of Great Power Politics*. New York: W. W. Norton, 2001.

Medalia, Jonathan. *"Bunker Busters": Robust Nuclear Earth Penetrator Issues, FY2005–FY2007*. Congressional Research Service (CRS) Report for Congress RL32347. Washington, DC: CRS, 21 February 2006.

———. *"Bunker Busters": Sources of Confusion in the Robust Nuclear Earth Penetrator Debate*. CRS Report for Congress RL325599. Washington, DC: CRS, 22 September 2004.

Menthe, Darrel. "Jurisdiction in Cyberspace: A Theory of International Spaces." *Michigan Telecommunication Technical Law Review* 4 (1998): 69–103. http://www.mttlr.org/volfour/menthe.html.

Miller, Benjamin. "Explaining Changes in U.S. Grand Strategy: 9/11, the Rise of Offensive Liberalism, and the War in Iraq." *Security Studies* 19, no. 1 (2010): 26–65.

Moghadam, Assaf. *The Roots of Terrorism*. New York: Chelsea House, 2006.

Montesquieu. *Considerations on the Causes of the Greatness of the Romans and Their Decline*. Translated by D. Lowenthal. Indianapolis, IN: Hackett Publishing Company, 1965.

Morgan, Patrick M. *Deterrence Now*. Cambridge, UK: Cambridge University Press, 2003.

Morgenthau, Hans. "The Fallacy of Thinking Conventionally about Nuclear Weapons." In *Arms Control and Technological Innovation*, edited by David Carlton and Carlo Schaerf, 256–64. New York: Wiley, 1976.

——. *Politics among Nations.* New York: Alfred A. Knopf, 1948.

——. *Politics among Nations: The Struggle for Power and Peace.* 5th ed. New York: Alfred A. Knopf, 1978.

Moskowitz, Clara. "Are Russia's Recent Space Woes a Sign of Larger Problems?" *SPACE.com*, 15 February 2012. http://www.space .com/14588-russian-space-failures-larger-problems.html.

Moustakis, Fotios, and Rudra Chaudhuri. "The Rumsfeld Doctrine and the Cost of US Unilateralism: Lessons Learned." *Defence Studies* 7, no. 3 (November 2007): 358–75.

Mowthorpe, Mathew J. "The United States Approach to Military Space during the Cold War." *Air & Space Power Chronicles,* 8 March 2001. http://www.airpower.maxwell.af.mil/airchronicles /cc/mowthorpe.html.

Mueller, John. *The Remnants of War.* Ithaca, NY: Cornell University Press, 2004.

——. *Retreat from Doomsday: The Obsolescence of Major War.* New York: Basic Books, 1989.

Mulaj, Klejda. *Violent Non-State Actors.* New York: Columbia University Press, 2009.

Murdock, Clark A. *The Department of Defense and the Nuclear Mission in the 21st Century: A Beyond–Goldwater-Nichols Phase 4 Report.* Washington, DC: CSIS, March 2008.

Myers, Christopher, and Jonathan Ball. "Space Transportation." *Space Web*, 2. http://home.att.net/-SpaceWeb/SPSM5900/Nat_Pol.htm.

Naim, Moises. "The Five Wars of Globalization." *Foreign Policy*, January /February 2003, 29–36.

Nance, Malcolm. *An End to Al Qaeda: Destroying bin Laden's Jihad and Restoring America's Honor.* New York: St. Martin's Press, 2010.

Narain, Sanjay, Gary Levin, Sharad Malik, and Vikram Kaul. "Declarative Infrastructure Configuration Synthesis and Debugging." *Journal of Network and Systems Management* 16, no. 3 (September 2008): 235–58.

Nardon, Laurence. *Satellite Imagery Control: An American Dilemma.* Paris: French Center on the United States, March 2002.

Naroll, Raoul, Vern L. Bullough, and Frada Naroll. *Military Deterrence in History: A Pilot Cross-Historical Survey.* Albany, NY: State University of New York Press, 1974.

The National Aeronautics Space Development Association. "To a New Phase of Japanese Rocket Development." NASDA Report No. 51, September 1996. http://www.nasda.go.jp/lib/nasda-news/1996/09/series_e.html.

"National Defense Authorization Act for FY 2003 Report (Excerpts Regarding NASA)." *SpaceRef*. http://www.spaceref.com/news/viewsr.html?pid=5539.

The National Defense Panel. *Transforming Defense: National Security in the 21st Century*, December 1997. http://www.fas.org/man/docs/ndp/toc.htm.

The National Intelligence Council. *Mapping the Global Future: Report of the National Intelligence Council's 2020 Project*. Undated, unclassified briefing.

The National Research Council. *Evaluation of Quantification of Margins and Uncertainties Methodology for Assessing and Certifying the Reliability of the Nuclear Stockpile*. Washington, DC: National Academies Press, 2008.

National Space Technology Council. "Fact Sheet, National Space Policy," 19 September 1996. http://www.au.af.mil/au/awc/awcgate/sep96.htm.

——. "National Space Policy Review, Fact Sheet," 28 June 2002. http://www.fas.org/irp/offdocs/nspd/nspd-15.htm.

Neumann, John von, and Oskar Morgenstern. *The Theory of Games and Economic Behavior*. Princeton, NJ: Princeton University Press, 1944.

Nichols, Thomas. *Eve of Destruction: The Coming Age of Preventive War*. Philadelphia: University of Pennsylvania Press, 2008.

Nincic, Miroslav. "Loss Aversion and the Domestic Context of Military Intervention." *Political Research Quarterly* 50, no. 1 (March 1997): 97–120.

"Nuclear Posture Review Report [Reconstructed] Submitted to Congress on 31 December 2001." Federation of American Scientists, 8 January 2002. http://www.fas.org/blog/ssp/united_states/NPR2001re.pdf.

Nuclear Weapons Council. "Procedural Guidelines for the Phase 6.X Process," 19 April 2000.

Obama, Pres. Barak. "Securing Our Nation's Cyber Infrastructure." Remarks. The White House, Washington, DC, 29 May 2009. http://www.whitehouse.gov/the_press_office/Remarks-by-the-President-on-Securing-Our-Nations-Cyber-Infrastructure/.

Odom, William E. "Whither the Soviet Union?" *Washington Quarterly* 4 (Spring 1981): 30–49.

Odom, William E., and Robert Dujarric. *America's Inadvertent Empire*. New Haven, CT: Yale University Press, 2004.

Odom, William, et al. *The Emerging Ballistic Missile Threat to the United States: Report of the Proliferation Study Team*. Fairfax, VA: National Institute for Public Policy, February 1993. http://www .dod.mil/pubs/foi/Science_and_Technology/Other/481.pdf.

Oelrich, Ivan. "Congressional Commission and Nuclear 'Requirements.'" *FAS Strategic Security Blog*, 6 May 2009. http://www.fas .org/blog/ssp/2009/05/1280.php#more-1280.

——. *Missions for Nuclear Weapons after the Cold War*. FAS Occasional Paper no. 3, January 2005. http://www.fas.org/pubs /_docs/01282005175922.pdf.

——. "A Response to Congresswoman Tauscher's Article on Nonproliferation Review." *FAS Strategic Security Blog*, 29 October 2007. http:// www.fas.org/blog/ssp/2007/10/a_response_to_congresswoman _ta.php.

Office of Science and Technology. "Fact Sheet, US National Space Policy," 31 August 2006. http://www.au.af.mil/au/awc/awcgate/whitehouse /ostp_space_policy06.pdf.

Office of the Secretary of Defense. *Military Power of the People's Republic of China*, 2009. http://www.defense.gov/pubs/pdfs/China_Military _Power_Report_2009.pdf.

——. *Quadrennial Defense Review (QDR) Report*, 30 September 2001. http://history.defense.gov/resources/QDR2001.pdf.

——. *Quadrennial Defense Review Report*, 6 February 2006. http:// history.defense.gov/resources/QDR2006.pdf.

——. *Quadrennial Defense Review Report*, January 2009. http://history .defense.gov/resources/QDR2009.pdf.

——. *Quadrennial Defense Review Report*, 12 February 2010. http:// www.defense.gov/qdr/images/QDR_as_of_12Feb10_1000.pdf.

——. *Unmanned Aircraft Systems Roadmap, 2005–2030*, 4 August 2005. https://www.fas.org/irp/program/collect/uav_roadmap2005.pdf.

Olson, Adm Eric T. "The Terror Threat: What It Will Take to Deter, Disrupt, and Defeat It." Speech. The Center for a New American Security, 3 March 2008. http://www.cnas.org/files/multimedia /documents/AdmOlson_CNAS_Transcript.pdf.

Omilecheva, Mariya. *Counter-Terrorism Policies in Central Asia*. New York: Routledge, 2011.

"The Operation Desert Shield/Desert Storm Timeline." American Forces Press Service. http://www.defenselink.mil/news/newsarticle.aspx?id=45404.

"Pak's N-bomb Prevented India from Attacking It after 26/11." *Press Trust of India*, 9 March 2009.

Paone, Chuck. "CITS [Combat Information Transport System] Key to Air Force Cyber Superiority Goal." 66th Air Base Wing Public Affairs, 28 May 2009. http://www.af.mil/news/story.asp?id=123151424.

Pape, Robert. "Coercion and Military Strategy: Why Denial Works and Punishment Doesn't." *Journal of Strategic Studies* 15, no. 4 (1992): 423–75.

———. "Suicide Terrorism and Democracy: What We've Learned since 9/11." *Policy Analysis* no. 582 (1 November 2006): 1–18.

Parker, Geoffrey. *The Cambridge Illustrated History of Warfare*. Cambridge, UK: Cambridge University Press, 2008.

Patterson, Thomas, J. Garry Clifford, Shane J. Maddock, Deborah Kisatsky, and Kenneth Hagan. *American Foreign Relations: Since 1895*. New York: Houghton Mifflin, 1999, 133–35.

Payne, Keith B. *Deterrence in the Second Nuclear Age*. Lexington: University Press of Kentucky, 1996.

———. *The Great American Gamble: Deterrence Theory and Practice from the Cold War to the Twenty-First Century*. Fairfax, VA: National Institute Press, 2008.

———. "The Schlesinger Shift: Return to Rationality." In *Nuclear Strategy: Flexibility and Stability*, edited by Keith B. Payne, C. Johnston Conover, and Bruce Bennett, 1–48. Santa Monica, CA: California Seminar on Arms Control and Foreign Policy, March 1979.

Payne, Keith B., et al. *Planning the Future U.S. Nuclear Force*. 2 vols. Fairfax, VA: National Institute Press, 2009.

———. *Rationale and Requirements for U.S. Nuclear Weapons and Arms Control*. Fairfax, VA: National Institute for Public Policy, 2001.

Payne, Keith, Kathleen Bailey, Colin Gray, Kurt Guthe, Robert Joseph, and Frederic Leykam. *Bioterrorism and a Strategy of Concomitant Deterrence*. Fairfax, VA: National Institute for Public Policy, September 2007.

Pena, Charles V. "US Commercial Space Programs: Future Priorities and Implications for National Security." In *Future Security in Space: Commercial, Military, and Arms Control Trade-Offs*, edited by James Clay Moltz, 8–10. Southhampton, UK: Center for Non-proliferation Studies, Mountbatten Centre for International Studies, University of Southampton, July 2002.

Peters, Anne, Lucy Koechlin, Till Förster, and Gretta Fenner Zinkernagel. *Non-State Actors as Standard Setters*. Cambridge, UK: Cambridge University Press, 2009.

Phillips, Matthew. "Uncertain Justice for Nuclear Terror: Deterrence of Anonymous Attacks through Attribution." *Orbis* 51, no. 3 (Summer 2007): 429–46.

Pickering, Sharon, Jude McCulloch, and David Wright-Neville. *Counter-Terrorism Policing*. New York: Springer, 2008.

Pinker, Steven. *The Better Angels of Our Nature: Why Violence Has Declined*. New York: Penguin Press, 2011.

Pipes, Richard. "Militarism and the Soviet State." *Daedalus* 109, no. 4 (Fall 1980): 1–12.

———. *Survival Is Not Enough: Soviet Realities and America's Future*. New York: Simon and Schuster, 1984.

Plato. *The Republic*. Translated by T. Griffith. Cambridge, UK: Cambridge University Press, 2000.

Pollack, Kenneth M. *The Persian Puzzle: The Conflict between Iran and America*. New York: Random House, 2004.

Polybius. *The Rise of the Roman Empire*. Translated by Ian Scott-Kilvert. London: Penguin Books, 1979.

"Polymorphic Cyber Defense—Active Repositioning in Cyberspace." Award notice, 13 March 2009. https://www.fbo.gov/spg/USAF /AFMC/AFRLRRS/Awards/FA875009C0051.html.

Posen, Barry R. *A Nuclear-Armed Iran: A Difficult but not Impossible Policy Problem*. New York: Century Foundation, 2006.

Post, Douglas. "Lessons Learned from ASCI [Advanced Strategic Computing Initiative]." Los Alamos National Laboratory, 30 March 2004. Abridged at http://www.csm.ornl.gov/meetings /SCNEworkshop/Post-IV.pdf.

Post, Jerrold M. "Deterrence in an Age of Asymmetric Rivals." In *Understanding the Bush Doctrine: Psychology and Strategy in an Age of Terrorism*, edited by Stanley A. Renshon and Peter Suedfeld, 153–74. New York: Routledge, 2007.

Preserving Nuclear Weapons Information. Lawrence Livermore Nuclear Weapons Information Project. https://www.llnl.gov/str/Lowns.html.

"Presidential Directive on National Space Policy, Fact Sheet," 11 February 1988. http://www.au.af.mil/au/awc/awcgate/policy88.htm.

Press, Daryl G. *Calculating Credibility: How Leaders Assess Military Threats.* Ithaca, NY: Cornell University Press, 2005.

Rabasa, Angel, Peter Chalk, Kim Cragin, Sara A. Daly, Heather S. Gregg, Theodore W. Karasik, Kevin A. O'Brien, and William Rosenau. *Beyond al Qaeda, Part 2: The Outer Ring of the Terrorist Universe.* Santa Monica, CA: RAND Corporation, 2006.

Reif, Kingston. "Nuclear Weapons: The Modernization Myth." *Bulletin of the Atomic Scientists,* 21 December 2009. http://thebulletin.org/web-edition/features/nuclear-weapons-the-modernization-myth.

Report of the Commission to Assess United States National Security, Space Management and Organization. Chapter 6, "Organizing and Managing the Future," May 2001. http://space.au.af.mil/space_commission/chapters/chapter6.pdf.

———. Chapter 7, "Conclusions of the Committee," May 2001. http://space.au.af.mil/space_commission/chapters/chapter7.pdf.

———. "Executive Summary," May 2001. http://space.au.af.mil/space_commission/executive_summary.pdf.

Report of the Secretary of Defense Task Force on DoD Nuclear Weapons Management, Phase II: Review of the DoD Nuclear Mission. Washington, DC: DOD, September 2008.

Report of The United States House of Representatives Select Committee on U.S. National Security and Military/Commercial Concerns with the People's Republic of China, volume 2, chapter 5, *Satellite Launches in the PRC: Hughes,* May 1999. http://www.house.gov/coxreport/pdf/ch5.pdf.

Rhodes, Richard. *Dark Sun: The Making of the Hydrogen Bomb.* New York: Simon & Schuster, 1994.

———. *The Making of the Atomic Bomb.* New York: Simon & Schuster, 1986.

Ricardo, David. *On the Principles of Political Economy and Taxation.* London: John Murray, 1817.

Rich, Ben. *Skunk Works.* Boston: Little, Brown & Co., 1994.

Richards, James. *Transnational Criminal Organizations, Cybercrime, and Money Laundering: A Handbook for Law Enforcement Officers, Auditors, and Financial Investigators.* Boca Raton, FL: CRC Press, 1999.

Richardson, Doug. *Stealth Warplanes*. Minneapolis, MN: Zenith Press, 2001.

Ricks, Thomas. *The Gamble: General David Petraeus and the American Military Adventure in Iraq, 2006–2008*. New York: Penguin Press, 2009.

Roberts, Brad. "Deterrence and WMD Terrorism: Calibrating Its Potential Contributions to Risk Reduction." In *Jihadists and Weapons of Mass Destruction*, edited by Gary Ackerman and Jeremy Tamsett, 259–284. Boca Raton, FL: CRC Press, 2009.

Robinson, Kristopher K., Edward M. Crenshaw, and J. Craig Jenkins. "Ideologies of Violence: The Social Origins of Islamist and Leftist Transnational Terrorism." *Social Forces* 84, no. 4 (June 2006): 2009–26.

Rosecrance, Richard. *The Rise of the Trading State*. New York: Basic Books, 1986.

Rubin, Barry. "The Containment Conundrum: How Dangerous Is a Nuclear Iran? The Right Kind of Containment." *Foreign Affairs* 89, no. 4 (July-August 2010): 160–68.

"Russia and Australia Working toward Space." *SpatialSource.com*, 15 March 2011. http://www.spatialsource.com.au/2011/03/15/article/PDFHLZULDP.html.

Sagan, Scott D. *The Limits of Safety: Organizations, Accidents, and Nuclear Weapons*. Princeton, NJ: Princeton University Press, 1993.

Sageman, Marc. *Understanding Terror Networks*. Philadelphia: University of Pennsylvania Press, 2004.

Sanger, David E., and Thom Shanker. "White House Is Rethinking Nuclear Policy." *New York Times*, 1 March 2010, 1.

Schaffer, Yehuda. "Detecting Terrorist Financing through Financial Intelligence: The Role of FIUs [Financial Intelligence Units]." In *Countering Terrorist Financing*, edited by Mark Pieth, Daniel Thelesklaf, and Radha Ivory, 41–55. Bern: Peter Lang, 2009.

Schaub, Gary, Jr. "Deterrence, Compellence, and Rational Decision Making." PhD diss., University of Pittsburgh, 2003.

Schelling, Thomas C. *Arms and Influence*. New Haven, CT: Yale University Press, 1966.

——. *The Strategy of Conflict*. Cambridge, MA: Harvard University Press, 1960.

Schifrin, Nick. "US Drone Strikes with Deadly Accuracy." *ABC News*, 19 November 2008. http://a.abcnews.com/print?id=6289748.

Schlesinger, James R. *European Security and the Nuclear Threat since 1945*. Santa Monica, CA: RAND Corporation, 1967.

Schroeder, Paul W. "Does the History of International Politics Go Anywhere?" In *Systems, Stability, and Statecraft: Essays on the International History of Modern Europe*, edited by Paul W. Schroeder, David Wetzel, Robert Jervis, and Jack S. Levy, 277–84. New York: Palgrave MacMillan, 2004.

Schumpeter, Joseph. *Capitalism, Socialism, and Democracy*. New York: Harper Perennial, 1962.

———. *Imperialism and Social Classes*. Cleveland, OH: World Publishing, 1955.

Schwartz, Gen Norton. "National Security Space and the Air Force." Address. Twenty-Eighth National Space Symposium, Colorado Springs, CO. 19 April 2012. http://www.af.mil/shared/media/document/AFD-120419-049.pdf.

Schweller, Randall L. "Bandwagoning for Profit: Bringing the Revisionist State Back In." *International Security* 19, no. 1 (Summer 1994): 72–107.

———. "Neorealism's Status Quo Bias: What Security Dilemma?" In *Realism: Restatements and Renewal*, edited by Benjamin Frankel, 90–121. London: Frank Cass, 1996.

Seay, Douglas. "What Are the Soviets' Objectives in Their Foreign, Military, and Arms Control Policies?" In *Nuclear Arguments: Understanding the Strategic Nuclear Arms and Arms Control Debates*, edited by Lynn Eden and Steven E. Miller, 47–108. Ithaca, NY: Cornell University Press, 1989.

Secretary of defense to the president. Draft memorandum, 6 December 1963, I-21–22. Document has been redacted and declassified.

———. Draft memorandum, 3 December 1964. Document has been redacted and declassified.

———. Draft memorandum, 1 November 1965. Document has been redacted and declassified.

———. Draft memorandum, 15 January 1968. Document has been redacted and declassified.

Secretary of the Air Force. *US Air Force White Paper on Long Range Bombers*. 1 March 1999. http://www.fas.org/nuke/guide/usa/bomber/bmap99.pdf.

Seidel, Robert W. "Books on the Bomb." *Isis* 81, no. 3 (September 1990): 519–37.

Seiler, Capt George J. *Strategic Nuclear Force Requirements and Issues.* Research Report no. AU-ARI-82-1. Maxwell AFB, AL: Air University Press, February 1983.

Selding, Peter B. de. "Europeans Blame US Government for Galileo Delay." *SPACENEWS International* 13, no. 3 (21 January 2002): 6.

Senate. *The Continuing Threat from Weapons of Mass Destruction: Hearings before the Armed Services Committee.* Appendix C: "Biological Agents." 104th Congress, 2nd sess., 1996. https://www.cia .gov/news-information/speeches-testimony/1996/go_appendixc _032796.html. (Statement of Dr. Gordon Oehler, Director, Nonproliferation Center.)

———. *Hearings on MX Missile Basing System and Related Issues.* 98th Cong., 1st sess., 1983. (Statement of Harold Brown, Secretary of Defense.)

———. *Hearings on Nuclear Terrorism: Confronting the Challenges of the Day After.* 110th Congress, 2nd sess., 2008. (Written statement of Dr. Cham Dallas, "Impact of Small Nuclear Weapons on Washington, DC: Outcomes and Emergency Response Recommendations.")

———. *The Safety and Reliability of the U.S. Nuclear Deterrent: Hearings before Governmental Affairs Subcommittee on International Security, Proliferation and Federal Services.* 105th Congress, 1st sess., 1997. (Statement of Vic Reis.)

———. *Testing and Operation Requirements for the B-2 Bomber: Hearings on the Safety and Reliability of the U.S. Nuclear Deterrent, Hearings before the Committee on Armed Services.* 101st Cong., 1st sess., 1989. (Statement of Gen. John T. Chain, Jr., USAF, Commander-In-Chief, Strategic Air Command.)

Sengupta, Somini. "India Launches Unmanned Orbiter to Moon." *New York Times.com,* 21 October 2008. http://www.nytimes .com/2008/10/22/world/asia/22indiamoon.html?oref=slogin &_r=0.

Sewall, Sarah. "Introduction to the University of Chicago Press Edition: A Radical Field Manual." In *The U.S. Army/Marine Corps Counterinsurgency Field Manual,* xxi–xliii. Chicago: University of Chicago Press, 2007.

Shaud, John A. "In Service to the Nation: Air Force Research Institute Strategic Concept for 2018–2023." *Strategic Studies Quarterly* 2, no. 4 (Winter 2008): 14–42.

Sheehan, James J. *Where Have All the Soldiers Gone? The Transformation of Modern Europe.* Boston: Houghton Mifflin, 2008.

Sheehan, Michael. *The Balance of Power: History & Theory*. New York: Routledge, 1996.

Shultz, Richard, and Andrea Dew. *Insurgents, Terrorists, and Militias: The Warriors of Contemporary Combat*. New York: Columbia University Press, 2006.

Siegfried, Charlene Haddock. "The Dangers of Unilateralism." *NWSA [National Women's Studies Association] Journal* 18, no. 3 (Fall 2006): 20–32.http://muse.jhu.edu/journals/nwsa_journal/v018/18.3seigfried.pdf.

Siemens PLM Software. "Case Study, SpaceX Delivers Outer Space at Bargain Rates," September 2010. http://www.plm.automation.siemens.com/en_us/about_us/success/case_study.cfm?Component=30328&ComponentTemplate=1481.

Simes, Dmitri K. "Assessing Soviet National Security Strategy." In *Understanding U.S. Strategy: A Reader*, edited by Terry L. Heynes, 210–12. Washington, DC: National Defense University Press, 1983.

Simon, Herbert A. *Administrative Behavior: A Study of Decision-Making Process in Administrative Organization*. 3rd ed. 1945. Reprint, New York: Free Press, 1976.

Slackman, Michael. *Target: Pearl Harbor*. Honolulu: University of Hawaii Press, 1990.

Smith, Adam. *An Inquiry into the Nature and Causes of the Wealth of Nations*. 1776. Reprint, Amherst, NY: Prometheus Books, 1991.

Snow, Donald. *Uncivil Wars: International Security and the New Internal Conflicts*. Boulder, CO: Lynne Reiner Publishers, 1996.

Snow, Donald, and Dennis Drew. *Making Twenty-First-Century Strategy*. Maxwell AFB, AL: Air University Press, 2006.

Snow, Nancy. *Information War*. Toronto: Hushion House, 2003.

Snyder, Glenn. *Deterrence and Defense: Toward a Theory of National Security*. Princeton, NJ: Princeton University Press, 1961.

Snyder, Robert S. "The U.S. and Third World Revolutionary States: Understanding the Breakdown in Relations." *International Studies Quarterly* 43, no. 2 (June 1999): 265–90.

"Spacelift: Spacelift Australia—SS-25 Missile." *SpaceDaily*, August 1999. http://www.spacedaily.com/news/aust-99e.html.

The Space Report: The Authoritative Guide to Global Space Activity, 2011. Colorado Springs: The Space Foundation, 2011.

SPOT Image Corporation. Website. http://www.spot.com/.

Steed, Brian. *Piercing the Fog of War*. Minneapolis, MN: Zenith Press, 2009.

Stenger, Richard. "Armadillo, Romanians Join $10 Million Space Race." *CNN.com*, 17 October 2002. http://www.cnn.com/2002 /TECH/space/10/17/xprize.contest/indes.html.

Stiglitz, Joseph. *Globalization and Its Discontents*. New York: W. W. Norton, 2002.

Stillion, John, and David Orletsky. *Airbase Vulnerability to Conventional Cruise-Missile and Ballistic-Missile Attacks: Technology, Scenarios, and US Air Force Responses*. Santa Monica, CA: RAND Corporation, 1999.

"Study Finds U.S. Not Ready for Nuke Hit." *Washington Times*, 21 March 2007, A-3.

Takeyh, Ray. *Guardians of the Revolution: Iran and the World in the Age of the Ayatollahs*. New York: Oxford University Press, 2009.

Taylor, Ian. "A Competitive Space." *Parliamentary Monitor Magazine*, August 1999. http://www.political.co.uk/iantaylor/articles%20 0899.htm.

Thompson, William R. *Causes of War*. Chichester, UK: Wiley Blackwell, 2010.

Thucydides., *The Peloponnesian War*. Translated by Rex Warner. London: Penguin Books, 1972.

Timmerman, Kenneth R. "The Day After Iran Gets the Bomb." in *Getting Ready for a Nuclear-Ready Iran*, edited by Henry Sokolski and Patrick Lawson, 113–29. Carlisle, PA: SSI, US Army War College, October 2005. http://www.strategicstudiesinstitute.army .mil/pdffiles/PUB629.pdf.

Tinnel, Laura S., O. S. Saydjari, and Joshua W. Haines. "An Integrated Cyber Panel System." In *Proceedings of the 2003 DARPA Information Survivability Conference and Exposition*, vol. 2, 32–34. http:// ieeexplore.ieee.org/stamp/stamp.jsp?tp=&arnumber=1194906.

Tirenin, Walt, and Don Faatz. "A Concept for Strategic Cyber Defense." In *Military Communications (MILCOM) Conference Proceedings*, 1999, 458–63. http://www.argreenhouse.com/society/TaCom/papers 99/16_1.pdf.

Tocqueville, Alexis de. *Democracy in America*. Translated by Harvey C. Mansfield and Delba Winthrop. Chicago: University of Chicago Press, 2000.

Tolbert, Julian. *Crony Attack: Strategic Attack's Silver Bullet?* Maxwell AFB, AL: School of Advanced Air and Space Studies, 2003.

"Top Official Deplores Decline of Russian Space Program." *Sydney Morning Herald*, 12 December 2002. http://www.smh.com.au /articles/2002/12/11/1039379887168.html.

Toynbee, Arnold J. *A Study of History*. Oxford: Oxford University Press, 1934–61.

Trager, Robert F., and Dessislava P. Zagorcheva., "Deterring Terrorism: It Can Be Done." *International Security*, Winter 2005/2006, 96–98.

Turner, Marlene E., and Anthony R. Pratkanis. "Theoretical Perspectives on Groupthink: A Twenty-Fifth Anniversary Appraisal." *Organizational Behavior and Human Decision Processes* 73, nos. 2/3 (February/March 1998): 103–4.

Ucko, David. *The New Counter-Insurgency Era*. Washington, DC: Georgetown University Press, 2009.

US Air Force Public Affairs. "Communications Airmen Meet to Discuss Career Field's Transformation," 9 June 2009. http://www .af.mil/news/story.asp?id=123153203.

US Air Force Scientific Advisory Board., *Defending and Operating in a Contested Cyber Domain.*, SAB-TR-08-01, August 2008.

US Air Force Strategic Environmental Assessment, 2010–2030. Washington, DC: US Air Force, 2011.

"US Airstrikes in Pakistan Called 'Very Effective.' " *CNN*, 18 May 2009. http://www.cnn.com/2009/POLITICS/05/18/cia.pakistan .airstrikes/.

US Strategic Command. *Deterrence Operations Joint Operating Concept*. Washington, DC: Department of Defense, 2006.

———. Policy, Doctrine and International Affairs Division. "Strategic Deterrence (SD) Joint Operating Concept (JOC) Version 2.0." PowerPoint presentation. http://www.dtic.mil/futurejointwarfare /strategic/sd_joc.ppt.

Vaisse, Justin. *Neoconservatism: The Biography of a Movement*. Cambridge, MA: Harvard University Press, 2010.

Vijayan, Jaikumar. "Data Security Risks Missing from Disaster Recovery Plans." *Computer World*. http://www.computerworld.com/s/article /105272/Data_security_risks_missing_from_disaster_recovery _plans.

Vick, Alan J. *Snakes in the Eagle's Nest*. Santa Monica, CA: RAND Corporation, 1995.

Wade, Nicholas. *Before the Dawn: Recovering the Lost History of Our Ancestors*. New York: Penguin Press, 2006.

Waltz, Kenneth. *Theory of International Politics*. Reading, MA: Addison-Wesley, 1979.

Ward, Colin. *Anarchism*. Oxford: Oxford University Press, 2004.

Warnke, Paul C. "Apes on a Treadmill." *Foreign Policy* 18 (Spring 1975): 12–29.

Watts, Barry D. *The Case for Long Range Strike: 21st Century Scenarios*. Washington, DC: CSBA, 31 December 2008.

———. *Long Range Strike: Imperatives, Urgency, and Options*. Washington, DC: CSBA, April 2005.

———. *Moving Forward On Long-Range Strike*. Washington, DC: CSBA, 27 September 2004.

Wehrey, Frederick, David E. Thaler, Nora Bensahel, Kim Cragin, Jerrold D. Green, Dalia Dassa Kaye, Nadia Oweidat, and Jennifer Li. *Dangerous but Not Omnipotent: Exploring the Reach and Limitations of Iranian Power in the Middle East*. Santa Monica, CA: RAND Corporation, 2009.

Wendt, Alexander. *Social Theory of International Politics*. Cambridge, UK: Cambridge University Press, 1999.

White, George. *Nation, State, and Territory*. Lanham, MD: Rowman and Littlefield, 2007.

Whitehouse, David. "Japan's Uncertain Space Future." BBC News, 29 August 2001. http://news.bbc.co.uk/2/hi/science/nature/1515095.stm.

The White House. *Cyberspace Policy Review: Assuring a Trusted and Resilient Information and Communications Infrastructure*, May 2009. http://www.whitehouse.gov/assets/documents/Cyberspace_Policy_Review_final.pdf.

———. *National Security Strategy*, May 2010. http://www.whitehouse.gov/sites/default/files/rss_viewer/national_security_strategy.pdf.

———. *The National Security Strategy for a New Century*, October 1999. http://www.au.af.mil/au/awc/awcgate/nss/nssr-1098.pdf.

———. *The National Security Strategy of the United States of America*, September 2002. http://nssarchive.us/NSSR/2002.pdf.

Wilkinson, Kate. "Japan's Evolving Space Program." *The National Bureau of Asian Research*, 9 September 2012. http://www.nbr.org/research/activity.aspx?id=173.

Wilkinson, Paul. *Terrorism versus Democracy*. New York: Routledge, 2006.

Windrem, Robert, and Alan Boyle. "China Space Shot Has Military Implications." *MSNBC.com*, 23 November 1999. http://www.msnbc.com/news/211770.asp?cp1=1.

Wohlstetter, Albert. *The Delicate Balance of Terror*. P-1472. Santa Monica, CA: RAND Corporation, 1958.

———. "How Much Is Enough? How Mad Is MAD?" In *Pacem in Terris III*, vol. 2, *The Military Dimensions of Foreign Policy*, edited by Fred Warner Neal and Mary Kersey Harvey, 37–43. Washington, DC: Center for the Study of Democratic Institutions, 1974.

———. "Sin and Games in America.," In *Game Theory and Related Approaches to Social Behavior: Selections*, edited by Martin Shubik, 209–25. New York: John Wiley and Sons, Inc., 1964.

Wohlstetter, Roberta. "Cuba and Pearl Harbor: Hindsight and Foresight." *Foreign Affairs* 43, no. 4 (July 1965): 691–707.

Wolf, Barry. *When the Weak Attack the Strong: Failures of Deterrence*. Santa Monica, CA: RAND Corporation, 1991.

Index

www.ingramcontent.com/pod-product-compliance
Lightning Source LLC
Chambersburg PA
CBHW082350270326
41935CB00013B/1576